Aspects of Contemporary Book Design

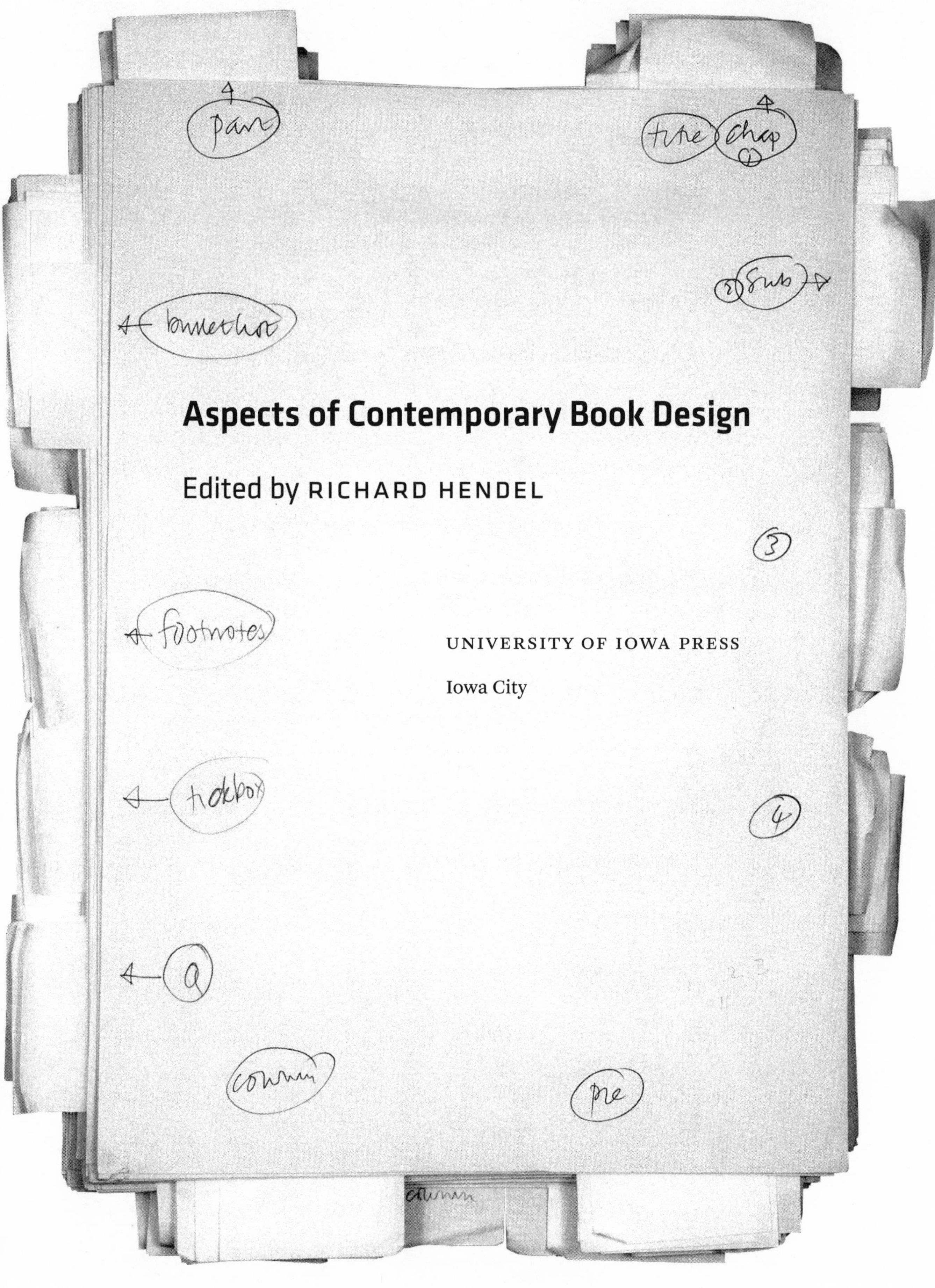

Aspects of Contemporary Book Design

Edited by RICHARD HENDEL

UNIVERSITY OF IOWA PRESS

Iowa City

University of Iowa Press, Iowa City 52242

www.uiowapress.org
Printed in the United States of America

This book is set in Arnhem, designed by Fred Smeijers, and Klavika, designed by Eric Olson. Typeset at Tseng Information Systems. Manufactured at Thomson-Shore, Dexter, Michigan.

Design by Richard Hendel

The University of Iowa Press is a member of Green Press Initiative and is committed to preserving natural resources.

Printed on acid-free paper

Paperback ISBN-13: 978-1-60938-175-2
Paperback ISBN-10: 1-60938-175-0
LCCN: 2012952179

Title page photo by Andrew Barker

To Vicky, yet again,

and in memory of

Richard Eckersley

and Alan Bartram,

from whom I learned

much, but obviously

not enough.

It is so much easier to *do* things

(like designing books) . . .

than to say *why* you did them.

— W. A. Dwiggins in an undated letter

to Alfred A. Knopf

Contents

Preface and Acknowledgments

Because these may be the final days of what we now know as book design, what follows may eventually turn out to be merely the reminder of a quaint aspect of graphic design. E-books have allegedly made reading more popular than ever, reinforcing what I have always secretly suspected, that design doesn't actually make much of a difference. Despite the obvious, I am glad there remain publishers who have not abandoned it. In the United States, most university presses still seem to care about the design of their books, as do a number of smaller publishers (Algonquin, for example). In England, the fine publisher Faber and Faber Ltd. no longer has a design manager for the interiors of their books.

In my quest to find designers whose work I knew and admired, I was grateful to find so many of them willing to take time to write something about how and why they do what they do. If, as Beatrice Warde prescribed, book design is (or should be) transparent, book designers themselves are nearly invisible. The graphic design stars who call themselves book designers are rarely the ones who are in the typographic trenches fretting over the typographic niceties of an encyclopedia of Caribbean religion.

My doubts about writing this book were assuaged from the beginning by the generosity of my colleagues. Robin Kinross gave me the suggestion to contact Andrew Barker. Were it not for Andrew I might have abandoned the project early on. He is perhaps as much responsible for this book as I. He has given me the wisest advice, helped me shape the direction of the book, and written far more than I could ever have wished for. When I needed more information about some topics, I turned to Andrew with his extensive experience. In every sense this book is as much his as it is mine.

Charles Ellertson is the most type-obsessed human being I have ever known. He sees flaws in the design of typefaces I frankly admit escape me. There is no one I know more knowledgeable than he about the way type for books should be set. We often meet to commiserate on how authors and editors don't understand us, and to wonder at why some designers choose such inappropriate typefaces. I'm sure he rarely approves of mine. It was Charles who found a problem with the design of the comma in the Garamond font I had used in my previous book and chose to alter it, causing a slight scandal of sorts (if you'll forgive the unintentional typographic pun).

Were it not for the generous assistance of Charles and his colleague Larry Tseng this book would never have seen the light of day.

Kent Lew's Whitman font is one of the best new book faces. What makes it so good is that Kent himself is a designer. Charles Ellertson has often noted that type designers too often seem not to realize what happens when their fonts are used for book work. Kent is in the great tradition of W. A. Dwiggins and Bruce Rogers: equally skilled at designing books and designing type.

Sean Magee is an editor who understands what designers do or should do. He actually likes designers and was my introduction to Ron Costley, John Ryder, and Alan Bartram. I've known few editors as astute as Sean in judging design.

Ron Costley is the purest designer I know. How he always manages to make every book so perfect, with nary a trick, shames me. Though he would not believe it, I always wonder what Ron will think about a design I am working on. Trying to find the proper balance between making the design obvious for American publishers (who want to see the design they are paying for) and honest enough for Ron, I'm sure I rarely get it quite right.

I owe many thanks to the designers and others I talked with in the past few years and those who have contributed to the text. The designers among them have all won numerous important awards, and I will say more about them in the following chapters: Julie Allred, Matt Avery, Mike Brehm, Kaelin Chappell Broadus, Eric Brooks, Kim Bryant, Amy Ruth Buchanan, Vin Dang, Abbey Gaterud, Debora Greger, Philip Gura, Sue Hall, Mindy Basinger Hill, Kristina Kachele, Robin Kinross, Maria Lindenfeldar, William Logan, Ron Maner, Molly Renda, Lou Robinson, Ashley Saleeba, Annie Shahan, Jill Shimabukuro, Kathleen Swaziola, Isaac Tobin, Robert Tombs, Jim Wageman, Cherie Westmoreland, Barbara Wiedemann, Barbara Williams, Anne Winslow, and Maia Wright.

I have had a long relationship as a freelance designer with the University of Iowa Press. One of the joys of working with them is their complete professionalism. Managing editor Charlotte Wright and copyeditor Bob Burchfield have put up with the eccentricity of this entire project with good humor and patience, for which I am more grateful than I deserve. For many years I have been lucky to work with design and production manager Karen Copp, who has the most eagle of eagle eyes and the greatest of integrity. Nothing escapes her vigilance in making sure work is done right.

Why the University of Iowa Press wanted to publish this book remains a bit of a mystery to me. They certainly are a quixotic lot, publishing poetry and short fiction. Holly Carver is, like Sean Magee, a designer's editor, and she has been the reason I've stuck with it.

Pages xiii and xiv: From the pre-Macintosh era, pencil layouts by Richard Eckersley for the University of Nebraska Press, ca. 1988, reproduced at 100%. Courtesy of Dika Eckersley.

4½pi

27pi

3½ pica head

CHAPTER 4

The Science of Harmony: Foundations For an Enlightened Systema

PABLUM

13pt small Caps, line 3
22pt b to b.
Ornament (A/W supplied)
34 pt b. to b. to chap. head
20/28 pt

Sink opening text to line 15.
36pt Bembo initial FL, aligned at base with second line of text. First word in 10/14 pt s.c., 1 unit letterspaced

27 pi 4½ pi 4½ pi

minimum 28pts, b. to b. –
Example caption, 9/12pt Bembo centered, to 12pi max. measure.
18pts # from baseline to top of figure, visually.
center figure on 27 picas.
from figure to text 28pts, b. to b. (min.)

Example 1

18pts

[Allegro]
Vln. 1
27
Vln. 2
f
Vla.
Bass
7 3 4
6 5
5 3
6 5

Aspects of Contemporary Book Design

Book Design on the Edge

When I began to think about putting together a new book on book design, I approached a publisher who had a series on writing and publishing to see if they might have any interest in my project. The acquiring editor for that list rejected my proposal claiming there was really "no future" in book design. Perhaps she was right, and this book may be an extended epitaph to a dead craft—not unlike being a Linotype operator. Was it Marshall McLuhan who claimed that when a technology is superseded it becomes an art form—how letterpress books, for example, became a kind of fine art?

> To a book conscious public, to a public that is willing to rank book design and production amongst the arts while still remembering that they are nobly and gloriously servile arts dedicated to the communication of thought—to such a public, the future will still bring books that look as if they had been designed with pride and intelligence.
> — Beatrice Warde, "The Design of Books"

Many years ago, in the days before the Macintosh, I had spent most of a weekend designing a title page for an obscure scholarly monograph. By late Sunday afternoon when I finally decided whatever I had done was good enough, my wife asked me if all that effort made any difference as it was unlikely anyone would pay much notice to a title page. Given the seeming lack of any considered design for most books, I suspect it made no difference. And now with the advent of the e-book, where readers can change fonts and sizes to suit themselves, I wonder if there will be any role at all for a designer.

Yet, at least in the first part of the second decade of the twenty-first century, there are still publishers who seem to care about the design of the printed book. As with my earlier book, *On Book Design*, I thought it might be instructive to interview other designers to learn how they work. None of this is meant to be taken as how to do it. Instead, my intention is to show how designers think about their work and why they make some of the choices they do. In my own work, I have realized how mutable are my own design philosophy (such that it is) and preferences. I am dismayed whenever I look back at work done years ago, wondering how I could have assumed that it was good. Even more dismaying is to look at a job fresh from the printer and see all the missed opportunities. A beginning designer once asked a colleague of mine how she knew when a design was done. She replied, "When you run out of time."

■ I have little patience for reading books about design—there is too much theory, too much design babble. I admit that I haven't read much design history either, so I was reluctant when I was asked by a publisher to write a wholly unnecessary foreword to Jan Tschichold's *The New Typography*. I greatly admire Tschichold, though I knew his writing only in translation. I was familiar only with what he had written long after he had repudiated his youthful manifesto. Rather than reveal my ignorance (and flattered to be asked), I finally read *The New Typography*. In it Tschichold advocated revolutionary stuff intended to challenge what he considered old and outworn design ideas. He complained about bland symmetry and the insensitive use of serif type. He suggested new rules for the new typography: use the fewest possible typefaces and fewest possible type sizes, do not letterspace lowercase, emphasize by using italic or bold of the same typeface, and use capitals only as an exception and then always carefully letterspaced.

When he eventually rejected the *way* in which he applied these rules, Tschichold realized that they applied just as well to more traditional book typography. Those principles, however, more or less sum up for me the basic core of where book design should begin.

■ This book concentrates on specific kinds of book design: poetry, fiction, plays, nonfiction, cookbooks, art books, reference books, and journals. I have invited other designers to write about the unique problems each of these present and to discuss how they have dealt with them. In addition, I have invited contributions from others who influence or who are influenced by designers: a typesetter who works with designers and editors, a designer of typefaces primarily used for text, and authors about being designed. Some of the chapters are set up as interviews, where one or more designers respond to my questions; some include interviews but are equally driven by their authors' own opinions; some are stand-alone essays that need no interview guidance from me. When relevant, I have included stories and examples from my own work. In all cases I have tried to preserve the designers' particular styles and voices.

I have little new to say about my own thoughts on book design. While I do not always do in practice what I truly believe, I truly believe what I *ought* to do. In this I am not, I think, unique. There are reasons (dubious and otherwise) why we slip into bad behavior. There are, as well, generational, cultural, and national considerations that influence our work. One Anglophilic critic of American book design considers it overdone to the point of being a kind of poorly executed magazine design. There is, perhaps, something valid to the criticism. Judging especially by the design for nonfiction books, American design has tended to be more graphically ambitious than that done in Britain. Certainly the design for scholarly books is, or has been since the beginning of the annual university presses book design competition. As I have often said, nothing encourages bad-behavior book design more than competitions.

This book is, at best, a snapshot of current practice from a random sample of designers whose work I admire. How we work and the fonts we like will no doubt change in the coming years. It is too early to tell at this stage how the design for e-books will influence how we work.

AT THE BEGINNING

Before starting work on a new project, a designer needs to have answers to some basic questions. Some of these are:

- What is this book about?
- Who is this book for?
- What is the expected trim size, characters per page, number of pages?
- Are there special typographic requirements (e.g., foreign languages, mathematical setting) in the text?
- What unique elements are there (e.g., kinds and levels of subheads, illustrations, epigraphs, prose extracts, verse extracts, etc.)?
- How much design attention does the publisher expect?
- Does the author, editor, or marketing department have specific requests or biases?
- What materials are there to work with? Can that pile of murky photos really be turned into an art book?
- What is the budget?
- What is the schedule?
- Who will typeset the book?
- Who has design approval?

Some of this sounds elementary, but without having answers it is easy to head off in completely the wrong direction. Freelance designers are often only given some of this information.

A few years ago I was asked to design a large and complicated bilingual book of Chinese poetry. The complication was that the poems were to be set in three columns: Chinese characters, Pinyin romanization, and English translation. I generally work very early in the morning, long before anyone would be at work at the publishing house. As every other book I had done for this publisher was 6×9 inches, I blithely assumed this one probably was. I worked out a system to make the three columns fit. The design was subsequently approved, and the job went to a typesetter. Many hundreds of pages were expertly set. The author seemed pleased, but it was only then the editor realized the publisher had wanted an 8.5×11 inch format and the job had to be completely redone.

HOW MUCH DO DESIGNERS KNOW BEFORE BEGINNING?

Designers rarely read all of a manuscript. Those who work for publishers rather than as freelancers often know more about a manuscript from discussions with acquiring editors and manuscript editors before they begin thinking about the design. Often editors have an unrealistic understanding of the structure of a manuscript or assume that an author's desires regarding design can be met realistically. A long and complicated text cannot be set in a large size of type with generous margins if it is also necessary to keep the book to a reasonable number of pages. Or all chapters cannot open with a double-page spread if the previous chapter ends on a verso page. Well, it could, but it would require the design solecism of a blank recto before the chapter opening spread.

Many designers of nonfiction at least read the introduction and some of the text. The designers I spoke with who design fiction say that when the jacket or cover design is done ahead of time, they might use that as a point of visual reference. Some authors know (or think they know) typefaces and request their books be set in one of their favorites. A production manager once told me that she was forbidden by the editor to use the typeface Palatino because the author detested it. When asked if the author had a typeface he did prefer, the editor pulled down a book from the shelf and said it was to be set in the font used in that book—which was, of course, Palatino.

An author I knew once told me he felt removed from his own words seeing them in type. One first-time fiction writer said he never looked at his finished book and only cared about what the jacket looked like. I am curious about why poets do not know more about typefaces since how a poem is set is often as important as the words themselves. When I asked the poets William Logan and Debora Greger how they felt about the typefaces used for their books, they said they were more concerned about the size of the typeface than the typeface itself, although William preferred fonts like Baskerville or Dante. I was once told that Elizabeth Bishop also preferred Baskerville, but I wonder if she knew the difference between Monotype Baskerville and Linotype Baskerville. They are quite different.

abgmABC
Monotype Baskerville

abgmABC
Baskerville Old Face

abgmABC
ITC New Baskerville

As basic as it may sound, at the very least a designer needs to know the expected trim size and how many pages the book is to make. In order to figure out the number of pages the designer needs an accurate castoff. For myself, even if the publisher has provided a castoff, I always try to get a sense of how many characters there are on an average manuscript page by setting a page of manuscript to see how it translates into a typeset page.

■ By the time most jobs come to the designer, too many decisions have already been made. All too often authors, acquiring editors, and marketing managers have unrealistic expectations about what the book should be (e.g., trying to fit a large manuscript into a reasonable number of pages, using low-resolution art assuming it will look good when printed).[1] It becomes the designer's problem to turn this mess into a sow's purse.

Whether it is the fault of inexperienced editors or recalcitrant authors, designers are often presented with nagging editorial problems. Seemingly simple yet obviously difficult situations often lurk at the very opening of a chapter. One chapter may have an epigraph or subtitle and the others none.

[1] I have never understood why an editor clever enough to know the difference between "that" and "which" (something I have never got the hang of) can't detect an out-of-focus photograph.

CASTOFF AND PRELIMINARY ESTIMATE Date__________

AUTHOR__________
TITLE__________
MS PAGES FOR CASTOFF__________ AVG CHARACTERS PER PG__________

Characters text and extract __________Ch @ pg__________ __________

	Pages
Front matter__________	______
Subheads__________X 4 lines each__________	______
Poetry/Line for Line__________	______
Photos__________	______
Maps__________	______
Tables__________	______
Lines of Notes __________Divided by__________lines per pg	______
Bibliography__________ Divided by__________lines per pg	______
Other__________	______
Index__________	______
Total pages	______

Trim Size: 6 1/8 x 9 1/4 Other__________
Stock: 50# Natures Natural Other__________
Casebound quantity__________ [] jacket [] no jackets
Notch paperbacks__________

Jackets CMYK plus film Other__________
Covers CMYK plus film Other__________
Text printer__________ Jacket/cover printer__________

Castoff form for an unedited manuscript used for preparing a preliminary production estimate.

The chapter might begin with a subhead. The very first word might begin with quotation marks. One chapter title might be a single word and the others many. Each of these situations creates a unique design problem. The editor or author can often make a case for each of these scenarios, and they are not always avoidable (I admit to allowing some of these very inconsistencies to creep into this book), but just as often they probably are. As are chapter titles that are obviously quotations, that technically, it could be argued, would require the use of quotation marks. However, using quotation marks in display type (especially American-style double quotation marks) seems both redundant and ugly. It assumes the reader hasn't the sense to sort out the idea that the titles are based on quotations.

One of the most useful documents for a designer is a transmittal sheet that indicates the kinds of extracts, the levels of subheads indicating the longest and shortest, a list of acronyms and abbreviations, and other anomalies in the text. This isn't because designers are too lazy to find these elements themselves, but they are far easier for the editor to identify while the manuscript is being edited. A list of abbreviations and acronyms gives the designer at least a chance of being able to style them as small caps rather than as full caps.

For good design to exist, there needs to be some compromise between editor and designer. There are some battles designers are unlikely to win, such as the use of single quotes instead of double quotes or spaced en dashes instead of closed-up em dashes. However, some editors insist on "rules" such as banning hyphenation at certain places (e.g., at the overleaf, at the end of a paragraph, or after the first two letters of a word) that can often create a situation even more egregious.

Tables are a special problem. They can be more problematic than almost any other part of the text. The author and editor should keep in mind that tables should fit the upright rectangle of a normal book page whenever possible. Editors should carefully consider the wording of column heads and stubs to see how the information can be compressed or abbreviated. An especially wide table that cannot be accommodated to fit on one page needs to be edited to see if it might be better to run across a spread rather than having to turn it. The designer George Mackie used to irritate editors by re-editing tables so they could easily fit upright on a single page. If only some editors could think more visually.

Running heads are meant as an indication of a chapter's content and need not be a literal reiteration of the entire chapter title (and subtitle). Far too often running heads can be much too long and awkward. Long running heads can seem to be just a line of disconnected text.

FORM AND CONTENT

The better an editor has clarified the form of the manuscript, the better a designer can transform it typographically. Book designers need to be able to understand the structure of the entire manuscript before they can begin the design. Too often designers are given only a small portion of what purports to be a representative sample of the manuscript; sometimes the sample is edited but frequently not. The designer is asked to build the design on the sample, not knowing how often certain elements such as subheads and extracts really occur. What may seem representative to an editor often isn't; frequently the sample represents the few anomalies in the text rather than the general style of the content. Working from an unedited manuscript, or before the title has been finally decided, can be dangerous. I was once asked to design a book about Ernest Hemingway with the title *Papa*, and, with such a short title, I used very large type on the title page and carried the oversize type as a device for the chapter openings. When the title later became *Picturing Hemingway*, that change completely scuttled the design.

I have often cited the example of how editing affects design by comparing the maps of the London and New York subway systems. John Beck, who devised the now iconic plan of the London Underground, had a far easier visual problem to solve because the system itself is so clearly edited. The New York subway system, by contrast, is far more complex in its structure, and so the challenge to explain it visually is a genuine dilemma; a map as good as Beck's has never been possible for New York.

Ideally, then, before the design can begin, the manuscript should be edited. The English typographer John Ryder wrote about the need for "visual editing." He felt that editors were concerned only with correcting spelling and grammar but were uncritical about how it all might look. Ryder felt that editors should be more critical of how something in the manuscript will appear in the printed book—the need to edit visually *before* the design process even begins.

There are two philosophical approaches to book design: there are those who feel a design should be timeless and neutral and others who feel it should reflect the content in a more obvious way (using typography or design elements relevant to what the book is about).

Designers who aim for neutral and timeless occasionally used to be called crystal goblet designers, after Beatrice Warde's eponymous essay. She had written that the design for books should be as transparent as a crystal goblet should be for wine. What Warde meant was that the design of the vessel should not call more attention to itself than its contents—the contents being more important than the form.

Warde was not alone in her attitude that the design for books should be different from other kinds of graphic design. More than other graphic designers, those who design books need to be aware of conventions of how people read.

Even within those conventions other approaches to book design aim to be more graphically conspicuous. While I personally believe that designers could make do with only a few text faces, the ever expanding availability of new typefaces is much too tempting. The designer Will Powers, for example, believed it was part of his mission to work with new type designers. He felt that books about America should be set in American typefaces. In one of his essays, he mused upon the "morality" of using John Downer's Iowan Old Style typeface in a book about Minnesota.

While that philosophical conundrum is perhaps a bit too arcane, there are situations where the choice of a special typeface would be suggested by the content (e.g., using a "French" typeface like Garamond for a book about French history or Bembo for a book about the Renaissance).

A mid-nineteenth-century font for a book about the Civil War would seem to be obviously the right choice—that is, until you see that is not necessarily the only way to do it. Richard Eckersley used a sans serif for a book about Civil War battlefields. Ron Costley used Sabon for a biography of Eric Gill, and Christopher Burke set his most useful study of Jan Tschichold in his own

Detail from *Eric Gill* by Fiona MacCarthy (Faber and Faber Ltd.), designed by Ron Costley using Sabon.

G VILLAGE 1907–13

n with the erotic, especially the images of
lso both sun worshippers. In 1910, their
tein had recently completed his frieze of
ınd female figures for the British Medical
nd. This work had caused a public furore.
sy in support of Epstein. Their joint plan
henge developed through that summer
and weekends down in Ditchling, with
dults and nude children. It is an interesting
taken by the census of Gill's diaries that
vas deleted (inefficiently); only the nude
ıain.
ing to collaborate on a series of immense
ds and giants in the Sussex landscape ('as

typeface Celeste when both Gill and Tschichold had themselves designed eminently useful book fonts. Designers can make the opposite mistake (or so it seems to me) by choosing something entirely inappropriate.

■ There are, of course, situations where conventional ideas about book design and readability can or should be violated, but in general most printed books are intended to be read as books have been read since the time of Gutenberg. Assuming that readability is the primary goal of book design, designers need to know how to use typefaces that are appropriate in design and arrangement.

The conventional rules of typography are allegedly based on what is best for reading and suggest what a good text page should look like. These rules state that an ideal page should have a top margin smaller than the bottom margin, and that the gutter margins should be smaller than the front margins (so that facing pages appear to be a unit). The supposition is that the length of line of text should be about sixty-five characters because a longer line of type causes visual problems—the eye has to pause too many times within the line, making movement from one line of type to the next difficult. These guidelines should not be slavishly followed, but neither should they be ignored.

■ Production considerations are equally as important as editing before the design can begin: the book's size, the expected number of pages, how the manuscript will be supplied to the designer, who will do the typesetting, who will be the printer. American book production has a certain range of standard formats. The designer needs to know what the publisher's intentions are regarding format and number of pages. Most of the time the publisher will have done an evaluation of the manuscript, estimating the average number of characters (i.e., letters and spaces) required to make the number of pages to make the book financially viable. Editors and authors always seem to measure the text in words rather than characters, but words are too imprecise a measure because of their obvious variation in length. One publisher I know requires 3,300 characters per page (in a 6×9 inch format); at the same time many serious designers find that impossible. The brilliant designer Richard Eckersley once told me that he thought anything over 2,800 was unworkable.

It now seems more exception than rule that editors supply computer files ready for typesetting so more designers than ever before now set their own type. Publishers seem to feel that it is more economical to keep much of the composition of their books in-house rather than send work to an outside typesetter.

Though this may be true for straightforward, uncomplicated text, professional typesetters are often far better at setting tabular material, foreign language, poetry, and other special content. Even more so, a high-quality typesetter will take special care with fonts, making slight adjustments that are seemingly imperceptible but make a qualitative improvement to the way even a straightforward, uncomplicated text page looks. When all the costs of dealing with an outside type shop are measured against all the costs of setting the job in-house, for me, the modest increase (if any) is worth the expense.

If the designer is not setting the type for a job, knowing who will typeset it is important for a number of reasons. Of primary importance is knowing which fonts the typesetter has. Digitized fonts are relatively inexpensive compared to the cost of metal type, but even so, a typesetter is likely to be reluctant to buy a font that might be used for one job and never again, to say nothing of the investment of time it takes to adjust a font. Though it seems that fonts "out of the box" look fine as they are, a knowledgeable typesetter experienced in book work will make adjustments to letter fit, kerned pairs, and even the length of descenders and ascenders, sometimes violating with good cause the often unnecessarily restricting End User License Agreement.

Personally, I design differently for different typesetters—rarely asking for an unusual font (even if it would be appropriate for aesthetics or content) or for complicated setting when I don't know anything about the typesetter.

■ Authors may spend many years writing their book, and they often have in mind the way they think books (especially their book) should look. Designers, of course, cannot know what the author's ideal book looks like. They try to solve the design based on the kind of criteria I have listed above. To save time and money, publishers often resort to using a standardized template for the design of many of their books. This is unfortunate because no two books fit totally comfortably into the same design. Certainly, it is not necessary for

RUNNING HEAD 17

revising descriptions of mechanisms. No one person created this mechanistic view or the experimental approach characteristic of its champions. In *The New Atlantis*, a work that inspired the social organization of science in the seventeenth century and beyond, Francis Bacon (1561–1626) described a utopian society sustained through the efforts of specialized scientists organized to discover and control nature's hidden causes. During that period, commonly referred to as the Scientific Revolution, thinkers came to see the natural world as a world of mechanisms, just as they came to see science as fundamentally organized around the search for mechanisms. As a consequence, the methods of science came increasingly to be evaluated in terms of their efficiency and reliability as tools in the search for mechanisms. The scientific project, in turn, was justified in many domains by the fact that knowledge of the hidden mechanisms of the natural world offers humans power over the forces of nature that dominate their lives.

Just when and how this mechanistic view of science entered the different fields of biology, specifically, and precisely how the idea of mechanism came to so thoroughly triumph as a way of thinking about explanation in biology, we shall not venture opinions. That it has so triumphed is indisputable. Neuroscientists study the mechanisms of spatial memory, the propagation of action potentials, and the opening and closing of ion channels in the neuronal membrane. Molecular biologists discovered the basic mechanisms of DNA replication and protein synthesis, and they continue to elucidate the myriad mechanisms of gene regulation. Medical researchers probe the genetic basis of cystic fibrosis and how nutrient deficiencies give rise to somatic symptoms. Evolutionary biologists study the mechanism of natural selection and the isolating mechanisms leading to speciation. Ecologists study nutrient cycling mechanisms and the way imbalances in nutrient cycling produce dead zones in places such as the Chesapeake Bay. Across the life sciences the goal is to open black boxes and to learn through experiment and observation which entities and activities are components in a mechanism and how those components are organized together to do something that none of them does in isolation.

Yet there is no tidy story to tell about how this idea took hold in biology. Some of the features of mechanistic biology are discussed in Aristotle's *Parts of Animals*, although we hesitate to call Aristotle (384-322 BC) a mechanist. Certainly, the break from Galen's theories of anatomy during the Renaissance, such as Vesalius's corrections to Galen's human anatomical diagrams and Harvey's demonstration that the blood circulates, share many of the marks of a commitment to the search for mechanisms and of the effort to codify experi-

revising descriptions of mechanisms. No one person created this mechanistic view or the experimental approach characteristic of its champions. In *The New Atlantis*, a work that inspired the social organization of science in the seventeenth century and beyond, Francis Bacon (1561–1626) described a utopian society sustained through the efforts of specialized scientists organized to discover and control nature's hidden causes. During that period, commonly referred to as the Scientific Revolution, thinkers came to see the natural world as a world of mechanisms, just as they came to see science as fundamentally organized around the search for mechanisms. As a consequence, the methods of science came increasingly to be evaluated in terms of their efficiency and reliability as tools in the search for mechanisms. The scientific project, in turn, was justified in many domains by the fact that knowledge of the hidden mechanisms of the natural world offers humans power over the forces of nature that dominate their lives.

Just when and how this mechanistic view of science entered the different fields of biology, specifically, and precisely how the idea of mechanism came to so thoroughly triumph as a way of thinking about explanation in biology, we shall not venture opinions. That it has so triumphed is indisputable. Neuroscientists study the mechanisms of spatial memory, the propagation of action potentials, and the opening and closing of ion channels in the neuronal membrane. Molecular biologists discovered the basic mechanisms of DNA replication and protein synthesis, and they continue to elucidate the myriad mechanisms of gene regulation. Medical researchers probe the genetic basis of cystic fibrosis and how nutrient deficiencies give rise to somatic symptoms. Evolutionary biologists study the mechanism of natural selection and the isolating mechanisms leading to speciation. Ecologists study nutrient cycling mechanisms and the way imbalances in nutrient cycling produce dead zones in places such as the Chesapeake Bay. Across the life sciences the goal is to open black boxes and to learn through experiment and observation which entities and activities are components in a mechanism and how those components are organized together to do something that none of them does in isolation.

Yet there is no tidy story to tell about how this idea took hold in biology. Some of the features of mechanistic biology are discussed in Aristotle's *Parts of Animals*, although we hesitate to call Aristotle (384-322 BC) a mechanist. Certainly, the break from Galen's theories of anatomy during the Renaissance, such as Vesalius's corrections to Galen's human anatomical diagrams and Harvey's demonstration that the blood circulates, share many of the marks of a commitment to the search for mechanisms and of the effort to codify experimental and observational methods for discovering mechanisms. In other

RUNNING FOOT 17

Using a running foot instead of a running head allows for an extra text line while preserving the feeling of a traditional larger bottom margin.

every book to be designed from scratch. Most designers keep a basic design in their heads (if not on their computers), and they can adapt that model more freely than if they had to work with a formal template.

STARTING WITH THE TYPEFACE

For myself, the core of the design is the typeface. I can't begin a design unless I know what text font seems right for a job. The choice of what to use depends on many criteria, some of which are:

- How tight does the text need to be? That is, how many characters on the page does the publisher require?
- What kind of special characters are in the manuscript?
- Is the book meant for specialist readers or for the general trade?
- What kind of display type would relate to it?
- How appropriate is the font for the content?

Many years ago, when I first began designing books my standard text page for a 6×9 format had approximately 2,500 characters, a very generous open page with good margins. Now I am routinely asked to get 2,900 to 3,000 characters on that same page. In order to keep the text from being so packed, I have resorted to using a running foot rather than a running head. Why this works (for me if not always for editors and authors) is that the traditional text page has a smaller head margin than a foot margin. The running foot at the bottom of the page occupies visually less space than a full text line might, and so the entire text block can move up to allow for an extra line of type.

Special characters in the text are less problematic now than they once were because OpenType versions of many text faces have nearly every variant of accented characters, small caps in roman and italic, oldstyle figures, lining figures, tabular figures, etc. Even so there are still some fonts that frustratingly do not have the one special version necessary (e.g., italic oldstyle figures).

If the book is meant for the general trade, the size of the type, the leading, and the measure need to seem to be more open than for a book intended for a specialist reader (where it is useful to pack as much information in as few pages as possible to keep production costs down). Books that are not necessarily meant to be read straight through (such as reference books) are usually designed to be extremely tight. A cookbook, on the other hand, needs to be far more generous in its layout assuming that the reader may be using it as an instruction manual.

Good text faces may not always have well-designed italic, boldface, or display sizes. A project with even a few levels of subheading would need good variants of the text face or a different font that related well with it. Not all text faces work when enlarged to use as headings (being too thin or too heavy), though increasingly new typefaces are offered with display versions.

How appropriate a font is to the content is a far more subjective criterion. Perhaps designers know more (or less) than they should. In a biography of the American composer Richard Rodgers, I could not imagine why the designer had chosen the very English typeface Joanna, which seemed so unsuitable for the content. It is not that every typeface is so specifically attached to its origins. Baskerville, for example, is as English as Joanna, but would have seemed a better choice even if it was not American. Too often designers feel some urge to use a "different" typeface without considering all the implications.

None of these issues can be considered in isolation. For production considerations, a publisher might need a very tight design for a book that is meant for a general audience; so the choice of a text face would mean choosing one that does not appear to look too small but also sets tightly enough to yield a high character count.

■ All book designers have favorite fonts, ones that they default to or rely on most of the time. When Linotype and Monotype in their metal versions were all that was available, there was not only a limited choice of font but also of available sizes for a particular font. Eleven-point type was as rare as an ivory-billed woodpecker, and ten and a half point type was but a dream. In those days it was a far easier business to decide which font and size to use.

It always surprises me that a type I think is impossible to work with is another designer's favorite. These "desert island" typeface love affairs don't last a lifetime because designers grow bored with them, the fonts go out of fashion, or they are supplanted by some newer (or older) font. In a 2012 survey I made of book designers' favorite typefaces, ones that I assumed were no longer used by any of us (like Palatino) or ineptly transformed into their digital versions (like Janson or Electra) were just such favorites of others. A font like Minion, ideal though it is for contemporary book work, hardly seemed to show up in my survey. Curiously enough though, it was the font used in most of the books selected in the last six years of the university presses' annual book show.

I no longer seem to rely on what were once my most favorite typefaces: Monotype Bulmer, Monotype Garamond, Linotype Baskerville. Bulmer and Garamond migrated in reasonable form to their digital versions. However, newer typefaces like Minion, available with every possible variant and accent mark, are so much more flexible to use. It takes me more than a few jobs to get to know a new font, and sometimes I never get comfortable with one. I have a library of typefaces I bought on the enthusiastic recommendation of other designers (Merlo, Dolly, Trinité) that I tried out a few times and wonder if I will ever use again. I have even more faces that I once loved (Ehrhardt, Trump, Galliard) and I have abandoned without good reason. Still, without some favorites to at least start with, I cannot begin a design.

■ I asked the designer Jim Wageman what influenced his choices of typeface. Wageman began as a university press editor and eventually became a director of art and design for major New York publishers of art and other illustrated books, as well as director of graphic design at the Museum of Modern Art. He wrote:

> *Congruity:* By which I mean the appropriateness of the typeface(s) to the subject matter and/or the graphic content of the book. At a basic level, this might relate to historical compatibility. For example, I'd hesitate to set a book on Botticelli in a Bodoni font. Both were Italian, of course, but they represent distinctly different eras and differing sensibilities. But historical accuracy probably isn't the overriding factor in most typeface selection, which for me has more to do with the sort of mood or emotion I'd hope the typeface would provoke in the reader. Usually this has to do with the display face, but text-face choice contributes to the overall visual "mood" as well. Cookbooks tend to allow for a greater range of suitable type choices in this regard than art books, for which the typography generally needs to be subservient to the artist's work

by not making too strong a statement on its own. Conversely, the display type for a cookbook may be called on to help establish some sort of unique visual look for the book. In all cases, however, the typeface selection needs to somehow create a visual mood that's compatible with the subject—even when that means staying suitably in the background as a neutral foil to the art.

Aesthetics (for lack of a better word): In a way, this relates to congruity and the evoking of an appropriate mood. The first book on book design I ever happened upon, years ago, was Hugh Williamson's *Methods of Book Design*, in which he advocates working from the inside out in developing the design, which I still consider good advice. Nonetheless, in recent years I've often begun the approach to a design by simply looking at the title set in a variety of typefaces, trying to assess the nuances of feeling each typeface may evoke. Another consideration on another level—particularly if the title is short—is how the individual letterforms look. Is there, for example, a capital "R," and, if so, how might I take advantage of that fact by selecting a typeface that has a particularly well-drawn or visually interesting and appropriate one?

More broadly, though, I think of "aesthetics" in this sense as typographic elegance or refinement—the kind of typography that many excellent designers provide for many museum catalogs, for instance, often incorporating fonts derived from classic Roman letterforms (Centaur, Trajan, Perpetua, etc.). More contemporary forms derive ultimately from the International or Swiss Style that emerged in the 1950s and '60s, Massimo Vignelli being one of its most eminent practitioners. With either of these approaches, the designer chooses to work within an established typographic tradition, looking to re-create a kind of classic appearance intended, presumably, to pretty much fit all subjects. This kind of typographic restraint is often appropriate and, when successfully executed, can result in a compelling and attractive setting for the artwork. The only problem I have with this approach is that in some cases it's as if the designer failed to respond to the artist's work depicted in the images going into the book. To posit an extreme example, it would be like being given a Keith Haring catalog to design and coming up with the usual classic Roman typeface and symmetrically balanced typography, a style that might be more appropriate for, say, a catalog of Gilbert Stuart's paintings. To me, the sort of one-size-fits-all approach that ignores the demands of the material can at times suggest a kind of indolent lack of responsiveness on the part of the designer.

I don't mean to suggest, though, that the type choices should somehow mirror or mimic the art, an approach that, if not handled carefully, can easily lead to its own ugly pitfalls. Conversely, particularly in books featuring historic art styles, a way of bringing renewed life to the subject can be accomplished by deliberately avoiding a historical look and instead placing the art in a fresh context reflective of our day and age.

There are of course many examples of books that exhibit this type of design strategy; one I can speak to was the catalog for what became a landmark exhibition on the Arts and Crafts Movement in America that opened at the Art Museum of Princeton University in 1972. Included in the show were ceramics, furniture, architectural details, and arts and crafts publications dating from the late nineteenth and early twentieth centuries. Reproducing the catalog images in some sort of re-creation of an Arts and Crafts–style design would likely have been cloying at best, not to mention inappropriate for an audience viewing them from the perspective of the late 20th century. The solution I chose was to create a "Swiss-style" grid with attendant flush-left, ragged-right setting—eschewing, however, what was at the time the virtually obligatory use of Helvetica and instead setting the nearly 300-page catalog in two weights of Hermann Zapf's Optima.

Simplicity: By which I mean that, particularly in the design of art books, often the best typographic approach would seem to be to get out of the way, so to speak, and let the art speak for itself. (Hello, Beatrice Warde!) In art books, giving prominence to the artwork is often furthered by the use of ample amounts of white space, but type "color" and the careful selection of type size and leading are important factors in this as well. Some of the handsome Roman serif faces (e.g., various Caslons, Jenson, Galliard, etc.) can be difficult to use in this kind of context, I think, since their color tends to create a "busy" look even in small sizes. Sans serif faces are an obvious choice, but many serif faces can also serve this purpose well—again, if sizes, weights, leading, and line length are judiciously considered.

As suggested earlier, not all books call for such simplicity of typographic design. Some in fact benefit enormously from the unique look that a distinctive typographic approach can create. One also thinks of the kind of strikingly creative graphic solutions that a brilliant typographer can bring to the art of bookmaking, the late Richard Eckersley's innovative typography for Avital Ronell's *Telephone Book: Technology, Schizophrenia, Electric Speech* being a prime example. For many of us lesser mortals, however, a general rule of thumb might well be: When in doubt, opt for restraint!

MISTAKES DESIGNERS MAKE

Though we designers make *many* mistakes, I asked some of them to list those they thought were the most egregious.

- Placing design above content. In other words, making the contents fit a design instead of allowing the contents to dictate the design. All designers have a problem giving up on a design concept that simply is not working.
- Not listening or not paying attention. As the designer Vin Dang said, "The book as an end product is arrived at through a confluence of many factors, decisions, and people, all of whom believe that their input, wishes, and demands are equally valid. Ask questions (even ones that seem basic). Listen to the answers. But also know when your experience needs to step in firmly so that the design illiterates aren't leading the way."
- Using too much design: choosing visual flair over readability—making things too complex, using too many typefaces or the wrong typefaces. As Beatrice Warde wrote, "There is nothing simple or dull in achieving the transparent page." Often this comes from trying to make a design an award winner instead of satisfying the needs of the book.

HOW MUCH DESIGN IS TOO MUCH DESIGN?

This is a conundrum if you are a freelance designer, for the client always wants to see value for money. There is the constant worry that if the design is not complicated or does not have some clever gimmick, the client will be disappointed. It is for this reason, perhaps, that American book design can seem so overdone. One of the reasons I like designing encyclopedias is because the object of the typography is to make the page as clear and uncluttered as possible while at the same time getting as much type on the page as necessary.

In *The New Typography* Jan Tschichold complained about the "non designed" book. He wanted designers to abandon what he considered to be an old-fashioned practice. His attempt was to encourage designers to find a new and more contemporary approach. Designers, though, are not free agents, and there is only so far that they can go given the considerations of author, editor, and reader. Tschichold then (in 1928) suggested that books should be set in sans serif type, an idea that few designers then (and now) have been able to do (except for art books, museum catalogs, and books about design). A young design intern of mine once attempted to use a sans serif font in a book about the Renaissance, arguing that the text was to be read now. This is not necessarily a totally invalid argument.

Even Tschichold himself later came to reject the idea that sans serif was the right typeface for books.

■ When the designer and the author disagree about a design, it is up to the publisher to decide who wins. Perhaps it is heretical for a designer to acknowledge that the tilt should always be toward the author (assuming what is wanted makes sense for the publisher). The author, after all, is responsible for creating the book in the first place. Designers need not be so territorial; there will always be another book to design. But, as I have written elsewhere, for an author, that book may be the only one.

Backwards and in High Heels

The Glamorous Work of Book Design

ANDREW BARKER

Before we begin, a note about terminology.

I've discovered quite a variety of names given to the roles of the people who participate in the process of making a book. For this reason I'm going to avoid using any terminology too particular. I'll refer to authors and to people who work in editorial, design, and production roles, and I hope that these terms will be understood without any need for explanation. Throughout I'll be speaking from the point of view of a designer, and I'll refer to the person for whom I'm designing as the client. This client will generally be someone who works in a publishing house, and despite using the term "client," what I say applies equally to a staff designer as to one who is self-employed or working for an agency or consultancy.

I think the only two pieces of jargon I haven't managed to do without are:

"U&lc," which means "upper- and lowercase." The term generally refers to lettering where lowercase letters (aka minuscules, small letters) are combined with capitals (aka majuscules, upper case) for the initial letters of words or sentences. Commonly the term is used to differentiate from words set entirely in capital letters.

"Baseline–baseline distance." This refers to the distance from the baseline that one line of type sits on to the baseline of the line of type below it. It may also be called "interlinear spacing" or "leading."[1]

Hopefully anyone who has spent any time at all studying typography will have already encountered these terms, but unexplained jargon that serves to exclude is not to be encouraged.

How did you come to be a book designer?

I come from a family of book-reading scientists; somehow I ended up not being a scientist, but both the book-reading and the scientific approach went on to influence my life. In my teens I had a part-time library job that afforded me ample opportunity not only to look at books but also to observe how people interacted with books. I left school with the intention of training to become a graphic designer.[2] To this end I went to the University of Reading to study typography and graphic communication. Ending up at Reading was largely serendipitous; at the time it offered the only university course of its kind in Europe. What I didn't know was that it produced a large number of the country's book designers, and I didn't know that I was necessarily going to end up

[1] Oh please, not "leading"! Leading is only possible with metal type, and not only that, the term is misapplied in computer programs. Properly 10.5 pt leading is 10.5 pt *in addition to* the body size of the type. So no, I won't be using the term "leading" unless I find myself talking about metal type. When working on a computer I shall refer to the baseline–baseline distance, a term that may be cumbersome, but it is at least unambiguous and accurate.

[2] I first thought of becoming a graphic designer at the age of eleven, talking to a friend in the lunch queue at school. At the time, all those years ago, we didn't use the term "graphic designer"; no, we used the term "commercial artist." How quaint.

being a book designer. I suspect that finding myself working in publishing was a combination of some whimsical notions on my part[1] and a typical student approach—taking the path of least resistance.

I've been working in book design since leaving Reading in 1987. For the first fifteen years of that working life I was staff at a sequence of publishing houses (Chatto & Windus, Faber and Faber Ltd., Gaia Books, Penguin Books). Ultimately I was design manager at Penguin Books. In 2003 I changed from member of staff to self-employed contractor/consultant brought in to work on specific projects. This means that at one time or another I've been a designer, manager of designers, client/commissioner of design, and external supplier of design services. So over the years I've looked at the activity of book design from a number of standpoints (and now I am getting to see how it feels to be an author too).

How much do you generally know about a book before you begin?
I don't know anything about the book before I begin; the beginning part is largely about finding out. Impatience to get on with the creative stuff sometimes makes me want to rush this preparation, but remembering the pain that can result from not doing this stage properly drives me to curb my impatience and get out my fine-tooth comb. I try to find out as much as I think I'll need to know. I try not to start any design work until I'm confident that I'm in full command of everything I need to know, but there's always that problem of being unaware of what one doesn't know. Experience teaches the questions that are most likely to give useful answers, but every book is different and anticipating everything one may need to know is not always straightforward. I try to be ready to accommodate new information if it arrives: occasionally it happens that during the design process new requirements are revealed that cannot be accommodated in the design approach as it stands. When this happens it may be necessary to undo some of the design thinking in order to take the design in a different direction, and this can take time that hadn't been allowed for, and that can have an impact on the cost or timing of the work. But these are generally the sorts of situations that cannot be predicted in advance and so have to be dealt with as they arise. Learn to think on the hoof and express vexation in private (not in front of children or guests and certainly not in front of the client).

The information a designer receives—and the degree of difficulty in uncovering it—varies. Clients tend not to hand over information in an easy-to-digest form; they are (understandably) looking at things from their point of view and not the designer's. The first thing that the client tells a designer, and how they present this, can be revealing—about their priorities, prejudices, expectations. There's a limit to how much reliance can be placed on such insights, but occasionally they can cast light when one is fumbling around in darkness.

[1] At that time most of my ideas were whimsical and formed largely from reading Thomas Hardy, Scott Fitzgerald, and *Wuthering Heights*; I should count myself lucky that my life has not been considerably more disastrous.

The key practical things I want to know before I start are the same for most book design:

- Is the page size decided? If so, what is it? If it isn't decided, is it my decision and are there any constraints or desires to take into account?
- Is there a number of pages to aim for? If so, how much latitude is acceptable?
- Are there any nontext components (for instance, illustrations, diagrams, tables, charts)? If so, are they supplied, or am I responsible for creating them?
- Am I typesetting the book or am I specifying for someone else to typeset?
- What is the schedule?
- Are there any production constraints (such as no bleeds allowed)?
- What is the structure of the text—how is the book physically organized?
- Are there any issues particular to this book (for instance, chapter 5 has a passage in Chinese, or the displayed extracts are of more importance than the linking text, or "the author's daughter did the illustrations and we know they're dreadful but there's no way to avoid using them so please make them look as good as possible")?

I like to know as much detail as possible about the structure of the text when I start work. Clients provide this information with differing degrees of comprehensiveness, so I prefer to check it out for myself. I like to have the entire and final manuscript before I start work, preferably as a paper copy and a digital file. If I have it, I always look through the entire manuscript before I start. I look at every page in order to see what textual components it contains. This can be tedious, but of course I'm not reading it, I'm scanning every page to find all the different elements lurking in there—such things as:

- Is it divided into parts?
- Are there chapters?
- What are the headings like (long, short, variable, including italicized elements, etc.)?
- Are there epigraphs?
- Are there subheadings within the text (how many levels, how are they distributed)?
- Are there lists?
- Are there text messages?
- Are there lists in text messages?
- And so on and so on.

I try to track down everything that needs to be designed and specified, and I keep track of how often each component occurs. I find this task easiest with a

This is a typical paper manuscript after I've been through it. This one had a lot of different components for me to flag. Working clockwise from the top left corner, the flags are for part headings, chapter headings (heading level 1), subheadings (heading level 2), text heading level 3, text heading level 4, pie charts, bar charts, my queries for the client, tickboxes, footnotes, bulleted lists. From flagging all of the elements like this I could easily see that all of the heading level 4 were in a single chapter, and that all of the pie charts and bar charts were in the first part of the book.

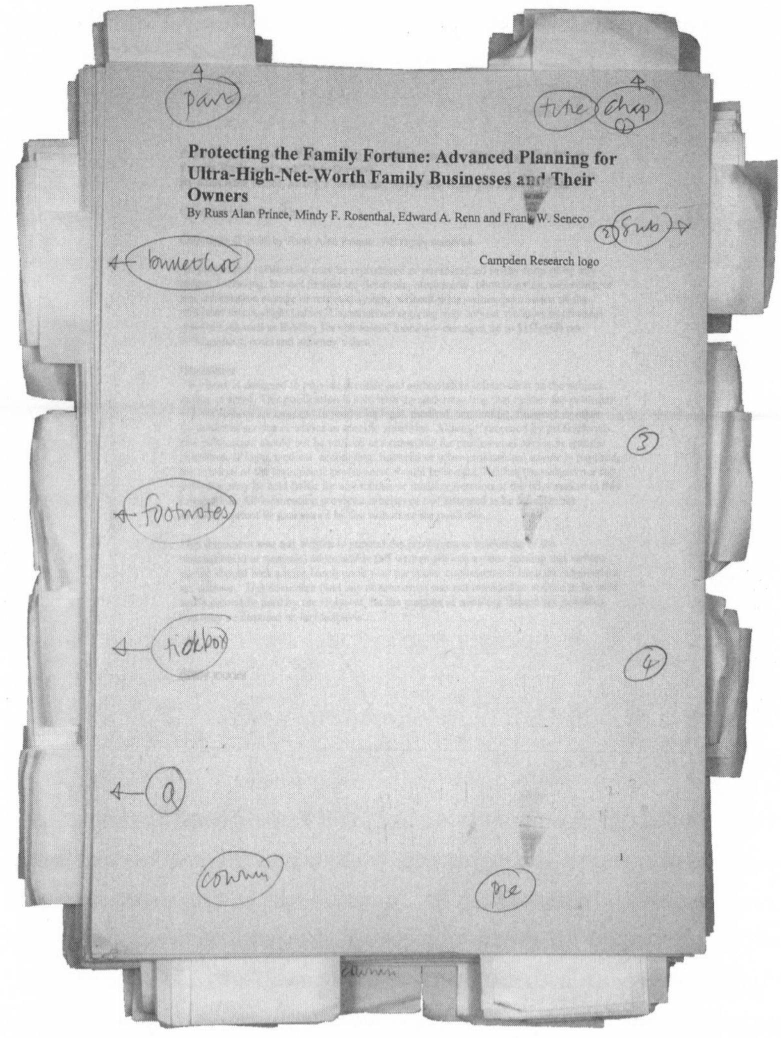

paper manuscript—I stick Post-it notes at different points on the page edges to flag different components, which means I can then see by glancing at the piled-up pages if, for instance, all the A-heads are in a single chapter, or if part two is actually 70 percent of a book with five parts. I've not found a way of doing this task so effectively with a digital file; I don't know if that's my age and ingrained habits, or if it really is easier on paper.

Of course, this is problematic if the book is not yet written. Then you have to rely on the client to tell you all that you need to know, and you can guarantee it is unlikely to be complete or comprehensive or detailed enough (unless you have the dream diligent client[1]). A consequence of knowing that there are gaps in what you know is that the design may have to be more generic and less responsive to the actual circumstances (because the actual circumstances are not clearly defined).

In addition to these practical, functional aspects, I need to know about the "look-and-feel" issues. This is potentially fraught because some clients

[1] In which case: be prepared, all other clients will be a bitter disappointment.

simply don't know how to talk about this, and trying to have the discussion can sometimes create problems rather than solving them—the chances are that I am talking to a member of the editorial staff who is more at home with words and ideas than with concrete visual/spatial judgments. In my experience, the best approach is cautious and tentative. A way into this conversation can be to ask whom the book is intended for; if that doesn't elicit enough information I might ask what sort of tone of voice the book has. If the client is prompt to start talking about ideas for how the book should look, then good. If the client doesn't take the conversation in that direction, I'm unlikely to push it any further because I've learned that clients can end up in a position where they feel obliged to have an opinion about look-and-feel when maybe they hadn't considered the subject before now, and that can be counterproductive as they scrabble for an opinion about something that they genuinely hadn't thought about (and why should they—isn't that what I've been asked to do?). With clients like this it is often best to show them something (a first visual) so they have something tangible to react against and hang their opinions on.

If the client can be clear about whom the book is for, that's good. If they can be clear about look-and-feel, that's even better. What can be dispiriting are those occasions when the client brings out a book and says "can you do it like this," especially when the design they want reproduced is unsuited to the new book (for instance, if the content is quite different, or it is a different page size, or a very different length). I don't think the situation is unique to book designers, doubtless hairdressers, interior designers, composers, and other people engaged in creative activities meet this same challenge! My approach is based on "the client is always right" or at least they must believe that they are. Gentle negotiation is always worth trying; failing that, covert persuasion or guidance may work. Sometimes you simply do what the client wishes, against your better judgment. Try not to weep too bitterly as you get paid.

The other place to find out about the tone of voice is in the text itself. Dipping into a few pages at random can be instructive in terms of the sort of content and how it is presented. (A book designer's working life is easier if he or she is at least moderately interested in reading and to a reasonable degree literate.) Having said this, bear in mind two things: (1) any interpretation of tone of voice from a reading of the text is subjective, and the designer may interpret what they read differently to how their client interprets it; and (2) the tone of voice in the text is not necessarily the tone of voice that the design should have. Yes. No. Really. It is possible that an editor may realize that the authorial tone of voice is not quite what they had been hoping to achieve (and maybe the editor, for one reason or another, has not been able to get the text entirely into line) and so the design is going to be used as a corrective for the authorial tone of voice. However, this is entering realms of subtlety into which briefing conversations between clients and book designers rarely stray in my experience. But worth bearing in mind nonetheless.

How much of a new manuscript do you read?
I read a few pages, to get a sense of flavor or tone of voice. Generally the budgets I work for don't allow time to read the whole book. I have designed some books whose content was of no interest to me at all, some that I found unintelligible,[1] and others where I had to try hard not to be drawn into reading the whole thing.

I found a quote recently:

> The book artist . . . must first and foremost have a pronounced feeling for literature, and be able when necessary to assess its level accurately; those who have only a visual gift and no interest in literature are unfit to become book designers because they will struggle to understand that the art deployed in their designs lacks respect for the literature that the designs should be serving.[2]

I'm not sure I'd put it so adamantly, but I agree somewhat with the sentiments. It surprises me how few book designers seem that interested in reading. Two examples of this: a designer I worked with used to refer to text as "the chinwag between the pictures" (hmmm, exactly); and while I was design manager at Penguin, recruiting for a new junior designer with the customary deluge of applications, I went through the applications with a simple list of three requirements, one of which was that applicants had to say they liked—or were interested in—books and reading. That little requirement whittled the applicants from several hundred down to fewer than ten. Is it so much to ask that book designers have some interest in reading?

I'm sure my friends and colleagues will agree when I say that I'm a mine of pointless and obscure information picked up from books I've worked on and inadvertently dipped into. For instance, I think I know more about the training of anchorite nuns than is likely to ever prove necessary to my life. I'm sure that I also misremember a portion of what I read while working, so I'm likely to be a source of misinformed opinions too!

What do you look for before beginning a design?
Inspiration [laughs hysterically]. I'm sure I put it away carefully in a drawer somewhere hereabouts.

What influences your choice of text font?
Two principal groups of factors, the same two as I was considering in the initial briefing and research:

[1] Neither of which is necessarily a problem in terms of designing the book.

[2] I believe that comes from Jan Tschichold, though I found it quoted in an article about Fernand Baudin by Charles Gautier in issue 21 of the journal *Etapes*.

1. The functional requirements of the book. For instance:
    - Does the typeface have the full character set that the book requires? Not all type manufacturers are equally diligent in terms of the range of characters supplied in a typeface. However, one of the good consequences of globalization is that typical character sets are becoming generally more comprehensive.
    - Am I going to have to use a lot of bold and/or italic? If so, I will need to check that the bold or italic or whatever it is I need is usable in extended passages.
    - Do I need to choose a typeface that is economical on space or good in very small sizes due to the excessive length of the manuscript?

These are the sorts of functional requirements that my initial investigation of the text will have uncovered; the exact demands of each book are different and have a direct bearing on typeface choice.

2. The look-and-feel requirements of the book. For instance:
    - Does the text have a particular tone of voice (bearing in mind the potential pitfalls of interpreting the tone of voice oneself)?
    - Does the content have a particular time and place or subject that one is likely to want to use to flavor the design? I remember once a conversation with another designer about the most appropriate typeface for setting a volume of early nineteenth-century Polish fiction; we were overheard by a production manager who thought us most strange.

These are typical of the sorts of look-and-feel questions I might ask.

Of these two groups of factors, the former is empirical and fairly straightforward to check; the latter is subjective and more difficult to talk about (and justify unequivocally) to clients.

By the way, I use the terms "flavor," "look-and-feel," and "tone of voice" broadly interchangeably. I'm assuming you understand what I mean by these terms, because peversely and quixotically I'm not going to explain this wooly terminology.

My choice of text face will probably also be influenced by fashion, what I've been looking at recently (things I've seen and liked or disliked) and what I have a taste for at any given time (which may be capricious, but why not, within reason).

I am often asked how typeface choices are made, and I'm tempted to say "whim." Partly that is a deliberately provocative answer playing into the notion of the empty-headed designer; it is also partly true, but that whimsical decision has a backbone of steel born of years of experience.

An additional consideration is whether the client will cover the cost of purchasing new fonts.

What influences your choice of display font?

First of all I ask: is the text face suitable for headings and other display material (functionally and aesthetically)? If the text font is suitable, that will usually be my first option for the display material in the book. I only consider a different font for display material if the text font isn't going to work (doesn't have the right look-and-feel or the right functional characteristics) or if I have aesthetic reasons for wanting to use something different for display material.

In considering display fonts, aesthetic considerations are likely to be of a different sort to those for text faces. With text one is considering how the type looks and works at relatively small sizes in long passages; the display font(s) are going to be considered in blocks of fewer words in larger sizes, and so individual characters have to bear greater scrutiny.

Of course the relationship of the text and display face is a significant consideration. I usually make the text face the primary decision and select the display face in relation to it. A few years ago, Trajan (Carol Twombly for Adobe, 1989) seemed to be all over the cover of any number of books, and this often drove a desire to use it for display inside books, but I found that at the sort of sizes suited to display inside books, Trajan often looked too weak in relation to text faces—it simply wasn't made for use at this sort of size in conjunction with text faces; its serifs looked too small and its thin strokes too thin in relation to most typical seriffed text faces. If one had no choice but to use Trajan (it happens), there seemed to be two options: Trajan had to be (1) made a *lot* bigger to be suitably weighty; or (2) made slightly bolder by putting a stroke around the character (I daresay I'm not meant to admit to such shocking practices, possibly as verboten as the letterspacing of lowercase italic—it worked though).

My general premise is that if one has a seriffed text face, the display face (if it isn't the same seriffed face) will be a sans serif or something equally contrasting to the text face. In my experience there are only rare occasions when the text and display can use different seriffed faces. I recently designed a book using Sabon (Jan Tschichold for Linotype, Monotype, and Stempel, 1967, based on the type of Claude Garamond) for the text and Bauer Bodoni (Heinrich Jost for Bauer Type Foundry, 1926, based on the type of Giambattista Bodoni) for the headings; it worked but the relationship of the two typefaces required careful management. Alternatively one can reverse the standard and use a sans serif for the text and a seriffed typeface for the headings. This can work well, if done with care and of course with a sans serif that is readable in extended passages.

Do you have "desert island" fonts—ones that you almost always use as a default? Which ones? Why?
Sabon is probably my most readily identifiable default. It is just such a good workhorse. It rarely lets me down, and I know how to get it to do what I require. It is tolerant of a range of printing circumstances. It is robust in construction. It has a readable italic. It has pleasing and workable old-style figures and small caps. But mainly it is close to being generic without being bland or dull; it is like the good book designer in that it does its job well but completely discreetly. It is good for series styles because it does not have too strong a flavor that is likely to clash with too many of the texts it has to be applied to.

After Sabon, I'd be likely to head for Adobe Caslon (Carol Twombly for Adobe, 1992, based on the type of William Caslon), Fresco and Fresco Sans (Fred Smeijers for OurType, 1998), Quadraat (Fred Smeijers for FontFont, 1997) and Quadraat Sans (Fred Smeijers for FontFont, 1998), Monotype Fournier (directed by Stanley Morison for Monotype, 1924, based on the type of Pierre Simon Fournier), Pragma ND (Christopher Burke for Neufville Digital, 2002), Monotype Plantin (directed by Frank Hinman Pierpont for Monotype, 1913, based on the type of Robert Granjon), and Minion (Robert Slimbach for Adobe, 2000). Why? Well, I like how they work. Like Sabon, they behave in ways that I can work with. Monotype Fournier may seem an idiosyncratic or frivolous choice, but it is surprisingly robust and always well behaved for me (and the italic old-style figures satisfy a profound need for frivolity). But I'd never confine myself to just this list. Ask me next week and the list may have changed a bit. I might drop Minion off the list and put New Caledonia (William Addison Dwiggins for Mergenthaler, 1938) in its place. Monotype Baskerville (directed by Stanley Morison for Monotype, 1923, based on the type of John Baskerville) and Monotype Garamond (directed by Stanley Morison for Monotype, 1922, based on the type of Jean Jannon) used to be on my list, but recently when I've tried them they were distinctly uncooperative. I'd like to work more with the Enschede fonts, particularly Collis (Christoph Noordzij, 1993), but they are too costly to be a reasonable proposition (I can't afford them, my clients can't afford them). There are new text faces produced practically every week and some look tempting, but there are so many of them that it is difficult to know where to start in the face of this apparently unstoppable deluge. On my current list of things I'd like an excuse to try are MVB Verdigris (Mark van Bronkhorst for MVBfonts, 2003), Malabar (Dan Reynolds for Linotype, 2009), Ginkgo (Alex Rütten for Linotype, 2008), Dolly (Bas Jacobs, Akiem Helmling, and Sami Kortemäki for Underware, 2001), Arnhem (Fred Smeijers for OurType, 2002), Expo Serif (Mark Jamra for TypeCulture, 2008), Skolar (David Březina for TypeTogether, 2009), Maiola (Veronika Burian for Type-

Together, 2010). And then there's some typefaces I look at and think, "Ewwww, I wouldn't even touch that wearing rubber gloves and a surgical mask."

How often do you look for a special text face? Why?
Well, I always stop to consider the decision of what typeface to use. I might try a number of different typefaces in the early stages of a design. I might look for a special typeface if the book that I'm working on has very particular functional requirements (particular accented characters, or lots of Greek setting, for instance) or if it requires a very particular look-and-feel. I might also look for a special typeface if I'm simply bored of looking at the same old selection—often searches like this send me back to the usual suspects when I've not been able to find anything that does that indefinable extra that I'm looking for (so I just have to make the design work that bit harder to achieve it).

Do you have a standard text page (on your Mac or in your head) in various formats that you usually use to begin a design, or do you always begin setting up a unique text page layout?
When I worked at Penguin I had a very fixed set of standards that eventually drove the series styles I set up. They were a necessary short cut to get through the volume of work while ensuring a basis of consistent appearance.

I used to have a set of standard or default pages, and they were often the starting point for my designs. How far the design departed from this starting point would depend on the needs of the particular book—some books are more suited to an off-the-shelf solution than others, but there are few that don't need some additional attention.

Recently I've been more inclined to start with a blank page for each new project. I think the standards that I was using are now so ingrained that I don't need a reminder of them. This way I don't have to spend time undoing the parts of the standard that don't work for the particular project I'm engaged with. Also, my standards tend more to a formula or set of principles, and so the unfolding of them can depend on the starting point—a different starting point will give rise to a different design, even out of the same set of principles.

Do you usually discuss the design with the author—either before or after sample pages?
More often than not I don't have direct contact with the author. Now that I work freelance my primary contact is most likely to be a member of staff in a production or design role; beyond that I may talk to an editor, but it is not usual to have direct contact with the author. Even when I worked as a staff designer I only infrequently had direct contact with an author. The author is one stakeholder among several, and how much they are heeded and hence how much input they have into the design of their book will depend on their

relative status—a well-known author whose books sell well commands more attention than a first-time author with no track record.

Any input authors have into the design of their book is likely to be mediated by an editor. It can be problematic when I present a design proposal to my client in the production department, who then takes it to the editor, who then takes it to the author, and then any feedback follows the same circuitous route in the opposite direction. In this sort of situation the comments that the designer receives may bear little relation to the design that prompted them or what was actually said. This can be frustrating, unsatisfactory, and difficult to unravel. Annoyingly it is not always possible to anticipate and avoid or preempt this happening, but that's life.

Some authors can be a joy to work with directly, and others can be more difficult—they often seem to be at the more extreme ends of this spectrum than the staff in publishing houses. Perhaps because they have a much more personal investment in their book, authors are inclined to be more protective and anxious. Authors sometimes appear extremely apprehensive of what a designer will do to their precious book—as if we're bound to do the most inappropriate and hateful thing because they expect all designers to be as high-handed and empty-headed as our comedy characterization. And so a designer may require much patience and diplomacy in their dealings with authors. Gaining the trust of an apprehensive author can be an uphill but worthwhile task. I have a great deal of respect for authors—they did write the book after all—and always endeavour to understand and accommodate their wishes. Authors and designers can struggle to find common ground or a shared language with which to communicate. I've spent quite some time pondering this and have formed the conclusion that authors generally mediate the world verbally and designers mediate the world visually and ne'er the twain shall meet. I have found that some authors (and editors) when shown a visual cannot "look at" the visual but have to read it. This is similar to the challenge of coaxing useful comments or feedback at the briefing. Of course, not all authors are difficult to deal with: I have met authors with whom it was possible to have a meaningful and productive conversation about the design of their book—often they come from a background in journalism or have already written several books and so have a better idea about what to expect and are used to the apparently brutal indifference their words may be subjected to.

Where do you normally begin a new project?
Strangely, I often start work face down in a large body of chlorinated water (oh for goodness' sake, a swimming pool) or half-asleep on the Piccadilly Line. I then have to try and recapture these moments seated at my desk.

Once I've found out everything that I think I need to know, I almost always start designing with whatever is the most typical page or whatever makes up the largest portion of the book; this is often the basic text page, and I work outward from there: basic text page, then additional textual components, then text headings, chapter openings, part openings, end matter, front matter, in that order. And it is always likely that within this sequence a component designed later in the process may cause an already-designed component to be revised.

Occasionally a book design might start with a concept. Often that's the bit that happened face down in the swimming pool or half-asleep (not half-asleep in the swimming pool; that's probably not a good idea). Actually it's more frequent than "occasionally" that a book design starts with a concept, but I prefer to let it happen of its own accord without paying too much overt attention to it, so it often happens in an unacknowledged way, and I have the concept without having actually paid it any direct attention. Like small shy creatures, my concepts are best left to do what they need to without being startled by scrutiny. I'm sure this is not how design is meant to happen; I'm meant to have a sketch-book in which I note ideas and collect samples of stuff, and make sketches of how something might look, and try out any number of different ideas, but I prefer to keep it all jammed in my head and let it all mix around untidily and promiscuously until some speculative hybrid forms itself, totters out of the debris, and slips shyly into my visuals.

If you are not setting the book, how differently would you design the book? Does it make a difference to you who the typesetter would be?
It would make a difference, for sure. If I'm setting the book myself, I know there are certain decisions that I can postpone until I'm doing the formatting and page makeup (and I know while I'm making up the book I can always go back and adjust decisions if they're not working). If the book is going to a typesetter, I try to ensure that everything is sorted out before sending the book out because opportunities to fix or fine-tune later are more limited. These are differences of process that can lead to differences of design outcome.

If I'm typesetting the book myself I might make a design that is more challenging to implement, knowing that I'll be able to make decisions appropriately during the typesetting that I couldn't sensibly expect anyone else to do for me (asking a typesetter to second-guess a designer is not in my experience a recipe for design happiness). And for a typesetter I might make the design more straightforward to reduce the likelihood of my instructions being misunderstood or things going wrong or not coming out well. A further difference depends on whether I know the typesetters or not—if it's a typesetter whom I know and trust I might leave more to their judgment; if it's a typesetter I don't know or one I've had not good experiences with before, I'd try to design within what I know (or can predict) of their abilities.

How differently do you think about the design of fiction versus nonfiction?
Well, every book is different. I don't think that I have generically different approaches to fiction and nonfiction, per se. What differences there are tend to start with the broad differences of content and structure in fiction and nonfiction. In general, fiction tends to be less complex with fewer textual components and other bits and pieces. However, that is not always true: popular nonfiction can be a lot less complex than some literary fiction. For instance, Wilkie Collins's novel *The Woman in White* has a particularly idiosyncratic structure with a sequence of part and chapter headings that is eccentric to the point of seeming random (but actually perfectly appropriate), plus all of the end matter you expect of a student edition: altogether a lot more design-intensive than some nonfiction with a straightforward structure.

Do you consider the subject of accessibility?
I'm not an expert on this subject, but it concerns me, and I'm surprised by how infrequently accessibility seems to enter discussions of book design in comparison to other sorts of design.

Since I started work as a designer, awareness of the different needs of disabled[1] people and the legislation around this issue has changed greatly. There's much greater awareness of the need to create design solutions that can be used by as many people as possible, including those who may have some sort of impairment—hence the prevalence of the terms "accessible" and "inclusive." Many countries now have legislation that can enforce that requirement. In the U.K. we now have the Equality Act, which consolidated all legislation to do with discrimination of any sort—whether by race, sexual orientation, (dis)ability, or whatever. Some elements of the design professions appear to have embraced the principles of the legislation with vigor, but I have seen it make little impact on the design of mainstream publishing. Notwithstanding this, I believe it is a subject that book designers should be mindful of, in part because it poses challenges for which there do not appear to be simple answers.

There is a point of view that proposes that the ideal design output is a single solution that is accessible to everyone, but that can be difficult to achieve, as some special requirements can be at odds with each other in what they need, meaning that a single universally accessible solution is not possible. A good example of this is found in the needs of the visually impaired person and the dyslexic person. The visually impaired person is likely to require the greatest possible figure-ground contrast—bright white paper and crisp type in dense black ink. On the other hand, the dyslexic person is likely to struggle with such high contrast; they are likely to want less contrast, perhaps even with a colored background. How can both requirements be satisfied? In situations

[1] I'd like to avoid the potentially pejorative term "disabled," but many alternatives sound too much like politically correct box-ticking, and the terminology in favor seems to change rather frequently.

like this, one may need multiple solutions, but if one has to make alternative solutions that are engineered to accommodate particular impairments, they must not be poor relatives—it is essential that the alternative versions give the user the same rich and full experience as the "principal" version; there is absolutely no reason for alternative versions to be in any way diminished or reduced in order to accommodate the demands of the disability.

The most obvious form of disability that the book designer will have to consider is visual impairment, but it doesn't stop there; you may also need to consider physical and cognitive impairments.

Visual Impairment

Research into and information on design for people with visual impairment often overlaps with research into legibility and readability:

Sophie Beier's recent book *Reading Letters: Designing for Legibility* (Amsterdam: BIS Publishers, 2012) is a good summary of research into designing for legibility.

Alex Poole's website gives a useful overview of his review of research into the legibility of serif versus sans serif typefaces (http://alexpoole.info/which-are-more-legible-serif-or-sans-serif-typefaces/).

Ole Lund's Ph.D. thesis, "Knowledge Construction in Typography: The Case of Legibility Research and the Legibility of Sans Serif Typefaces" (available through the British Library Electronic Theses Online Service), covers similar ground.

See It Right: Making Information Accessible for People with Sight Problems is published in the U.K. by the Royal National Institute for Blind People (RNIB) and is a good starting point but contains some statements that seem surprising:

> *There is no scientific evidence to suggest that one category [either seriffed or sans serif typefaces] is easier for people with sight problems to read than the other, but there is anecdotal evidence that suggests a clear sans serif typeface is preferable.*
>
> *Most typefaces in common use in books and newspapers, whether serif or sans serif, are easy to read.*
>
> *Most books are set in semibold serif typefaces.*

Part of the problem with this serif versus sans serif debate is that there are legible and illegible typefaces in both categories, and there are so many other factors to consider (type size, line length, word spacing, and contrast, to name a few). The third of these statements I find the most worrying. I think that most books in seriffed typefaces are set in a weight usually called "roman," "normal," or "regular." If these seriffed typefaces have a semibold weight,

I doubt that it is regularly used for book setting. With sans serif typefaces, weight naming is rather more variable, but I'd still expect to use a weight called "roman," or "regular," or less likely "medium," but if I was setting a book in a weight called semibold I'd be wondering who was responsible for the naming of the weights. I understand that the RNIB's advice is aimed at discouraging the use of lighter weights of type for text setting, but I wonder if the user uncritically following this advice is too likely to come unstuck.

I wonder to what extent designers were involved in the writing of *See It Right*; it looks as if they were not consulted in the design of the publication—it may be that the book follows its own guidance, but the result is not in this instance an attractive publication. This really should have been a model demonstrating that good accessible design can also be appealing.

Possibly e-book readers are an attractive option for the visually impaired because of the possibility of increasing the text size; however, many of the e-book readers fall down by offering displeasing typefaces, poor relationship of line spacing to word spacing, no hyphenation, and diminished figure-ground contrast, all of which may hinder ease of reading whether visually impaired or not. Hopefully all of these things will improve over time.

Physical Impairment

This is not often considered in relation to book design, but it is a factor in the handling of a book.[1] I have a friend with arthritis whose wrists are so weak that she can no longer hold a large book in her hands, so she must read only lightweight books, or sit at a table in order to read a heavier book, and if the book is tightly bound she will struggle to keep the pages open.

All aspects of the design and production of a book may have a bearing on how physically accessible it is.

Returning to the subject of e-book readers, I wonder how easy the controls are to use for someone with limited motor skills.

Cognitive Impairment

Cognitive impairments are as diverse as visual and physical impairments in the sorts of conditions encompassed and the sorts of accommodations required. One might be considering people who have, for instance, dyslexia, processing impairments, dementia, stroke victims, or people taking certain types of medication, all of which are different in the effects they have on cognitive abilities.

A greater part of the responsibility for ensuring accessibility to people with cognitive impairment falls to the author and editor of the book—they need to make the content as clear as it can be. And then the designer has to ensure that the design is also as clear as possible and serves the content as well as possible. I have found few guidelines dealing with the accessibility of printed

[1] Books are three-dimensional objects; they exist in time and space, they have weight and texture, even smell and taste. It is impossible to read a book without handling it, feeling its weight, discovering the exact flexibility of the pages as you turn them over.

documents for people with cognitive impairments; where found, they tend to include factors such as: clear document structure reflected in the design, exclusion of distracting design features, clear navigation devices. This list might sound as if it were driving in the direction of a somewhat reduced design; however, it has also been suggested that in addition to the above list a design that gives a full and rich sensory experience can aid understanding and retention exactly because the sensory stimulation is so much broader. What is important is that the rich and full sensory experience must be directed towards making the content clear and still avoid distraction and confusion. And as I wrote earlier, accessible versions of documents should not be regarded as poor relatives.

Can you tell us something about your approach to sizes and measurements?
Over the last few years I have made increasing use of type sizes and measurements that are not whole numbers of points or picas, by which I mean I'm as likely to choose (for instance) a text size of 10.648 pt as 10.5 or 11 pt. "Why?" I hear you say. Well, first of all, measurement systems are ultimately arbitrary in their unit size—just change the units in the document in InDesign or Quark on your Mac from points to millimeters and watch the dimensions all become awkward numbers to three decimal places. So is there any real reason why 10 pt is better than 10.648 pt?

I use awkward point sizes for particular reasons, usually because of their relation to other elements of the book and the design. Often all of the layout dimensions that I now use are derived from the trimmed page size of the particular book. For instance, in my recent work the baseline–baseline distance in the main text block is probably a whole increment of the total page depth. Let me illustrate this with examples from a recent project:

- The main text was 11.8/14.74 pt and that 14.74 pt baseline–baseline distance was equal to 1/45 of the full page depth.
- Text line 1 sat on a baseline 58.96 pts from the top of the page; that's the text baseline–baseline distance multiplied by 4 (four lines down from the top edge of the page).
- Chapter headings in the book are 23.6/22.11 pt—this heading type size is 2 times the text size, and the baseline–baseline distance is 1.5 times the text baseline–baseline distance (I find headings often work better with less interlinear space than text setting).
- In the same book the end matter was set down to 8.85/11.055 pt, which the arithmetically minded will immediately spot is three quarters of 11.8/14.74 (the text size and baseline–baseline distance).

I could go on, but hopefully you get the point.

I work a lot with document grids that look like squared paper, and everything fits into that grid, and the rectangles that make up the grid exactly fit the trimmed page. I often start with a grid that divides the width and depth of the page into nine (and then into ninths of that). Why ninths? Well, I've found that dividing the page width into ninths gives a grid that seems to give useful-sized intervals (especially if that grid is then divided into quarters or ninths). Actually I'd much rather use a grid that divided the page width into eight (and eighths thereof), but practice has revealed that eighths don't work so well as ninths. The vertical grid that divides the page depth by nine (and ninths thereof, too) is less prone to straightforward usefulness than the horizontal grid, but I replace it with baseline–baseline distances that are an increment of the full page depth (and often that baseline grid is further divided into quarters).

InDesign and Quark have both been able to do this sort of arithmetic for years—everyone knows that if you type 10*1.5 into the font size window, it automatically calculates 10 × 1.5 = 15 for you. How easy is that; no need to do your own arithmetic, ever! And you can specify measurements to up to three decimal places. You can put your grid on every page of the document. And you don't have to remember the numbers. Your Mac does all this for you—so why not use it?

The final arbiter is always "does it look right?" If it doesn't look right I change it, probably for a different numerical pattern, until it looks right.

Maybe you're thinking that this all sounds like a postmodern parlor game—sudoku for book designers or something. Well, it works for me. I hope that utilizing these proportional relationships makes the books look better, and it helps to make structure and order out of the components and their relationships to each other in the potentially shapeless manuscripts that land on my desk. Try it; it's fun. No? OK so maybe I am strange.

This approach is an ongoing project that I've been gradually developing over the last few years. The following case studies show (among other things) snapshots of different points during the development of this approach, and I've also included in the case studies some comments on how I might have adjusted the dimensions I used to bring them in line with my current practice, partly to retrospectively satisfy my own curiosity but also hopefully to shed more light on this apparently eccentric practice of mine.

CASE STUDY: PENGUIN CLASSICS SERIES STYLE

During 2002–2003 I worked on a new series style for the insides of Penguin Classics. I had been working at Penguin for nearly ten years; designing the insides of Penguin Classics had been part of my work since joining the company. When I first started designing Penguin Classics there was no explicit design direction for them; my decision when I first got my hands on their design was to give them a resolutely traditional styling. After I had been working on

London's main artery is also the second longest river in England. The Thames rises in Gloucestershire, and meanders through Oxfordshire and Berkshire to London. There it was easily forded in ancient times, a factor that led the Romans to set up camp in what is now the City of London c. AD 43. The Thames became its main transport network and by the 19th century was filled with ships unloading goods at one of the world's busiest ports. Since the closure of the docks and the building of fast roads in the second half of the 20th century the Thames has emptied of craft, although in recent years much of the land along its banks has been reborn for residential and commercial use.¶

■ The Thames section covers sites and buildings of interest by the river in Greater London.¶

north bank: Spelthorne to Thurrock (Greater London boundaries)¶

HAMPTON¶

A small pleasant village at the far western edge of the Greater London boundary set at some distance from the tourist-happy enclave of Hampton Court¶

St Mary, Thames Street. The Tomb of Susannah Thomas who died in 1731 captivates visitors to the village church for it reads: "Dying unmarried, she left her fortune to her next Heirs in Blood, under the restriction of their being Protestants, and in failure of such Issue to Charitable Uses." In Jerome K Jerome's much-loved Thames sojourn, Three Men In A Boat (1889), one passage runs: "Harris wanted me to get out at Hampton Church to go and see Mrs Thomas's Tomb. 'Who is Mrs Thomas?' I asked. 'How should I know' replied Harris. 'She's a lady that's got a funny tomb and I want to see it.'"¶

Garrick's Temple to Shakespeare, Hampton Court Road, near Hogarth Way. Classically built in 1756 and with a domed roof, this small folly by the river just to the east of Hampton was constructed by the great actor David Garrick and contains relics that supposedly belonged to the writer including his gloves and a signet ring sporting the initials "W. S."¶

Garrick's Villa, Hampton Court Road, near Hogarth Way. Almost destroyed by fire in 2008, this was the 18th-century actor's riverside home, where he entertained Dr Johnson and the King of Denmark. Just as the poet Alexander Pope had constructed a grotto under the grounds of his Twickenham villa Garrick created one running under his Hampton villa towards the river. The house was converted to flats in 1922.¶

Tagg's Island, ½ mile west of Hampton Bridge. An idyllic private island with Britain's only floating B&B previously known as Walnut Tree Ait. It is named after Tom Tagg who hired out boats here in the mid-19th century. He built the Thames Hotel here in 1872 and it was later remodelled by Fred Karno, mentor to Charlie Chaplin, into a music hall, the Karsino. While Karno struggled to fill the Karsino soldiers on the Western Front during the Great War sang: "We are Fred Karno's Army. The ragtime infantry/ Fred Karno is our captain, Charlie Chaplin our O.C./And when we get to Berlin, the Kaiser will say 'Hoch hoch, Mein Gott'/ what a jolly fine lot, Are the boys in Company A."¶

» After the War, custom picked up as punters journeyed to hear the banter from acts such as Harry Weldon and Jack Melville:¶

WELDON: Are you married?¶

MELVILLE: Yes, sixteen wives, no kids.¶

WELDON: Ridiculous. No man in England is allowed sixteen wives.¶

MELVILLE: Yes he is. It says so in the Marriage Service: "Four richer, four poorer, four better, four worse."¶

» Karno lived in a houseboat, the Astoria, which is moored nearby and which is now owned by Pink Floyd guitarist Dave Gilmour where parts of Pink Floyd's *The Division Bell* were recorded.¶

Hampton Bridge. An 1930s bridge by Edwin Lutyens which replaced earlier connec-

124 Central London EC1, WC1-2

London's main artery is also the second longest river in England. The Thames rises in Gloucestershire, and meanders through Oxfordshire and Berkshire to London. There it was easily forded in ancient times, a factor that led the Romans to set up camp in what is now the City of London c. AD 43. The Thames became its main transport network and by the 19th century was filled with ships unloading goods at one of the world's busiest ports. Since the closure of the docks and the building of fast roads in the second half of the 20th century the Thames has emptied of craft, although in recent years much of the land along its banks has been reborn for residential and commercial use.

● The Thames section covers sites and buildings of interest by the river in Greater London.

north bank: Spelthorne to Thurrock (Greater London boundaries)

HAMPTON

A small pleasant village at the far western edge of the Greater London boundary set at some distance from the tourist-happy enclave of Hampton Court

St Mary, Thames Street. The Tomb of Susannah Thomas who died in 1731 captivates visitors to the village church for it reads: "Dying unmarried, she left her fortune to her next Heirs in Blood, under the restriction of their being Protestants, and in failure of such Issue to Charitable Uses." In Jerome K Jerome's much-loved Thames sojourn, Three Men In A Boat (1889), one passage runs: "Harris wanted me to get out at Hampton Church to go and see Mrs Thomas's Tomb. 'Who is Mrs Thomas?' I asked. 'How should I know' replied Harris. 'She's a lady that's got a funny tomb and I want to see it.'"

Garrick's Temple to Shakespeare, Hampton Court Road, near Hogarth Way. Classically built in 1756 and with a domed roof, this small folly by the river just to the east of Hampton was constructed by the great actor David Garrick and contains relics that supposedly belonged to the writer including his gloves and a signet ring sporting the initials "W. S.".

Garrick's Villa, Hampton Court Road, near Hogarth Way. Almost destroyed by fire in 2008, this was the 18th century actor's riverside home, where he entertained Dr Johnson and the King of Denmark. Just as the poet Alexander Pope had constructed a grotto under the grounds of his Twickenham villa Garrick created one running under his Hampton villa towards the river. The house was converted to flats in 1922.

Tagg's Island, ½ mile west of Hampton Bridge. An idyllic private island with Britain's only floating B&B previously known as Walnut Tree Ait. It is named after Tom Tagg who hired out boats here in the mid-19th century. He built the Thames Hotel here in 1872 and it was later remodelled by Fred Karno, mentor to Charlie Chaplin, into a music hall, the Karsino. While Karno struggled to fill the Karsino soldiers on the Western Front during the Great War sang: "We are Fred Karno's Army, The ragtime infantry/ Fred Karno is our captain, Charlie Chaplin our O. C./And when we get to Berlin, the Kaiser will say 'Hoch hoch, Mein Gott'/ what a jolly fine lot, Are the boys in Company A."

After the War, custom picked up as punters journeyed to hear the banter from acts such as Harry Weldon and Jack Melville:

WELDON: Are you married?
MELVILLE: Yes, sixteen wives, no kids.
WELDON: Ridiculous. No man in England is allowed sixteen wives.
MELVILLE: Yes he is. It says so in the Marriage Service: "Four richer, four poorer, four better, four worse!"

Karno lived in a houseboat, the Astoria, which is moored nearby and which is now owned by Pink Floyd guitarist Dave Gilmour where parts of Pink Floyd's *The Division Bell* were recorded.

Hampton Bridge. An 1930s bridge by Edwin Lutyens which replaced earlier connec-

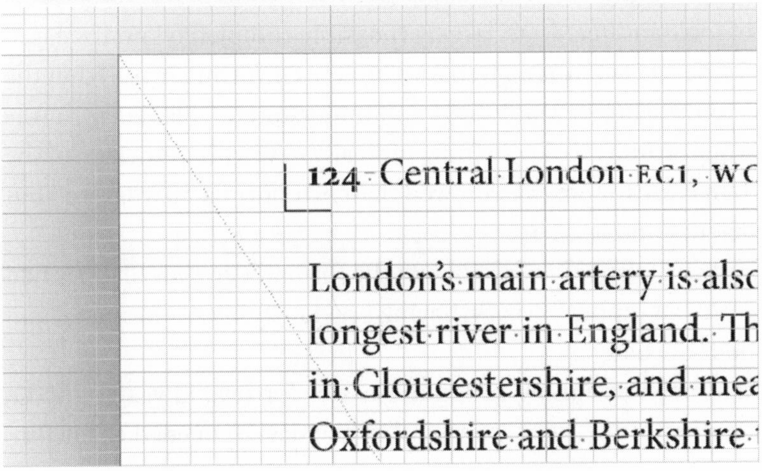

124 Central London EC1, WC

London's main artery is also

longest river in England. Th

in Gloucestershire, and mea

Oxfordshire and Berkshire

These three images show screenshots from a typical page of a visual. You can see how the grid increments exactly fit the page width and depth, and all parts of the design exactly sit on that grid—the running head and page number, the little rule device, the text area (the first image shows the page with guides turned on; the second image shows the same page with guides turned off so you can see more clearly what's actually on the page; and the third image shows a zoomed-in detail of the top of the page).

them for three or four years I had evolved a working series style for Penguin Classics. This previous series style had considerable flexibility—it gave a basic text page, a set of heading styles, and described an approach, but allowed the designer to choose a suitable typeface and adjust headings and other components as necessary for the content of the particular volume. In 2002, in conjunction with the redesign of the covers for Penguin Classics, the decision was made to make the design of the insides much more regularized, in order to keep down costs by allowing more straightforward volumes to go directly to the typesetter with minimal (or no) design intervention.

It might seem strange for me—the design manager—to agree to something that was likely to reduce the design workload and as a result potentially reduce the number of designers employed, but I could foresee that only the most straightforward volumes would do without design intervention (and these volumes are the least interesting to work on in design terms). Also, this strategy of minimizing design time on individual titles was not unique to Penguin Classics—the same thing was being done in a number of different parts of Penguin Books, and in other publishing companies—there was little likelihood of success in my trying to stop the tide. But it may be worth noting that all of the text designers at Penguin were made redundant not long after the completion of the Classics series style. Maybe that was a coincidence.

A Design Brief?

It is hard to recall, several years later, what the starting point for the design was. I don't recollect a briefing meeting; possibly it was fairly cursory because I already knew so much of what the design functionally needed to cope with (briefings were often fairly minimal). Probably the brief was to come up with a series style that required less individual book-by-book attention from designers, would get as many words as possible onto the page without compromising the size of type, and would keep the Americans happy (never an easy thing, to come up with a design that satisfies both American and U.K. audiences).[1]

The issue of look-and-feel went largely (possibly completely) undiscussed at the time. I suspect that it was a given for both the editor and myself that the design would continue to be traditional and understated. This redesign was seen not as an opportunity to do anything radically new with the design of the Classics but to make a system that allowed them to continue to work well but with more efficiency and less cost.

Another given with Penguin Classics was the format. Penguin Classics had been b-format[2] for a number of years (having previously been a-format[3]), and that wasn't about to change.

Because I had been designing Penguin Classics for several years, I had a good understanding of the full scope of what the design needed to encom-

[1] American books always appear more "designed" than British books; they have more typographical devices, rules, ornaments, drop capitals—anything that the designer can do to trumpet their presence to the world. I was indoctrinated with a very different approach: that of making a design work with the most minimal of means—not adding anything to the page that was unnecessary and only adding additional "stuff" at all if it was the only way to get the design to work.

[2] b-format = 198 mm high × 129 mm wide.

[3] a-format = 181 mm high × 111 mm wide.

pass in terms of functionality—down to the detail of, for instance, knowing that a footnote might contain quoted verse drama and so a typographical specification was required even for esoteric things like verse drama extracts in footnotes.

In designing this series style and the typesetting specification, I had to cover a range of scenarios:

- The most straightforward books go directly to the typesetters without being seen by a designer. This means that the typesetting specification must be intelligible to the typesetter, and that the editor must mark up the manuscript using terminology and names consistent with those used in the typesetting specification.
- Some books fall within the series style but go to a designer before going to the typesetter because they are sufficiently complex to require input from a designer. This means that the typesetting specification must be intelligible to a designer who will select what parts to pass on to the typesetter and ensure that the editor's terminology matches the typesetting specification.
- Some books are very complex and contain elements that are not encompassed within the series style. These books clearly require design input, and the designer (not necessarily me) has to be able to understand the series style in sufficient depth to be able to extrapolate what to do in situations that fall outside of the scope of the series style.

Typesetters, designers, and editors all had to be able to make use of the series style typesetting specification document. I knew the typesetters who were at that stage typesetting the classics (and very good they were, too—Rowlands Phototypesetting, no longer in business and much missed); however, I had to anticipate the likelihood of other typesetters taking on the work, and I could not predict how competent they might be. Also I could not predict how competent any intervening designers might be. I know from experience that trying to understand another designer's thought process can be rather like trying to finish cooking a dinner that someone else started, and in their kitchen—nothing is quite where you expect it or done in the way you expect, and probably doesn't taste quite right either. So, I wanted to make the series style as thorough and comprehensive as possible, and presented as clearly as possible, making it easy to find what one needed. The balance of how much information to give was difficult to decide: too much information and the user may give up looking and maybe assume that what they are trying to find isn't there; too little information and the user has to make guesses to fill in the missing information. Writing and designing the typesetting specification document for the series style proved to be a substantial part of the project; if

I had to do it all again, there is more that I would change about the specification document than about the series style itself.

Part of my project was to ensure that the editorial staff knew and understood how the new series style worked and what to call the various components. This had one side-benefit: the editors would be able to anticipate what the outcome from their instructions should look like (they could check in the style document what a verse drama extract in a footnote would turn out like, rather than just indicating in the manuscript that there was a verse drama extract in the footnote and hoping the designer would deal with it appropriately).

Some Rejected Design Approaches

Early in the design process, it crossed my mind to consider making the design radically different—maybe ranged left headings, maybe ranged left unjustified text, maybe even sans serif text.[1] This amounted to little more than idle speculation on my part though because I was certain that the editors would barely glance at such proposals before rejecting them (in the eleven years I worked full time at Penguin, I designed only a handful of books that didn't have main text set justified in a traditional seriffed typeface).

I gave more consideration to the idea of using typography to mark the difference between main text and apparatus.[2] Given that the main text has a very different status to the apparatus, I thought that this might help the reader to appreciate what was the original author's work and what was supporting material. I considered two strategies for differentiation:

- using a sans serif typeface for all apparatus and editorial interventions
- having all apparatus set down (that is, setting down the front matter to match the end matter).

While I could see benefits to using some sort of typographical differentiation, I dissuaded myself for two reasons. First of all I was not convinced that it would be an easy job to persuade the editors of the value of such a scheme, and I didn't want to antagonize them or make them more anxious than was absolutely necessary—I needed to choose my battles wisely.[3] Secondly, sometimes the line between authorial text and editorial intervention can be less than clear. To give a hypothetical example: maybe part titles were added to a book long ago by the editor of the first edition and the author hated them, but they've been included ever since. Would they count as part of the original text, or part of the editorial intervention? I could see such scope for muddle that I thought it best to steer clear.

Typeface Choice

One of my first design decisions was to choose Sabon for the text face.

In the previous series style for Classics the choice of typeface had been left

[1] This is radical! Sans serif text in a Penguin Classic! There might have been riots in the Strand!

[2] By "apparatus" I mean all of the supporting editorial material: this encompasses any introductions or other front matter, any footnotes or editorial comments in the main text, and any end matter such as endnotes, bibliography, commentary, and so on—all the stuff that wasn't written by the author as part of the original book.

[3] Or as wisely as I could; it's not something I'd claim to be particularly good at.

to the designer of the particular volume (to choose something with an appropriate flavor for the time and place of the main text of the volume), but this was no longer an option. I had to choose a single typeface that would suit all of the Penguin Classics canon.

I chose Sabon for its robustness, its usability at small sizes, and its self-effacing lack of very particular flavor; I chose it for its readable italic, and good small caps and old-style numerals.

I planned to use Sabon for the whole volume—both text and display setting. This approach matched the previous Classics series style. It seems to look more traditional and understated in a way that is suited to the overall ethos of Penguin Classics. To be honest, I didn't seriously consider using a different display face—there was no clear reason to do so, and the introduction of another typeface into the complex structure of the Classics was (in my opinion) likely to create more problems than it solved.

A Basic Text Page: Text, Running Heads, Page Numbers

Having made a provisional choice of typeface,[1] the next step was to design a basic text page.

This design of the basic text page was driven strongly by U.K. and U.S. commissioning editors who wanted to get more words on the page and make the text size bigger. Usually getting more words on the page results in making the type smaller, so trying to get more words on the page while making the type bigger, not smaller, was going to be interesting to resolve, wasn't it? At the time it was relatively unusual for Penguin U.S. to have any input into the design of books at Penguin U.K. I had no direct contact with the U.S. editor(s)—what I heard from them was mediated by the U.K. editor. Despite the editorial wish to get as many words per page in as big a size as possible, I was concerned that the basic text page shouldn't give the impression of having too much text jammed onto it. So, in addition to the two potentially contradictory wishes of the editors, I added a third demand all of my own. Oh yes, I'm wild, don't try to stop me.

In order to maximize the depth available for the text block on the page (an attempt to increase the number of words per page), I put the page number at the top of the page, sitting it on the same baseline as the running head. Previously Classics had their running head above the text block and the page number below it, both centered on the text measure—a classic page layout but obviously allowing less depth for the main text block whereas consolidating page number and running head in the same space on the page left more room available for main text. I have a total aversion to the default that seems to crop up so often that puts running head and page number both at the top of the page with centered running heads and the page number ranged out to the fore-edge—I find it dated and awkward.[2] For Penguin Classics

[1] At this stage the typeface choice really was provisional, but I didn't have any reason to reconsider it at any stage during the design process.

[2] No indeed. I. really. do. hate. it. In a nails-dragged-down-a-blackboard sort of way, I do not understand why this car crash of an arrangement is used so often; it is awkward to look at and so easy to avoid. So, now you know.

Opposite:
These illustrations compare the previous standard design and the new standard. The text size is bigger; the pages are definitely blacker and heavier in the new design, but it does not look uncomfortably full.

I ranged the page numbers out to the fore-edge and ranged the running heads to the back margin. In my opinion this creates a better balance on spreads and pages—ranging both running heads and page numbers out to the edges of the text width works well to counterbalance elements centered in the text width. In the Classics the running heads customarily give the book title on the left-hand page and the chapter title on the right-hand page, and having the running heads ranged toward each other around the spine seems to create a meaningful relationship between the running heads on the pages of a spread.

For the text block itself, we went through a number of iterations as I tried to satisfy the editors' wishes to have a big text size as well as more words per page and my wish to keep some sense of space in the pages. Previously the Classics default had been 10/12.5 pt Monotype Bembo, × 23 pica measure × 36 lines. I changed this to 10.25/12.25 pt Sabon × 23 pica measure × 38 lines. The difference between 10/12.5 and 10.25/12.25 pt may not seem much, but the version of Sabon we were using is unusually big on its body, so it is actually a significant increase in text size. The pages are denser-looking for sure, but they are not uncomfortable to read—it worked out better than I was anticipating (dreading), and I was relieved to not have to cram even more words onto the page.

Returning to the running heads and page numbers, the size of these components has to be considered in relation to the text size. There is much variety in how designers regard the relationship between running heads, page numbers, and the text they accompany. My starting premises are: that the running heads and page numbers are navigational devices that are subservient to the main content/text, even if they are decorative they must still be able to perform their navigational function, and that it is important to be able to locate and read running heads and page numbers when one needs to, but they should not demand the reader's attention at other times.

The fact that these components are in the margin[1] gives them some conspicuousness and makes it relatively easy for the reader to spot them, particularly if they are in the sort of locations they customarily occupy and are designed in the sorts of ways that readers expect. That—in my opinion—should be sufficient, and it is rare that I would want to make them particularly emphatic beyond that (do that and you risk them starting to look like text headings or somehow more important than the text and that may confuse readers). Running heads and page numbers tend to look a bit too emphatic to me if they are the same size as the text, so my practice is to make them a bit smaller than the main text size—typically 90 percent of it. I made the running heads and folios smaller than usual in the Classics, for three reasons:

- The text was larger than I would customarily specify for this page size, and my default proportions resulted in running heads and folios that simply looked too big on the page.

[1]Running heads and page numbers could go elsewhere than in the margin, but the options are limited, and it would probably make them more difficult to find and identify.

"It's a mineral, I *think*," said Alice.

"Of course it is," said the Duchess, who seemed ready to agree to everything that Alice said: "there's a large mustard-mine near here. And the moral of that is—'The more there is of mine, the less there is of yours.'"

"Oh, I know!" exclaimed Alice, who had not attended to this last remark. "It's a vegetable. It doesn't look like one, but it is."

"I quite agree with you," said the Duchess; "and the moral of that is—'Be what you would seem to be'[8]—or, if you'd like it put more simply—'Never imagine yourself not to be otherwise than what it might appear to others that what you were or might have been was not otherwise than what you had been would have appeared to them to be otherwise.'"

"I think I should understand that better," Alice said very politely, "if I had it written down: but I ca'n't quite follow it as you say it."

"That's nothing to what I could say if I chose," the Duchess replied, in a pleased tone.

"Pray don't trouble yourself to say it any longer than that," said Alice.

"Oh, don't talk about trouble!" said the Duchess. "I make you a present of everything I've said as yet."

"A cheap sort of present!" thought Alice. "I'm glad people don't give birthday-presents like that!" But she did not venture to say it out loud.

"Thinking again?" the Duchess asked, with another dig of her sharp little chin.

"I've a right to think," said Alice sharply, for she was beginning to feel a little worried.

"Just about as much right," said the Duchess, "as pigs have to fly;[9] and the m——"

But here, to Alice's great surprise, the Duchess's voice died away, even in the middle of her favourite word 'moral,' and the arm that was linked into hers began to tremble. Alice looked up, and there stood the Queen in front of them, with her arms folded, frowning like a thunderstorm.

"A fine day, your Majesty!" the Duchess began in a low, weak voice.

"Now, I give you fair warning," shouted the Queen, stamping on

the ground as she spoke; "either you or your head must be off, and that in about half no time! Take your choice!"

The Duchess took her choice, and was gone in a moment.

"Let's go on with the game," the Queen said to Alice; and Alice was too much frightened to say a word, but slowly followed her back to the croquet-ground.

The other guests had taken advantage of the Queen's absence, and were resting in the shade: however, the moment they saw her, they hurried back to the game, the Queen merely remarking that a moment's delay would cost them their lives.

All the time they were playing the Queen never left off quarreling with the other players, and shouting "Off with his head!" or "Off with her head!" Those whom she sentenced[10] were taken into custody by the soldiers, who of course had to leave off being arches to do this, so that, by the end of half an hour or so, there were no arches left, and all the players, except the King, the Queen, and Alice, were in custody and under sentence of execution.

Then the Queen left off, quite out of breath, and said to Alice "Have you seen the Mock Turtle yet?"

"No," said Alice. "I don't even know what a Mock Turtle is."

"It's the thing Mock Turtle Soup is made from,"[11] said the Queen.

"I never saw one, or heard of one," said Alice.

"Come on, then," said the Queen, "and he shall tell you his history."

As they walked off together, Alice heard the King say in a low voice, to the company generally, "You are all pardoned." "Come, *that's* a good thing!" she said to herself, for she had felt quite unhappy at the number of executions the Queen had ordered.

They very soon came upon a Gryphon,[12] lying fast asleep in the sun. (If you don't know what a Gryphon is, look at the picture.) "Up, lazy thing!" said the Queen, "and take this young lady to see the Mock Turtle, and to hear his history. I must go back and see after some executions I have ordered;" and she walked off, leaving Alice alone with the Gryphon. Alice did not quite like the look of the creature, but on the whole she thought it would be quite as safe to stay with it as to go after that savage Queen: so she waited.

The Gryphon sat up and rubbed its eyes: then it watched the Queen

He gave permission for the works of Titus Labienus, Cremutius Cordus, and Cassius Severus, which had been banned by order of the Senate, to be routed out and republished – stating it to be entirely in his interest that posterity should be in full possession of all historical facts; also, he revived Augustus' practice, discontinued by Tiberius, of publishing an imperial budget; invested the magistrates with full authority, not requiring them to apply for his confirmation of sentences; and strictly and scrupulously scanned the list of knights but, though publicly dismounting any who had behaved in a wicked or scandalous manner, merely omitted the names of those guilty of lesser misbehaviour from the list which he read out. Gaius' creation of a fifth judicial division aided jurors to keep abreast of their work; his reviving of the electoral system was designed to restore popular control over the magistracy. He honoured faithfully and uncritically every one of the bequests in Tiberius' will, though this had been set aside by the Senate, and in that of his maternal great-grandmother Livia, which Tiberius had suppressed; abolished the Italian half-per-cent auction tax; and paid compensation to a great many people whose houses had been damaged by fire. Any king whom he restored to the throne was awarded the arrears of taxes and revenue that had accumulated since his deposition – Antiochus of Commagene, for example, got a refund of a million gold pieces from the Public Treasury. To show his interest in every kind of noble action he awarded 8,000 gold pieces to a freedwoman who, though put to extreme torture, had not revealed her patron's guilt. These acts won him many official honours, among them a golden shield, carried once a year to the Capitol by the priestly colleges marching in procession, and followed by the Senate, while children of noble birth chanted an anthem in praise of his virtues. By a senatorial decree the festival of Parilia,[3] was transferred to the day of his accession, as though Rome had now been born again.

17. Gaius held four consulships: the earliest for two months, from 1 July; the next for the whole month of January; the third for the first thirteen days of January; and the fourth for the first seven. Only the last two were in sequence.[4] He assumed his third consulship without a colleague. Some historians describe this as

a high-handed breach of precedent; but unfairly, because he was then quartered at Lugdunum, where the news that his fellow Consul-elect had died in Rome, just before the New Year, had not reached him in time. He twice presented every member of the commons with three gold pieces; and twice invited all the senators and knights, with their wives and children, to an extravagant banquet. At the first of these banquets he gave every man a toga and every woman a red or purple scarf. He also added to the gaiety of Rome by extending the customary four days of the Saturnalia, with a fifth, known as 'Youth Day'.

18. Gaius held several gladiatorial contests, some in Statilius Taurus' amphitheatre, and others in the Enclosure; diversifying them with prize-fights between the best boxers of Africa and Campania, and occasionally allowing magistrates or friends to preside at these instead of doing so himself. Again, he staged a great number of different theatrical shows of various kinds and in various buildings – sometimes at night, with the whole city illuminated – and would scatter vouchers among the audience entitling them to all sorts of gifts, over and above the basket of food which was everyone's due. At one banquet, noticing with what extraordinary gusto a knight seated opposite dug into the food, he sent him his own heaped plate as well; and rewarded a senator, who had been similarly enjoying himself, with a praetorship, though it was not yet his turn to hold this office. Many all-day Games were celebrated in the Circus and, between races, Gaius introduced panther-baiting and the Trojan war-dance. For certain special Games, when all the charioteers were men of senatorial rank, he had the Circus decorated in red and green. Once, while he was inspecting the Circus equipment, from the Gelotian House which overlooks it, a group of people standing in the near-by balconies called out: 'What about a day's racing, Caesar?' So, on the spur of the moment, he gave immediate orders for games to be held.

19. One of his spectacles was on such a fantastic scale that nothing like it had ever been seen before. He collected all available merchant ships and anchored them in two lines, close together, the whole way from Baiae to the mole at Puteoli, a distance of more than three and a half Roman miles. Then he

Close-up of running head and main text. As you can see, the running head is set in small caps that are smaller than the main text size. While I'd usually make running heads smaller than text, the size difference here is greater than I'd normally consider—this was because the text size was quite large for the page size, and the running heads looked too heavy if they were any bigger than this.

GAIUS (CALIGULA)

a high-handed breach of precedent; but u
then quartered at Lugdunum, where th
Consul-elect had died in Rome, just bef
not reached him in time. He twice prese
the commons with three gold pieces; ar
senators and knights, with their wive
extravagant banquet. At the first of these

- The need to accommodate long running heads: obviously in the design of a series style I couldn't predict how long running heads were going to be, but I knew from experience the sort of range they generally fell into, and I was concerned about fitting in some longer running heads, and obviously making the running heads smaller was one way of being able to accommodate more characters.
- Sabon has small caps that are unusually big in relation to the x-height.

I found that what looked best in this instance was for the running heads to be 8.25 pt and the page numbers 8.5 pt (alongside 10.25 pt text).

The running heads are in letterspaced small caps because that is a continuation of what Classics had previously done, and it looked right. Making the running heads upper- and lowercase would have made it easier to accommodate long running heads, but wouldn't have looked right and would have made the running heads more confusable with main text. Page numbers were old-style figures because I always use them rather than ranging figures if I can.

In the Classics series style, the running heads and page numbers sit 21 pt baseline–baseline above text line 1 of the text block. This is more than the half-line space I would have allowed for a centered running head, but when running heads are aligned with the edge of the main text, they often need to be spaced farther away from the text block in order to avoid looking as if they are part of the text block . . . but then not so far away that they look lost and floating in space. After some tests, I decided that 21 pt looked like the right sort of distance.[1]

[1] If I were doing this today, I might make that distance 21.4375 pt because (drum roll) that is 1.75 times the baseline–baseline distance. But actually if I were doing this today I might have made the baseline–baseline distance 12.202 pt because that is 1/46 of the full page depth, and then the running heads and page numbers would have sat on a baseline 21.3535 pt above text line 1. But I digress.

Other Elements of Main Text

After provisionally defining the basic text page, I had to deal with all of the other components of the body text:

- Body text with hanging indent
- Verse
- Prose drama
- Verse drama
- Prose extracts
- Correspondence extracts
- Verse extracts
- Prose drama extracts
- Verse drama extracts
- Marginal line numbers
- Footnotes
- Prose extracts in footnotes
- Correspondence in footnotes
- Verse extracts in footnotes
- Prose drama extracts in footnotes
- Verse drama extracts in footnotes

This is the sort of list that delights completer-finishers (and fills the rest of us with dread). You'll notice that all of the extract types in the main text are repeated in the footnotes; we'll meet the same extract list again when we get to the design of the end matter.

This serves to illuminate another challenge of the project—the design had to be not only systematic horizontally (meaning, for instance, that the design of verse drama had to be consistent with the design of prose drama and so on) but also systematic vertically (meaning, for instance, that the design of prose drama in the main text had to visually and structurally relate to the design of prose drama extracts, and prose drama extracts in the footnotes, and in the endnotes, and so on). This was a self-imposed constraint, but this sort of systematic approach to structural elements is intended to help readers by being consistent; I know of no research that backs up this notion of mine, but I live in hope.

Making the design horizontally and vertically systematic generated a highly interrelated design in which making a change to one part of the design could have reverberations throughout the rest of the design. For instance: change the typography for speakers' names in prose drama and you have to reflect that change in speakers' names in verse drama, and all drama extracts in the main text, in footnotes, and in end matter, and so on. However, it had another consequence: much of the decision making about the design became something like painting-by-numbers: if I do this with the design of component X, then the design of components Y and Z has to match. In some respects this helped to rationalize the design process, but it made writing the specification a singularly convoluted task as I had to make sure that the things that needed to be consistent stayed consistent as the design developed and were actually specified consistently (in terms of both intent and language used).

The design of the other elements of the main text did not in general excite a great deal of concern from the editors. I was able to proceed without too much negotiation. This is a summary of some of my considerations in the design of these other elements.

Prose with Hanging Indents

The indent matches the standard paragraph indent, and other indents used elsewhere—such as the indents in verse, in drama, and in some end matter. This style is not often used within the main text but can be handy for apparatus that take the form of listings (bibliographies, for instance).

Drama

Drama in Penguin Classics typically includes: speakers' names, speech itself (and this can be verse or prose or both, and may contain songs or quoted matter), and stage directions.

I intended to make the treatment of these categories of component as consistent as possible throughout all types of drama, both in the main text and apparatus (footnotes, introduction, endnotes, displayed extracts).

Following what had been a relatively consistent practice in the Classics, I chose to have speakers' names full out in small caps, with speech in roman indented on the left (same indent as hanging indents), and stage directions in italics indented further.

There was a further question of verse drama, a question that I agonized over when I came to deal with all types of verse, as you will see below.

Extracts

Extracts were to be 1 pt smaller than main text, on the same baseline–baseline distance, with a line space above and below. Extracts were also indented left and right by the same indent as a paragraph first line (the standard indent).

I put extracts on the same baseline–baseline distance as the main text in order to ensure the consistent backing-up of pages (so that the "shadow" of any show-through from one page to the next remains in step with and concealed by the text you're looking at). The use of a line space above and below the extract also serves to keep all the text on the same baseline grid.

Sometimes a whole line space above and below extracts can look too gappy. As an alternative I sometimes use a half-line space (in terms of the show-through, this means that the extract, while not in step with the main text on the page it backs up, is consistently out of step, and then after the extract the main text is back in step); however, I knew that in Classics the use of a half-line space was not always going to work, for instance—without getting ahead of ourselves—I knew that I'd probably be using a line space to indicate stanza spaces in verse and verse extracts (more about that later) and that it would look a bit strange and create illogical groupings if a verse extract had a line space for a stanza space but half-line spaces between the extract and the main text. So, even though the line space above and below extracts may look a bit gappy, the alternatives bring worse problems with them.

In general, if some portion of text is identified as being different by being set down and with space above and below—as extracts are in the Classics—I would not normally regard it as necessary to also indent the text. In my opinion the setting down and space above and below are sufficient to signal difference to the reader without requiring indention too. I generally try to avoid indenting text because it can create awkward crenellations in the left and right edges of the text block. Some volumes of the Classics have introductions that are very liberally peppered with displayed extracts, and this profusion of extracts exacerbates this crenellation effect. However, the commissioning editor was adamant that extracts had to be set down, with space above and below, *and* indented, so that is what we had to do. And that of course set a precedent for the treatment of extracts elsewhere—such as in footnotes and end matter.

And drama extracts and verse drama extracts required the general extract style to be hybridized with the drama and verse drama styles.

Footnotes

Footnotes are not encouraged in Classics but are occasionally unavoidable either because they are part of the original text and cannot be undone or they are the best solution to what needs to be explained. The footnotes are 8.25/9.875 pt, smaller than extracts and main text as is customary. The awkward baseline–baseline distance keeps the same proportional relationship between type size and baseline–baseline distance as the main text (about 80 percent of the main text size and 80 percent of the main text baseline–baseline distance).

In general the Classics series style sets footnotes to the full text width; however, numbered footnotes are not set to this width. This was an instance where a later stage of the design process caused me to revisit earlier decisions: when later on I came to deal with endnotes (which are related to the main text by a numbering system) I had to put their cue numbers hanging in a column to the left of the note text, and this column had to be reasonably wide to

The relationship between the type size and the baseline–baseline distance is consistent for both main text and footnotes.

'May thirty devils take this horn-bearing cuckold, this Marrano, this devil's own sorcerer, this caster of spells for Antichrist! Let's get back to our king. I'm certain he will not be pleased with us if ever he learns that we ventured into the haunt of this be-cassocked devil. I'm sorry I ever came. I would gladly give a hundred golden nobles – and fourteen commoners – if only the thing which used to break wind in the bottom of my trunk-hose would at this very moment shine up his moustaches with its squitterings! True God! He's made me

14. Some technical terms now little known: *haruspicine*: the *haruspex* examined entrails; *extispicine*: the *extispex* did likewise; the *oscines* are the birds from whose song or cry divinations were made; the 'tripudiation solistime' (*tripudium solistimum*) is a measured, solemn liturgical dance.

allow for note numbers of up to three digits followed by a full point and a space. This approach of having the note numbers in a separate column is not one that I find particularly satisfactory, but it was the solution preferred by the editor. Having taken this approach with the endnotes, I applied the same principle to numbered footnotes (oooh look: systematic vertically); this required that numbered footnotes indent 18.75 pt to allow for note numbers of up to three figures in footnote-sized type followed by a full point and space. This indention is greater than the standard paragraph first-line indent, but matches the indent given to verse turnover lines.

Verse

As with other elements of the design, I intended for verse of all types (including verse drama, and verse extracts and verse drama extracts) to share a family similarity that derived from the main text style.

Typography for verse could be the subject of an entire book. Verse carries more of its meaning in its organization on the page than prose does: the requirements can be so particular that they often require individual treatment. Penguin Classics run the entire gamut of types of verse—and not only volumes whose main text is entirely verse, but also some containing a mixture of verse and prose. The Classics series style had to work equally well and consistently for all types of verse as well as prose/verse combinations. Previously in Penguin Classics verse had been treated in a way that was inconsistent with the rest of the Classics—for a host of legacy reasons that I won't go into—and I took this redesign as an opportunity to bring the treatment of verse in line with the rest of the Classics series style.

Broadly I planned for verse to be a ranged left block of main text-sized type centered in the text measure—a classic solution. This simple objective immediately brings up a host of questions:

- because the right-hand edge of the block of verse text is often ragged with particularly uneven line lengths, the process of centering becomes a subjective visual judgment, and having to make that judgment for each piece of verse slows down the process of typesetting;
- what do you do with separate poems on the same page—do they align or do they take their own centering?
- what do you do with a poem that runs over several pages—is each page centered separately?
- what about poet-devised schemes of indention?
- what about turnover lines?
- what are the rules for breaking verse at the foot of a page?

These questions are not unique to Penguin Classics; they apply to much verse setting. By the time I came to work on this series style for Penguin Classics, I had worked on the design of numerous volumes of verse (both within Penguin Classics and without), so I had some practice in devising solutions to these questions and the consequences of these solutions. Despite having wrestled with these questions over a number of years, I was far from having reached definitive conclusions to them,[1] but I had a grasp of the scope of the problem and saw my task as ensuring that the most typical and likely verse scenarios were addressed systematically and consistently in the specification.

Verse setting was one area of Classics design that I anticipated was likely to still require individual design attention. This limited the amount of detail the specification had to include, but it nonetheless had to set a robust foundation to allow other designers to be able to specify additional elements of verse for Classics with some degree of consistency.

Considering stanza spaces, the default tends to be a line space. This can look too gappy, so I have occasionally used a half-line space, which tightens up the overall appearance without having too messy an effect on text back-up—it is exactly out of step. But for the Classics I decided to leave stanza spaces as full line spaces because one of the disadvantages of half-line stanza spaces is that they do not combine well with elaborate indention schemes—the stanza space can end up looking like a not-quite-right interruption in the indention scheme. It might have been slightly more economical to use a half-line space for stanza spaces, but this was one instance where I decided that on balance the likelihood of things not looking good or intelligible was more important than the saving of space.

Verse drama presented a slightly different set of challenges to regular verse, mainly to do with the use of centering and how it related to elements of the drama style. If verse drama is centered, what do you do with the speakers' names—do they remain ranged left full out, or do they wander in and out if the centering varies from page to page? The difficulty for the typesetters,

[1] I still haven't to this day.

visual confusion, and unattractive results that centering of verse drama had the potential to cause meant that I could see no centered solution that was likely to work sufficiently well for enough of the time and so I took the decision that verse drama would not be centered but would range left indented as for prose drama. This made verse drama inconsistent with other sorts of verse[1] but consistent with other sorts of drama. I allowed this inconsistency because a large proportion of the verse drama in Classics is written in iambic pentameters or other metrical patterns with relatively even line lengths, meaning that although the line lengths do not fill the measure, they are on the whole relatively even and regular. Like verse, verse drama can never look completely tidy and regular, because of the requirements and shape of the content, but to some extent that raggedness is beside the point; the important thing is for the content to be as accessible and intelligible as possible.

An alternative approach to verse drama is to have the speaker's name centered on the line above the speech, allowing for the centering of the verse to be independent of the placing of the speaker's name. However, I find this sort of arrangement not particularly user-friendly. I have not seen any research into the usability of drama setting, but my (hopefully relatively well informed) second-guessing is that centering the speakers' names makes them less easy to spot and makes awkward the jump from the speaker's name to the start of the speech. It might at first seem that centered speakers' names are functioning similarly to centered headings, but I think that the relationship between a speaker's name and their speech is not the same as that between a heading and the text following it, and what works for headings does not necessarily work equally well for speakers' names. So I did not adopt this method.

A further complication arises when verse drama contains songs. Shakespeare's a one for doing this. The song needs to be typographically differentiated from the verse drama around it, and it is all too easy for this to look muddled, especially if an editor has started marking what should be centered and where space should go, without fully thinking through what it will look like and how things will end up looking when visually grouped by the insertion of space. The typography of songs in verse drama also deserves an entire book of its own—though I'm not sure how many people would feel the need to read such a book. However, suffice it to say that if the verse drama is ranged left, centering the song is a useful strategy for distinguishing it from the verse drama (so long as it is centered within the width of the text lines above and below rather than the full measure)—another good reason for having the verse drama ranged left.

Is your head spinning? Mine was, regularly, during the process of designing and then specifying the Classics series style. I found it was something that I could concentrate on for only limited periods of time without becoming seriously gaga, delicate flower that I am.

[1] I'm sure there'll be rioting in the Strand yet again.

Line Numbers

And then of course there are line numbers to consider. Any sort of text can have line numbers—all flavors of verse and prose. Nothing particularly contentious was done with the design of line numbers. I chose to put them in the fore-edge margin,[1] in footnote-sized type. The only exception to this was line numbers in verse, which I sat within the main text area ranged out to the fore-edge margin. This decision to pull the line numbers into the text area on verse setting was driven by the fact that in general verse lines are shorter than the full text width, and if the line numbers are out in the fore-edge margin they are likely to end up unhelpfully distant from the lines of verse they relate to. There was of course the possibility that long lines of verse could clash with line numbers, but I took the judgment that this was a less frequent problem than line numbers looking too distant. Consequently, the typesetting specification had to include instructions on what to do in the instances where verse lines were too long, and of course these instructions had to be different for right- and left-hand pages:

> If this happens on a recto page, the long line should be forced to turn over; and on verso pages if the left-hand edge of the verse is going to clash with the line numbers, then the part of the poem that falls on that page indents to align 9 pt in from the end of the line numbers on that page.

Headings

Having dealt with all of the text components of the main text, I moved on to consider the headings that accompany the main text. The actual process was not so neatly compartmentalized; as I mentioned before there was some back-and-forth as early decisions had to be revisited in the light of later decisions, but none of these revisions were earth-shattering.

In general, the typical Penguin Classic has chapter headings and they start new pages, and the front matter probably has chapter headings, plus subheads in the text. So how difficult is that to design? Well, not at all, thank you for asking. The series style had to be optimized for these sorts of books, but also had to work well for the less frequent others with elaborate and complex sets of headings—such as, for instance, a volume divided into books, each of those books divided into parts, each of those parts divided into chapters, and each of those chapters divided into sections. And this has to be accommodated within the same typographical structures that work well for the book just divided into chapters.

One thing to mention before I start talking about individual heading styles is that I intended for all levels of heading to be centered—parts, chapters, A-heads, all of them. Some designers seem to be happy to have text headings ranged left beneath centered chapter and part headings, but I find that a visu-

[1] Oh look, more unavoidable jargon! In case it isn't self-explanatory, the fore-edge is the outside edge of the page—the left-hand edge of the left-hand page and the right-hand edge of the right-hand page. The fore-edge margins are where you traditionally put your thumbs to hold the book open. And where you scribble notes in textbooks. This note is on the fore-edge of this page.

Line numbers were positioned slightly differently for verse and prose. Moving line numbers into the text area had visual advantages for verse but complicated the specification for the typesetters by the instructions to deal with long verse lines clashing with line numbers. These illustrations are taken from the visuals in the specification document.

CHAPTER I 237

'Oh! Mr. Bennet, you are wanted immediately; we are all in an uproar. You must come and make Lizzy marry Mr. Collins, for she vows she will not have him, and if you do not make haste he will change his mind and not have her.'[1]

Mr. Bennet raised his eyes from the book as she entered, and fixed them on her face with a calm unconcern which was not in the least altered by her communication.

'I have not the pleasure of understanding you,' said he, when she had finished her speech. 'Of what are you talking?'

'Of Mr. Collins and Lizzy. Lizzy declares she will not have Mr. Collins, and Mr. Collins begins to say that he will not have Lizzy.'

'And what am I to do on the occasion? – It seems an hopeless business.'

'Speak to Lizzy about it yourself. Tell her that you insist upon her marrying him.'

'Let her be called down. She shall hear my opinion.'

Mrs. Bennet rang the bell,[2] and Miss Elizabeth was summoned to the library.

'Come here, child,' cried her father as she appeared. 'I have sent for you on an affair of importance. I understand that Mr. Collins has made you an offer of marriage. Is it true?' Elizabeth replied that it was. 'Very well – and this offer of marriage you have refused?'

'I have, Sir.'

'Very well. We now come to the point. Your mother insists upon your accepting it. Is it not so, Mrs. Bennet?'

'Yes, or I will never see her again.'

'An unhappy alternative is before you, Elizabeth. From this day you must be a stranger to one of your parents.[3] – Your mother will never see you again if you do not marry Mr. Collins, and I will never see you again if you do.'

Elizabeth could not but smile at such a conclusion of such a beginning; but Mrs. Bennet, who had persuaded herself that her husband regarded the situation as she wished, was excessively disappointed.

'What do you mean, Mr. Bennet, by talking in this way? You promised me to insist upon her marrying him.'

236 SAMUEL COLERIDGE TAYLOR

And there were gardens bright with sinuous rills
Where blossomed many an incense-bearing tree;
And here were forests ancient as the hills,
Enfolding sunny spots of greenery.

But oh! that deep romatic chasm which slanted
Down the green hill athwart a cedarn cover!
A savage place! as holy and enchanted
As e'er beneath a waning moon was haunted
By woman wailing for her demon-lover!
And from this chasm, with ceaseless turmoil seething,
As if this earth in thick fast pants were breathing,
A mighty fountain momently was forced:
Amid whose swift half-intermitted burst
Huge fragments vaulted like rebounding hail,
Or chaffy grain beneath the thresher's flail:
And mid these dancing rocks at once and ever
It flung up momently the sacred river.
Five miles meandering with a mazy motion
Through wood and dale the sacred river ran,
Then reached the caverns measureless to man,
And sank in tumult to a lifeless ocean:
And 'mid this tumult Kubla heard from far
Ancestral voices prophesying war!

The shadow of the dome of pleasure
Floated midway on the waves;
Where was heard the mingled measure
From the fountain and the caves.
It was a miracle of rare device,
A sunny pleasure-dome with caves of ice!

A damsel with a dulcimer
In a vision once I saw:
It was an Abyssinian maid,
And on her dulcimer she played,
Singing of Mount Abora.
Could I revive within me

EDWIN ARLINGTON ROBINSON 237

The searching rays of wisdom that reach through
The mist of shame's infirm credulity,
And infinitely wonder if hard words
Like mine have any message for the dead.

XIII

I grant you friendship is a royal thing,
But none shall ever know that royalty
For what it is till he has realized
His best friend in himself. 'T is then, perforce,
That man's unfettered faith indemnifies
Of its own conscious freedom the old shame,
And love's revealed infinitude supplants
Of its own wealth and wisdom the old scorn.

XIV

Though the sick beast infect us, we are fraught
Forever with indissoluble Truth,
Wherein redress reveals itself divine,
Transitional, transcendent. Grief and loss,
disease and desolation, are the dreams
Of wasted excellence; and every dream
has in it something of an ageless fact
That flouts deformity and laughs at years.

XV

We lack the courage to be where we are: –
We love too much to travel on old roads,
To triumph on old fields; we love too much
To consecrate the magic of dead things,
And yieldingly to linger by long walls
Of ruin, where the ruinous moonlight
that sheds a lying glory on old stones
Befriends us with an wizard's enmity.

ally awkward thing to do. It baffles me. I can see no reason for it at all, and conspicuous reasons for not doing it. So take it as given from now on that all headings in Penguin Classics (with the obvious exception of shoulder heads) will be centered.

My usual practice is to start with the text headings, sort them out, and then work my way upward through the hierarchy of headings until I reach the top. With the Classics series style, there was more to-ing and fro-ing than might usually be the case within the hierarchy of headings as I tried to get the set to work in as many different permutations as possible.

One factor I had to take into account carefully was to ensure that the headings were not too greedy in the amount of space they used. This was to ensure that longer books were not longer than necessary and hence as easy to afford and handle as possible.

Text Headings

I chose to allow for three levels of heading within the text (by which I mean headings hierarchically below the chapter heads). I have an untested theory that most readers cannot deal with more than three levels of heading in the text, and so decided to limit what was available to three levels.

It is customary with these sorts of headings to label them "A," "B," and "C," with "A" being at the top of the hierarchy and "C" at the bottom. One consequence of this is that when editors apply these styles, they always start with "A" and work their way downward through as many levels as they require for the particular volume (they are, not unreasonably, unwilling to mark headings as B-heads if they haven't already included A-heads). So "A" becomes the most frequently used style, and since it is at the top of this bit of the hierarchy it is likely to be the most emphatic and generally the most space-hungry of the levels of heading. I didn't necessarily want the most emphatic level of heading to be the most frequently used, and I certainly didn't want to use more space than was necessary. So, I wanted to see if I could make the middle-level heading—the "B" level—the default, with the possibility of adding the heading level above or below (or both) depending on what best matched the requirements of the particular volume. For instance, if the headings are very frequent (at least one per page, say) it looks a bit much if they are too big or emphatic, or if the headings are very wordy they maybe don't want to be so big, but if the headings are infrequent and pithy then maybe they are better served by being large or more emphatic.

To drive this idea of the middle-level heading being the default, I called that level of heading "H" ("H" is for "heading"); the top-level heading is "H+1," and the bottom-level heading is "H-1," creating a hopefully self-explanatory series of "H+1," "H," and "H-1." The editors seemed to have no trouble understanding and applying this system, which was a relief.

Opposite: The illustrations in the specification document showing the three levels of text heading: "H+1," "H," and "H-1," and showing the positioning of an "H+1" heading when it falls at the top of a page and the spacing to use when it is directly adjacent to an "H" or "H-1" heading. At the top of the page the "H+1" heading has been dropped down slightly so it is below text line one of the text area; this is to avoid it getting too close to the running head and page number, and to ensure that the text that follows it sits on the baseline grid. When pairs of headings coincide, the spacing between them is closed up to a distance that visually "makes sense" and keeps the text after the headings on the baseline grid.

I used both typography and vertical space to make clear the hierarchy of the three levels of text heading (no surprises there).

Starting with the H level of heading (the middle one), I made this heading 11.25/12.25 pt roman U&lc with 16.335 pt extra vertical space above and 8.165 pt extra vertical space below. These accompany the main text of 10.25/12.25 pt. The baseline–baseline distance is the same as main text, but the type size is slightly larger. I wanted to keep the baseline–baseline distance consistent for the same backing-up reasons as discussed earlier. And I have found that headings look best with less interlinear spacing than text, so 11.25/12.25 pt for headings is larger than the text but on the same baseline–baseline distance. The difference between 10.25 and 11.25 pt may not seem like much, but it is enough to make them look bigger than the text, and being U&lc allows them to accommodate a lot of characters on a single line, which helps them to be quite economical of space even when the headings are wordy.

The vertical spaces specified above and below the heading may look like horrid amounts, but these spaces add up to two lines, with two-thirds of that space above and one-third below—meaning that the text after the heading is still on the baseline grid and will back up. Although the vertical spaces may seem awkward numerical values, they were driven by my wish to make the spacing around the three levels of text heading a visually logical and consistent sequence. This H head has a two-line space around it, with two-thirds above and one-third below; the H+1 heading has a three-line space around it, with two-thirds above and one-third below; and the H-1 heading has a single line space around it, with two-thirds above and one-third below. See how gloriously simple the principle is.

H+1 heads are 11.25 pt roman capitals, but because capitals take up more visual depth than U&lc, the baseline–baseline distance is increased to 18.375 pt (one and a half lines of main text), but the intention is that few of these headings will run to a second line.

H-1 heads are 11.25/12.25 pt italic U&lc.

So that is how the typography and the spacing both work to signal the hierarchy—more space equals higher up the hierarchy, and capitals are higher up the hierarchy than roman U&lc, which is higher up the hierarchy than italic U&lc. The capitals–roman–italic typographical hierarchy seems self-evident to the average reader. I wouldn't like to hazard a guess how this intuitive understanding comes about, but it seems very widespread among readers using the Latin alphabet.

Two further issues that the specification had to address in relation to the text headings were how to deal with combinations of headings (when an H+1 heading is directly followed by an H heading, and so on) and treatment of headings when they fall at the top of the text block.

With heading combinations, a problem arises in that the spacing specified have comic fragments on literary themes), but the *Frogs* has a special place in the history of criticism. In it we have parody and criticism of tragedy, but also parody of criticism itself. This is particularly evident in the scene in which each poet finds fault with the other's prologues, where we are given a lengthy demonstration of the detailed criticism of poetry and language which had become fashionable in intellectual circles. Euripides objects to the tautology in Aeschylus' line, 'Lo, to this land I come and do return',[11] and Aeschylus retaliates by ridiculing Euripides for saying that Oedipus 'became' the most unfortunate of men, he was so all along, and so on. Dionysus, in true layman's fashion, pronounces the criticism brilliant, but adds that he doesn't understand a word of it (1168).[12]

Much of Aristophanes' satirizing of Euripides, both in the *Frogs* and elsewhere, centres on his newfangled intellectualism and the sophistic spirit which pervades his plays. Like the Socrates of the *Clouds*, Aristophanes' Euripides embodies the new mood of scepticism, with its subversive attitude towards morality and tradition, which characterized Athenian society in the late fifth century BC. That mood was particularly associated with the sophists, itinerant teachers who travelled through the Greek world offering instruction on a variety of subjects, which included the study of language, the analysis of poetry, and, most significantly for the history of criticism, the techniques of oratory.

GORGIAS AND THE SOPHISTS

One of the most famous and influential of these early teachers of rhetoric was Gorgias of Leontini, who visited Athens in 427 BC and amazed the Athenians with is dazzling speeches. In his *Encomium of Helen*,[13] a rhetorical display piece in defence of Helen of Troy, he produces a number of reasons why Helen should not be blamed for eloping with paris. One possible line of argument, developed at considerable length, is that she was persuaded to do so by the irresistible power of speech, *logos*. Speech, Gorgias claims, is a great master, with the power to

have comic fragments on literary themes), but the *Frogs* has a special place in the history of criticism. In it we have parody and criticism of tragedy, but also parody of criticism itself. This is particularly evident in the scene in which each poet finds fault with the other's prologues, where we are given a lengthy demonstration of the detailed criticism of poetry and language which had become fashionable in intellectual circles. Euripides objects to the tautology in Aeschylus' line, 'Lo, to this land I come and do return', and Aeschylus retaliates by ridiculing Euripides for saying that Oedipus 'became' the most unfortunate of men, he was so all along, and so on. Dionysus, in true layman's fashion, pronounces the criticism brilliant, but adds that he doesn't understand a word of it (1168).

Much of Aristophanes' satirizing of Euripides, both in the *Frogs* and elsewhere, centres on his newfangled intellectualism and the sophistic spirit which pervades his plays. Like the Socrates of the *Clouds*, Aristophanes' Euripides embodies the new mood of scepticism, with its subversive attitude towards morality and tradition, which characterized Athenian society in the late fifth century BC. That mood was particularly associated with the sophists, itinerant teachers who travelled through the Greek world offering instruction on a variety of subjects, which included the study of language, the analysis of poetry, and, most significantly for the history of criticism, the techniques of oratory.

Gorgias and the Sophists

One of the most famous and influential of these early teachers of rhetoric was Gorgias of Leontini, who visited Athens in 427 BC and amazed the Athenians with is dazzling speeches. In his *Encomium of Helen*, a rhetorical display piece in defence of Helen of Troy, he produces a number of reasons why Helen should not be blamed for eloping with paris. One possible line of argument, developed at considerable length, is that she was persuaded to do so by the irresistible power of speech, *logos*. Speech, Gorgias claims, is a great master, with the power to stop fear, remove sorrow, create joy and increase pity. All poet-

have comic fragments on literary themes), but the *Frogs* has a special place in the history of criticism. In it we have parody and criticism of tragedy, but also parody of criticism itself. This is particularly evident in the scene in which each poet finds fault with the other's prologues, where we are given a lengthy demonstration of the detailed criticism of poetry and language which had become fashionable in intellectual circles. Euripides objects to the tautology in Aeschylus' line, 'Lo, to this land I come and do return', and Aeschylus retaliates by ridiculing Euripides for saying that Oedipus 'became' the most unfortunate of men, he was so all along, and so on. Dionysus, in true layman's fashion, pronounces the criticism brilliant, but adds that he doesn't understand a word of it (1168).

Much of Aristophanes' satirizing of Euripides, both in the *Frogs* and elsewhere, centres on his newfangled intellectualism and the sophistic spirit which pervades his plays. Like the Socrates of the *Clouds*, Aristophanes' Euripides embodies the new mood of scepticism, with its subversive attitude towards morality and tradition, which characterized Athenian society in the late fifth century BC. That mood was particularly associated with the sophists, itinerant teachers who travelled through the Greek world offering instruction on a variety of subjects, which included the study of language, the analysis of poetry, and, most significantly for the history of criticism, the techniques of oratory.

Gorgias and the Sophists

One of the most famous and influential of these early teachers of rhetoric was Gorgias of Leontini, who visited Athens in 427 BC and amazed the Athenians with is dazzling speeches. In his *Encomium of Helen*, a rhetorical display piece in defence of Helen of Troy, he produces a number of reasons why Helen should not be blamed for eloping with paris. One possible line of argument, developed at considerable length, is that she was persuaded to do so by the irresistible power of speech, *logos*. Speech, Gorgias claims, is a great master, with the power to stop fear, remove sorrow, create joy and increase pity. All poetry is speech in metre, and everyone recognizes the remarkable

GORGIAS AND THE SOPHISTS

It may be theat they have comic fragments on literary themes), but the *Frogs* has a special place in the history of criticism. In it we have parody and criticism of tragedy, but also parody of criticism itself. This is particularly evident in the scene in which each poet finds fault with the other's prologues, where we are given a lengthy demonstration of the detailed criticism of poetry and language which had become fashionable in intellectual circles.

HOMER AND THE EARLY GREEK POETS

Styistic Similarities

Euripides objects to the tautology in Aeschylus' line, 'Lo, to this land I come and do return', and Aeschylus retaliates by ridiculing Euripides for saying that Oedipus 'became' the most unfortunate of men, he was so all along, and so on. Dionysus, in true layman's fashion, pronounces the criticism brilliant, but adds that he doesn't understand a word of it (1168).

ARISTOPHANES

Expectations of Comedy

Much of Aristophanes' satirizing of Euripides, both in the *Frogs* and elsewhere, centres on his newfangled intellectualism and the sophistic spirit which pervades his plays. Like the Socrates of the *Clouds*, Aristophanes' Euripides embodies the new mood of scepticism, with its subversive attitude towards morality and tradition, which characterized Athenian society in the late fifth century BC. That mood was particularly associated with the sophists, itinerant teachers who travelled through the Greek world offering instruction on a variety of subjects, which included the study of language, the analysis of to go with individual headings creates too-big vertical gaps between the headings if, for instance, the space below an H+1 heading is added to the space above an H heading. This is a problem that has to be resolved for any heading hierarchy. As is usual in these sorts of specification documents, I supplied a set of conditional instructions such as "if an H+1 is followed by an H, there is only 10.21 pt extra vertical space between them," one instruction for each possible permutation. The challenge is visual and arithmetical—to make the spacing look visually right while at the same time keeping the relationship to the baseline grid.

When a text heading falls at the top of a text block, it can create problems with the running head and page number. If the heading sits on text line 1 it might look too close to the running head and result in the text below it not sitting on the baseline grid. Again, these are not unusual problems to encounter with headings in text. I wrote a set of further exceptions that specify how much each heading should drop in order to keep the main text on the baseline grid and avoid the running head and the heading looking too close. As with heading combinations, the challenge is both visual and arithmetical. Similar exception instructions had to be written to cover what happens when the text headings immediately follow a chapter or part heading, again to ensure that they looked "right" and maintained the text chapter/part drop but also kept the main text on the baseline grid.

Headings for Verse

Again, the special needs of verse demanded their own treatment. Headings in verse are not like those in prose: instead of being akin to subheadings in text, they are poem titles or titles of groups of poems, so instead of being one of a series of subheadings within a large chunk of stuff, each one is the heading to a relatively autonomous chunk of stuff (usually a poem). This requires that they are marked by a more significant break than a text head. And then of course there are stanza numbers to take into account too, and even where there aren't stanza numbers there are stanza breaks, which have a bearing on the spacing appropriate for headings—a stanza space looks wrong if it looks bigger than the space between a poem title and the start of the poem.

I have designed enough books of poetry (particularly anthologies) to know that heading schemes for poems can be surprisingly variable. You might think "you have a poem, it has a title" and that may be the case most of the time, but a minority of poems have bloody-minded heading structures that defy rationalization. This is probably exactly right for the poem but can be a headache for the designer. First you have to figure out the poet's intentions and then figure out how to give them typographical form. Knowing that whatever I came up with could never cover all eventualities, and having already concluded that verse volumes were likely to require individual design attention,

I designed a set of headings that I hoped would provide a robust starting point for whoever had to design verse volumes for Penguin Classics.

Working, as usual, from the bottom of the hierarchy upward, stanza numbers/heads are specified to be text-size small caps centered, with a line space above and no extra vertical space below—as understated as they could possibly be. Because these headings have no space below them, they look fine if they sit on text line 1 when they fall at the top of a text block.

Following the pattern of text heading structures, I called stanza numbers/heads "S," and then created an "S+1" head, which was specified to be "used for numbers/titles in sonnet sequences or other poems divided into sections or where one number/title has several stanzas following it." These S+1 heads have space below as well as above. They were created because the standard stanza number—sitting with no extra space between it and the verse below it—ceases to be effective if it relates to several stanzas; it looks like it only relates to the first of the stanzas because of the visual effect of grouping and spacing. The typography of S+1 heads is pretty much like poem titles, but with less space above them.

Poem titles themselves use the same size as was used for text heads —11.25/12.25 pt. However, for the verse heads I decided to use italic U&lc. For some reason poem titles often look better in italics than in roman; I'm not sure I could say why without ending up with some slightly idiotic statement such as "they look more poetic." Notwithstanding the cause, the effect seems appropriate for the overall "look" of Penguin Classics. These headings demand a full line space below; it couldn't be less because of the line space used for stanza spaces—and a two-line space above—so the same spacing as an H+1 head, as I said before, verse needs a more emphatic break between poems than that between subsections of prose.

Poem titles were coded as "V" heads (probably V for "verse"); I also created "V+1" heads to be used for the titles of groups of poems. To put them visually in the right hierarchical relationship to the V heads, these were made italic capitals and with greater amounts of space above and below than V heads.

In addition to these I created subheads ("Vsub") to go with poem titles and to be used for any additional heading components such as dates, or subtitles (poem titles often have appendages of this sort). These were specified as text-size ital U&lc, centered, directly below the V head with no extra vertical space between, and a line space directly below the Vsub head. If I had been designing an individual volume, I might have been inclined to do something more imaginative with this level of heading (put it in small caps, for instance), but given the range of material this was going to have to work for, any solution with too much visual character was likely to be the wrong character too much of the time, so the solution is slightly dull but reliable.

And then of course some poems have epigraphs, too. These are treated in

Song made in lieu of many ornaments,
With which my love should duly have been decked,
Which cutting off through hasty accidents,
Ye would not stay your due time to expect,
But promised both to recompense,
Be unto her a goodly ornament,
And for a short time an endless moniment.

FOUR HYMNS

A Hymn in Honour of Love

Love, that long since hast to thy mighty power,
Perforce subdue my poor captived heart,
And raging now therein with restless store,
Does tyrannise in every weaker part;
Fain would I seek to ease my bitter smart,
By any service I might do to thee,
Or aught that else might to thee pleasing be.

And now t'assuage the force of this new flame,
And make thee more propitious in my need,
I mean to sing the praises of thy name,
And thy victorious conquests to areed;
By which thou madest many hearts to bleed
Of mighty Victors, with wide wounds embrewed,
And by they cruel darts to thee subdued.

Only I fear my wits enfeebled late,
Through the sharp sorrows, which thou hast me bred,
Should faint, and words should fail me, to relate
The wondrous triumphs of thy great godhead.
But if thou wouldst vouchsafe to overspread

War shall yet be, but warriors
Are now operatives; War's made
Less grand than Peace,
And a singe runs through lace and feather.

Shiloh
A Requiem
(April, 1862)

Skimming lightly, wheeling still,
The swallows fly low
Over the field in clouded days,
The forest-field of Shiloh –
Over the field where April rain
Solaced the parched ones stratched in pain
Through the pause of night
That followed the Sunday fight
Around the church of Shiloh –
The church so lone, the log-built one,
That echoed many a parting groan
And natural prayer
Of dying foement mingled there –
Foemen at morn, but friends at eve –
Fame or country least their care:
(What like a bullet can undecieve!)
But now they lie low,
While over them the swallows skim,
And all is hushed a Shiloh.

Malvern Hill
(July, 1862)

Ye elms that wave on Malvern Hill
In prime of morn and May,
Recall ye how McClellan's men
Here stood at bay?

II

Wherefore, with this belief, held like a blade, –
Gathering my strength and purpose, fair and slow,
I wait; resolved to carry it to the heart
of that dark doubt in one collected blow;
And stand at guard with spirit undismayed,
Nor fear the Opposer's anger, arms, or art;
when, from a hiding near, behold him start
With a fresh weapon of my weakness made;
And goad me with myself, and urge the attack,
While I strike short, and still give back and back
While the foe rages. then from that disgrace
He points to where they sit that have won the race,
Laurel by laurel wreathing, face o'er face,
And leaves me lower still; for, ranked in place,

III

And borne with theirs, my proudest thoughts do seem
Bald at the best, and dim; a barren gleam
Among the immortal stars, and faint and brief
As north-light flitting in the dreary north.
'what have thy dreams, – a vague, prospective worth?
An import imminent? or dost thou deem
thy life so fair, that thou wouldst set it forth
Before the day? or art thou wise in grief,
Has fruitful Sorrow swept thee with her wing?'
To-day I heard a sweet voice carolling
In the wood-land paths, with laugh and careless cry,
Leading her happy mates. Apart I stept;
And, while the laugh and song went lightly by,
In the wild bushes i sat down and wept.

The searching rays of wisdom that reach through
The mist of shame's infirm credulity,
And infinitely wonder if hard words
Like mine have any message for the dead.

XIII

I grant you friendship is a royal thing,
But none shall ever know that royalty
For what it is till he has realized
His best friend in himself. 'T is then, perforce,
That man's unfettered faith indemnifies
Of its own conscious freedom the old shame,
And love's revealed infinitude supplants
Of its own wealth and wisdom the old scorn.

XIV

Though the sick beast infect us, we are fraught
Forever with indissoluble Truth,
Wherein redress reveals itself divine,
Transitional, transcendent. Grief and loss,
disease and desolation, are the dreams
Of wasted excellence; and every dream
has in it something of an ageless fact
That flouts deformity and laughs at years.

XV

We lack the courage to be where we are: –
We love too much to travel on old roads,
To triumph on old fields; we love too much
To consecrate the magic of dead things,
And yieldingly to linger by long walls
Of ruin, where the ruinous moonlight
that sheds a lying glory on old stones
Befriends us with an wizard's enmity.

a manner related to the treatment of epigraphs elsewhere (on chapter or part heads, which we will get to soon). It was at moments like this that I was most tempted to just write in the specification, "Oh figure it out yourself can't you."

The treatment of epigraphs, needless to say, is related to the design of displayed extracts (because epigraphs and extracts have the same sort of category of content).

The specification included the instruction that headings designed to go with verse could not be combined with text headings or run-on chapter heads (yes, we'll come to them, eventually); it was obvious to me that this combination wouldn't work, but I couldn't guarantee that someone else would necessarily figure that out.

Opposite: The illustrations in the specification document showing the varieties of headings for verse. There are "V+1" headings for groups of poems, "V" headings for individual poems, "Vsub" as subheads for poems, "S+1" headings for those instances that are somewhere between a poem title and a stanza number, and "S" headings for straightforward stanza numbers.

Chapters and Parts

Now, having designed all of the headings to go within text (prose and verse), it was the moment to consider headings farther up the hierarchy. We finally reach the chapter and part headings. The customary approach is that a chapter starts a new page, and a part has a separate half title on a new right-hand page with the text starting on the following right-hand page; however, I anticipated that we would also need a style for chapters that didn't start new pages, and a style for parts where they didn't have a separate half title. I also decided that the front and end matter would have a slightly different chapter head style to the main text—I wanted a small signal of the different status of the main text in relation to front and end matter: the main text is by the author—it is the key part of the book—the front and end matter are usually by the volume editor and act in a supporting role to the main text. I marked this difference by making the main text chapter heads roman capitals and the front and end matter chapter heads roman U&lc. Not a major difference, but a modest signal to the reader of the different status.

Following my preoccupation with arithmetical progressions, the type size used for chapters and parts is 1.5 times that used for text heads (16.875 pt). The baseline–baseline distance is not in proportion with this though; 1.5 times the H+1 baseline–baseline distance is 27.5625 pt, and that looked too gappy, so I closed it up to 24.5 pt (twice the main text baseline–baseline distance), which looked right and kept it on the baseline grid. This heading can have proportionally less interlinear spacing because it is bigger and because it has more space between it and the text. I decided that this same type size worked for parts as well as chapters, and that the difference of being on a separate part title was enough to signal the hierarchical difference between the part and the chapter. Oh, and maybe the words "part" and "chapter"—don't forget that the content can carry some of the burden of meaning, the typography doesn't have to do it all.

Standard part headings are coded "PN" for part number and "PT" for part

BOOK THREE

COURTSHIP AND MARRIAGE (1256–9)

XII
DOMITIAN

On 24 October, AD 51, a month before his father,[1] as Consul-elect, was due to take office, Domitian was born in Pomegranate Street, which formed part of the sixth district of Rome. later he converted his birthplace to the Temple of the Flavians. he is said to have spent a poverty-stricken and rather degraded youth: without even any silver on the family table. At all events it is an established fact that Claudius Pollio, an ex-praetor and the target of Nero's satire *The One-Eyed Man*, used to show his guests a letter in Domitian's handwriting, which he had kept, promising to go to bed with im. It is also often insisted that Domitian was sexually abused by his eventual successor, the Emperor Nerva.

During the war against Vitellius, Domitian with his uncle Sabinus and part of the forces under him, fled to the Capitol; but when the enemy burst in and set the temple on fire, Domitian concealed himself all night in the caretaker's quarters and, at daybreak, disguised as a devotee of Isis, took refuge among the priests of that rather questionable order. 'Oh! Mr. Bennet, you are wanted immediately; we are all in an uproar. You must come and make Lizzy marry Mr. Collins, for she vows she will not have him, and if you do not make haste he will change his mind and not have her.'

Mr. Bennet raised his eyes from the book as she entered, and fixed them on her face with a calm unconcern which was not in the least altered by her communication.

'I have not the pleasure of understanding you,' said he, when she had finished her speech. 'Of what are you talking?'

'Of Mr. Collins and Lizzy. Lizzy declares she will not have

BOOK V
A JUDICIAL ERROR

CHAPTER I

Fyodor Pavlovich Karamazov

'Oh! Mr. Bennet, you are wanted immediately; we are all in an uproar. You must come and make Lizzy marry Mr. Collins, for she vows she will not have him, and if you do not make haste he will change his mind and not have her.'[1]

Mr. Bennet raised his eyes from the book as she entered, and fixed them on her face with a calm unconcern which was not in the least altered by her communication.

'I have not the pleasure of understanding you,' said he, when she had finished her speech. 'Of what are you talking?'

'Of Mr. Collins and Lizzy. Lizzy declares she will not have Mr. Collins, and Mr. Collins begins to say that he will not have Lizzy.'

'And what am I to do on the occasion? – It seems an hopeless business.'

'Speak to Lizzy about it yourself. Tell her that you insist upon her marrying him.'

'Let her be called down. She shall hear my opinion.'

Mrs. Bennet rang the bell,[2] and Miss Elizabeth was summoned to the library.

'Come here, child,' cried her father as she appeared. 'I have sent for you on an affair of importance. I understand that Mr. Collins has made you an offer of marriage. Is it true?' Elizabeth replied that it was. 'Very well – and this offer of marriage you have refused?'

'Oh! Mr. Bennet, you are wanted immediately; we are all in an uproar. You must come and make Lizzy marry Mr. Collins, for she vows she will not have him, and if you do not make haste he will change his mind and not have her.'[15]

Mr. Bennet raised his eyes from the book as she entered, and fixed them on her face with a calm unconcern which was not in the least altered by her communication.

'I have not the pleasure of understanding you,' said he, when she had finished her speech. 'Of what are you talking?'

'Of Mr. Collins and Lizzy. Lizzy declares she will not have Mr. Collins, and Mr. Collins begins to say that he will not have Lizzy.'

'And what am I to do on the occasion? – It seems an hopeless business.'

CHAPTER 18

Briefly illustrative of two Points; – First the Power of Hysterics, and, Secondly, the Force of Circumstance

For two days after the *dejeune* at Mrs Hunter's, the Pickwickians remained at Eatanswill, anxiously awaiting the arrival of some intelligence from their revered leader. Mr Tupman and Mr Snodgrass were once again left to their own means of amusement; for Mr Winkle, in compliance with the most pressing invitation, continued to reside at Mr Potts house, and to devote his time to the companionship of his amiable lady.

'Speak to Lizzy about it yourself. Tell her that you insist upon her marrying him.'

'Let her be called down. She shall hear my opinion.'

Mrs. Bennet rang the bell,[1] and Miss Elizabeth was summoned to the library.

'Come here, child,' cried her father as she appeared. 'I have sent for you on an affair of importance. I understand that Mr. Collins has made you an offer of marriage. Is it true?' Elizabeth title. Where part headings don't get their own half titles, these are coded "PN-1" and "PT-1" following the system used elsewhere, and their specification is very similar to the standard chapter head. Of course, "PN-1" and "PT-1" can't be used in conjunction with the standard chapter headings: they have to be used in conjunction with the run-on chapter headings (chapters that do not start a new page).

The run-on chapter styles are much more economical than the standard chapter titles—having more in common with text headings in terms of scale and typography. Chapter titles in run-on headings often seem to be much more discursive; for this reason ital U&lc seemed better suited than roman U&lc or capitals.

Of course, any chapter or part heading can be accompanied by an epigraph. These were designed in a way that is related to displayed extracts—they are similarly set down but to a narrower measure to allow for the fact that the headings they accompany are generally narrower than the full text measure.

Finally I had to also consider how to treat headings in drama. These generally take the form of act or scene headings. In a bit of judicious recycling I discovered that the chapter title specification worked for act headings, and run-on chapter titles worked for scene heads.

Opposite: Illustrations in the specification document showing the treatment of parts and chapters. There are standard parts with part title pages, and standard chapters that start a new page, and then there are variants for chapters that don't start a new page, and parts that start a new page but with no separate part title.

Illustration from the specification document showing the treatment of act and scene headings.

ACT V

Scene i

[The scene is set before the temple of Demeter and Persephone at Eleusis after the disastrous Argive expedition against Thebes. AETHRA, *mother of* THESEUS, *is seated against an altar surrounded by the* CHORUS, *the mothers of the seven dead champions of Argos who have been refused burial by the victors. At the doors of the temple in an attitude of despair are* ADRASTUS, *who had led the expedition as Argos' king, and the* SONS *of the dead warriors. These boys form a secondary* CHORUS *to that of their mothers. The women of the* CHORUS *are attended by handmaidens.*]

CLÉANTE Where are you rushing off to?

ORGON Lord, how do I know?

CLÉANTE it seems to me that we should start by putting our heads together and think of what needs to be done in the circumstances.

ORGON It's the casket that worries me most. I'm more concerned about that than anything else.

CLÉANTE is there some important secret attaching to the casket?

ORGON Argas, a friend I miss greatly, left it with me for safekeeping. he gave it into my charge, swearing me to total secrecy. he chose me for this purpose when he fled the country. It contains documents, so he said, on which his life and property depended.

CLÉANTE Then why did you entrust them to someone else?

ORGON: Because of a scruple of conscience. I went straight to

End Matter

Having dealt with the main text, it was now time to move on to the end matter. From my previous work on Penguin Classics I knew that end matter is often substantial, explaining and supporting the main text through notes, a bibliography, possibly some appendixes, and other sections depending on the content of the individual volume.

It is customary for end matter to be set smaller than the main text of a book. For books of this format it is typically set down by about 10 percent, and that is broadly what I chose to do. For main text of 10.25/12.25 pt I set the end matter in 9.25/11 pt, to the same measure, with as many lines as would fit into the same depth as the main text.

As with the main text, the starting point for the design of the components of the end matter was the basic text block, from which I followed the formulae established in the main text to extrapolate the design for other sorts of text I was likely to require.

For the end matter I created a set of additional

NOTES 237

part: as a boy he had spent miserable months working at the 'amiable' Mr Warren's shoe-blacking factory; here he favours Warren's competitors.

4. *Doctors' Commons*: Between 1829 and 1831 Dickens had been a reporter on the proceedings of Doctors' Commons, where doctors of civil law provided the judges and advocates in the Admiralty Court and various ecclesiastical courts. *Sketches by Boz* contains a chapter on Doctors' Commons, as does *David Copperfield* (Chapter 23).

5. *I saw no more of my cousin*: Collins' notes mention an account by Sir David Baird, which seems to be *The Life of General Sir David Baird, Bart.*, by Theodore Hook (London: Bentley, 1833), 'collated from the voluminous papers and extensive correspondence' of its subject. This relates (pp. 200–201) how a Colonel Wallace was sent by the general to investigate reports of looting in the 'treasury', which:

> had been pointed out to General Baird, and he had posted a strong guard over it, but a door had been discovered which opened into it from another court of the palace, through which the marauders entered.
>
> Colonel Wallace, on his arrival, found the place filled with soldiers and (to their shame be it said) officers, loading themselves with gold and jewels. One gentleman in particular, when he perceived Colonel Wallace and the aid[e]-de-camp approaching, affected to be highly incensed against the men, and actively employed in preventing the pillage, while at the very moment they saw him filling his own pockets.

6. *blunt*: Cash.

7. *Belle Savage*: Coaching inn at the foot of Ludgate Hill.

8. *'In hurry ... I come back'*: The opening of a song in Kane O'Hara's adaptation of the burlesque *Tom Thumb* by Henry Fielding (1707–54). O'Hara's 'burletta' dates from 1780, but a new edition had been published in 1829.

9. *mizzle*; vanish.

10. *Victor General's*: Lay official employed to assist a bishop or archbishop in supervising ecclesiastical business.

11. *amicus curiæ ... ad captandum*: Friend of the court, or one requested to advise the court; and for the purpose of captivating, i.e. a bribe, respectively.

12. *Barnwell and –*: Dickens and Sam are between them playing on

Illustrations from the specification document showing the treatment of notes in the end matter. Putting the note numbers in their own column on the left occupies more space than one might expect due to the need to make this space wide enough to accommodate three-digit numbers (plus full stop and space after). Indenting extracts left and right uses yet more space. And then there's the question of where centered headings are centered—on the full width or the note width.

text styles that echoed those created for the main text. Do you remember the list that started: verse, prose drama, verse drama, prose extracts, etc., etc.? Yes, them, all over again, for the end matter.

The relationship of these styles to the end matter matches their treatment in the main text. So, for instance, verse in end matter is the same text size as end matter, and the rest of the rules about centering, indentation schemes, stanza spaces, and so on all echo those specified for verse in the main text.

Usually, the most substantial feature of end matter in Penguin Classics is the notes section, and this required particular attention. Typically the notes are cued in the text by numbers: a superior figure in the text identifies the presence of an endnote; in the endnotes, each note starts with a number that matches the superior figure in the text. These notes may also contain the full range of extracts—prose, verse, correspondence, prose drama, verse drama. Individual notes may be a short sentence, or several paragraphs.

My default approach to this sort of endnotes is to put the note number full out in bold old-style figures, with all subsequent lines also full out (except for the first line of a subsequent paragraph, which takes the standard first-line indent) and no extra vertical space between notes. For this approach to work, it is dependent on the bold figures being sufficiently bold. It is a relatively restrained approach, but in the absence of any user testing I am confident that readers are able to use it comfortably. However, the commissioning editor was not happy with this approach and insisted that the note numbers be put in a separate column to the left of the note text. This is not an approach that I am particularly keen on, but it was not negotiable. My concerns about this approach are:

- Because the column for note numbers has to be able to accommodate three figures (for note numbers often go over 100) plus a full stop and a word space, it ends up being a wide column that not only occupies a lot of space but also means that the single- and double-digit note numbers are unhelpfully distant from the note they relate to.
- It is uneconomical on space—one ends up with a column of largely empty space down the left edge of the text block; also extracts have to be further indented left and right which wastes yet more space.
- The note numbers are overemphatic—I agree they need to be easily accessible, but this solution is a sledgehammer to crack a small nut,

and I'm not sure that the accessibility-advantage of this scheme is sufficient to merit the increase in page length it generates.
- As well as these functional issues, I find it difficult to make it look elegant, and whether headings are ranged or centered, it is difficult to know what to range them with or center them within in order to create order and balance.

The same arrangement was applied to numbered footnotes in the main text, for reasons of consistency. Though as discussed earlier, footnotes in text are discouraged.

From experience I knew that most of the sorts of content in the end matter would be accommodated within this set of styles described above. Exceptional sorts of end matter with different typographical requirements were the sort of thing that I was going to have to leave to the designer assigned to any particular volume—for them to come up with a solution extrapolated from the principles I had created.

Following my systematic program, I turned next to the headings within end matter. As already mentioned, the end matter (in common with the front matter) used chapter headings that were slightly different in style to the main text chapter headings. I knew that the end matter was unlikely to require a level of heading above chapter headings (parts) and so didn't create a part-heading style within front and end matter. As for headings within text, I created a set that was analogous to the headings created for use in the main text: it contained three levels of heading called "EH+1," "EH," and "EH-1." The typography and spacing of the three levels mirror that of the three levels of heading in the main text, scaled down to end matter size.

I decided that endnotes would require their own particular set of headings. In general, the headings within endnotes are the same as those in the main text: if the main text is divided into chapters, so will the endnotes be divided into chapters using the same numbers and names; if the main text is divided into parts, the endnotes will be similarly divided, using the same numbers and names; and so on. For this reason, I created a set of headings for use in endnotes to allow the typography of the headings to echo those in the main text. So, a chapter heading in the main text in letterspaced capitals is reflected in the endnotes by a heading using the same words in letterspaced capitals (but clearly in a smaller size than the chapter heading itself and not starting a new

NOTES 237

part: as a boy he had spent miserable months working at the 'amiable' Mr Warren's shoe-blacking factory; here he favours Warren's competitors.

34. *Doctors' Commons*: Between 1829 and 1831 Dickens had been a reporter on the proceedings of Doctors' Commons, where doctors of civil law provided the judges and advocates in the Admiralty Court and various ecclesiastical courts. *Sketches by Boz* contains a chapter on Doctors' Commons, as does *David Copperfield* (Chapter 23).
35. *Old Bailey Proctors*: Sam is referring to attorneys at the chief criminal court. But he is confusing terms. Strictly, proctors work in courts administering civil or canon law only.
36. *blunt*: Cash.
37. *Belle Savage*: Coaching inn at the foot of Ludgate Hill.
38. '*In hurry … I come back*': The opening of a song in Kane O'Hara's adaptation of the burlesque *Tom Thumb* by Henry Fielding (1707–54). O'Hara's 'burletta' dates from 1780, but a new edition had been published in 1829.
39. *mizzle*: Vanish.
40. *Victor General's*: Lay official employed to assist a bishop or archbishop in supervising ecclesiastical business.
41. *amicus curiæ … ad captandum*: Friend of the court, or one requested to advise the court; and for the purpose of captivating, i.e. a bribe, respectively.

VOLUME 4

CHAPTER TWELVE

HETTY'S EXPECTATIONS

1. *Barnwell and –*: Dickens and Sam are between them playing on a striking coincidence. The little man, Perker, is about to cite a case from *Reports of Cases in the Court of the King's Bench* (1817–34), written by R. V. Barnewall and others. Sam takes this legal authority for the famous fictional felon George Barnwell, the subject both of George Lillo's 1731 tragedy, *The London Merchant*, and of the *Ballad of George Barnwell*, an apprentice who robbed his employer and murdered his uncle after being seduced by the whore Milwood. Both Milwood and Barnwell are hanged, or 'scragged' as Sam puts it.
2. *porter's knot*: Knotted rope harness, worn by porters when car-

Illustration from the specification document showing the treatment of headings in the endnotes. Because the content and organization of these headings reflects the structure of the main book, their typography reflects that of the headings in the main book too.

page). I think the echo of the letter and word shapes helps the reader to connect the heading in the endnotes to the heading in the main text. I don't know of any research on the subject, but such a strategy imposes order and structure and can't do any harm, can it?

So, that was the end matter pretty much done. Now there was just the front matter left to do.

Front Matter

As with the end matter, the front matter contains a relatively limited range of components, some of which are always included; others appear with greater or less frequency. During the time I worked on the Classics, the editorial staff began to take a more proactive approach to the organizing of the front and end matter. The manuscripts arriving to be designed and typeset became more consistent in structure and organization—rather than leaving it to the individual editor to reinvent the wheel for each volume.

And so it became more predictable that each volume would contain:

- half-title page
- title page
- title verso/imprint details
- contents list
- acknowledgments
- abbreviations
- chronology
- introduction
- further reading
- note on the text

The greater regularity made it easier to anticipate what would be required of the series style.

The text- (rather than display-) based items on the list could be accommodated within the styles already specified, mainly main text and main text with hanging indent.

The displayed elements required more consideration, but again, the work was generally to extrapolate from what had already been designed, in ways applicable to these new elements. Notable among them were the title page and contents list.

Title Page

I was concerned that the title pages of the individual volumes needed to work well—each looking good on their own terms as well as carrying the series style. The principal challenge was the variability of what has to be included on the title page—not just the elements that had to appear (or not) but the length of each element and their status in relation to each other.

The elements are:

- Author: not all volumes have a named author, but some have more than one; the name may be a single word, or several.
- Title: all volumes have a title; it may be a single word, or several.
- Subtitle: some volumes have a subtitle; it can run to more than a single line.
- Editorial bylines: all volumes have editorial bylines in the form of "Introduction and Notes by John Smith"; but this may extend to several people who have all had different involvement in the volume.
- Imprint: all volumes say Penguin Books at the bottom of the title page.

This may seem like a limited and controllable set of elements, and in some ways it is, but that small number of components, their variability, and the nature of the material made it a less easily resolved challenge. As with the rest of the series style, it was necessary to develop an approach that was optimized for the most typical but could also accommodate the most problematic instance.

Obviously, author and title are the most important elements; their importance relative to each other can vary from one volume to another. I had to find a way to make them both prominent and differentiated, and something that would continue to work across a wide range of possible circumstances.

My approach was to put the author first, in large-size small caps printed in gray (as a tint of black), with the title below in roman U&lc in a size slightly smaller than that used for the small caps of the author name, followed by the subtitle in smaller italic U&lc. Below that, the editorial byline is in text-size italic U&lc with names in small caps. And at the bottom of the text area, "Penguin Books" is in slightly-larger-than-text-size small caps.

I used small caps for the author name, rather than normal capitals because small caps are a bit bolder—their thin strokes are not so thin, the serifs are a bit chunkier, and the characters are wider than normal roman capitals (when you make the cap sizes the same), and they looked better balanced against the title.

The gray for the author name slightly tones down the boldness of the large-sized small caps to balance them better against the book title typography. The gray adds variety and a change of texture to the page; it adds liveliness that stops the title page looking too monotonous; it also further differentiates the author name and the volume title (as well as one being small caps and the other being U&lc).

When I started work in publishing, I don't recall ever seeing type printed in gray (as a tint of black) on standard trade text paper. Paper and printing tech-

Opposite: Illustrations from the specification document showing title pages, as well as showing a typical case; these show how the style copes with long names, subtitles, and other extra matter, and even the surprisingly frequent instances of no author name.

nology were not sufficiently reliable to make it possible. As time passed things improved, and printing type as a tint became part of the designer's repertoire. I can remember when it still used to be a bit of a lottery: anything darker than 50 percent was likely to print as indistinguishable from solid black, and anything lighter than 15 percent was likely to vanish. But now things have improved, and tints printed on text paper are much more reliable.[1]

The use of small caps for names within ital U&lc in the editorial bylines is deliberately a bit old-fashioned. Small caps were originally developed as the capitals to use with italic lowercase by Aldus Manutius and his punchcutter, Francesco Griffo, in Venice at the start of the sixteenth century. My use of small caps here is not the same as Aldus's,[2] but it still has something of that not-quite-of-this-time flavor. It also helps to make the editorial names a little easier to find amid the italics. This was not something that was new to editorial bylines on Penguin Classics; it was something that my previous series styles for them had already included.

The exact type sizes specified for the components of the title pages, and the spacing between them, were the subject of careful consideration, to ensure that the title pages continued to make sense when the components varied significantly in length or were absent. Since the series style was introduced, if I find myself standing in a bookshop in front of a shelf of Penguin Classics I'm inclined to start randomly picking them off the shelves and checking their title pages to see how they are working out, and in general they look good.[3] Even more so than some other elements of the series style, title pages are something of a gamble (or shot in the dark) as to how they will actually turn out in such a vast series, but I have to say I'm relieved that I've yet to see anything disastrous (if you have seen some, you can keep them to yourselves thankyouverymuch).

Contents List

Knowing the variability of the contents of a Penguin Classic, I was somewhat worried about how I was going to make a sensible specification for the contents list that was going to cover as many eventualities as possible, while at the same time making them look good and make sense.

I see many books marred by ill-thought-out contents lists. Too often they look like an afterthought. Too often the design looks unrelated to the design of the rest of the book. And too often they give insufficient insight into the content, structure, and organization of the book. This is one part of the book where the editor and the designer may need to discuss and negotiate what is included and how it is displayed.

In order to best illustrate the specification for the contents list I'm simply going to quote what I wrote in the specification document:

[1] Now where's the fun in that—no more Russian roulette with vanishing headings?
[2] And the customary usage of italics today is not the same as Aldus's—he didn't use them for emphasis but because they were more economical on space than roman U&lc.
[3] Even if I say so myself.

HERODOTUS

The Histories

Translated by AUBREY DE SÉLINCOURT
Revised with an Introduction and Notes by
JOHN MARINCOLA

PENGUIN BOOKS

FYODOR DOSTOYEVSKY

Crime and Punishment

Translated with an Introduction and Notes by
DAVID McDUFF

PENGUIN BOOKS

GUSTAVE FLAUBERT

Madame Bovary

Provincial Lives

Translated with an Introduction by
GEOFFREY WALL
Preface by MICHÈLE ROBERTS

SECOND EDITION

PENGUIN BOOKS

Classical Literary Criticism

Edited by
PENELOPE MURRAY *and* T. S. DORSCH
with an Introduction and Notes by
PENELOPE MURRAY

PENGUIN BOOKS

The contents list will undoubtedly require more design intervention to make it work sensibly, but as a starting point the most likely components are listed below.

If the specification below is making the contents look nonsensical, the best thing to do is to see what it looks like all (with the exception of the heading) in text-size rom U&lc.

If the items listed are very long or variable in length it may be advisable to force over the longest lines to improve the shape/sense of the block.

Whatever design intervention is necessary please be sure that the primary motive is one of making the text easy to use and as intelligible as possible.

The contents list may run to more than one page: it is generally desirable to have the contents all on one page, but do not force this if the copy is simply too long.

All items in the list align left and page numbers align right with space between the columns closed up to one 10.25 pt em, and the whole block centered in the text measure.

ALL FRONT/END MATTER CHAPTER TITLES IN THE LIST
body text size rom U&lc

ALL MAIN TEXT CHAPTER TITLES IN THE LIST
body text size rom caps letterspaced 10/200 em
12.25 pt extra vertical space between front matter and main text in list
6.125 pt extra vertical space between each main text chapter title in the list
12.25 pt extra vertical space between main text and end matter in list
if the chapter titles follow the book title in the contents list, the book title should be in 14/15.25 pt rom U&lc, centered in text measure, with 12.25 pt extra vertical space above and 6.125 pt extra vertical space below

ALL OTHER COMPONENTS IN THE LIST
U&lc/caps/ital to reflect the typographic treatment of these headings where they occur in the book
mainly in body text size
but with more important heading levels in 11.25 pt and less important heading levels in 9.25 pt
it may be useful to indent the sublists

PAGE NUMBERS
body text size old-style figures and rom lowercase

And this was accompanied by illustrations of sample contents lists.

Contents

Contents

The specification document illustrated only two contents lists. Although contents pages may vary greatly from one volume to the next, the principles that drive them are relatively simple. The typography of the components of the list all visually refer to the typography of the headings where they appear in the book, and the only components likely to be included in the contents list are the front and end matter chapter headings, book or part titles, and chapter headings from the main text. The two contents lists illustrated show the difference between a contents list that lists all of the chapters of the main text and one that doesn't.

Conclusion

And that, broadly, is the series style. The document that explains the series style runs to 87 A4 pages, spiral bound, with transparent frosted polypropylene front cover. The first 18 pages explain and specify all of the detail; the remaining 69 pages are sample pages that illustrate the design—throughout the 18 pages of specification there are cross-references to the relevant sample pages.

Producing the typesetting specification document was a task as large as creating the series style. A lot of the sample pages were produced during the design process as a way of test-driving the specification and checking how the components performed in relation to each other. In creating the document I was very lucky to be working with editorial staff who were as engaged with the task as I was and were willing not only to comment on the design of the series style but also to read my specification document for clarity and consistency (even if they could not be expected to understand all of the typographical terminology). The document went through a number of draft stages as we established what the series style needed to cover, how it should do it, and how I should express and organize that specification.

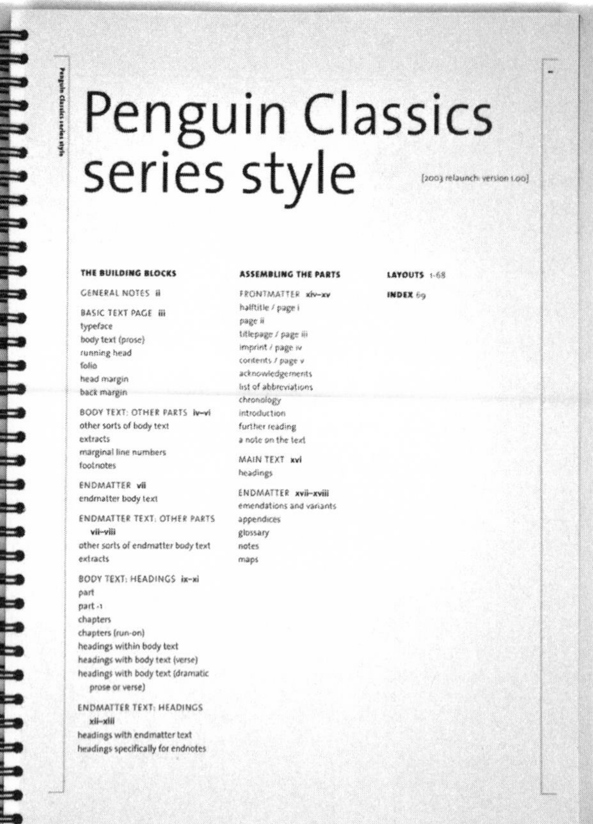

Penguin Classics series style

Penguin Classics series style

[2003 relaunch: version 1.00]

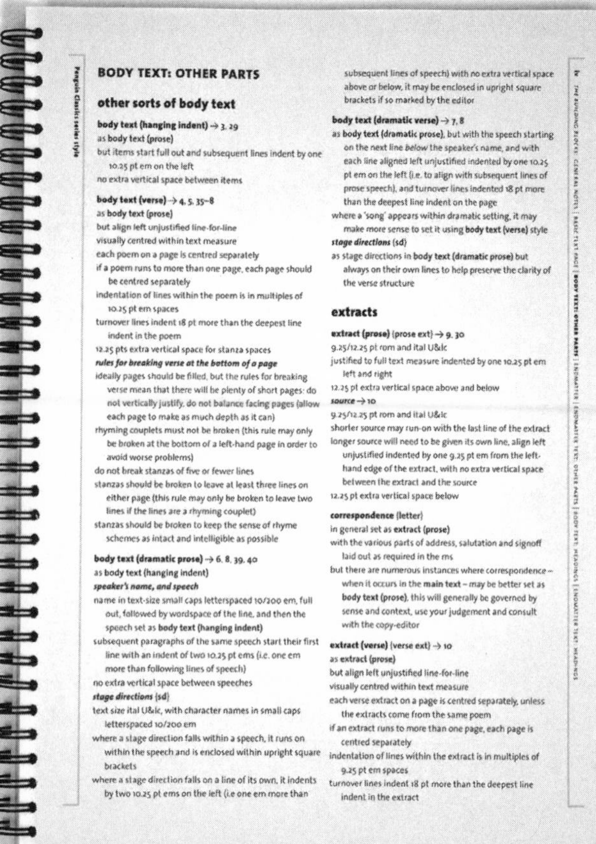

Penguin Classics series style

BODY TEXT: OTHER PARTS

other sorts of body text

body text (hanging indent) → 3, 29
as **body text (prose)**
but items start full out and subsequent lines indent by one 10.25 pt em on the left
no extra vertical space between items

body text (verse) → 4, 5, 35–8
as **body text (prose)**
but align left unjustified line-for-line
visually centred within text measure
each poem on a page is centred separately
if a poem runs to more than one page, each page should be centred separately
indentation of lines within the poem is in multiples of 10.25 pt em spaces
turnover lines indent 18 pt more than the deepest line indent in the poem
12.25 pts extra vertical space for stanza spaces
rules for breaking verse at the bottom of a page
ideally pages should be filled, but the rules for breaking verse mean that there will be plenty of short pages: do not vertically justify, do not balance facing pages (allow each page to make as much depth as it can)
rhyming couplets must not be broken (this rule may only be broken at the bottom of a left-hand page in order to avoid worse problems)
do not break stanzas of five or fewer lines
stanzas should be broken to leave at least three lines on either page (this rule may only be broken to leave two lines if the lines are a rhyming couplet)
stanzas should be broken to keep the sense of rhyme schemes as intact and intelligible as possible

body text (dramatic prose) → 6, 8, 39, 40
as **body text (hanging indent)**
speaker's name, and speech
name in text-size small caps letterspaced 10/200 em, full out, followed by wordspace of the line, and then the speech set as **body text (hanging indent)**
subsequent paragraphs of the same speech start their first line with an indent of two 10.25 pt ems (i.e. one em more than following lines of speech)
no extra vertical space between speeches
stage directions (sd)
text size ital U&lc, with character names in small caps letterspaced 10/200 em
where a stage direction falls within a speech, it runs on within the speech and is enclosed within upright square brackets
where a stage direction falls on a line of its own, it indents by two 10.25 pt ems on the left (i.e one em more than subsequent lines of speech) with no extra vertical space above or below, it may be enclosed in upright square brackets if so marked by the editor

body text (dramatic verse) → 7, 8
as **body text (dramatic prose)**, but with the speech starting on the next line *below* the speaker's name, and with each line aligned left unjustified indented by one 10.25 pt em on the left (i.e. to align with subsequent lines of prose speech), and turnover lines indented 18 pt more than the deepest line indent on the page
where a 'song' appears within dramatic setting, it may make more sense to set it using **body text (verse)** style
stage directions (sd)
as stage directions in **body text (dramatic prose)** but always on their own lines to help preserve the clarity of the verse structure

extracts

extract (prose) (prose ext) → 9, 30
9.25/12.25 pt rom and ital U&lc
justified to full text measure indented by one 10.25 pt em left and right
12.25 pt extra vertical space above and below
source → 10
9.25/12.25 pt rom and ital U&lc
shorter source may run-on with the last line of the extract
longer source will need to be given its own line, align left unjustified indented by one 9.25 pt em from the left-hand edge of the extract, with no extra vertical space between the extract and the source
12.25 pt extra vertical space below

correspondence (letter)
in general set as **extract (prose)**
with the various parts of address, salutation and signoff laid out as required in the ms
but there are numerous instances where correspondence – when it occurs in the **main text** – may be better set as **body text (prose)**, this will generally be governed by sense and context, use your judgement and consult with the copy-editor

extract (verse) (verse ext) → 10
as **extract (prose)**
but align left unjustified line-for-line
visually centred within text measure
each verse extract on a page is centred separately, unless the extracts come from the same poem
if an extract runs to more than one page, each page is centred separately
indentation of lines within the extract is in multiples of 9.25 pt em spaces
turnover lines indent 18 pt more than the deepest line indent in the extract

iv THE BUILDING BLOCKS: GENERAL NOTES | BASIC TEXT PAGE | **BODY TEXT: OTHER PARTS** | ENDMATTER | ENDMATTER TEXT: OTHER PARTS | BODY TEXT: HEADINGS | ENDMATTER TEXT: HEADINGS

The specification document itself, first page and a page of the specification inside. The entire document is set in TheSans.

An additional version of the series style was developed to deal with volumes that were exceptionally long and needed a smaller text size to fit them in a reasonable number of pages. In this version, the same formulae were used, but extrapolating from a smaller starting text size.

And, boy, was I happy when it was done. That was me doing cartwheels down the Strand.

CASE STUDY: *TINKER TAILOR SOLDIER SPY*

I designed this book for the Folio Society in 2009. The Folio Society is a U.K.-based publishing house that largely sells through subscription by mail order. They mainly produce their own editions of existing books. Their objective is to produce books with high design and production values.

This was not the first book that I designed for the Folio Society, and so I already had an understanding of their design values. When briefed to design this book, I already had some knowledge of the writing of John le Carré. As part of my brief I was given the binding concept for the book, the manuscript (as electronic file), and a small amount of handover documentation, which included the trimmed page size decided for the book.

In terms of practical/functional questions about the book, I could find out all that I needed to know from the manuscript and the handover documents. I found out that:

- The book is divided into three untitled parts.
- Each part starts a new page with a separate half title.
- The parts are divided into numbered but untitled chapters.
- The chapters are generally quite short.
- The chapters do not start new pages (with such short chapters it would have made the book much longer and gappy-looking if they did so).
- The prelims are minimal, comprising half title, title, imprint, list of illustrations, and dedication.
- No end matter.
- The text itself is a mixture of dialogue and paragraphs of prose.
- The dialogue has a lot of one- and two-line speeches.
- The text contains section breaks.
- I was also instructed that there were to be no running heads.

In terms of look-and-feel factors, my information came from the binding concept and what I knew of le Carré's fiction, in particular this novel, which is one of his best-known.

The binding concept was to use cloth printed with a flat light gray color, and blocked in dull dark red with a row of silhouettes of the upper halves of the bodies of four men in a row along the bottom third of the front board. Overall the impression was plain, austere, and muted, with a sort of mid-twentieth-century English period flavor.

Le Carré's fiction deals with espionage from the point of view of the British secret service. Unlike the glamorous and exciting world of James Bond, le Carré's fiction takes place in a somewhat morally ambiguous, not always effective, postwar, Cold War environment. The atmosphere is closer to Graham Greene than Ian Fleming. Aspects of the writing that I was particularly keen to make evident in the design were: the sense of a slightly worn-out world, on the

The binding, using the same typeface as the display inside the book.

way to becoming shabby—a physical manifestation of being perhaps morally threadbare; and a sense of underlying conflict between old and new orders, between an older, traditional, conservative (with a small "c") world and a new modern dynamic world still coming into being.

I wanted to reflect the flavor of the novel—as I saw it—within the typography of the novel. The binding concept seemed already in tune with these ideas. However, there wasn't a great deal available within the typography to give this look and feel to—there was not really much other than either the text or the minimal headings to apply flavor to.

I had in mind that somehow the text and the headings were going to embody the underlying conflict I saw in le Carré's fictional world.

I started with establishing the text area on the page. I wanted a relatively traditional text page in terms of text area and margins. I chose to use Monotype Imprint (Frank Hinman Pierpoint for Monotype, 1912) as the text face. It isn't a face I use very frequently; I find it always looks a bit dated, and this was exactly the effect I wanted. This represented for me the old order.

I chose to set the headings in Transport D. This typeface is based on the lettering originally developed for British road signs in 1957–63 by Jock Kinnear and Margaret Calvert. It is part of the mid-twentieth-century British project of modernization through large state-run projects and social engineering. It has a flavor that is particular both in time and place.

I also chose to make the headings ranged left—they are not centered, as one might expect in such a traditional text page—this again was emphasizing the underlying conflict: centered headings seem formal and perhaps imperious, whereas ranged left headings can seem more modern and even informal. And finally, Transport D is quite black and robustly constructed in comparison with Imprint. Everything about the text and headings is contrived to accentuate their contrast.

Looking more closely at the text itself, I had been given a number of pages to aim for, and I found that it was quite generous in relation to the amount of text, so I could put more space between the lines of text than I might normally do (certainly more than in Penguin Classics). Actually, the interlinear space is such that the baseline–baseline distance is exactly twice the cap-height of the text. This is a little more than I might customarily use, but I didn't want to make the margins any more generous or increase the text size, and so the only way to make the text fill the requisite number of pages was to put more space between the lines of text. I didn't want to make the text size bigger because I thought that the slight meanness of the text size used and the resulting sense of parsimony chimed well with the picture of a world still recovering from the privations of war and rationing.

The Folio Society had asked me to typeset the book for them as well as designing it. And although the text was largely quite straightforward, it had

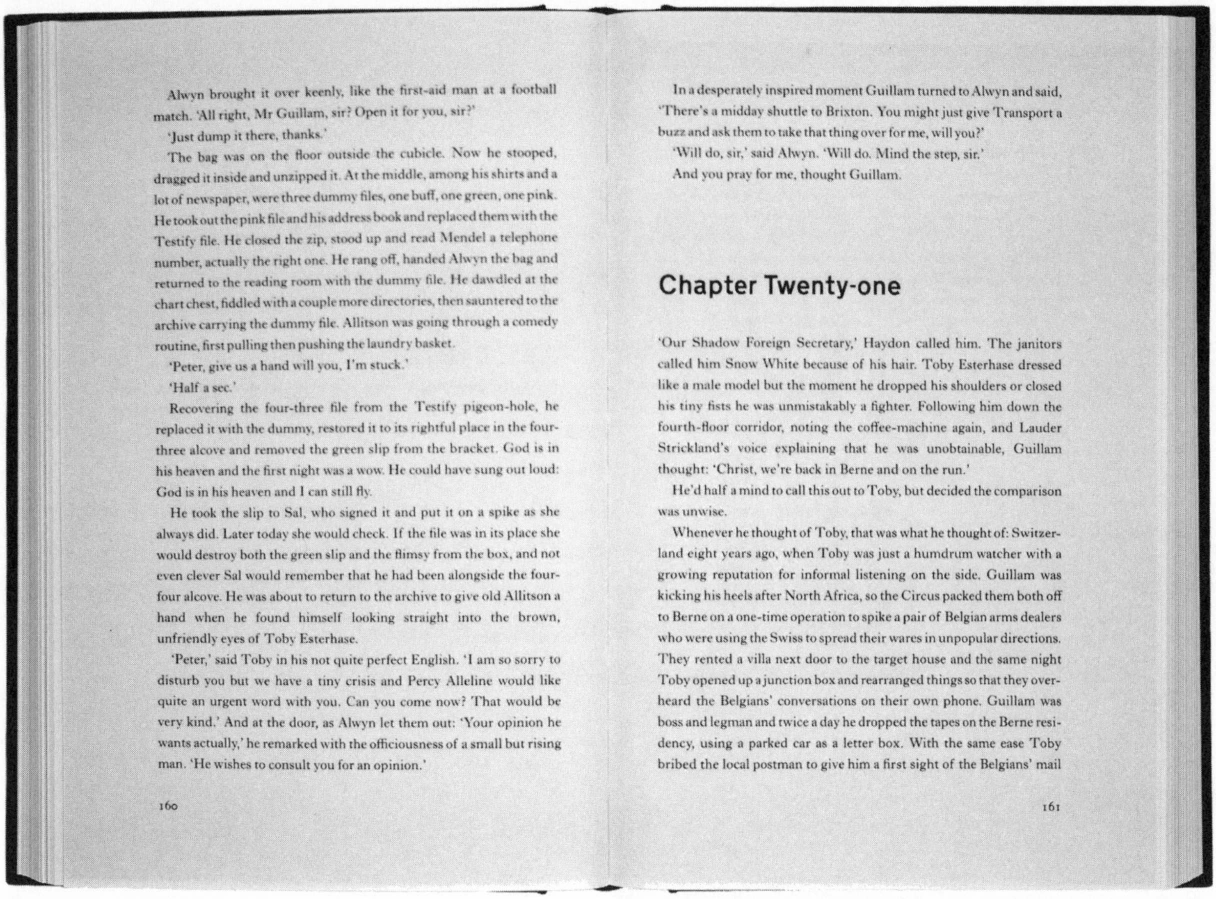

Alwyn brought it over keenly, like the first-aid man at a football match. 'All right, Mr Guillam, sir? Open it for you, sir?'

'Just dump it there, thanks.'

The bag was on the floor outside the cubicle. Now he stooped, dragged it inside and unzipped it. At the middle, among his shirts and a lot of newspaper, were three dummy files, one buff, one green, one pink. He took out the pink file and his address book and replaced them with the Testify file. He closed the zip, stood up and read Mendel a telephone number, actually the right one. He rang off, handed Alwyn the bag and returned to the reading room with the dummy file. He dawdled at the chart chest, fiddled with a couple more directories, then sauntered to the archive carrying the dummy file. Allitson was going through a comedy routine, first pulling then pushing the laundry basket.

'Peter, give us a hand will you, I'm stuck.'

'Half a sec.'

Recovering the four-three file from the Testify pigeon-hole, he replaced it with the dummy, restored it to its rightful place in the four-three alcove and removed the green slip from the bracket. God is in his heaven and the first night was a wow. He could have sung out loud: God is in his heaven and I can still fly.

He took the slip to Sal, who signed it and put it on a spike as she always did. Later today she would check. If the file was in its place she would destroy both the green slip and the flimsy from the box, and not even clever Sal would remember that he had been alongside the four-four alcove. He was about to return to the archive to give old Allitson a hand when he found himself looking straight into the brown, unfriendly eyes of Toby Esterhase.

'Peter,' said Toby in his not quite perfect English. 'I am so sorry to disturb you but we have a tiny crisis and Percy Alleline would like quite an urgent word with you. Can you come now? That would be very kind.' And at the door, as Alwyn let them out: 'Your opinion he wants actually,' he remarked with the officiousness of a small but rising man. 'He wishes to consult you for an opinion.'

160

In a desperately inspired moment Guillam turned to Alwyn and said, 'There's a midday shuttle to Brixton. You might just give Transport a buzz and ask them to take that thing over for me, will you?'

'Will do, sir,' said Alwyn. 'Will do. Mind the step, sir.'

And you pray for me, thought Guillam.

Chapter Twenty-one

'Our Shadow Foreign Secretary,' Haydon called him. The janitors called him Snow White because of his hair. Toby Esterhase dressed like a male model but the moment he dropped his shoulders or closed his tiny fists he was unmistakably a fighter. Following him down the fourth-floor corridor, noting the coffee-machine again, and Lauder Strickland's voice explaining that he was unobtainable, Guillam thought: 'Christ, we're back in Berne and on the run.'

He'd half a mind to call this out to Toby, but decided the comparison was unwise.

Whenever he thought of Toby, that was what he thought of: Switzerland eight years ago, when Toby was just a humdrum watcher with a growing reputation for informal listening on the side. Guillam was kicking his heels after North Africa, so the Circus packed them both off to Berne on a one-time operation to spike a pair of Belgian arms dealers who were using the Swiss to spread their wares in unpopular directions. They rented a villa next door to the target house and the same night Toby opened up a junction box and rearranged things so that they overheard the Belgians' conversations on their own phone. Guillam was boss and legman and twice a day he dropped the tapes on the Berne residency, using a parked car as a letter box. With the same ease Toby bribed the local postman to give him a first sight of the Belgians' mail

161

Smiley, his eye had settled on a different game. It was a toy, made of two steel rods like the shafts of a pair of tongs. The trick was to roll a steel ball along them. The further you rolled it the more points you won when it fell into one of the holes underneath.

'The other reason you might not have told us, I suppose, is that you burned them. You burned the *British* passports, I mean, not the Swiss ones.'

A typical text spread with a chapter opening and a close-up of the text face. The contrast between the text face and the display face was deliberately intended to reflect something of what I saw in the book. I used Imprint for the text setting, not a typeface I've used much recently, but it had the right period flavor for my intentions. I was able to be generous with space—something that is rarely the case in trade publishing.

one challenge hidden within it—all that dialogue. One of the problems with setting large chunks of dialogue is that many of the "paragraphs" are only a couple of lines long. The last line of a paragraph cannot go at the top of a page, but if most of the paragraphs only contain a couple of lines, the scope for making and saving lines to avoid short lines at the top of a page is very limited. I found with this volume, as I have found previously, that setting large chunks of dialogue is surprisingly slow because it requires a lot of to-ing and fro-ing and fiddling to find ways to avoid widows and orphans (as they are quaintly called).

The only other thing to say about this volume is that on the title page and part titles I chose to range everything right. I do this sometimes if the default ranging left of these pages results in everything falling into the spine. Given

Title page, ranged right to stop it slipping into the spine (as would have happened if ranged left), and helping to mask show-through from the imprint page.

that these are always right-hand pages, making them ranged right puts everything in a more visible position on the page, and on the title page it can help to conceal any show-through from the imprint page (which will be ranged left if it's that sort of book).

I also chose to set the lines of the title with very little interlinear spacing. This slightly hinders the readability of these lines, but to counter that I made lines of the heading different shades of gray to help differentiate them, and it is a well-known and simple title, so hopefully it does not present too much of a challenge to readers. The title page of a volume like this is possibly the only place in a book that I'd permit myself such pattern-making.

I was glad to see that the finished binding of the book had used Transport D, too.

CASE STUDY: CD GUIDES

Prehistory, Mainly Classical

Penguin Books has been producing a guide to recordings of classical music for many years, starting when recordings were on vinyl, progressing in subsequent editions through cassettes, to CDs, and now to downloads. Because recordings are continually being issued, the publication has to be updated every year or two. And as the years have passed, the number of recordings has increased, making each edition bigger and more time-consuming to produce than the last. The project remains viable because it has—to the best of my knowledge—continued to be profitable.

At some point Penguin also started to produce a comparable guide to recordings of jazz music.

I can't remember when I started work on the classical music guide, probably not long after I joined Penguin in 1991. At first I was asked to oversee a new edition following the design of the previous edition. And that is what I did, minimal intervention to keep it on track. But I could see ways in which the design could be improved, and I negotiated to do that for the next edition.

The content of the book follows a regular structure. The book is made up of reviews of recordings of classical music, the elements of the reviews are consistently structured, and the way that the reviews are organized is consistent.

Within each review you find these components in the order in which they are listed here:

- Titles of works on the recording. This functions as the heading of the entry. It can be very variable; if the recording contains only a single symphony obviously this will be a short heading, but if it contains a large number of individual works clearly it will be much longer and in the case of boxed sets of multiple discs longer still.
- Discography. This contains not only the code given to the recording by its manufacturer but also information about the artists who perform on the recording (orchestra, conductor, soloists, etc.).
- The review itself. This is written in paragraphs of straightforward prose.

This is how the reviews are arranged within the book:

- All of the recordings by a single composer are grouped together under a composer heading, and those headings are put in the form of "SURNAME, first name (birth and death dates)."
- The composers are sorted alphabetically.
- Under each composer heading the reviews are always sorted into a consistent sequence: symphonies come first, in numerical order; concertos, chamber works, and other forms are always sorted into a fixed order. When a composer has a large number of reviews, the groups are given

subheadings (such as, for instance, "Symphonies," "Chamber works," "Vocal music"), so that it is easier for readers to find their way through these longer sequences of reviews; these subheadings are not included for composers with fewer reviews because they are not necessary.
- When several recordings of the same work are reviewed, the reviews are consolidated into a single entry: there is a single heading giving the title of the work, followed by several discographies, followed by a review that discusses the different recordings.

That's all pretty straightforward. But there are exceptions and "yes but not quite" stuff.

- Some of the composers aren't composers at all; they are conductors or performing artists significant enough to merit grouping their recordings together in their own section. In the heading given to each of these artists, instead of birth and death dates, we are told their instrument (for instrumental soloists), vocal range (for singers), or orchestra (for conductors).
- Some recordings have been given a title by the recording company—for instance, "Japanese Orchestral Favourites." These titles are included at the start of the heading listing the titles of works.
- Some recordings contain groups of things—such as arias or cantatas—this means that within headings there can be groups of items such as "arias: blah, blah, blah; cantatas: blah, blah, blah, blah."
- Sometimes, the various works on a recording are not all performed by the same artists—different artists or different permutations of artists perform different works on the one CD. How this is dealt with is explained later when I discuss the design of discographies in more detail.
- Of course, some recordings contain works by more than one composer, so the heading has to reference those other composers and works (which are reviewed elsewhere in the CD guide, under their own composer heading).
- Some recordings may be by one composer, but orchestrated by someone else or finished by someone else; this and all similar situations are reflected in the heading.

And How Many Times Did I Redesign the Classical CD Guide?

Three times have I redesigned it! With further tinkering in between.[1]

The structure of the entries has not changed much in the time that I've worked on the guide, and some of the bone structure of the typography has been relatively constant too. For much of its life the book has been two column—because the type is small and the page relatively wide, single column

[1] Does this mean that the first two designs I gave it didn't work and had to be replaced? Not really; that wasn't the reason for the redesigns. The redesigns happened because times change, tastes change, editorial staff change.

first played this together at the 1947 'Prague Spring', and their Paris account affords an admirable opportunity for contrasting the golden tone of the one with the (on this occasion) seraphic playing of the other. Of course the sound calls for some tolerance, but this film is a rarity and is to be treasured. Rostropovich, playing with enormous intensity the *Bourrées* from the *Third Suite for Solo Cello*, recorded in December 1962, is a welcome bonus.

Double Violin Concerto in D min., BWV 1043

(M) *** RCA (ADD) 09026 63531-2. Heifetz, Friedman, London New SO, Sargent – BRAHMS: *Double Concerto;* MOZART: *Sinfonia concertante, K.364* ***

It is good to have Heifetz's 1961 stereo recording of the *Double Concerto* as a worthy successor to Menuhin's two versions. Sargent's tempi in the outer movements are brisk but are none the worse for that, and the Elysian dialogue of the slow movement, with Heifetz's pupil Erick Friedman a natural partner, is hardly less inspired and much better recorded.

Detail of my first redesign of the Classical CD Guide, using Minion and Scala Sans. Titles of works, discography, and review—these elements make up most of the book. The '(M)' at the start of the discography is an abbreviation that means this is a mid-priced recording. It was part of a set of abbreviations in parentheses that identified recordings that were new (N), bargains (B), super-bargains (BB), or mid-price (M), and following them is a star rating for the recording.

the golden tone of the one with the (on this occasion) seraphic playing of the other. Of course the sound calls for some tolerance, but this film is a rarity and is to be treasured. **Rostropovich**, playing with enormous intensity the *Bourrées* from the *Third Suite for Solo Cello*, recorded in December 1962, is a welcome bonus.

Double Violin Concerto in D min., BWV 1043

Ⓜ *** RCA **SACD** (ADD) 88697 04605-2. Heifetz, Friedman, London New SO, Sargent – BRAHMS: *Double Concerto;* MOZART: *Sinfonia concertante, K.364* ***

It is good to have **Heifetz's** 1961 stereo recording of the *Double Concerto* as a worthy successor to Menuhin's two versions. Sargent's tempi in the outer movements are brisk but are none the worse for that, and the Elysian dialogue of the slow movement, with Heifetz's pupil Erick Friedman a

Detail of my second redesign of the Classical CD Guide, using Nexus Serif and Nexus Sans. The overall layout has stayed the same, but typefaces and exact sizes have changed. I also replaced the abbreviations in parentheses with a set of symbols, just to prevent them from getting so lost in the discography.

would be awkward to read, though I do recall having to make visuals to prove this to an editor at some point.

When I started work on the guide, the design that I inherited was all in some version of Times New Roman (Victor Lardent and Stanley Morison—or perhaps Starling Burgess—for Monotype and The Times, 1932). My first adjustments to the book continued to use Times.

The first time I fully redesigned the book, I changed the typeface to Minion (Robert Slimbach for Adobe, 1990), with discographies in Scala Sans (Martin Majoor for FontShop, 1993).

I chose Minion partly because it was a relatively new arrival. At that time new typefaces did not arrive with such frequency as they do now, and the arrival of a new, usable text typeface was particularly noteworthy. Having been using pretty much the same repertoire of text faces for the whole of my career up to this point, infatuation with the new arrival was unsurprising, fickle thing that I am. Minion also has a good italic and good bold weights, both of which were important for this book.

I chose Scala Sans for the discographies for a number of reasons: I wanted to use a sans serif for the discographies to help signal the difference of this component—"this is the functional bit of information"; I also wanted a sans serif with old-style figures, and sans serifs with old-style figures were something of a rarity at the time. Fresco Sans has the added advantage of being a humanist-style sans, which made it (in my opinion) better for text setting and a good companion for Minion. Why, you may ask, didn't I use Scala as the seriffed typeface to accompany Scala Sans? Well, I can't really remember after so many years, but it may have been something as pedestrian as Penguin simply not having Scala at the time.[1]

The second time I redesigned the book, I changed the typefaces again. This time I used Nexus Serif and Nexus Sans (Martin Majoor for FontShop, 2004). Yes, this time I used a matching serif and sans. Of course, Nexus Sans is similar to Fresco Sans—both were designed by Martin Majoor. The serif and sans were used in the same relationship to each other as in the previous design.

With every new edition of the CD guide, there were anxieties about the number of pages: the book was invariably making the maximum number of pages that could be bound. So each redesign had to squeeze as much onto the page as possible. The designs achieved economies by the obvious strategy of making the type as small as possible. Also, we kept margins as small as was reasonable—to allow as much of the page as possible to be available for text. Also, using two columns increased the number of words per page (changing a page from single-column to double-column will generally make it accommodate more words, even if the text area stays the same, strange though this may at first seem).

[1] In a large organization, the process of purchasing new fonts can be time consuming and constrained—the purchase has to be justified and approved. Consideration of the number of licenses required may knock back some purchases, and "well, I might like to use it" is a pretty lame business case to present in favor of a purchase. Since the trickle of new typefaces turned into a flood and costs came down, it has become easier to justify and make font purchases.

The other way we squeezed more words onto the page was by being parsimonious with vertical space between elements. Now, of course, we all know that using space is one of the most reliable ways of helping readers to understand the grouping of elements—a bigger space between things signals that those things are not as closely related as the things that have only small space between them. But there was little spare space available, so I had to be really careful with how it was distributed. This meant that the smallest vertical spaces had to be really small, in order to stop the bigger spaces getting too big. If, say, space A has to be identifiably bigger than space B, then space B has to be in turn identifiably bigger than space C, which has to be identifiably bigger than space D. If space D is moderately big, space A has to be really big; whereas if space D is quite small, space A can be relatively smaller too.

By 2010 the number of classical releases was such that they could no longer fit within a single volume. So Penguin took the decision to reconfigure the classical guide into only the thousand best recordings—to make it selective rather than comprehensive and thereby make the book a more manageable size. Penguin also decided to do the same thing with the jazz guide, and to give them the same design. Up to this point the jazz guide had had its own design, given to it very capably by Richard Marston, one of the other then staff designers at Penguin.

Once More unto the Breach . . . Classically . . .

I was asked (by now freelance and no longer staff at Penguin) to design a single new look for the insides of both classical and jazz guides in their new incarnation as selective rather than comprehensive guides. As part of the transformation, the trimmed page size was reduced; previously they had been royal height but about an inch wider, now they became standard royal (234 mm high × 153 mm wide).

In working on this most recent redesign intended for both classical and jazz guides, I started with the classical guide, because this was the first one that I was sent any text for. The brief that I was given didn't extend much beyond the request to make it only single column and the same design for jazz and classical guides.

My first visuals were in Nexus Serif and Nexus Sans, in essence a scaling up of the typography of the previous classical CD guides. The manuscript I was sent, and the number of pages I was told to aim for, meant that the text size could be a reasonable size for single column on a royal page.

. . . Continuing in a Jazz Idiom

After these first visuals, which were approved with little negotiation, there was a considerable pause. The next thing that happened was that a portion of the manuscript for the jazz guide arrived, with a publication date in advance of

138 SURNAME, Firstname

Brandenburg Concertos 1–6; Orchestral Suites 1–4.

Ⓜ EMI 5 099921297052. Busch Chamber Players, Adolf Busch.

The Busch family was among the most illustrious of the inter-war years; Fritz Busch was one of the leading conductors in Europe, Adolf one of its most important chamber musicians and Herman a distinguished cellist. The Busch Chamber Players recorded the *Brandenburg Concertos* in the mid-1930s and they remain among the most thought-provoking and imaginative accounts. The string portamenti, sweet-tone vibrato, rallentandos and piano continuo may put some listeners off, but not R.L. – although E.G. has reservations. Yet these readings have a radiance and a joy in music-making that completely transcend their sonic limitations, which are remarkably few given the provenance and they still serve as a reminder that these 'inauthentic' years have something to teach us. Few have matched Leon Goossen's poignant solos in the slow movement of No. 1 and Rudolf Serkin's playing in No. 5 has wonderful delicacy and imagination. This naturalness of expression is never more telling than in **Marcel Moyse's** contribution to the *B minor Suite* and a richness of feeling from all concerned that make this reissue a special document.

Among more recent recordings, those wanting a first class period instrument version of the *Four Suites* can turn to **Martin Pearlman** and the **Boston Baroque** on Telarc (CD 80619) while those favouring modern instruments and a bargain price, might consider **Marriner's** stylish analogue 1972 set with the **ASMF** (Decca 430 378-2). As a compromise between the two approaches Trevor Pinnock "eager to cut through any narrow perceptions of period style", offers an entirely fresh, authentic approach with the European Brandenburg Ensemble (on Avie AV 2119 - 2 discs) leading his group of 16 musicians elegantly on the harpsichord.

Violin Concertos 1–2; (i) Double Violin Concerto, BWV 1041-3; (ii) Double Concerto for Violin and Oboe, BWV 1060

Ⓜ ⑩⓪ Ph. 420 700-2 Grumiaux with (i) Krebbers; (ii) Holliger; Les Soloists Romandes, Gerecz (ii) New Philh. O, de Waart

These four solo concertos must surely be considered among Bach's most inspired instrumental works, particularly the *Double Violin Concerto* with its elysian interplay between the two soloists. Here

SURNAME, Firstname 139

Grumiaux, a masterly Bach player in his own right, responds to his partnership with another great artist, Hermann Krebbers (who also gave us a justly celebrated record of the Beethoven concerto). The account of the *Concerto for Violin and Oboe* is hardly less felicitous, and the two solo concertos are equally memorable when the recording is so naturally balanced.

(Unaccompanied) Cello Suites 1–6, BWV 1007-12

EMI **DVD** DVA 5 99159-9 (2) Rostropovich

Whether on DVD (filmed against the comparatively severe backcloth of the Basilique Sainte-Madeleine, Véselay in France) or on the companion CD version, both of which are included here Rostropovich 's performances are masterly and all-involving, drawing distinctions between each work in his spoken introductions, although one can choose to hear the music without the commentaries. Unsurpassed and unsurpassable. There is also a CD-only set, offered less expensively on EMI 5 18158-2, which is just as welcome.

Unaccompanied Violin Sonatas 1–3, BWV 1001, 1003, & 1005; Violin Partitas 1–3, BWV 1003, 1004, & 1006

Hyp. CDA 67691/2. Alina Ibragimova

The young Russian virtuoso Alina Ibragimova has been making waves for some time but in these accounts of the Bach solo sonatas and partitas her mastery is very striking indeed. Hers are traditional readings and pay no homage to the authentic instrument lobby. She brings a refined, quiet sensitivity to the slow sarabandes of the *First* and *Second Partitas* as well as the slow openings of the three sonatas, and finds great spirit and incisiveness in the more vigorous movements. There is elegance and character in every single piece. We have a special affection for Grumiaux (Philips 438 736-2) and Milstein (DG 457 702-2) in these works, but this modern version from Hyperion is outstanding in every way.

Goldberg Variations, BWV 988

Sony 696998924322 Perahia (piano)

VAI (ADD) VAIA 1029 Turek (piano)

We are agreed that **Murray Perahia's** set of the *Goldberg Variations* is

The first visuals for my third redesign. Redesigning both classical and jazz guides, I started with the classical guide. Now that the guide has become selective rather than comprehensive it has become shorter, so there's rather less of it to fit in the available space. My starting point was to take the typography of the previous design and resize it, taking into account the new page size and the number of pages they wanted to make.

the classical guide. So I switched my attention to the jazz guide and took my new design for the classical guide and applied it to the jazz guide. I discovered something significant: the structure of the entries was different—I had expected they would be the same.

While the jazz guide is like the classical guide in that it is organized with the artist name as the main heading, followed by recording name, discography, and review within each entry, there is nothing else similar about their organization. Working from the top of the structure downward:

- The jazz guide is not organized alphabetically but chronologically, divided into decades with a chapter heading for each decade. This layer of chapter headings is absent from the classical guide (even though the classical guide is organized alphabetically, there is no heading or break between alpha sections).
- The composer names are not given in the "CHOPIN, Frédéric (1810–49)" format of the classical guide, but are just the name in the standard order of "Chris Barber." Other details are on a separate line below and

are much more extensive than in the classical guide; not only are birth and death dates given but also places, plus instrument(s) played.

- The recording headings are shorter and more regular than in the classical guide—for the simple reason that jazz CDs have "proper" names (such as *Kind of Blue*) rather than simply listing all of the works on the recording.
- The discographies are relatively similar, but all of the additional information about artists playing on the recording is on a new line (or lines) below.
- Each review starts with a displayed anecdote about the artist or the recording, generally several sentences long.
- Because the recordings are ordered chronologically rather than by artist, the recordings by a single artist are not grouped together, and any other recordings by the same artist that are reviewed within the book are signposted by a cross-reference.
- Additionally, it occurred to me that the overall "tone of voice" in the typography of the classical guide was not right for the jazz guide. Both subject matter and authorial tones of voice are quite different in the two guides.

The different heading structures in the two books meant that the typography for the headings was clearly going to have to be different despite the fact that the two books were meant to share the same design. And the books maybe needed different tones of voice in the design too. I discussed these issues with Penguin, and we agreed that I would create designs for the jazz guide and the classical guide that were related but not identical.

I proposed to do this by the fairly standard means of creating a basic design that I could flex by changing heading styles to reflect functional differences of organization and aesthetic differences of tone of voice and content. Basically what I intended to do was to use more sans serif type for the jazz guide to give it a more modern feel in contrast with the traditional predominantly seriffed typography I planned to use for the classical guide. This sort of differentiation strategy is not exactly rocket science; it might even be regarded as rather clichéd, but there is no point in making signs and signals that nobody understands.

The next visuals I produced were for the jazz guide because there was a more immediate need for them. They showed the text in Nexus Serif with headings and discography using Akzidenz Grotesk (originally released by Berthold in 1896). Akzidenz is a typeface I've always been intrigued by but rarely had much opportunity to use. I thought it had a modernist urban vigor[1] that seemed appropriate for jazz.

And then two things happened:

[1] Well how do *you* talk about the rather subjective flavors of a particular typeface?

232 THE PENGUIN GUIDE TO JAZZ RECORDINGS

take a recording credit, and Watson plays a closing solo version of Lindberg's 'Ceilings', an unexpected but very effective end to the set. There are a couple of improvised numbers in the middle of the set, gaspingly short but not a note too long. Mangelsdorff's 'The Horn Is A Lady' and 'Fersengeld' are subtly done and what one takes from the very first track is an impression of three players comfortably bridging the avant-garde and jazz tradition. Lindberg went on to make an album that meditated on the legacy of Ives and Gottschalk. Those concerns aren't far away here. In fact, Ives is a very good composer to keep in mind while listening to John Lindberg, the same couthy wit, the same structural daring, the same sense that everything is possible, but only within understood bounds. Exhilarating.

DAVE McKENNA

Born May 30 1930, Moonsocket, Rhode Island; died October 18 2008, Moonsocket, Rhode Island

PIANO

A Handful of Stars

Concord CCD 4580

McKenna (p solo). June 1992.

Dave McKenna said (1986): **"Some one praised my 'technique', but all I was doing was playing the song, and it needed all those things. I don't think I have much technique, not like some of the great players and the new, good players. I just try to deliver the song I think I know."**

McKenna hulked over the keyboard, a big man with an imposing presence. One of the most dominant mainstream players on the scene, his immense reach and two-handed style distributed theme statements across the width of the keyboard. He possibly quite rightly demurred at comments about his apparent virtuosity because often what he did was quite physical, flat-thumbing three notes at once in the middle of an otherwise open-plan passage, or playing a locked-hand accent that seems to interrupt an otherwise flowing passage of arpeggios. McKenna never sounded inept or amateurish, though. His improvisations proceeded with impressive logic.

He worked with Charlie Ventura, Boots Mussulli, Woody Herman and Gene Krupa, all situations that required a firm hand, and he was nearly 30 before he began recording on his own account. Concord took him up in a big way and Carl Jefferson allowed him to develop his favourite programmes of thematically related songs. These only look contrived on paper, like a 'Knowledge Medley' which takes in 'Apple For The Teacher', 'I Didn't Know What Time It Was', 'I Wish I Knew', 'You'll Never Know', and so on but works superbly in performance, where titles don't really matter. McKenna's attitude seemed to be that with so many great songs out there, one principle of organization was a good ans any other. He gave Concord a set of Hoagy Carmichael tunes in 1983, an Arthur Schwartz tribute a little later. He did a Maybeck recital in that beautiful Berkeley hall, and then in began.

Our favourite of the medley-records is A Handful of Stars, not because it's meltingly romantic, but on the contrary because McKenna takes 'Star Eyes' at a clip and squeezes the mush out of others. His touch always seems appropriate to the moment, and the choice of material, which stretches to the Brazilian pop song 'Estrela Estrela' is always imaginative. The Concord catalogue is much reduced, and though the new owners have brought back some classic items, here's one that cries out for reissue.

THE 1990S 233

STEVE GROSSMAN

Born January 18 1951, New York City

TENOR & SOPRANO SAXOPHONE

I'm Confessin'

Dreyfus FDM 36902

Grossman; Harold Land (ts); Fred Henke (p); Reggie Johnson (b); Jimmy Cobb (d). June–July 1992.

Steve Grossman said (1993): **"I got going on Charlie Parker when I was about eight years old. Then I started checking out John Coltrane, and that has continued pretty much ever since.**

Grossman was working with Miles Davis in his teens, making appearances on the Fillmore live records and the Jack Johnson sessions and it's tempting to suggest that his career peaked too early. Grossman has been out of the American loop for much of the time since, making

The first visuals for my third redesign, applied to the jazz guide. It is exactly the same as the classical guide, with changes made only where necessary due to the different heading structure, and with Akzidenz Grotesk substituted for some of the display setting to reflect a difference between jazz and classical styles.

- I received the complete manuscript for the jazz guide and calculated the number of pages it would make, using the most recent design. It turned out that the jazz guide was considerably longer than the classical guide. Even though both guides contain reviews of 1,000 recordings, the jazz guide has more heading components for each review, and the reviews themselves are longer.
- I started to wonder if Nexus was the right choice of text face for this project. OK, maybe at this point I should admit that when I saw the first printed copies of the previous redesign of the classical guide, I found that Nexus Serif had not turned out quite as I was expecting. Of course I'd looked at numerous visuals on-screen and printed out (I had typeset about thirty pages of the book as a "test drive" to see how the typography worked over an extended sequence of pages, so I had certainly looked at a lot of it), but there's always that final step of the actual typesetting printed on the actual paper. And while nobody said to me that they didn't like it, and while it is perfectly readable, and

while Nexus Serif is a perfectly fine typeface, it didn't work quite as I expected. All of which means that maybe I was predisposed to look for something different.

So, when I had a discussion with Penguin about the length of the book, they said that the jazz guide still had to make 600-ish pages, even though it was so much longer than the classical guide. I pointed out that this meant significant design changes to get a lot more words on the page, and at this point I raised the possibility of changing the typefaces too. Penguin was perfectly happy for me to look at alternative typefaces as part of the design changes I was going to have to make.

So, what I did was to change the typeface and scale down the typography to get more words per page. I presented Penguin with three options, all of which used a single new typographic design but varied in the text block they put on the page:

- Option 1 used exactly the same margins as had been agreed previously for the classical guide (when the type was bigger and economy wasn't such an issue), but with a smaller text size it fit many more words into that same block of space. This gave an average of 520 words per page.
- Option 2 reduced the margins by as much as I thought was suitable for the page size and pushed the line length as long as it could go for the now-small type size. This gave an average of 566 words per page.
- Option 3 took the same margins as option 2 but split it into two columns. This gave an average of 682 words per page.

Look at that, the only difference between options 2 and 3 is that option 3 is double-column, and see how many more words per page it accommodates.

My preference was for option 3 because it not only gave the best number of words per page, but also it allowed for a line length that was shorter and closer to the optimum line length for reading ease. Penguin chose option 2. I wouldn't begin to second-guess their reasoning, but I have noticed among editors a strong resistance to two-column setting. If I was designing a book of literary essays, serious nonfiction, or fiction I would agree that two-column setting gives the reader the wrong sort of impression of what the book contains. However, for a book such as a guide to recorded music, which is much more likely to be referred to purposefully (answering questions of the sort: "I'm looking for the best recording of Mahler's third symphony" or "What's the best place to start if I want to get to know the music of Woody Herman," for instance) and where it is unlikely that the reader will read the book from cover to cover for the pleasure of the content, then two-column setting seems perfectly appropriate. Anyhow, whatever, that's just my opinion; Penguin preferred the single-column version.

The second visuals for my third redesign, in three options. The jazz guide had proved rather longer than the classical guide, so I had to try and get more words onto each page, and I had reconsidered the question of typefaces. All of these options now use Fresco and Fresco Sans, in the same sorts of typographical articulation as the previous designs; the three options differ in the text area they put on the page and whether it is one- or two-column.

keep in mind while listening to John Lindberg, the same couthy wit, the same structural daring, the same sense that everything is possible, but only within understood bounds. Exhilarating.

See also String Trio of New York, **Rebirth of a Feeling**

DAVE McKENNA

Born May 30 1930, Moonsocket, Rhode Island; died October 18 2008, Moonsocket, Rhode Island
Piano

A Handful of Stars

Concord CCD 4580
McKenna (p solo). June 1992.

Dave McKenna said (1986): **"Some one praised my 'technique', but all I was doing was playing the song, and it needed all those things. I don't think I have much technique, not like some of the great players and the new, good players. I just try to deliver the song I think I know."**

McKenna hulked over the keyboard, a big man with an imposing presence. One of the most dominant mainstream players on the scene, his immense reach and two-handed style dis-

A Different Typeface

After some pondering and trying out a number of typefaces, I chose Fresco and Fresco Sans (Fred Smeijers for OurType, 1998). Why did I choose the Fresco family? Well, the seriffed version works well in text setting even at small sizes (such as I was going to require); it has bold weights and italics that work well. In large sizes the pen-drawn origins of the characters become clear, and it looks delightful. Also the sans serif has a clear relation to the seriffed version; the character shapes clearly relate and the sans serif itself makes a very good text face, and finally, the bold and light weights of the sans serif have immensely pleasing character shapes.

Typographic Detail in the Jazz Guide

The task of dealing with all of the components of each entry took some time and attention. These are the components that are repeated in each entry in the jazz guide:

- Artist name (heading)
- Birth and death dates and places
- Instrument(s) played
- Recording name (heading)
- Discography
- Personnel on the recording
- Displayed anecdote
- Review text
- Cross-reference to other recordings by the same artist

The review text was the main text component and the starting point for all of the typography.

The text size I used is 8.1/10.5 pt. If I were doing this job today, I would probably make the baseline–baseline distance 10.528 pt. WHY (I hear you cry) would I consider making such a ridiculous and eye-watering adjustment? Well, deep breath, 10.528 is exactly 1/63 of the page depth. It probably makes no difference to anyone anywhere on the planet (and maybe extraterrestrials) if I choose 10.528 rather than 10.5 pt, but it now offends my sense of structure and order to have a baseline grid that is not in step with the page depth. You might think that this sounds like an insane limitation, but I have yet to find a situation when it has made me feel like I'm designing with my hands tied. Of course, it doesn't have to be 1/63 of the page depth, try 1/62 or 1/64 if you want a bit more or a bit less, and so on.

The text size of 8.1 pt gives a capital height that is just a bit more than half of 10.5 pt. This is—dare I say it, try not to swoon dear reader—a visual judgment. Gosh, yes, really, I make this judgment based on what looks right. Of course, there's any amount of to-ing and fro-ing until I have the right balance of text size, baseline–baseline distance, and lines per page. Maybe it sounds like a load of math, but hey your computer can do it for you. And use the document grids in InDesign; they make possible my obsessive design strategies.

But we haven't finished yet. Again, if I were designing this book today, instead of using indents in multiples of a pica or an em, I'd use multiples of 12.047 pt. Stop sighing, stop rolling your eyes heavenward; 12.047 pt is 1/36 of the page width. No I didn't choose it because it is just the figures 63 switched round (oh, how arbitrary would that be[1]) but because it is a quarter of a ninth of the page width.

Returning to the vertical grid, I think you can probably predict that the text depth won't be just plonked by eye within the page depth. Of course not, if the vertical grid exactly fits the page depth, and the text block sits on that: text line 1 of the text area aligns with line 5 of the vertical grid that starts at the top edge of the page. There, wasn't that easy. Of course, it's not always so straightforward; sometimes visually the best position is to put the baseline grid on a half-line of the vertical grid. Not quite perfectly fit together, but close enough, and it looks right in those instances. Ah, well.

As for text width and inner and outer margins, well, whatever looks best, so long as it sits on the grid. My starting point has a tendency to be 4/36 for the inner margin and 6/36 for the outer margin, with a top margin about equal to the inner margin and a bottom margin about equal to or greater than the outer margin—as the vertical grid will allow.

So, now that we have our tightly contrived text page, we have to figure out what to do with all of those other textual components.

Working outward from the main text, I set the displayed anecdote that occurs before each review in text size Fresco Sans bold horizontally scaled to 95 percent. I'm not normally a fan of fiddling with the horizontal scaling of a typeface mainly because it quickly starts doing bad things to the stroke thicknesses and letter shapes, but I did it quite a bit in this design—expanding and contracting by 5 percent—mainly as a way of fine tuning the balance between the many elements. Five percent was enough to make a difference to how emphatic (or not) the type looked without doing really bad things to stroke thicknesses and letter shapes, and Fresco is very forgiving of such rough treatment. I wanted the displayed quotes to stand out emphatically from the main text, and putting them in bold sans did that; condensing the type slightly pulled back the contrast just a little.

Personnel and discography information I put in 7.3/10.5 pt Fresco Sans normal horizontally scaled to 95 percent. I put this in the sans serif, for the same reason as in previous editions of the classical guide, because this is detailed factual information that many readers will skip over most of the time;

[1] Yes, that's irony.

tracks from a live Californian set recorded in 1962. These don't add much to a record that is already classic Santamaria.

CHARLES MINGUS&

Born 22 April 1922, Nogales, Arizona; died 5 January 1979, Cuernavaca, Mexico
Double bass, piano

The Black Saint And The Sinner Lady

Impulse! 051174-2
Mingus; Rolf Ericson, Richard Williams (t); Quentin Jackson, Don Butterfield (tba); Jerome Richardson (as, bs, f); Booker Ervin (ts); Dick Hafer (ts, f); Charlie Mariano (as); Jaki Byard (p); Dannie Richmond (d). January 1963.

Sue Mingus says: **'In some fashion, Charles absorbed Bob Hammer's rehearsal band for a six-week gig he had at the Village Vanguard in 1963, which provided a unique opportunity to work out, night after night, on one of his greatest compositions, *The Black Saint And The Sinner Lady.* During that six-week period, the piece grew and developed and changed and took on the colours and musical personalities of the musicians in the band as evidenced in the recording. Musicologist Andrew Homzy has noted how entirely different the original written score is compared to the actual recording, typical of Mingus's incorporation of ideas and sounds of his band members as the music developed.'**

Almost everything about *Black Saint* is distinctive: the long form, the use of dubbing, the liner-note by Mingus's psychiatrist. On its release, Impulse! altered its usual slogan, 'The new wave of jazz is on Impulse!', to read 'folk', in line with Mingus's decision to call the group the Charles Mingus New Folk Band. Ellingtonian in ambition and scope, and in the disposition of horns, the piece has a majestic, dancing presence, and Charlie Mariano's alto solos and overdubs on 'Mode D/E/F' are unbelievably intense. There is evidence that Mingus's desire to make a single continuous performance (and it should be remembered that even Ellington's large-scale compositions were relatively brief) failed to meet favour with

Detail of the typography in the jazz guide: a lot of elements to differentiate within a small amount of space.

that is also why it was set down and condensed slightly—all intending to minimize this information for those who want to skip over it but keeping it perfectly readable for those who want to access the content. Also, some personnel lists are very long, and condensing the type was a way of shaving a line off of the longer instances.

The recording name is in 10.5/10.5 pt Fresco Sans bold U&lc horizontally scaled to 105 percent. This was the biggest I could make the heading while keeping it on the same baseline-baseline distance as the main text (in general headings can be set with less interlinear spacing than text). Expanding the type slightly pushed it in the opposite direction to condensing it—making it a little more emphatic—which the heading needed.

The decision to make the recording name Fresco Sans bold horizontally scaled to 105 percent was taken at the same time as the decision to do the same to the artist name. The artist name is higher up the hierarchy than the recording name, so I made it bigger and all capitals—it marks the beginning of each entry, so it needs to be an emphatic marker of the beginning. Not only is it the biggest, boldest bit of typography in the entry, it has more space above it than is found between any other parts of the entry. Space and grouping work in conjunction with the typography to signal the start of the entry.

The artist name is in 13.125/15.75 pt; you'll notice 15.75 pt is exactly one-and-a-half times the standard baseline–baseline distance. If the heading had been U&lc, I might have considered following the pattern of the recording name by making it 15.75/15.75 pt; however, this heading is all capitals and so requires relatively more interlinear spacing. The type size I used—13.125 pt—is one-and-a-quarter times the size of the recording name, oh yes, and it looked right too.

And finally, the birth and death dates and places are in 7.3/10.5 pt Fresco italic U&lc, the same type size as used for the discography. This information is set directly after the artist name with no extra vertical space between. Normally one might expect more space after a heading like the artist name because it is the most significant level of heading and has a fairly big space above it, but in this case, the birth and death dates and places relate very closely to the artist name—they are specific to the artist rather than to the recording, so they are grouped tightly with the artist name, using the visual strategy of spatial relationships to demonstrate actual relationships within the content.

Maybe now would be a good time to talk about the use of vertical space within the entries. Do you recall that I wrote earlier about the baseline grid being divided into quarters? Well, the reason is that in a book like this I specify all vertical spaces in increments of a quarter of the baseline grid (2.625 pt). Normally, one tries to keep text on a regular baseline grid because it helps pages to back up regularly and thereby look better concealing any show-through. Sometimes, one might specify half line spaces if space is tight or if a line space looks too big—it is still in the same rhythm as the baseline grid, and any show-through is at least regular and retains the possibility of ending up back in step if there's another half line space on the same page. In the case of this book, space was tight; each entry contained a load of components, and so I decided that even half-line spaces would make the whole structure too loose and use too much space. So I resorted to quarter line spaces—this still has some relationship to the baseline grid and retains the possibility of ending up back in step. A quarter-line space is about the smallest vertical space whose presence can be readily spotted.

There are three-and-a-half line spaces above the artist name (and you'll remember that the artist name is on one-and-a-half times the standard baseline–baseline distance, so it actually starts a whole number of lines below the end of the previous entry). There's a line space between the birth and death dates and places and the recording name. Then there's a half-line space above the quote and a quarter-line space below it.

The editor was adamant that pages should make the full depth and columns should balance. With so many components that have space around them and limitations on where columns can break, columns often end up a bit short. It is my habit to simply allow this; the irregular bottom margin does not offend me, and I'm much more keen to keep the vertical spacing within the text block even. However, the editor was not of the same opinion, and so in order to fulfill his requirements as well as maintaining my wish to not upset the evenness of the vertical spacing too much, these are the vertical justification instructions I gave to the typesetters:

In general, facing pages should balance
Pages that don't have to balance:
- the last page in a chapter
- a page that has the end of a recording entry at the bottom of the page

Balanced facing pages do not have to make full depth, can be up to two lines short or up to a half-line long, so long as they balance

Where can recording entries be broken:
- before the artist name
- between instrument and CD name
- between details and anecdote
- within anecdote (leaving at least two lines at the start and end)
- between anecdote and review
- within review (leaving at least two lines at the start and end, normal paragraph breaking applies elsewhere within)
- after cross-reference

Pages can be made to balance by adjusting vertical space:
- above artist name (min 18.875 pt, max 36.75 pt)
- between instrument and CD name (min 7.875 pt, max 13.125 pt)

These are the only points at which vertical space can be adjusted, if you find that this cannot be made to work, please contact the designer immediately

Adjust vertical space in increments of 2.625 pt

Where vertical space has to be adjusted, try to keep the same depth for all instances of that sort of vertical space ("above artist name," or "between instrument and CD name") on that page, or at least try to avoid them being different to each other by more than 2.625 pt

And they made a remarkably good job of it.

Cross-references in the Jazz Guide

There's one final element that I've not mentioned yet—the cross-references—they look minor but are actually important and took quite a bit of work to get right. Because the book is chronological, the same artist can have entries in different places in the book. For example, Gerry Mulligan has entries on pages 245, 324, 388, and 605. Each entry carries cross-references to the other recordings by the same artist, but these are at the end of the entry, and I was worried that they would only be found by the more diligent readers, particularly in instances where the entry goes over the page, putting cross-reference overleaf and thereby invisible as one looks at the artist name at the start of the entry. My suggestion that the cross-references would be more user-friendly if they were immediately after the birth and death dates and places was not well received—my reasoning was that they would thereby be more appropriately grouped with the artist information rather than the information specific to this recording. However, I did get approval to put a signpost in the artist heading to alert people to the fact that there are other recordings in a cross-reference at the end of the entry.

This signpost takes the form of a superscript character, and I wanted to make it something that was as intuitive as possible to understand. I tried all sorts of things: asterisks, arrows, ampersands, the word "more," and permutations of these elements, including some custom ligatured versions of them. In the end we selected to use an Adobe Caslon italic ampersand as a superior figure after the artist name (and to help make the link we repeat this character at the start of the cross-reference at the end of the entry).

A part of the reason for selecting this character was the formal pleasure of setting a small florid character against the unadorned bulk of the Fresco Sans bold capitals. I would have liked a signal that worked more clearly and intuitively to direct readers to the cross-reference at the end of the entry, but hopefully it at least alerts them at the start of the entry to the fact that there's something going on, and the ampersand signals that it has to do with there being more stuff to be found. This cross-reference symbol is explained in the introduction, but of course most readers will never find that explanation, and will only ever figure out what the symbol means by using the book and using a bit of common sense.[1] It would be illuminating to try user-testing a range of symbols to see how effective they proved to be, but of course publishing is conducted on a shoestring that cannot accommodate the costs of such activities.

I'm not going to talk about the rest of the book—part-headings, prelims, and so on, because there's not a great deal to say that is particularly interesting.

[1] Relying on users' common sense leaves the designer a hostage to fortune. Never a good situation to be in.

Running Heads and Page Numbers

And I'm only briefly going to talk about the running heads and page numbers. These are grouped at the top of the page, because that takes up less room than

Detail illustrations of six of the large range of cross-reference symbols I tried out for the jazz guide.

the traditional arrangement of running heads at the top of the page and page numbers at the bottom (same reasoning as in the Penguin Classics). The page numbers are ranged full out to the fore-edge margin and the running heads ranged just inside them. I put a short horizontal rule below the page numbers because I thought that visually separating the page numbers from the main text would help readers. The main text area contains a scattering of numbers (dates, discographies, etc.); it also contains a lot of bits of vertical space, so I could see how easy it might be for the reader's eye to trip over the page numbers if they were not fenced off from the main text on the page. Also, the rule gives some regularity and structure to pages that might otherwise look scrappy. The rule provides a fixed point from which each page can hang. And as is my wont, the typography of the running heads reflected the typography of the part heads that they referenced.

Returning to the Classical Guide

Some time after the jazz guide had been finished, the edited manuscript for the classical guide was sent to me. It was not ideal to have only one book or the other at a time while trying to create a design to encompass both of them, but such is life. I already knew the classical guide was likely to be structured differently to the jazz guide and shorter in length. And it was both of these things. The last work I had done on the design of the classical guide had been in Nexus and using a type size larger than what the jazz guide now used. So, the first thing I did was to see what happened when the manuscript was distractedly, but with the title-track, one of a cycle of 'Sienna'-related compositions, and the closing 'Dis Place' Cowell lets loose his remarkable harmonic and rhythmic intelligence.

HANK JONES

Born 31 July 1918, Vicksburg, Mississippi; died 16 May 2010, New York City
Piano

Lazy Afternoon

Concord CCD 4391
Jones; Ken Peplowski (as, cl); Dave Holland (b); Keith Copeland (d). July 1989.

Hank Jones said (1990): **'Tatum was always number one, but I listened to Teddy Wilson and admired that very elegant approach. When bebop – and I don't like the word – came along, some of that elegance was thrown away, and that was a pity.'**

The oldest, and last surviving, of the Jones brothers is as quiet and unassuming as Elvin was extrovert, but he shares something of Thad's sophistication. Hank served his time in

poured into the jazz guide design. Before getting too embroiled in the details of design changes required, I looked at the length, and sure enough it was considerably shorter than the jazz guide. I discussed this with Penguin, and it was my hope that I'd be able to at least pull back the text area to a slightly shorter line length, if not adjust the whole design starting with a bigger type size, but Penguin wanted to keep the text area and text size just the same. So "all" I had to do was figure out how to treat the heading structure.

I've already explained the differences and similarities between the jazz guide and the classical guide. And as I've already said, it was my intention to give the classical guide a more traditional look in comparison with the jazz guide, and I planned to do this by changing the sans serif headings to seriffed headings. In many respects my design took the lessons learned from previous designs of the classical guide and applied them to the typographical base that sat behind the jazz guide.

As ever, I started by working on the most commonly occurring element in the book—the review text. This presented little problem: like the jazz guide, this was straightforward prose and could use the same typography as the jazz guide.

The discography was treated the same as in the jazz guide, which had been based on my previous designs for classical guides anyhow. One improvement I made—a point I had missed on the jazz guide—was to use ranging figures in the discography. Mostly in text I'd use old-style figures, but in the discographies the identifying code for each CD is usually a mix of capital letters and numbers, and of course, with capital letters, ranging figures look more comfortable and consistent than old-style figures.

of *Petrushka*, again reflecting Howells's response to the Diaghilev Ballets Russes' appearances in London. Helped by rich, atmospheric sound, Richard Hickox draws performances that are both brilliant and warmly persuasive from the LSO, with Moray Welsh a movingly expressive soloist in the concertante works. A most attractive bargain reissue, joining together two equally desirable discs.

(i–ii) ***Elegy for Viola, String Quartet & String Orchestra***; (i) ***Merry-Eye***; ***Music for a Prince: Corydon's Dance***; ***Scherzo in Arden***; (iii) ***Procession for Small Orchestra***

Lyrita (ADD) SRCD 245. Boult, with (i) New Philh. O; (ii) Herbert Downes; (iii) LPO (with **WARLOCK**: *An Old Song for Small Orchestra*. **HADLEY**: *One Morning in Spring*) - **BUTTERWORTH**: *The Banks of Green Willow*, etc.

Of these short pieces the *Elegy* is much the most searching, a thoughtful and expressive inspiration, playing on textual contrasts such as make VW's *Tallis Fantasia* so moving in its restrained way. Written in 1917, it represents the sort of response to the First World War that one also finds in Vaughan Williams's *Pastoral Symphony*. The other pieces are relatively slight, but they present a welcome sample of the work of a highly discriminating composer. *Merry-Eye* offers

Comparison of the typography used for the discographies in the jazz guide and classical guide. Having done the jazz guide, I spotted that I should have specified ranging figures (rather than old-style figures, which were the default for the book) just for the discographies so that the numbers matched the strings of capital letters they frequently accompanied. This example of a classical discography also includes a cross-reference, serving a different purpose to the cross-references in the jazz giude.

Cross-references in the Classical Guide

Like the jazz guide, the classical guide has cross-references, but here they are completely different. Whereas cross-references in the jazz guide refer to other recordings by the same artist, in the classical guide they refer to works by other composers on the same CD, so that the reader knows where to go to find the reviews of the rest of the tracks on the CD. These cross-references are within the discography. This is a feature that previous classical guides had included, so it came as no surprise to me, and my treatment of these cross-references is based on the treatment in previous editions. The cross-reference is made up of the composer surname (with first name only if necessary to differentiate from other composers with the same surname) plus the name of the work. To articulate this I used typography that echoes that of the headings giving the composer surname and the name of the work—by which I mean composer names are in Fresco bold capitals and the names of works are in Fresco italic U&lc. This helps to make them easier to spot in discographies (which are set in Fresco Sans regular), and retains the weight differentiation between composer and work as shown in the headings themselves, but made a little less emphatic (bold and normal instead of black and bold). This was fiddly to specify and typeset (this is when a thorough coding job on the manuscript comes in handy), but I decided it was sufficiently helpful to readers to be worth doing. Not only did it mean that the typography of the cross-references contained visual echoes of the things referred to, but also the typographic differentiation helped the cross-references stand out and thereby be easier to spot. It would have been otherwise easy for a reader to overlook them.

The only other components sufficiently different to the jazz guide to be worth describing here are the headings giving composer names and the titles of the works.

Composer Name Headings

These headings follow the structure of previous editions of the classical guides in giving surname in capitals followed by first name(s) in U&lc and then birth and death dates—for instance, "CHOPIN, Frédéric (1810–49)." I chose to put the name in Fresco black. I'd not normally consider such a bold weight of a seriffed typeface, particularly in a traditional-styled design, because they often look less than great, but Fresco black is considerably better than the heavier weights of many seriffed faces; I thought it looked good and made a suitably emphatic beginning to each composer entry. Some of the composer entries can go on for pages and pages, and the composer names are key elements in macronavigation[1] of the book, so they needed to be really clear and conspicuous—the first thing the reader spots on the page. The birth and death dates were put in the regular weight and text size, because they needed to not distract from the composer name (even though they were on the same line).

Title of Work Headings

The title of work headings provided a rather more awkward challenge. As someone who listens to classical music, I had on occasion actually used editions of the classical guide,[2] and one of the problems that I'd noticed and not been able to resolve satisfactorily in previous editions was the question of how to deal with the plentiful instances where a single CD contains a large number of separate works. I had found it was often difficult to identify where the name of one work ended and the next began. Now that might sound really dumb, but you should try reading them. Here's an example:

> Allabreve in D, BWV 589; Aria in F, BWV 587; Canzona in D min., BWV 588; Canonic Variations on "Vom Himmel hoch," BWV 769; Chorale Partitas, BWV 766–70; Clavier-Übung (Prelude & Fugue in E flat, BWV 552/1–2 & Chorale settings, BWV 669–89; 4 Duets, BWV 802–5); Concertos for organ solo (after Ernst) BWV 592; (after Vivaldi), BWV 593, 594 & 596; (after the Prince of Sachen-Weimar), BWV 592. Fantasia, BWV 562; BWV 563 (con imitazione); BWV 570; BWV 572; Fantasia and Fugue, BWV 537 & BWV 540 & 542; Fugue on a theme by Giovanni Legrenzi, BWV 574; Fugues, BWV 574, BWV 577–8; Fugue on a theme of Corelli, BWV 579; Orgelbüchlein: Chorales BWV 599–644; Kirnberger Chorales, BWV 691–713 & Chorale settings, BWV 714–41 & BWV 753; 764, BWV AnH. ll/55 & without BWV number. 18 Leipzig Chorales, BWV 651–68; 6 Schübler Chorales, BWV 645–50; 18 Chorales of diverse kinds, BWV 659–67; Passacaglia & Fugue in C minor, BWV 582; Pastorale, BWV 590; Pedal-Exercitium, BWV 598; Preludes, BWV 568; 569 (con organo pleno); Preludes & Fugues, BWV 531–46; 543; 551; 535a; Toccatas and Fugues (Dorian), BWV 538; 540; in D min., BWV 565; BWV 566; Toccata, Adagio & Fugue, BWV 564; Trio Sonatas 1–6 BWV 525–30; Trios, BWV 583 & BWV 586

[1] Macronavigation: let's say that's the navigation of the book as a whole, finding the section of the book that has the stuff you're looking for. And micronavigation would be finding the exact place you need within the relevant section or page.

[2] What! No! Really! A designer actually using a book he's designed. Wonders will never cease.

Lawks-a-mercy how could anyone find their way through that thorny thicket? That's long but it's by no means the longest entry, and do you see what I mean about how difficult it is to find the beginning and end of each individual work, and spot a particular work in that list?

One thing that helps the reader is the presence of opus numbers (in the case of this Bach example, BWV numbers): each work ends with its opus number, and they provide a set of landmarks to help one navigate this seemingly impenetrable mass of stuff. However, not all artists have opus numbers, and occasionally an artist with opus numbers will have a few works without opus numbers for their works, so using these to navigate is by no means foolproof.

Perhaps a less confusing way to treat this material would be to put the name of each work on its own line; however, I didn't suggest that as an option because I could see how many extra lines that would make. Possibly with this new selective edition where length was no longer such a constraint, I might have suggested it. But I didn't; increased length isn't the only problem unleashed by using a one-work-per-line approach. If laid out this way, the longer headings look awkward and not much like headings. Also, there are some entries that defy such a strategy. What would one do, for instance, with "Concertos for organ solo (after Ernst) BWV 592; (after Vivaldi), BWV 593, 594 & 596; (after the Prince of Sachen-Weimar), BWV 592"? These are a number of separate works that are all organ concertos, so presumably they should all be on separate lines (following the one-work-per-line policy), but then they become divorced from the "Concertos for solo organ" prefix, which is rather important to them. Maybe one would end up with something like this, reformatting the earlier example:

Allabreve in D, BWV 589;
Aria in F, BWV 587;
Canzona in D min., BWV 588;
Canonic Variations on "Vom Himmel hoch," BWV 769;
Chorale Partitas, BWV 766–70;
Clavier-Übung (Prelude & Fugue in E flat, BWV 552/1–2 & Chorale settings,
  BWV 669–89; 4 Duets, BWV 802–5);
Concertos for organ solo (after Ernst) BWV 592;
    (after Vivaldi), BWV 593, 594 & 596;
    (after the Prince of Sachsen-Weimar), BWV 592.
    Fantasia, BWV 562;
    BWV 563 (con imitazione);
    BWV 570;
    BWV 572;
Fantasia and Fugue, BWV 537 & BWV 540 & 542;
Fugue on a theme by Giovanni Legrenzi, BWV 574;

Fugues, BWV 574, BWV 577–8;
Fugue on a theme of Corelli, BWV 579;
Orgelbüchlein: Chorales BWV 599–644;
Kirnberger Chorales, BWV 691–713 & Chorale settings, BWV 714–41 & BWV 753; 764, BWV AnH. ll/55 & without BWV number.
18 Leipzig Chorales, BWV 651–68;
6 Schübler Chorales, BWV 645–50;
18 Chorales of diverse kinds, BWV 659–67;
Passacaglia & Fugue in C minor, BWV 582;
Pastorale, BWV 590;
Pedal-Exercitium, BWV 598;
Preludes, BWV 568; 569 (con organo pleno);
Preludes & Fugues, BWV 531–46; 543; 551; 535a;
Toccatas and Fugues (Dorian), BWV 538; 540;
    n D min., BWV 565;
    BWV 566;
Toccata, Adagio & Fugue, BWV 564;
Trio Sonatas 1–6 BWV 525–30;
Trios, BWV 583 & BWV 586

That's a first shot at laying out such a list; I'm not sure it's entirely correct and consistent. There are some subentries that have separate lines but are indented (that's what I've done, for instance, with the concertos for solo organ that I described just now), but maybe they should all be run-on on a single line. And look at the Clavier-Übung and Kirnberger Chorales entries—what on earth is going on there? Should this be a number of subentries? Or what? Do you see the can of worms that this layout might open? It would undoubtedly require substantial editorial assistance—just when they thought they'd finished the editing. Not to mention making the heading much longer. So, no, I took the decision to take this approach no further.

One thing that you might have spotted in the example above is that the punctuation is a clue to the start and end of each work. In general works are separated by semicolons, or occasionally a full stop. The full stops tend to occur when there has been a sequence of works with a sort of headword, for instance:

Flute Concertos: in D min., Wq.22; in A min., Wq.26; in B flat, Wq.167; in A, Wq.168; in A, Wq.168; in G, Wq.169. Sonata for solo flute, Wq.132

If we lay this out list-wise we get something like this:

Flute Concertos:
    in D min., Wq.22;
    in A min., Wq.26;

in B flat, Wq.167;
in A, Wq.168;
in A, Wq.168;
in G, Wq.169.
Sonata for solo flute, Wq.132

So, as is more apparent when laid out like this, works are generally separated by a semicolon or a full stop. Just to confound this a little, full stops, as you can see above, are also used in abbreviations such as "op." for "opus" with which the book is liberally sprinkled. Anyhow, thinking about a way to reinforce and amplify the role that the punctuation plays in separating works, I decided to try using some typographical differentiation within these headings. In previous incarnations of this book, these headings had been entirely in bold italic. I decided to retain this, but to set only the names of works in Fresco bold italic, and to use Fresco Sans normal for everything else. This means that the punctuation between works is in Fresco Sans normal (all other punctuation within a work title is in Fresco bold italic), and other elements too—such as "(original version, revised Gendron)"—all supporting material is in Fresco Sans normal.

Detail of a title of work heading, showing the differentiation of titles of work from the other "stuff" in the heading. The other "stuff" is mainly punctuation, which separates the title of one piece of work from the next. Of course, unhelpfully, titles also contain punctuation, so the punctuation within the title matches the typography of the heading (in Fresco bold italic); punctuation that separates titles of works is in Fresco Sans normal, and other nontitle stuff such as "(arr. Schneider)" is also in Fresco Sans normal. I don't really expect any user of this book to be conscious of the typographic subtlety, but I hope that it will help them unravel these awkward tangles of titles without them being aware of the assistance they are being given.

expression, using the widest dynamic range down to the most delicate *pianissimos*, intensifies the impact of each performance, magnetic and concentrated as if recorded live.

Violin Sonata; ***Canto popolare***; ***La Capricieuse, Op. 17***; ***Chanson de matin, Op. 15/2***; ***Chanson de nuit, Op. 15/1***; ***Mot d'amour, Op. 13/1***; ***Offertoire, Op. 11*** (arr. Schneider); ***Salut d'amour, Op. 12***; ***Sospiri, Op. 70***; ***Sursum corda, Op. 11***
Chan. 9624. Mordkovitch, Milford

Along with the *Cello Concerto*, the *Piano Quintet* and the *String Quartet*, the *Sonata* belongs to Elgar's last creative period; all were composed at Brinkwells during 1918–19. Considering its

You might remember that I mentioned back in the mists of time that sometimes the recording might include a number of different soloists or orchestras or whatever, and these are enumerated in the discography and linked to the relevant works in the recording by using roman numerals. It looks like this:

(i) Cello Concerto 9 in B flat (original version, revised Gendron); (ii–iii) Flute Concerto in D, Op. 27 (attrib.; now thought to be by Franz Pokorny); (iv) Symphonies 3 in C; 5 in B flat, Op. 12/3 & 5; (v) Guitar Quintets 4 in D (Fandango); 9 in C (La Ritarata de Madrid); (vi) String Quartet in D, Op. 6/1; (iii) String Quintet in E, Op. 13/5: Minuet (only) Decca 438 377–2 (2).

(i) Gendron, LPO, Casals; (ii) Gazzelloni; (iii) I Musici; (iv) New Philh. O, Leppard; (v) Pepe Romero, ASMF Chamber Ens.; (vi) Italian Qt

To help you unravel this stuff, maybe I could start by saying that the first work—*Cello Concerto 9 in B flat*—was performed by Gendron, LPO, and Casals.[1] And the second work—the flute concerto—is performed by Gazzeloni and I Musici. Does the use of bracketed roman numerals make sense?

So, anyhow, these roman numerals and their brackets were of course set in Fresco Sans normal rather than Fresco bold italic.

Oh yes, and because life wasn't complicated enough already, the characters in Fresco bold italic were vertically scaled to 105 percent, and the characters in Fresco Sans normal were vertically scaled to 95 percent. I didn't specify what to do with word spaces; maybe I should have done so, but you know, I didn't want to overdo it (crikey no!).

My hope was that the names of the works would become easier to pick out and separate out among the clutter and undergrowth. Again, user testing would help us to know, but doubtless none of the readers will think to give Penguin any feedback about this (and even if they do give Penguin any feedback, will it get fed back to anyone who might know what to do with the information?).[2]

More Echoes

I discussed earlier the cross-references in the discography and how the typography echoed that of the headings they reference. Well, there is one other instance where I needed to use a variant on this treatment of cross-references. I also mentioned earlier that not all of the recordings are grouped by composer; some are grouped by performer(s)—generally a soloist or a conductor. Very often a recording in this category is of works by several composers, and rather than split the review into little chunks within the reviews grouped under each composer (as is the practice with other CDs containing the work of more than one composer), there is just the one review under the artist heading. And so the heading style used for the title of work, discussed at length above, has yet another circumstance to deal with: that of multiple composer names within a single heading. I decided to treat these in a way that echoed the typography of the composer headings and cross-references: the composer names are in Fresco black capitals in the midst of the titles of works in Fresco bold italic U&lc. The use of black in addition to the capitalization served to differentiate between the composer names and the titles of works around them, even though they are all run together, so hopefully it is easier to navigate these lists and spot individual works by particular composers within them.

As with the jazz guide, I'm not going to discuss the rest of the components of this book. The front matter was typical of many standard works of reference or nonfiction. The running heads and page numbers are very similar to those in the jazz guide, and like the jazz guide the running heads echo the typography of the heading that they take their content from.

[1] The list of abbreviations in the book tells us that "LPO" is the London Philharmonic Orchestra, but it is left up to the reader to figure out that "Gendron" is Maurice Gendron the conductor and "Casals" is Pablo Casals the cellist.

[2] On the subject of feedback and its scarcity, have you noticed how rarely the design of a book gets mentioned in reviews? Maybe that's good in a crystal goblet sort of way, but it gives us designers little feedback to work with.

Vassily Sinaisky and the BBC Philharmonic are pure magic. Although not the best known, a piece like *From the Apocalypse* is hardly less inspired. The *Eight Russian Folksongs* are especially attractive, with their splashes of local colour, and the dance pieces are equally colourful in their imaginative orchestral dress. The performances are matched by recording of equal richness and luminosity.

LIPATTI, Dinu (piano)

CHOPIN: ***Sonata 3 in B min., Op. 58***; ***Barcarolle***; ***2 Études***; ***Mazurka; 13 Waltzes***; ***Piano Concerto 1***. **BACH**: ***Concerto in D min.,*** cond. Ackermann; ***Partita in B flat***. **BARTÓK** ***Concerto 3*** (with Paul Sacher). **BRAHMS**: ***Waltzes*** (with Nadia Boulanger). **ENESCU**: ***Sonata 3***. **GRIEG**: ***Concerto*** (with Galliera). **LISZT**: ***Concerto 1*** (with Ansermet); ***Années de pèlerinage: Sonetto 104 del Petrarca***. **MOZART**: ***Concerto 21 in C, K.467*** (with Karajan). **RAVEL**. ***Alborada del gracioso***. **D. SCARLATTI**: ***Sonatas Kk. 9 & 380***. **SCHUBERT**: ***2 Impromptus***. **SCHUMANN**: ***Concerto*** (with Karajan)
(B) EMI Classics mono 207318 2 (7)

During his short life (1917–50) the great Romanian pianist attained a legendary standing, and the relatively few recordings he made have rarely been out of circulation. The present collection includes rarities such as the *Third Sonata* of Enescu, who incidentally was his godfather as well as sonata partner in wartime Bucharest, and some Brahms *Waltzes* recorded in 1937 with Nadia Boulanger, with whom he studied. Lipatti's Chopin was in a class of its own and

Detail of a title of work heading where the "composer" is actually a performing artist and the recording contains the work of many composers. The composers' names within the title of work heading again echo the composers' names headings by being in a bolder weight and in capitals; as ever the intention is to help readers unravel these complex headings and navigate their way through them more easily. By the way, dear reader, have you spotted the error in this entry that none of the proofreading picked up? Yes, on line two of the recording title, "BACH" is in the wrong weight (raises eyes to heaven and mutters silently "you can't get the staff . . ."). Well, there were one thousand of these headings to check, and there are a lot in each of them to check aren't there, so please try not to think too badly of me or any of the other people who checked the proofs!

GLOBE UNITY ORCHESTRA&

Formed 1966
Ensemble

Globe Unity 67 & 70

Atavistic Unheard Music Series 223
Manfred Schoof (c, t, flhn); Kenny Wheeler (t, flhn); Jürg Grau, Claude Deron, Tomasz Stańko, Bernard Vitet (t); Paul Rutherford (tb, thn); Jiggs Wigham, Albert Mangelsdorff, Malcolm Griffiths (tb); Kris Wanders (as, bcl); Gerd Dudek (ts, ss, cl, f); Evan Parker (ts, ss); Michel Pilz (ss, bcl, f); Peter Brötzmann (ts, as, bs); Heinz Sauer (bs, ts, as); Willem Breuker (bs, cl); Alexander von Schlippenbach (p, perc); Karl Berger (vib); Derek Bailey (g); Willy Lietzmann (tba); Buschi Niebergall (b, btb); Peter Kowald (b, tba); Han Bennink (d, perc, shellhorn); Jaki Liebezeit, Mani Neumeier, Sven-Åke Johansson, Paul Lovens (d). October 1967–November 1970.

Alexander von Schlippenbach said (1966): **'From the divine indifference of the spheres emerge the solos with all the impulse of revolt. The lines they trace are the images of life.'**

Though it isn't often discussed in wider contextual terms, Globe Unity was a phenomenon very much of its times – combining postwar political radicalism with a pan-cultural, almost cosmic view informed by the example of Karlheinz Stockhausen and Sun Ra – which managed to sustain that spirit over the next four decades. Schlippenbach's most ambitious ensemble has sustained itself with rare concerts and even rarer records. Although there has been a revolving cast of players throughout the group's existence, a few hardy spirits act as points of reference. What a great find 67 & 70 was, two sets by huge editions of the Orchestra, one from Donaueschingen, the other from Berlin, both recorded by German radio. 'Globe Unity 67', which runs for 34 minutes, is a glorious pandaemonium of sound, the 19-strong group making a magnificent racket which scarcely lets up, but which, on careful listening, revolves around a relatively harmonious structure. The 1970 performance seems tamer in comparison, yet in formal terms this is the more freewheeling and radical piece and it's interesting to follow the parallels in working philosophy observed by the London Jazz Composers' Orchestra, whose first model was American but which existed in the same orbit as Globe Unity, moving from composition to free playing and then back to something like structure.

& *See also* **ALEXANDER VON SCHLIPPENBACH, Pakistani Pomade** (1972; p. 401), **Monk's Casino** (2003–2004; p. 683); **LONDON JAZZ COMPOSERS' ORCHESTRA, Ode** (1972; p. 393)

THELONIOUS MONK&

Born 10 October 1917, Rocky Mount, North Carolina; died 17 February 1982, Weehawken, New Jersey
Piano

Underground

Columbia Legacy 513559 2
Monk; Charlie Rouse (ts); Larry Gales (b); Ben Riley (d); Jon Hendricks (v). November 1967, February 1968.

The pianist's son, T. S. Monk, said (1998): **'You have to remember that he was considered some kind of Bolshevik, a dangerous revolutionary who was out to break things down. There's a political dimension to this music no one talks about, and because Thelonious didn't talk to the press, they made up their own version of him.'**

Columbia shrewdly signed Monk just as he was making the transition from underground to mainstream, which is why there's a certain irony in the choice of *Underground* as the title four decades. The sound is first class. At DG Double price, this sweeps the board in this repertoire.

Elijah

Chan. 8774/5 (2). White, Plowright, Finnie, A. Davies, L. Symphony Ch., LSO, Hickox

Richard Hickox with the London Symphony Chorus and the LSO secures a performance that both pays tribute to the English choral tradition in this work and presents it dramatically as a kind of religious opera. Willard White may not be ideally steady in his delivery, sometimes attacking notes from below, but he sings consistently with fervour. Rosalind Plowright and Arthur Davies combine purity of tone with operatic expressiveness, and Linda Finnie, while not matching the example of Dame Janet Baker in the classic EMI recording, sings with comparable dedication and directness in the solo, *O rest in the Lord*. The chorus fearlessly underlines the high contrasts of dynamic demanded in the score. The Chandos recording, full and immediate yet atmospheric too, enhances the drama.

St Paul, Op. 36

Ⓜ Chan. 10516 (2). Gritton, Rigby, Banks, Coleman-Wright, BBC Nat. Ch. & O of Wales, Hickox

Richard Hickox's version, recorded live in Cardiff with BBC Welsh forces, completely avoids sentimentality, finding a freshness which effectively echoes the Bach *Passions* in punctuating the story of St Paul with chorales and the occasional '*turba*' or crowd chorus. In brushing any Victorian cobwebs away, Hickox tends to favour speeds on the fast side, never sounding hurried but, more importantly, never sounding heavy or pompous as other German versions often do. Choral singing is excellent, and among the soloists, Susan Gritton and Jean Rigby are first rate, though the tenor, Barry Banks, is a little strained and Peter Coleman-Wright sounds rather gritty as recorded, though never wobbly. The warmth and clarity of the recording add to the freshness. It is now offered at mid-price with full texts and translations.

MENOTTI, Gian Carlo (1911–2007)

Amahl and the Night Visitors (opera, complete)

That's Entertainment CDTER 1124. Haywood, Dobson, Watson, Painter, Rainbird, ROHCG Ch. & O, Syrus

Recorded under the supervision of the composer himself, this is a fresh and highly dramatic performance, very well sung and marked by atmospheric digital sound of striking realism. Central to the success of the performance is the astonishingly assured and sensitively musical singing of the boy treble, James Rainbird, as Amahl, while Lorna Haywood sings warmly and strongly as the Mother, with a strong trio of Kings.

MESSAGER, André (1853–1929)

Les Deux Pigeons

Ⓜ Australian Decca Eloquence 476 2448. Welsh Nat. Op. O, Bonynge

Messager's charming gypsy ballet was premièred at the Paris Opéra in 1886 on the same bill as Donizetti's *La Favorita*. But it swiftly established its independence, to remain on the repertoire and be revived (with new choreography by Fredrick Ashton) by the Sadler's Wells Company in 1961. We are familiar with the suite, but this is the first complete recording. The music is light but cleverly scored, after the manner of Delibes; agreeably tuneful, it does not

Previous spread: Pages from the finished jazz guide and classical guide, showing their similarities (same typeface families, same basic text type size and text area, same treatments for running heads and page numbers) and differences (heading structures, heading typography).

A Brief Conclusion

All of my work on the CD guides, and the painstaking effort taken over differentiation of elements, was done with the aim of making the complex content as easy and intuitive to use as possible, and at the same time attractive and appealing. I'd love to hear from users of the books about how they have found them to use.

Designing Nonfiction

Design considerations for books of nonfiction vary as widely as their subject matter—from texts as relatively straightforward as a biography to complex reference books. Budget pressure and time pressure have both pushed publishers into wanting to standardize design as much as possible. While they are not the ideal, format designs in the hands of an experienced designer can work reasonably well. Elsewhere in this book Sue Hall and Andrew Barker address the issue of planning for future projects without actually knowing what they might be.

Even with format or model designs, many projects need some involvement by an editor or designer. And, of course, there will always be special projects that cannot fit into some standardized format such as guidebooks, reference books, multiauthored books, and books that reproduce many varieties of documents.

Guidebooks can be especially complex, giving architect names, dates, street addresses, and directions. For the *AIA Guide to the Architecture of Washington, D.C.*, the publisher asked me to keep the design as tight as possible. Most of the entries were brief but contained a lot of different information (location, dates of contruction and renovations, architects' names, contact information, and descriptions). With a two-column format, I wanted to use a condensed sans serif, but many of them did not have every variant I needed. In the end I compromised on URW Franklin Gothic Condensed Book even though there were no italic old-style figures or italic small caps. I was not sure I would need them, but the typesetter I worked with created them for this project.

Documenting Intimate Matters reproduced a large variety of primary documents. Nearly every chapter required special design considerations. There was no way to force everything into a unified format. Some of the documents required centered elements, while others needed eccentric indentions.

Avital Ronell's *The Telephone Book*, designed by Richard Eckersley, could never have fit into a format and still have done what the author required. Here the designer was a co-equal collaborator with the author.

There are still publishers, mostly at university presses such as Chicago and Duke, that design every new title. For many years Duke University Press has maintained a strong design presence, from the days of John Menapace and Mary Mendell to the present staff. Cherie Westmoreland (recently retired from the press) and Amy Ruth Buchanan have won many awards, often finding inspiration from within even the most academic monographs.

Throughout this procedure the designer can only achieve coherence and unity by subjecting every detail to the test of suitability—suitability to subject, author, publisher, market, mechanical processes of origination and reproduction, and, of course, to costing.
— John Ryder,
The Case for Legibility

From *The Telephone Book* by Avital Ronell (University of Nebraska Press), designed by Richard Eckersley.

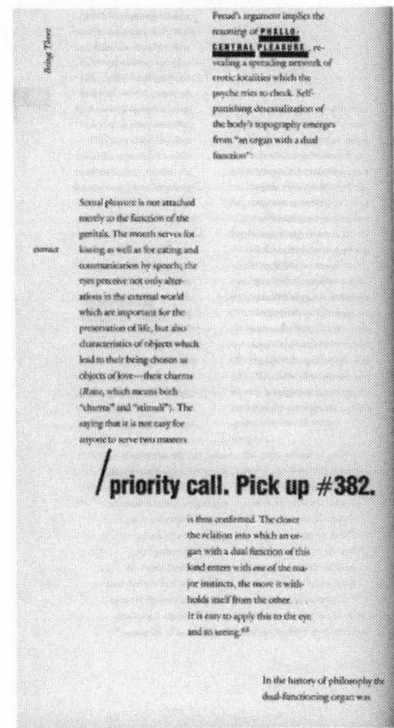

Being There

Freud's argument implies the recasting of **PHALLO-CENTRAL PLEASURE**, revealing a spreading network of erotic localities which the psyche tries to check. Self-punishing desexualization of the body's topography emerges from "an organ with a dual function":

contact

Sexual pleasure is not attached merely to the function of the genitals. The mouth serves for kissing as well as for eating and communication by speech; the eyes perceive not only alterations in the external world which are important for the preservation of life, but also characteristics of objects which lead to their being chosen as objects of love—their charms (*Reize*, which means both "charms" and "stimuli"). The saying that it is not easy for anyone to serve two masters

/priority call. Pick up #382.

is thus confirmed. The closer the relation into which an organ with a dual function of this kind enters with *one* of the major instincts, the more it withholds itself from the other. . . . It is easy to apply this to the eye and to seeing.[68]

In the history of philosophy the dual-functioning organ was

A3 Cannon House Office Building
New Jersey and Independence Avenues, SE

1908—CARRÈRE & HASTINGS
1913—ADDITION: ARCHITECT OF THE CAPITOL, WITH CARRÈRE & HASTINGS
1932—RENOVATION: ARCHITECT OF THE CAPITOL, WITH ALLIED ARCHITECTS

The commission to erect freestanding office buildings for the Senate and the House was divided between the two principals of one architectural firm. Thomas Hastings was responsible for the House Office Building (pictured here), later named for Speaker Joseph Cannon; John Carrère took the lead on the design of its Senate counterpart [see A-8]. The result was a set of fraternal Beaux-Arts twins that, with their giant columns and gleaming Vermont marble, visually merged to form a unified backdrop for the Capitol, at least until the more sober Longworth Building and the irredeemably hideous Rayburn Building came along and spoiled the view.

A4 Library of Congress (Thomas Jefferson Building)
1st Street and Independence Avenue, SE

1888-97—JOHN L. SMITHMEYER & PAUL J. PELZ; INTERIORS: EDWARD PEARCE CASEY
1910-65—RENOVATIONS AND ADDITIONS: VARIOUS ARCHITECTS
1986-97—RESTORATION: ARTHUR COTTON MOORE/ASSOCIATES

Tel: (202) 707-5458
www.loc.gov

As the government was preparing to move to the new federal city in 1800, Congress approved an expenditure of $5,000 to buy books and create a library for its own use. Housed within the Capitol, these original tomes were destroyed during the British invasion of 1814. To replace them, former president Thomas Jefferson, who declared that "there is, in fact, no subject to which a Member of Congress may not have occasion to refer," sold his remarkably broad-based private library of precisely 6,487 volumes to the government. From this core, the Library of Congress has evolved into the largest and best-equipped library in the world, containing more than 144 million items.

The institution's growth was slow and steady until Congress passed the Copyright Act of 1870, which required that the library receive two copies of every book, drawing, photograph, map, or other item submitted to the government for copyright protection. The legislation immediately resulted in a flood of new acquisitions—some 20,000 in the first year alone—exceeding the capacity of the library space inside the Capitol, so in 1873, Congress authorized a competition for a new, stand-alone facility. The team of John L. Smithmeyer and Paul Pelz won first place with a sedate, Italian Renaissance Revival design that did not inspire much enthusiasm. Over the following 13 years, Smithmeyer and Pelz continued to tinker with the design, exploring a wide variety of styles—including French Renaissance, German Renaissance, and "Victorian Gothic"—like teenagers trying on different outfits before a date. Congress finally agreed to a specific proposal and authorized construction in 1886, but there were more delays, and the library was not completed until 1897, 26 years after the original competition.

The executed design is, at least on the exterior, a rather stodgy Beaux-Arts affair that combines aspects of the architects' French and Italian schemes but ultimately is pervaded by a baronial, Germanic aura. The entrance pavilion, nonetheless, was almost certainly inspired by the elegant Paris Opera House by Charles Garnier. The key similarities include the arched doorways on the main level; the five central bays above, framed by paired columns, with circular openings above the windows; and the projecting bays on either side, topped by arched pediments. While Garnier's original conveys a kind of delicate grandeur, however, Smithmeyer & Pelz's interpretation seems overwrought and bombastic. One significant difference is that the Opera House is set right at street level, while the Library of Congress is raised on a podium, contributing to a sense of aloofness. The architect and critic Russell Sturgis lambasted the library's entrance as representing "that false idea of grandeur which consists mainly in hoisting a building up from a reasonable level of the ground, mainly in order to secure for it a monstrous flight of steps which must be surmounted before the main door can be reached."

The library's exterior may be awkward, but once inside, even the most skeptical visitor is likely to be dazzled. The principal interior spaces, which were overseen by Edward Pearce Casey after both Smithmeyer and Pelz were dismissed from the project, are among the most regal rooms in Washington. Casey led a team of more than 50 sculptors and painters, who brought the architecture to life through an artistic program of appropriately encyclopedic proportions. The heroic Great Hall is replete with mosaics and statuary set amid a sea of marble, stained glass, and bronze. Paired columns support arches that seem to spring effortlessly into the air.

The Main Reading Room, topped by a 160-foot-high dome, is the grand finale. The room's octagonal shape was dictated by Ainsworth Spofford, the Librarian of Congress during the building's construction, to reflect a new system for organizing books into eight categories. A mind-boggling assortment of allegorical sculptures and paintings provides intellectual inspiration for the reader, should any be needed. Here, the opening of a book becomes a noble rite.

A5 Folger Shakespeare Library
201 East Capitol Street, SE

1932—PAUL PHILIPPE CRET; CONSULTING ARCHITECT: ALEXANDER B. TROWBRIDGE
1983—ADDITIONS AND RENOVATIONS: HARTMAN-COX ARCHITECTS

Tel: (202) 544-4600
www.folger.edu

When he wasn't raking in money as an oil tycoon, Henry Clay Folger and his wife, Emily Jordan Folger, were busy amassing the world's largest collection of Shakespeare's printed works and related material. Once Henry retired as chairman of the Standard Oil Company of New York in 1928, he turned his full at-

Text spread from *AIA Guide to the Architecture of Washington, D.C.* by G. Martin Moeller, Jr. (The Johns Hopkins University Press). Trim: 5 ×10. Text: 8.9/11 Franklin Gothic Condensed. The condensed Franklin Gothic is not the most elegant sans serif font but was one of the few that had oldstyle figures and small caps. The building headings and running heads are in dark blue.

6 William Byrd, Virginia Planter (1710–1712)

William Byrd was a wealthy planter and slave owner who lived in eighteenth-century Virginia. Byrd's diaries have been read by historians as evidence of white patriarchal insecurity as it defined itself in opposition to white women and enslaved African American women. Byrd wrote about the sexual experiences he had with his wives, prostitutes, enslaved women, and servants. How do his descriptions speak to his identity as an elite white man? What can his diaries tell us about the experiences of enslaved women and men, especially with regards to family and intimacy?

February 22, 1709

I rose at 7 o'clock and read a chapter in Hebrew and 200 verses in Homer's Odyssey. I said my prayers, and ate milk for breakfast. I threatened Anaka with a whipping if she did not confess the intrigue between Daniel and Nurse, but she prevented by a confession. I chided Nurse severely about it, but she denied, with an impudent face, protesting that Daniel only lay on the bed for the sake of the child. . . .

June 17, 1710

. . . I set my closet right. I ate tongue and chicken for dinner. In the afternoon I caused L-s-n to be whipped for beating his wife and Jenny was whipped for being his whore. In the evening I took a walk about the plantation. I said my prayers and drank some new milk from the cow. . . .

Some one in this country has tried to set me at variance with Mr. De Bienville but my irreproachable conduct and the protection of Mr. De Boisbriant have got me out of this trouble.

I am with respect, Sir,
Your, etc.,
Chassin.

April 29, 1711

I rose about 6 o'clock and read nothing because I wished to prepare for my going out of town. I said my prayers and ate rice milk for breakfast. I settled all my affairs and then went to Mr. Bland's to take my leave, which I did about 9 o'clock. Then I rode to my sister Custis' and found them pretty well, only my sister was melancholy. I comforted her as well as I could and then took a walk with my sister and brother in the orchard. About one o'clock

24

4th (5th day) Was at Meeting. . . . I drank Tea at I. Pemberton's with S. Morris & H. Logan. Met in the evening with the latter accidentally at A. Benezitt's. Waited upon her to I. P. jun', where we Supped; then accompanied her to her Brother's & had an opportunity of some Converse with her. Made proposals of waiting upon her at home & of Asking her parents' Consent if such attention was not Absolutely Disagreeable to her. I was in a good deal of Confusion, but her Good Nature Bore with it, without Endeavouring to Encrease it, And Though I could not perceive that she was willing I should take that Step, she Consented to receive another Letter from me upon my promising not to take that for any Encouragement &c.

5th (6th day) I wrote a long Letter to Dear Hannah, & Got her brother William to Undertake the Delivery of it. I told her in it my mind very fully—the Grounds upon which I had formed my unalterable Resolution of having her if possible—and as there was some difficulty whether my waiting upon her parents would be disagreeable or not, I begged the favor of a Line or two upon that Subject, promising the Utmost Secrecy. . . .

Letter of John Smith to Hannah Logan
Philad[elphia], 12 mo: 5th, 1747–8.
DEAR FRIEND

According to the Sentiments I Entertain of Friendship, that pan of it which can bear with the weakness, and put the best Construction upon the failings of One Another Manifests the truest and most Exalted height of that Celestial Virtue.

I conclude with Observing that Marriage is a Solemn thing, but where undertaken with upright, honest Intentions the Blessing of the Almighty Solemnly sought had therein, it must certainly be the happiest State of Life. And I must tell thee that my views in desiring to have thee mine, are so far [from] being mercenary, that should thou Incline to an Alteration with respect to place of Residence, Manner of Living, Business or anything Else, this Inclination shall be punctually Complied with. I pray God to pour down his choicest Blessings upon thy head—and with the Salutation of the Tenderest Regard,

I Remain,
Thy Truly Affectionate Friend,
JOHN SMITH.

The Marital and Reproductive Matrix, 1600–1800 25

All these experimenters in the art of controlling propagation may be reduced in principle to three classes, viz.:

1. Those that seek to prevent the intercourse of the sexes, such as Malthus and the Shakers.
2. Those that seek to prevent the natural effects of the propagative act, viz., the French inventors [of contraceptives] and Owen.
3. Those that seek to destroy the living results of the propagative act, viz., the abortionists and child-killers.

Now it may seem to you that any new scheme of control over propagation must inevitably fall to one of these three classes; but I assure you that we have a method that does not fairly belong to any of them.

Psycho-Physiological Comparison of the Sexes

It is not merely in the organs of generation that Nature has placed the differences between the sexes. She has deeply engraved them throughout the entire organization.

❖

A principal of a high school in Iowa was a married man many years before he knew that the sexual relation was ever sustained during pregnancy.

Those desiring the best reproduction of themselves should learn:
That every mother should be set apart during pregnancy for the antenatal culture of her child.
That control of appetite is the first step in human culture.
That no man should become a father who can not and will not observe the demands of temperance in all things for the benefit of his child.

There is always the danger that she may enter on illicit relations; or, failing to find an outlet for her spirits, become apathetic and hysterical. Every girl should be in possession of a moderate sum for her own use in order that she need not be so ready to accept promiscuous overtures.

Agencies for Recreation
DANCING

The leading amusement ideal of the adolescent girl is the dance-hall. After that, in order of popularity may be mentioned restaurants and cafes, the moving-picture shows, the theaters; in some communities skating-rinks; and promenading the streets. Coming from the monotony of work, and from oftentimes dreary home surroundings, the dance-hall, with its

32 PART ONE

2 Dr. Clelia Mosher, Mosher Survey (1892)

Dr. Clelia Mosher received her medical degree from the Johns Hopkins University in 1900. Mosher interviewed forty-five college-educated white women about their sexual attitudes and experiences, leaving us a rich record of the voices of women to contrast with the male medical prescriptive constructions of female sexuality found in Cooke. The surveys included a broad range of questions, from demographic questions to frequency of sexual intercourse to methods of birth control. The sample below includes a selection of questions and responses from four of the survey respondents: numbers 22, 24, 32, and 33.

No. 22

23. What do you believe to be the true purpose of intercourse? . . .
(b) Pleasure?
In its right place and a minor purpose.
(c) Reproduction?
Yes, main reason.
(d) What other reasons beside reproduction are sufficient to warrant intercourse?

In the married condition my ideas as to the reasons for it have changed materially from what they were before marriage. I then thought reproduction was the only object & that once brought about [i.e., after conception], intercourse should cease. But in my experience the habitual bodily expression of love has a deep psychological effect in making possible complete mental sympathy.

First child was conceived immediately before the monthly period and the second after the eighteenth day from first appearance of menses.

No. 32

22. Is intercourse agreeable to you or not?
Not.
Do you always have a venereal orgasm?
Occasionally. . . .
23. What do you believe to be the true purpose of intercourse?

33

From *Documenting Intimate Matters* edited by Thomas A. Foster (University of Chicago Press). Trim: 6 × 9. Text: 11.3/13.5 Arno Pro. Arno is neutral enough in style with all the variants to deal with documents dating from the seventeenth century to the twenty-first.

CHERIE WESTMORELAND

How much do you generally know about a book before you begin?
In the early '90s I would design using the unedited manuscript. The design process has changed a lot. Everything is moving very fast now, maybe too fast. Now I do my text designs in InDesign CS5, flowing in the edited Word files. The information I have before I begin a design comes from a few sources:

> The manuscript transmittal: a document prepared by the acquisitions editor for each book project that includes a general description of the book's content; the estimated number of book pages that is desired; if it's in a series, how many illustrations, tables, figures, halftones does it have? Is there a color insert? What is the desired schedule?
>
> The marketing questionnaire (prepared by the Marketing Department and filled out by the author) gives additional information including a short and long description of the book—the marketing launch meeting where the acquisitions editor introduces the book and there is discussion about how the book will be marketed. What is the primary audience for the book? Will it be used in classes? Is it a trade book?

How much of a new manuscript do you read?
I have very little time to actually read the manuscript, although I may read part of the introduction. Basically I want to know what kind of book it is. Historical? Narrative? Theoretical? "Cutting edge"? (in which case I will try to do something original or more experimental with the design).

Do you usually discuss the design with the author—
either before or after sample pages?
I rarely interact with the authors regarding the text design. Occasionally I will send sample pages to an author.

What do you look for before beginning a design?
Where do you normally begin a project? From the basic text page
out to the title page? From the title page through the book, etc.?
The manuscript editor will have noted unusual elements and also made a list of the codes used. I begin by carefully looking at the contents page. This usually gives me a lot of information about the structure and complexity of the manuscript. Is it a multiauthor, edited collection? Are there multiple levels of subheads? The more complicated the manuscript, the simpler I try to keep the design. Quickly paging through the manuscript is useful, but I don't usually have time to do this carefully page by page.

Do you have a standard text page (on your Mac or in your head) in the various formats that you usually use to begin a design? Or do you always begin setting up a unique text page layout?

The standard Duke University Press trim sizes are between 5½ × 8½ inches up to 6⅛ × 9¼ inches. When I begin a text design my first consideration is how many characters per page are desired. The castoff and production estimates for the project specify this, usually between 2,400, 2,600, or 2,800 characters per page. I am more likely to start a design from scratch if I am not limited by a large character count. There is a direct correlation between characters per page and trim; if I need to get 2,800 characters on a page the trim will be 6⅛ × 9¼. The desired character count of course also affects the text font choice. I usually design a text page first to make sure that I will be able to achieve the right number of characters per page, which can seriously limit my choice of a text font.

How often do you look for a special text face?

Rarely. I think it is important to mention that a new and more limiting factor in text font choice now is that fonts are getting more and more expensive now that we have moved into the world of e-books. End User License Agreements (EULAS) generally discourage use of the fonts. This is particularly a problem for nonprofit academic publishers. Jan Tschichold advocated using only a few typefaces, and for text fonts that's pretty much what I do. I'm limited to the few Duke has purchased.

Do you set your own books or do you send to a dedicated typesetting firm? Does it make a difference to you who the typesetter would be?

Usually I know which typesetter I am going to send a project to, due to schedule requirements and the nature of the project. I rarely typeset the books that I design. As a result my InDesign files are not as carefully created as they would be if I were typesetting my own books. I don't worry about consistency in setting up character styles. I am using InDesign as a creative tool.

What influences your choice of a text face? Do you have "desert island" fonts—ones you almost always use as a default? Which ones? Why do prefer them?

The choice of typesetter often affects my font choice, limiting me to those fonts that the typesetters I work with have experience in setting well. These include Minion, Scala, Quadraat, Carter & Cone Galliard, Fournier, Bembo, and more recently Chaparral Pro, Whitman, Warnock Pro, and Arno Pro. When choosing the text font I also look through the manuscript to see if there are a lot of acronyms, numbers or dates, or significant use of italics.

After deciding on the trim size and coming up with some possible fonts

I design a basic text page, keeping in mind the desired character count. For some projects I decide on a font and just run with it. For a book I was working on recently, the word "Katmandu" was in the subtitle and for some reason I immediately thought of Arno Pro. I tried it and it worked well for that book.

What influences your choice of display font?
Sometimes a recurring character (i.e., Q, Z, or swash capitals) will lead me to choose a particular display font. For sans serif display fonts some of my favorites include Gill Sans, Helvetica Neue, Quadraat Sans, and Sumner Stone's Magma Compact.

After I have designed the text block, I usually design the contents page. This lets me see at a glance what some of my limitations will be in choosing the display font(s): Are there part pages? Are the chapter titles really long (in which case I probably wouldn't use a big point size or letterspaced caps)? Are there long chapter subtitles? Are there acronyms, dates, italics? More than one chapter author? The more complex the manuscript in terms of elements, the simpler the design.

I like to incorporate ornaments into text designs when I can. Ornaments have to be chosen carefully and used sparingly. Experience has taught me to make sure that any ornament that I use can easily be removed without requiring redesign, as an author may intensely dislike my choice of any ornamental device.

CHILDREN OF FATE

Childhood, Class, and the State in Chile, 1850–1930

Nara B. Milanich

Duke University Press Durham and London

2009

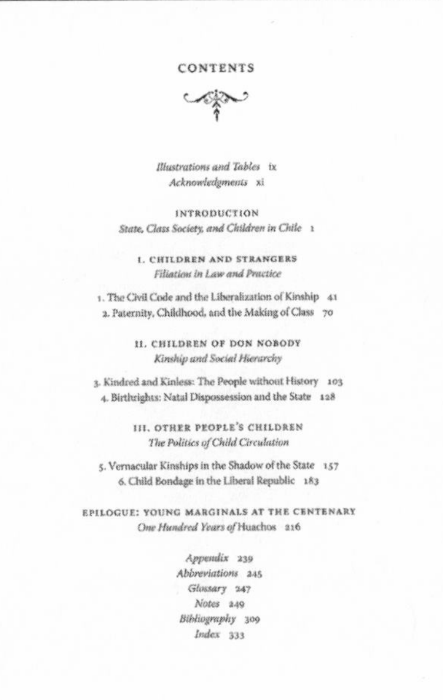

CONTENTS

CHAPTER 3

Kindred and Kinless:

The People without History

Autobiography of an Orphan

"It was the year 1868, if my memory serves me, since I was at most four years old. I remember we were a bunch of little kids amusing ourselves in the sun and eating some wafers . . . that the *madrecitas* made. [*Madrecitas* is] what we called the nuns of Providencia, who when all was said and done were our real mothers since we didn't know any others." So begins the extraordinary tale *The Orphan: True Story Recounted by a Foundling of the Casa de Maternidad de Santiago*. Published serially in a provincial newspaper in 1897 and the following year as a book, the narrative recounts the life of Pablo Pérez, who claimed to have been reared in the Casa de Huérfanos, Santiago's massive public orphanage.[1] The author describes his early childhood in the institution, which in the late nineteenth century housed as many as 9 percent of the children born in the city, as well as his subsequent years laboring in private homes as a young servant. The story then follows the shipwrecks, earthquakes, and other swashbuckling adventures of a self-reliant young orphan forced to make his way alone in the world. The narration is intertwined with the milestones of late-nineteenth-century Chilean history. A self-styled "good liberal," Pérez fights in the War of the Pacific against Peru and Bolivia and militates on behalf of doomed President José Manuel Balmaceda in the 1891 civil war. Apropos of his own marital difficulties, his autobiography is also a spirited exhortation in favor of legal divorce, a perennial cause of Chilean liberals.

Part adventure story, part political treatise, Pérez's autobiography

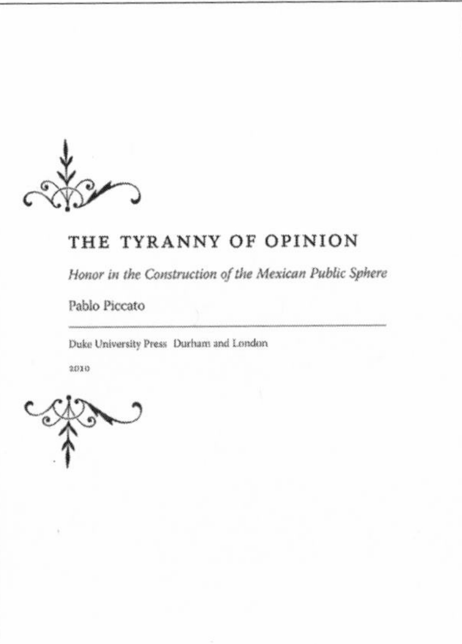

THE TYRANNY OF OPINION

Honor in the Construction of the Mexican Public Sphere

Pablo Piccato

Duke University Press Durham and London

2010

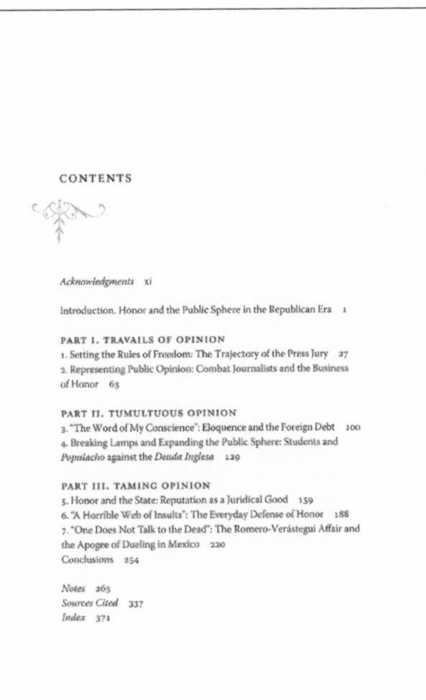

CONTENTS

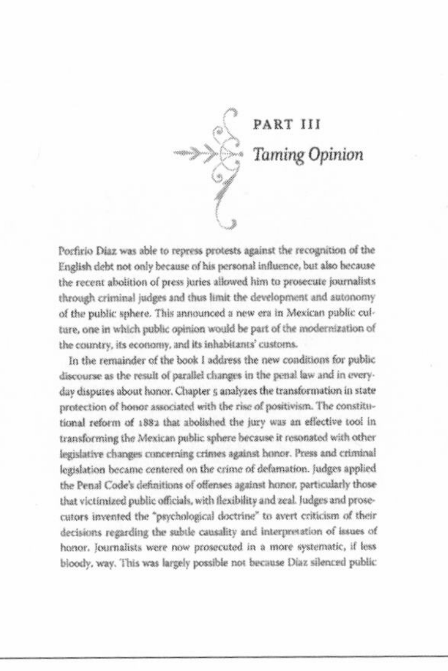

PART III
Taming Opinion

Porfirio Díaz was able to repress protests against the recognition of the English debt not only because of his personal influence, but also because the recent abolition of press juries allowed him to prosecute journalists through criminal judges and thus limit the development and autonomy of the public sphere. This announced a new era in Mexican public culture, one in which public opinion would be part of the modernization of the country, its economy, and its inhabitants' customs.

In the remainder of the book I address the new conditions for public discourse as the result of parallel changes in the penal law and in everyday disputes about honor. Chapter 5 analyzes the transformation in state protection of honor associated with the rise of positivism. The constitutional reform of 1882 that abolished the jury was an effective tool in transforming the Mexican public sphere because it resonated with other legislative changes concerning crimes against honor. Press and criminal legislation became centered on the crime of defamation. Judges applied the Penal Code's definitions of offenses against honor, particularly those that victimized public officials, with flexibility and zeal. Judges and prosecutors invented the "psychological doctrine" to avert criticism of their decisions regarding the subtle causality and interpretation of issues of honor. Journalists were now prosecuted in a more systematic, if less bloody, way. This was largely possible not because Díaz silenced public

Here are two text designs that both have Warnock Pro as the text font and Whitman as the display. These layouts show the way in which I recycle a design, or create a variation. One is a centered design, and the other is flush left. I even took the same ornament and altered it for reuse. Obviously not "cutting edge design," but appropriate for the content and nature of these two books and helpful when the schedule demands it.

Dolly Mixtures

THE REMAKING OF GENEALOGY Sarah Franklin

Duke University Press Durham and London 2007

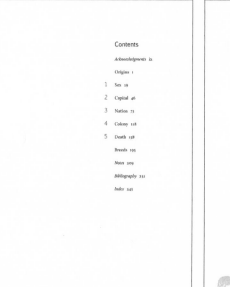

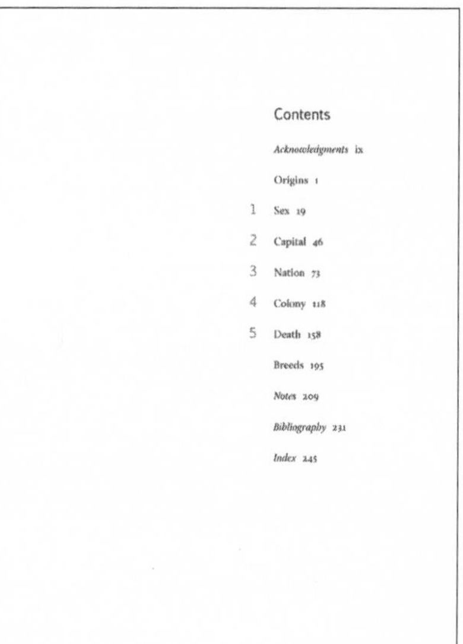

Contents

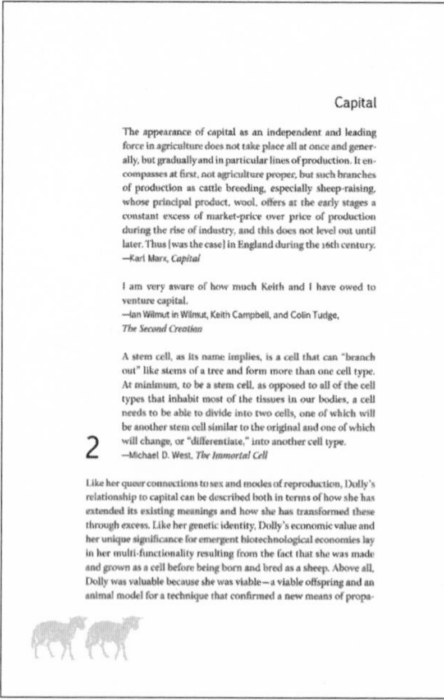

Capital

The appearance of capital as an independent and leading force in agriculture does not take place all at once and generally, but gradually and in particular lines of production. It encompasses at first, not agriculture proper, but such branches of production as cattle breeding, especially sheep-raising, whose principal product, wool, offers at the early stages a constant excess of market-price over price of production during the rise of industry, and this does not level out until later. Thus [was the case] in England during the 16th century.
—Karl Marx, *Capital*

I am very aware of how much Keith and I have owed to venture capital.
—Ian Wilmut in Wilmut, Keith Campbell, and Colin Tudge, *The Second Creation*

A stem cell, as its name implies, is a cell that can "branch out" like stems of a tree and form more than one cell type. At minimum, to be a stem cell, as opposed to all of the cell types that inhabit most of the tissues in our bodies, a cell needs to be able to divide into two cells, one of which will be another stem cell similar to the original and one of which will change, or "differentiate," into another cell type.
—Michael D. West, *The Immortal Cell*

2

Like her queer connections to sex and modes of reproduction, Dolly's relationship to capital can be described both in terms of how she has extended its existing meanings and how she has transformed these through excess. Like her genetic identity, Dolly's economic value and her unique significance for emergent biotechnological economies lay in her multi-functionality resulting from the fact that she was made and grown as a cell before being born and bred as a sheep. Above all, Dolly was valuable because she was viable—a viable offspring and an animal model for a technique that confirmed a new means of propa-

TO MARTHA POTTER BROOKS, "TYPPI" (1912–99), for being a rare breed

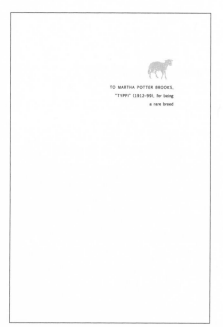

Pages from *Dolly Mixtures* by Sarah Franklin (Duke University Press).
For this book about clones, I cloned a lamb as an ornamental device. Trim: 6.125 × 9.25.
Text: Cycles with Euphemia display.

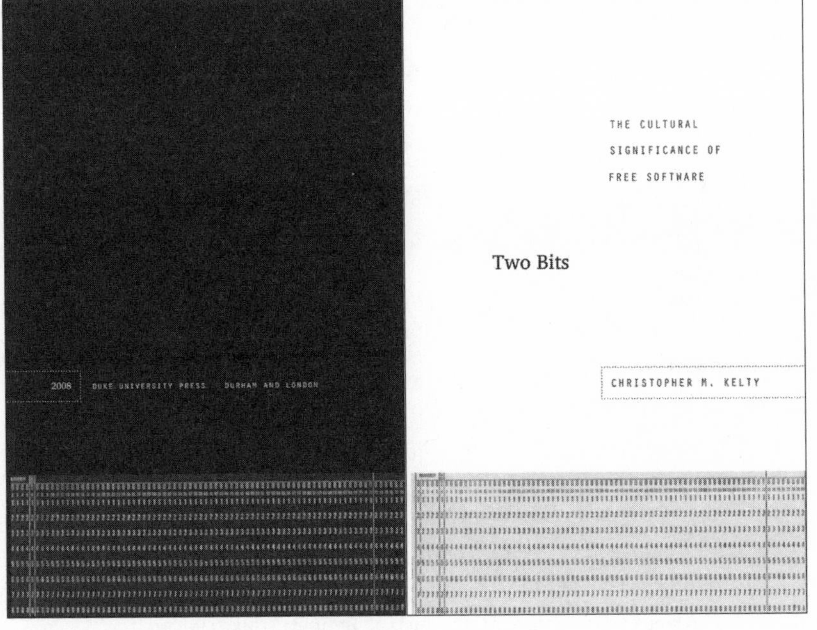

2008 DUKE UNIVERSITY PRESS DURHAM AND LONDON
THE CULTURAL
SIGNIFICANCE OF
FREE SOFTWARE
Two Bits
CHRISTOPHER M. KELTY

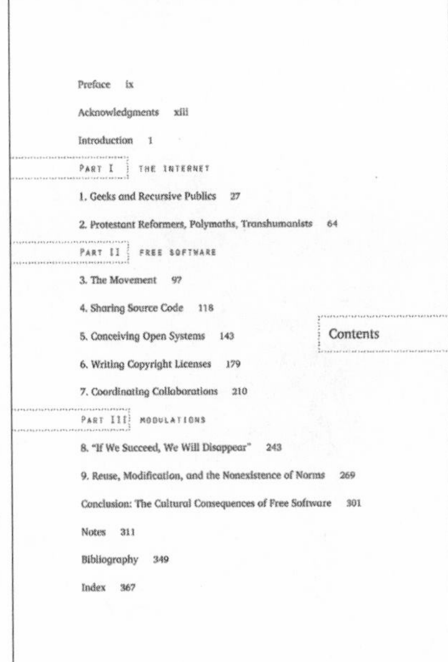

Contents

PART I THE INTERNET

The concept of the state, like most concepts which are introduced by "The," is both too rigid and too tied up with controversies to be of ready use. It is a concept which can be approached by a flank movement more easily than by a frontal attack. The moment we utter the words "The State" a score of intellectual ghosts rise to obscure our vision. Without our intention and without our notice, the notion of "The State" draws us imperceptibly into a consideration of the logical relationship of various ideas to one another, and away from the facts of human activity. It is better, if possible, to start from the latter and see if we are not led thereby into an idea of something which will turn out to implicate the marks and signs which characterize political behavior.
—JOHN DEWEY, *The Public and Its Problems*

Geeks and Recursive Publics 1.

Since about 1997, I have been living with geeks online and off. I have been drawn from Boston to Bangalore to Berlin to Houston to Palo Alto, from conferences and workshops to launch parties, pubs, and Internet Relay Chats (IRCs). All along the way in my research questions of commitment and practice, of ideology and imagination have arisen, even as the exact nature of the connections between these people and ideas remained obscure to me: what binds geeks together? As my fieldwork pulled me from a Boston start-up company that worked with radiological images to media labs in Berlin to young entrepreneurial elites in Bangalore, my logistical question eventually developed into an analytical concept: geeks are bound together as a recursive public.

How did I come to understand geeks as a public constituted around the technical and moral ideas of order that allow them to associate with one another? Through this question, one can start to understand the larger narrative of *Two Bits*: that of Free Software

From the Facts of Human Activity

Boston, May 2003. Starbucks. Sean and Adrian are on their way to pick me up for dinner. I've already had too much coffee, so I sit at the window reading the paper. Eventually Adrian calls to find out where I am, I tell him, and he promises to show up in fifteen minutes. I get bored and go outside to wait, watch the traffic go by. More or less right on time (only post-dotcom is Adrian ever on time), Sean's new blue VW Beetle rolls into view. Adrian jumps out of the passenger seat and into the back, and I get in. Sean has been driving for a little over a year. He seems confident, cautious, but meanders through the streets of Cambridge. We are destined for Winchester, a township on the Charles River, in order to go to an Indian restaurant that one of Sean's friends has recommended. When I ask how they are doing, they say, "Good, good." Adrian offers, "Well, Sean's better than he has been in two years." "Really?" I say, impressed.

Sean says, "Well, happier than at least the last year. I, well, let me put it this way: forgive me father for I have sinned, I still have unclean thoughts about some of the upper management in the company, I occasionally think they are not doing things in the best interest of the company, and I see them as self-serving and sometimes wish them ill." In this rolling blue confessional Sean describes some of the people who I am familiar with whom he now tries very hard not to think about. I look at him and say, "Ten Hail Marys and ten Our Fathers, and you will be absolved, my child." Turning to Adrian, I ask, "And what about you?" Adrian continues the joke: "I, too, have sinned. I have reached the point where I can see absolutely nothing good coming of this company but that I can keep my investments in it long enough to pay for my children's college tuition." I say, "You, my son, I cannot help." Sean says, "Well, funny thing about tainted money . . . there just taint enough of it."

I am awestruck. When I met Sean and Adrian, in 1997, their start-up company, Amicas, was full of spit, with five employees working out of Adrian's living room and big plans to revolutionize the medical-imaging world. They had connived to get Massachusetts General Hospital to install their rudimentary system and let it compete with the big corporate sloths that normally stalked back offices: General Electric, Agfa, Siemens. It was these behemoths, according to Sean and Adrian, that were bilking hospitals

GEEKS AND RECURSIVE PUBLICS 31

Two Bits by Christopher M. Kelty (Duke University Press). The subject of free software led me to choose Charis, an open-source font, for the text display (with Orator for some of the display type), and also inspired the "digital" design elements. Trim: 6.125 × 9.25.

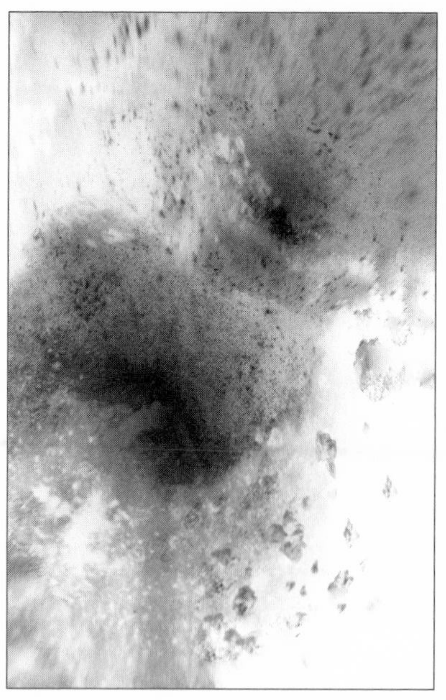

JANE BENNETT

Vibrant Matter

A Political Ecology of Things

Duke University Press Durham and London 2010

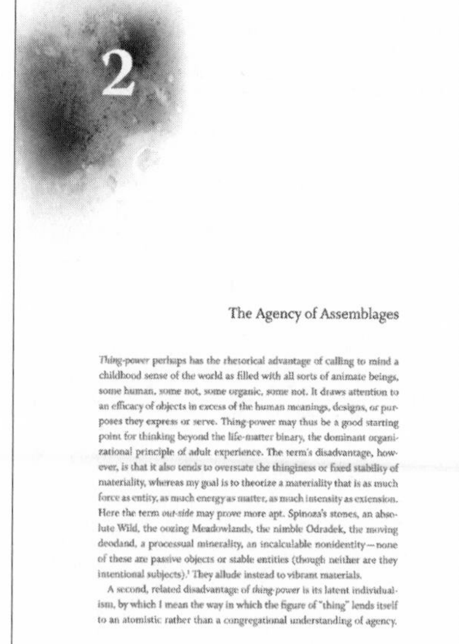

2

The Agency of Assemblages

Thing-power perhaps has the rhetorical advantage of calling to mind a childhood sense of the world as filled with all sorts of animate beings, some human, some not, some organic, some not. It draws attention to an efficacy of objects in excess of the human meanings, designs, or purposes they express or serve. Thing-power may thus be a good starting point for thinking beyond the life-matter binary, the dominant organizational principle of adult experience. The term's disadvantage, however, is that it also tends to overstate the thinginess or fixed stability of materiality, whereas my goal is to theorize a materiality that is as much force as entity, as much energy as matter, as much intensity as extension. Here the term *out-side* may prove more apt. Spinoza's stones, an absolute Wild, the oozing Meadowlands, the nimble Odradek, the moving deodand, a processual minerality, an incalculable nonidentity—none of these are passive objects or stable entities (though neither are they intentional subjects).[1] They allude instead to vibrant materials.

A second, related disadvantage of *thing-power* is its latent individualism, by which I mean the way in which the figure of "thing" lends itself to an atomistic rather than a congregational understanding of agency.

The Force of Things

In the wake of Michel Foucault's death in 1984, there was an explosion of scholarship on the body and its social construction, on the operations of biopower. These genealogical (in the Nietzschean sense) studies exposed the various micropolitical and macropolitical techniques through which the human body was disciplined, normalized, sped up and slowed down, gendered, sexed, nationalized, globalized, rendered disposable, or otherwise composed. The initial insight was to reveal how cultural practices produce what is experienced as the "natural," but many theorists also insisted on the *material recalcitrance* of such cultural productions.[1] Though gender, for example, was a congealed bodily effect of historical norms and repetitions, its status as artifact does *not* imply an easy susceptibility to human understanding, reform, or control. The point was that cultural forms are themselves powerful, material assemblages with *resistant force*.

In what follows, I, too, will feature the negative power or recalcitrance of things. But I will also seek to highlight a positive, productive power of their own. And, instead of focusing on collectives conceived primarily

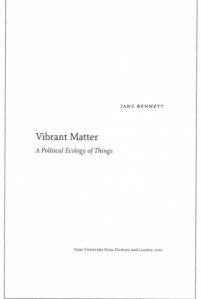

Pages from *Vibrant Matter* by Jane Bennett (Duke University Press). Here I created the art for the title page spread and chapter openings in Photoshop (each one is different). Trim: 5.875 × 9. Text: 10.3/14 Whitman × 23p6 measure.

AMY RUTH BUCHANAN

How much do you generally know about a book before you begin?

I've been at Duke long enough that I can get a reasonable read on a manuscript by looking at the art program (that is, the illustrations that are to appear in the book, along with their captions and any notes about how they should be handled), the table of contents, and the transmittal notes compiled by the acquiring editor. I know what kinds of books each editor acquires, and after more than fifteen years at Duke I know a decent portion of the authors, too, so when I see a book by, say, a well-known Latin American studies scholar, or a leading light in queer theory, I sort of know what I am in for. What I listed above is what I look at when I am picking, along with my fellow designers, which books I want to work on. At Duke we do get to pick, but the list we each end up with is not always stable. We shuffle things around to each other or occasionally to freelance designers as needed to make the schedules work. Nevertheless, having some say over what I work on is crucial. Years ago a former department manager mused aloud about the possibility of going to a "next in line" form of assignment: that is, you send a book off to typesetting and—bam—you get whatever is next in line. I remember the despair I felt at this prospect. Fortunately, the proposal never went anywhere.

Once the manuscript is picked? In an ideal world I would pore over it, read it, and make my design-troubleshooting list while it's in copyediting. In the real world it often sits on my shelf until the launch meeting (and now that we have gone partly paperless, where it "sits" is on a file server, so it's even more out of sight than it used to be), which is when the acquiring editors meet with the marketing department, the production and design manager, and the assistant managing editor and designer assigned to the book, to present the book and discuss its schedule and marketing plan. At this meeting I hope to get a clearer picture of where the book fits into the overall list, what the audience is, what the sales expectations are, how important the author is in his or her field or to the press, and how everyone at the table feels about any cover art suggested by the author. More recently, we have added a separate meeting devoted to discussing cover art only. This has been a huge help in moving the schedules forward so that we can design the cover well in advance of the book, though switching the order of things (cover first, then interior design) has been a significant shift for me. I know it is good for the press and for marketing the book, but I do not necessarily think it results in the most integrated book design.

How much of a new manuscript do you read?

I would have hated to admit it to Richard Eckersley (who once chastised a roomful of designers at a jacket design workshop for this very sin), but sometimes the answer is: not much. For example, I recently designed a book about the history of tuberculosis in Buenos Aires. I didn't need to read much of that to get the picture. It was not a boring book by any means, but reading for comprehension wasn't necessary to come up with a nice, appropriate, Duke-like design for it. If it's an author or topic in which I have a particular interest, I will usually read the introduction at least. And I do quite a bit of scattered reading as I do my initial page-through, taking notes toward the design. This is especially important in an illustrated book. I try to look at the art callouts and read the surrounding text to get an idea of what work the illustration is doing. This helps me make good decisions in my art layouts. Most importantly, as a designer I do a different kind of reading: a reading for structure. Structure is, of course, what interior typography is all about: finding a way to build a strong scaffolding on which the various elements of the book can hang cleanly and legibly.

What do you look for before beginning a design?
Years ago I made a checklist of the elements I look for on page-through as an aid for a beginning book designer. I don't actually use the checklist myself—it's all in my head. But it was a useful exercise to see all the elements of a manuscript that affect a design:

- What character count was assumed in the cast-off and budget? Our standard at Duke is 2,600 characters per page, but this can go higher or lower depending on the targeted book length. Is it a multiauthor edited volume or a single-author work? At the start, do I have a feel for typefaces for this project?
- Is it in a series? Does the series have a logo? Does it have extra front matter such as a list of illustrations or abbreviations?
- Does it have part titles? With or without part numbers? With or without introductory part title text?
- How many chapter titles are there? Should they be new recto, or recto/verso? Are the introduction and conclusion (or prologue and epilogue) styled similarly? Are chapter subtitles used consistently? Are there epigraphs? Does the text start with an A-head? Is the author requesting art at the very beginning of a chapter? What are the longest and shortest running heads?
- Does the main text include lots of numbers? Acronyms? Proper names and other capitalized words? Italics? Small caps? Do I need true italic small caps? Special characters?
- Are there numerous extracts? What kind? How long? Poetry? How will the poetry source line be treated? Dialogue? How are speaker names treated? Are there lists? Are they numbered, unnumbered, or em-

dashed? Any unusual elements like field notes, narratives, letters, or sidebars?

- How many levels of subheads? Are any of them stacked (a + b, b + c)? Are there text epigraphs immediately following subheads? What are the longest and shortest subheads? Do the subheads use numbers, roman numerals, italics, or quote marks?
- Are the notes at the end of chapter, end of book, or foot of page? Are there subheads in the notes? Does the treatment of chapter numbers in the A-heads need to match the treatment on the chapter opening page? Are there extracts in the notes? Are there unnumbered notes? Does the bibliography have subheads or odd elements?
- Are table elements properly coded? Do they make sense?
- Is the art program accompanied by complete numbered printouts of each piece, an art inventory, and captions? Has any art been moved, deleted, or otherwise renumbered? Are there cropping instructions from the author or editor? Are there any restrictions on art by the copyright holder I need to know about? Is there a color insert? How is the art distributed: evenly paced, clumped? Which pieces of art are called out together or within a single page? How is the art called out in the text? Figure numbers or no figure numbers? Which illustrations are most important? How are they discussed? Which need full-page reproduction?

Out of that long list I'd say the most important things I look for are chapter openings, subheads, and art.

Some examples of how items on this checklist might steer my design: If a book has long passages of italics, I won't choose Galliard. I love Galliard's italic face, but it is too spiky and distinctive for reading long passages. If the subheads frequently have italicized words in them, such as book or film titles, I might not design the book with subheads in italics, because I will end up with all those italic terms reversed to roman. If a book has a significant amount of italicized small caps I will choose a face with true, drawn italic small caps, such as Minion. And so forth. The aim, always, is to avoid designing myself into a corner. It's very annoying to be finishing up composition specs only to see that the nice short back matter title "Bibliography" is, in this book, "Suggestions for Further Reading," and that my nifty back matter title design, which is of course closely tied to my chapter opening design and thus my title page, won't work at all. Thorough page-through notes are my best defense against getting into this pickle.

What influences your choice of a text face?

Some of the things I mentioned above, things I note in my page-through such as the frequent use of italic small caps or special characters, will influence my choice. Which typesetter I think will be setting it has an impact, too. Some typesetters set certain faces better than others. Text faces are expensive, and we rarely buy new ones. So we learn to work with what we have. My workhorse typefaces are probably Minion, FontFont Quadraat, and Carter & Cone Galliard. I'd guess that in 2010, about half of my books were set in those faces. I used Scala a lot until I got a little burned out on it, but I do still use it. I am using Chaparral Pro more and more—it has a chipper, slightly casual feel that works well with some of our titles. I have played around, too, with a face that's kin to Chaparral, PMN Caecilia. When I first started designing books in Chaparral, Charles Ellertson, my fount of font wisdom at Tseng Information Systems, suggested I try Caecilia, I think because he had started to feel more comfortable setting it himself. Caecilia is the default font on the Kindle, and I would like to learn a bit about it in hopes that I can work comfortably within the Kindle's current limitations when designing for e-books. I am fond of Monotype Dante, which I first tried out because Cherie Westmoreland designed an important series of ours, the Latin America Readers, in Dante. I feel like I have done some nice books in Dante, but I am still figuring out how to use it properly.

My list of less-used but still useful typefaces would include Bembo (Charles Ellertson's version); Fournier and Perpetua (two very different faces I think of as "pretty" and use for certain titles with a lyrical bent); Arno (I have never been a big user of Jenson but I am trying to warm to Arno—it seems stubborn not to use a nice, Adobe-bundled OpenType face with all the bells and whistles); and Sabon (I used to use it quite a bit but haven't in years—maybe it's time to pick it up again). Adobe Garamond? I have never really mastered it. I will set a book in Monotype Garamond (which Robert Bringhurst reminds me is not a Garamond at all) once in a while just to flex that particular muscle in my design hand, but it's so distinctive and the italics so unruly. The italic caps in particular are so piggish. I am not very deft with Garamond, either real or misnamed. But I have started to use Garamond Premier Pro a bit. Adobe Caslon I seem to use for non-Duke books but not for Duke books. I can't exactly say why.

So beyond the list of considerations above, how do I pick? As I am paging through the book I just get a feeling: this is a Quadraat book, this is a Galliard book. A new book will remind me of another Duke book, and I think I semiconsciously remember what face I set that older book in, so it feels right for the new book too. It's one of the many shortcuts I have fallen into. Other habits can start to feel like clichés. I often set Asian studies books in Quadraat. Something of the calligraphic flair in Quadraat must make me think of Asian letterforms. This is admittedly silly. A book on contemporary Japanese film might have about as much to do with sumi-e calligraphy as a book on modern Italian film has to do with illuminated manuscripts. Luckily Quadraat is a truly beautiful and versatile text face so I don't think in this case my design cliché leads to bad design (at least, I hope I am not falling into what Rob Giampietro, in his excellent piece on the use of Neuland to signify "African American," cleverly calls "stereotypography").

I don't play with period typography much, partly because my typographic history education is spotty, and partly because it just doesn't seem necessary for the type of theory-driven books we publish at Duke. If we do a book on the American Revolution, it won't be a straight history. If it looks right to use Caslon, I will, but I don't feel duty-bound to make a nod to typographic history. That doesn't mean I am immune to the appeal of the occasional design in-joke. Several years ago I designed a book on the history of videotaping, subtitled *Bootleg Histories of Videotape and Copyright*. For the display face I used Arial, which some designers might consider a bootleg Helvetica. I thought that was pretty funny, and it looked good, too.

Do you have "desert island" fonts—ones that you almost always use as a default? Which ones? Why? How often do you look for a special text face? Why?

I suppose my desert island text face is Minion. I like it, I like the x-height, I like the italics, I like the figures, and I like the small caps. It is reliable. My relationship to display faces is more complicated. I'd hesitate to call any of them desert island picks because I really wouldn't want to be stranded with any of them (no offense, Gill Sans). One of my frequent fliers is indeed Gill Sans Bold caps set small and generously letterspaced; I think that always looks pretty nice and can usually transcend the faint whiff of 1950s that lingers about it. Franklin Gothic Extra Condensed caps is another stand-by, though it's very much a love-hate situation. Speaking of love-hate, Erik Spiekermann's Meta can drive me crazy. Yet I keep using it. It is a handy face that is free of the sometimes-dated look of Gill, Frutiger, Helvetica, or Futura. It's kind of blandly modern, and I really mean that in an admiring way, but the nomenclature is confusing (where do I find the italic bold small caps again?), and the letterspacing can be wonky.

I don't really look for new text faces these days simply because we usually can't afford to buy them. I swoon over Enschede's Trinité but it's very pricey, so I enjoy it vicariously through other designers and typesetters. Though I feel very out of touch with all the new display faces out there, I am starting to play around with some free, open-source faces such as those from the League of Movable Type and other foundries. A few years ago I turned my nose up at free fonts, for both aesthetic and ethical reasons. Now, the reality of budget constraints and my frustration with restrictive EULAs has happily coincided with a big leap forward in the quality of free, open-source offerings.

Do you have a "standard" text page (on your Mac or in your head) in various formats that you usually use to begin a design? Or do you always begin setting up a unique text page layout?
The standard Duke text design that hovers in my consciousness is something like this: 6⅛ × 9¼, 9.8/14 × 25p Minion, 38–39 lines per page. Running feet in old-style figures and small caps text, flush outside left and right. A-heads in italics, flush left, 1½ line spaces above, ½ line space below. Extract indent left 1p, ½ line space above and below. Back matter goes down in size and leading at least one point. That basic template can accommodate a lot of books.

In practice what I do is reuse old InDesign layouts. After I have determined the trim size and text face, I look for a recent title with a similar level of complexity and hopefully the same trim size and open it up. After resaving the file, I highlight all the marginal specs and make them blue. As I type over and refine them for the new design, I change them to black. That's my very low-tech way of trying not to introduce errors and inconsistencies in my layouts as a result of recycling a previous InDesign layout. I delete all the previous design's dummy text and start placing the new book's Word files. Once I have the right selection of files placed (and because of the notes I took during page-through, I know which chapter openings I need to lay out for samples and which chapters have the tricky text elements I want to make sure to dummy for the typesetter), I tag everything with my previously defined paragraph and character styles. This method took some getting used to: my inclination would be to jump in and start adjusting and designing as soon as the Word files had been dropped in. But I have found that although it is counterintuitive and feels forced to start off tagging things (because it makes the pages look like sloppy versions of the old design), if I do it, my work will be so much easier. Once everything is tagged I start designing, selecting "redefine style" as I go along. If I start with a robust paragraph and character style palette, this can be a fairly smooth process. Designing the text spread does not always come first though in theory it should, because that's when I realize I may need to go back to my master page and adjust the basic grid.

Do you usually discuss the design with the author—either before or after sample pages?
No. On a handful of occasions I've had an author object to my text design or some element therein. If I can change it without affecting page makeup at first page proofs, I will. For instance, I once did a design for a book of feminist theory that paired blocky, black condensed sans caps (probably the aforementioned Franklin Gothic Extra Condensed!) with a swashy ornament. I was after extreme contrast, no doubt under the abiding influence of the title page of Jan Tschichold's *Typographische Gestaltung* with its marvelous (to me) use

of swashy script and black slab serif (I have ripped off, or tried to rip off, that title page several times). The author was not amused and insisted I scrub the ornament from the design. She found it too feminine. I disagreed (see: John Hancock), but I complied. What remained of my design was a bit clunky, but the author was senior in her field, and it was a battle I was not going to win. Years earlier I had a similar incident with a book on nuns in colonial Peru. I used a flower ornament, inspired by some images of potted flowers set in the niches of the ancient convent walls. The author objected, explaining that it was hard enough to be taken seriously as a female historian writing a woman-centered history, and that my girly (my word, not hers) design wasn't helping matters. In this case the author was right; the flowers came out, and the author and I have remained fans of each other's work ever since. I recently designed her latest book, and it was 100 percent flower-free.

Where do you normally begin a new project?
From the basic text page out to the title page?
From the title page through the book, etc.?
I don't have a standard progression. I will usually try to settle a nice combination of text face and display idea in my head first. The idea is: sans or serif display? All caps? All lowercase? Ornament? Dramatic use of white space? Or extreme alignment to very top of page? Epigraphs above or below chapter title? Etc. Sometimes I will see the page structure in my head; this often occurs in my free time! I'll see, for instance, how the title page could have a retro-cool blocky centered design, how that might carry over into a blocky centered table of contents where the text is flush left and the block shape is defined by flush right page numbers preceded by old-fashioned dotted leaders. I will then imagine how this might continue to a centered chapter opening layout with some sort of dotted rule element (I love polka dots, both sartorially and typographically), but then maybe I would choose not to carry through the centered motif on the text page, opting for my usual flush-left A-head and flush-outside running feet. From that sort of general, fuzzy mental sketch, I try to decide which element will be most challenging and thus rule the design: the title page or the chapter opening page? I start there and work out until I have a reasonable level of consistency of design from half title to CIP page. I think the correct answer to this question is probably "start at the text page," but because I work in a pretty narrow range of trim sizes and character counts, I feel reasonably confident in my text pages, or rather, I feel reasonably confident that whatever trim and typefaces I choose, I can make a nice, balanced text spread for the design. I do freelance work in addition to my job at Duke, and it's in that work that I get to play with different trim sizes.

If you are not setting the book, how differently would you design the book? Does it make a difference to you who the typesetter would be?
At Duke I am never setting the book, so my designs must always take typesetting into account. As I mentioned in my discussion of text faces, some typesetters set certain faces better than others. Some have a steady, experienced hand at proper kerning—especially of display faces, which tend to have much worse "out of the box" kerning—while others need much more direction on kerning, and I don't always have the time to give it, much to my distress. In my freelance work I do sometimes set the book myself, and the main difference is I can be blessedly looser in my specs. Good spec-writing means anticipating all sorts of page-making challenges by writing specs that are strong without being rigid. This kind of spec-writing is tedious, especially when you are sending a book to a compositor who really wants very exacting specs (as opposed to a typesetter who just knows what you want, even when you don't). When I am setting the book myself, I can breathe a bit, because I know that I will get to make each individual spread work within my grid without having to spell out all possible iterations of the layout. Working at the other end of the design-control spectrum, doing design for another press and an unknown typesetter can be nerve-racking. Sometimes it is nerve-racking enough that I will leave my name out of the credits, not because I assume the publisher won't do a lovely production job, but because if a bothersome error makes it through proofing I don't want it to look like my error. Once I did a text and cover design for a press known for good design. When my advance copy of the book arrived it was beautifully typeset, printed, and bound, but a series page had been added in page proofs with little consideration for its relation to the title page. That was disappointing. But I appreciate the schedule constraints publishers work under—sometimes you just have to keep things moving.

Reading Boyishly by Carol Mavor
First, some history. I was hired at Duke as a production assistant. I had an art history background but no training in graphic design. One day my boss, Mary Mendell, found me on the floor of my office stamping a design on kraft paper to make wrapping paper. Instead of asking why I was wrapping a gift on company time (slow day?), she said, "Hey, would you like to design a book?" The manuscript she gave me was almost comically unsuited for a beginner: a massive tome on German constitutional jurisprudence with something like five levels of unwieldy subheads. But Mary is very smart, and this book was actually a great crash course in book design. I learned a lot about vertical spacing working with all those subheads, a lot about character counts trying to keep the page count on target, and a lot about the work of scholarly book design trying to make structural sense of a book on a subject I myself did not fully understand. Starting with that book, and by looking carefully at Mary's

and Cherie Westmoreland's book designs and specs, I slowly absorbed book design. Mary didn't explicitly instruct me so much as she gave me opportunities to learn by watching and doing. An important part of my self-teaching came via BiblioFind, the late, great online used bookseller. There I hoarded dozens of books in my shopping cart: books on book design and type, books by or about famous book designers and typographers, any and everything I could find on Bruce Rogers, Jan Tschichold, P. J. Conkwright, W. A. Dwiggins, and many, many others. The books I actually bought from that overflowing shopping cart became treasured textbooks. One of them was Adrian Wilson's *The Design of Books*. In that book there's a photograph of Wilson seated at an L-shaped desk with an author. They are working side by side, separate but together. For many years this was my fantasy of book design, to work side by side with authors to help their books take shape.

In the real world of publishing, most of us designers would see that scenario as a nightmare. We want author input but not too much input. We want cover art suggestions but we don't want to hear the dreaded "my husband is a graphic designer . . ." But still the L-shaped desk lingers in my book design dreams. The closest I have ever come is this book, *Reading Boyishly* by Carol Mavor. At Duke I have had the pleasure of designing books for several former professors and fellow students, as well as for authors I read and revered as an undergraduate. But designing this book by Mavor, my undergraduate mentor and close friend, was particularly rewarding.

To quote from the cover, *Reading Boyishly* is "an homage to four boyish men and one boy—J. M. Barrie, Roland Barthes, Marcel Proust, D. W. Winnicott, and the young photographer Jacques Henri Lartigue." It is lavishly illustrated with 215 illustrations. The first design choice, and the most important one, was to make it a squat, fat book. Mavor described the book, in her marketing questionnaire, as "overstuffed." In this book, Mavor embraces excess: too many chapters, too many illustrations, too many allusions. This too-muchness is what we were after. We had a production subvention so that meant we could make the trim size smaller (5¾ × 8 inches), the character count lower, and the book longer, while still affording a nice paper to show off the gorgeous art.

Mavor's first book for Duke University Press, designed by Mary Mendell, had been set in Eric Gill's Perpetua, which suited her topic (Victorian photography). I wanted an elegant, even pretty, text face with graceful italics, so my first thought was to try Perpetua. But the French-ness of the book (Barthes, Lartigue, and Proust) set me to thinking of Fournier, which I had used for Mavor's second book, *Becoming*. I mocked up some pages, and it worked beautifully. Next, a display face. Meta seemed right to counter the prettiness of Fournier and keep it all looking contemporary. Plus, I had a sense of this winding up alongside fancier art books in museum bookstores, and somehow

Meta seemed right for that, too. A little Poetica ornament that combined a swash and a colon acted as design punctuation, marking the start of section breaks, filling in for em dashes at the start of chapter epigraph source lines, and appearing in mirrored pairs under each caption.

The biggest design idea that Mavor brought to the project was her desire to print segments of the text in blue (which appear as gray in the figures here). The color blue is the focus of one of the chapters, titled "Beautiful, Boring, and Blue," and flashes of blue appear throughout the book, from the blue marbles in Joseph Cornell's boxes to the greenish-blue Polaroid at the start of Roland Barthes's *Camera Lucida*. *Reading Boyishly* employs an unusual style of captioning illustrations: each illustration is accompanied by a fragment from the text that refers to the image. The image titles and credits proper appear in a list at the back of the book, with each entry keyed to page numbers. This freed me up to size the art generously. It also inspired me to treat the captions more like poetry: I set them centered, broken into nice rounded shapes, with the Poetica ornaments printed in blue below. Then in the running text, the text fragments that had been used as captions are printed in blue. Thus the blue text functions as a pointer finger, leading the reader to the art. Many of the illustrations are used in highly allusive ways, so callouts by figure number were neither needed nor appropriate. For example, the first illustration in the book is a contemporary photograph of a swan-shaped boat. The text refers to Proust's *Swann's Way*. There is no discussion of the photograph itself; it is there as a poetic echo of and comment on the text.

Two motifs that wind throughout the book are ribbons (or, variously, cords, threads, and strings) and bubbles. For the title and chapter opening pages, my first thought was to have some sort of tangled string winding through and around the chapter title and epigraphs. I think my inspiration was a book I had seen in the 1998 AAUP Book, Jacket, and Journal Show, *The Voice Imitator* by Thomas Bernhard, published by University of Chicago Press. That book's designer used marvelous, energetic, scribbled lines as art on the cover. Where the Bernhard scribbles were violent, I wanted something balletic but still tangled. I struggled to make this work (my admiration for the effortless look of the Chicago design increasing with each not-right attempt) until I hit on a different, and more appropriate, design inspiration: the famous concrete poetry of Lewis Carroll's "Mouse's Tale" poem in *Alice's Adventures in Wonderland* (Mavor's first book, *Pleasures Taken*, also published by Duke, examined Carroll's photographs of young girls, and she returns to Alice again and again in her writing).

Here was type itself made into ribbon. So that is what I did: each of *Reading Boyishly*'s twelve chapters opens recto with the chapter title and epigraphs carefully broken into an undulating ribbon down the

"The Mouse's Tale" in the 1866 edition of Lewis Carroll's *Alice's Adventures in Wonderland* (D. Appleton).

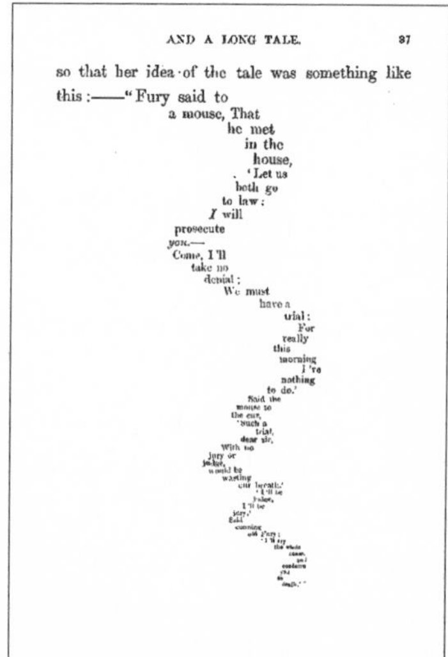
AND A LONG TALE. 97

so that her idea of the tale was something like
this :——"Fury said to
a mouse, That
he met
in the
house,
'Let us
both go
to law :
I will
prosecute
you.—
Come, I'll
take no
denial :
We must
have a
trial :
For
really
this
morning
I've
nothing
to do.'
Said the
mouse to
the cur,
'Such a
trial,
dear sir,
With no
jury or
judge,
would be
wasting
our breath.'

MARINA WARNER ONCE REFERRED to my voice, my writing voice that is, as being in partnership with the "new hedonists."[1] Just who those new hedonists are, I am not sure, but I do know who the original hedonist to whom she refers is: Roland Barthes. (As Barthes once said in an interview: "In my case, I have taken on the responsibility of *a certain hedonism*, the return of a philosophy discredited and repressed for centuries: first of all by Christian morality, then again by positivistic, rationalistic morality.")[2] And it is most certainly true that I eat him up. I have an appetite for Barthes who had an appetite for Proust.

As both hedonist *and* structuralist, Barthes's full language crumbles and whips between "egoism and terrorism, actor and policeman."[3] Puffed, glazed, and fluted by the "hopelessly irresolvable choice he faced as writer and teacher," [4] monster and critic, Barthes suffered and took pleasure in a game of two languages. Such play makes Barthes a promising gourmand, a sweet and savory character. As Barthes writes at the beginning of *Roland Barthes by Roland Barthes*: "It must all be considered as if spoken by a character in a novel."[5] Likewise, but in an inversion, Marcel Proust's *In Search of Lost Time* began, not as a novel, but as a hybrid form of literary criticism against the author Sainte-Beuve, entitled *Contre Sainte-Beuve*. (*Contre Sainte-Beuve* was never finished.) Confused as to whether he was or should be working on a novel or a critical study of Sainte-Beuve, Proust writes in one of his working notebooks: "Should I make it a novel, or a philosophical study—am I a novelist?"[6] Like some of Barthes's writing (*Roland Barthes by Roland Barthes*, *Camera Lucida*, *A Lover's Discourse*, *Empire of Signs*), *Contre Sainte-Beuve* is as much autobiographical as it is critical as it is "novel."

When reading *Contre Sainte-Beuve*, I am delighted by parts that I recognize from *Swann's Way* (the first book of the many-volumed *Search*). Amid the heated attacks on its so-called subject (Sainte-Beuve), I find elements of the *Search*: the memories of the bedrooms that the Narrator had slept in; the water closet that smells of orrisroot (but with a more focused masturbation scene in *Sainte-Beuve*); and a taste of magic madeleine (served up as dry toast with tea in *Sainte-Beuve*).

2 *introduction*

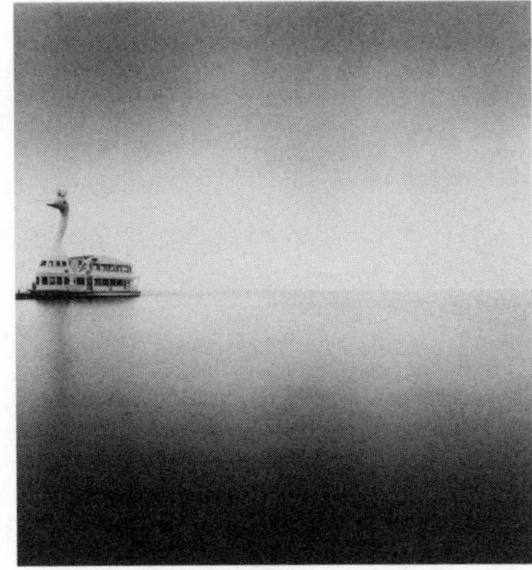

"When reading *Contre Sainte-Beuve*, I am delighted by parts that I recognize from *Swann's Way*."

A text page spread from *Reading Boyishly* by Carol Mavor (Duke University Press). Trim: 5.75 × 8. Text: 10.7/14 × 24 MT Fournier.

page. These were all dummied by me and then entrusted to the skilled hands of my typesetter at Tseng Information Systems in Durham. More flashes of blue appear on the chapter pages, and each one also has one perfect round bubble featuring a detail of an illustration from the chapter. The position of the bubble bounces around from chapter to chapter, as bubbles will do.

Rounding out the ribbony, bubbly, fat, blue design is the front matter. The title page echoes the chapter opening in a ribbon of type. The round bubble features a nest with five eggs to refer to our five "boys." The verso is a solid bleed of the blue. The table of contents shows the ribbon shape and the blue type to best effect: the chapter numbers are spelled out in all lowercase italics and set in blue. This helps them recede, but not disappear, so that the unevenly long chapter titles are immediately legible and easy to read.

Pacing of the art was essential to the way the book was meant to be experienced. Because some of the art had no explicit reference in the text, it needed to fall in the right place, and because the ratio of art to text was so high, the inevitable clusters of images needed to feel meaningful and dynamic, not haphazard or unavoidable. Art sizes ranged from smallish and centered to full chapter two

WINNICOTT'S

ABCS

AND

STRING

BOY

But then the memory—
not yet of the place in which
I was, but of various other
places where I had lived and
might now very possibly be—
would come like a rope let down
from heaven to draw me up out of
the abyss of not-being . . .
Proust, *In Search of Lost Time*

chapter five

NESTING:

THE

BOYISH

LABOR

OF

J. M. BARRIE

MRS DARLING: My dear,
when I came into this room
to-night I saw a face
at the window.
MR DARLING: A face at the
window, three floors up?
Pooh!
MRS DARLING: It was
the face of a little boy;
he was trying to get in.
George, this is not the first time
I have seen that boy.
J. M. Barrie, *Peter Pan*

Like faces in windows
calling you home,
like flying, like flight.
Eliza Minot, *The Tiny One*

chapter eight

SOUFFLÉ/

SOUFFLE

"The Ambassador,"
my mother told her
[Françoise], "assured me
that he knows nowhere where
one can get cold beef and
soufflés as good as yours."
Proust, *In Search of Lost Time*

Françoise: "It was very
nicely done . . . the soufflés
had plenty of cream."
Proust, *In Search of Lost Time*

Chapter openings from *Reading Boyishly* by Carol Mavor (Duke University Press).

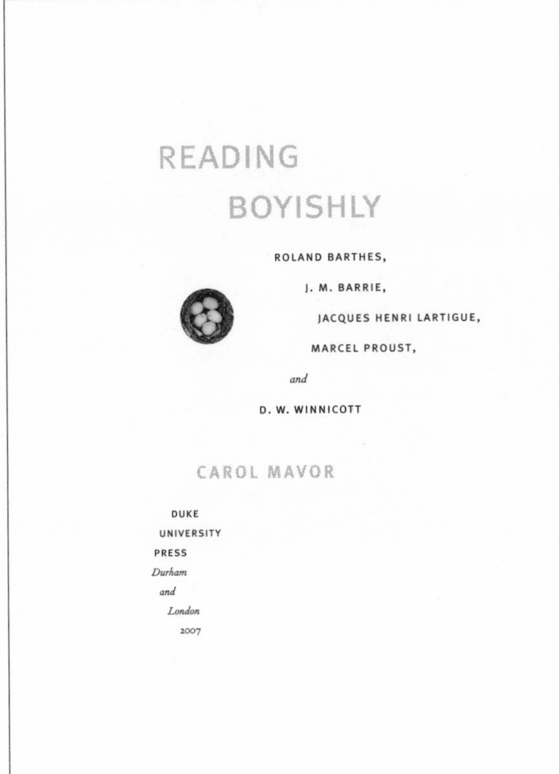

READING
BOYISHLY

ROLAND BARTHES,
J. M. BARRIE,
JACQUES HENRI LARTIGUE,
MARCEL PROUST,
and
D. W. WINNICOTT

CAROL MAVOR

DUKE
UNIVERSITY
PRESS
Durham
and
London
2007

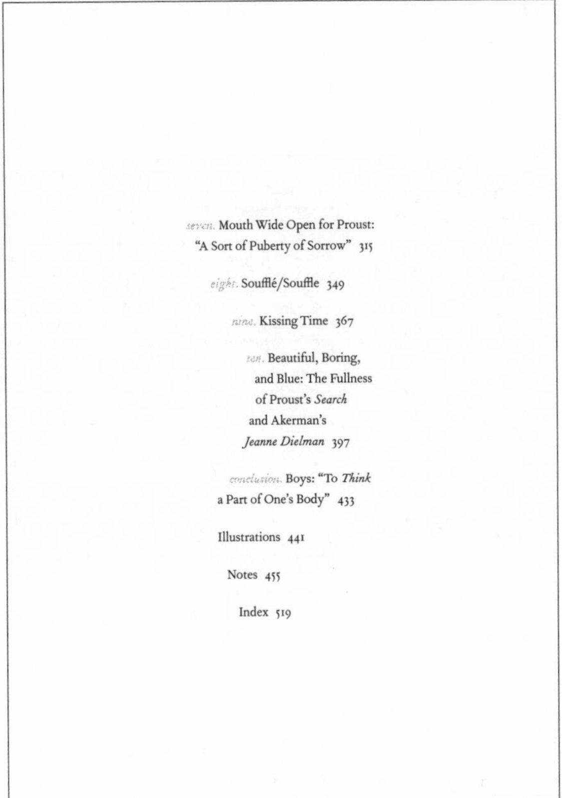

Title page and the table of contents from *Reading Boyishly* by Carol Mavor (Duke University Press).

left-right bleed, with the occasional cut-in positioned in the outer margin. I dummied nearly the whole book and then, once again, trusted my typesetter to make it all work. While the book was printed on a four-color press, we could not afford to have all the color art prepped and proofed in full color, so in consultation with the author I picked approximately thirty-five pieces to print in color.

The cover design carried through some but not all of the interior design elements. The mouse-tail type is gone in favor of a simpler centered design. Five circular details in a row feature three boys, a plane, and a bird (birds and flight being two other important motifs in the book). The background is tinted a bit to match the interior paper color, and the back background is solid blue.

Cruel Optimism by Lauren Berlant

I do not want to leave the impression that *Reading Boyishly* typifies the kind of work I do every day. It doesn't. It was printed in China on very nice paper, with color throughout. I spent a lot of extra time dummying it because of the huge art program. None of that is normal for Duke Press. The design I did for

Text page and jacket from *Reading Boyishly* by Carol Mavor (Duke University Press).

saw. (Barthes's lovely line from *Camera Lucida* surfaces: "My stories are a way of shutting my eyes."[20]) But when his "eye-trap" began to fade, at the tender of age of six, he fell ill. (The doctor diagnosed growing pains.) "It was dating from this convalescence that I would try, with human means, to revive my beautiful ever-vanished 'angel snare.' . . . I tried to photograph everything and paint everything."[21] Like a victim of nostalgia with throat and lung tissues thickened and purulent—like Michelet whose "eating" of history was troubled and propelled by his migraines[22]—like Barthes whose time in the sanatorium allowed his tubercular body to record hundreds of passages from Michelet's writings on index cards, which he then rearranged like playing cards to compose fragmented texts that rather magically projected the books that he was yet to write—like the asthmatic Proust writing and rewriting in his cork-lined room—a real illness or an imagined illness enabled Lartigue with the *chronic* time of disease (specifically, it seems, the disease of nostalgia, here a rarity in that it has already infected, affected, the body of a young child) that afforded him (along with his class) his gigantic creativity. Using photography's predilection for collectomania and his own for the miniature, the child-like, Lartigue snared his bourgeois *Belle Époque*, including the boyish self-portrait in which he plays with a self-made miniature hydroglider, complete with propeller (he sports his famous impish grin; to take the picture he placed his camera on a floating board in the tub, set the exposure and focus, and had Maman snap the picture); *real* racing cars that look as if they drove out from his bedroom floor and grew once they hit the road outside, like the Delage (which could travel at the fantastic speed of thirty-five miles an hour); ladies that look like dolls, promenading in fine feathery, featuring hats that are just as much of an engineering invention as fashion innovation, with unbelievably stylish small dogs at their side who look more like their velveteen cousins than the real thing; the family's pet rabbit as animistic plush toy riding in the miniature roller coaster built by his brother Zissou. As Lartigue wrote in a small black book whose earliest entries were written around 1911, the time he began keeping a record of all of his daily tricks, errands, weather, fashions, illnesses: "'All the pretty or curious things give me so much pleasure. Thanks to photography I can hold

Splitting 93

"before the five were . . . his"

(and certainly a range of objects throughout the Ogilvy-Barrie home in tiny Kirriemuir) darkening "Jimmie's" life only to be replaced (or perhaps more accurately reinforced) with the shadows of the Llewelyn Davies boys. David Barrie's shadow nests in the shadows of "the five"—and their shadows nest like swallows under the eyes (the eaves) of Barrie. Next to his diminutive size, Barrie's most notable characteristic were the dark rings under his eyes.

The shock of David's death was so great that Barrie's mother became emotionally lost, spiritually if not physically gone, for a painfully long time. Of course, it is no coincidence that David of *The Little White Bird* shares the name of Barrie's brother who had died tragically at such a young age. David Barrie was the first boy to never grow up and in his shoes grew the forever-boy-David of *The Little White Bird*, and Peter Pan himself. But even before the five were legally his, the Llewelyn Davies boys were part of the weaving of Barrie's nest, his nest of boyish labor that he began felting and weaving when his brother David did not grow up.

Nesting 203

ART/CULTURAL STUDIES

An homage to four boyish men and one boy—J. M. Barrie, Roland Barthes, Marcel Proust, D. W. Winnicott, and the young photographer Jacques Henri Lartigue—*Reading Boyishly* is a meditation on the threads that unite mothers and sons and on the writers and artists who create from those threads art that captures an irretrievable past.

"It is rare for such an informative book to be so evocative, and indeed for such a wide-ranging book to be at once so subtle and so precise. *Reading Boyishly* allows mothers and sons to be as close as they are—as close as they somewhere know themselves to be; and allows that this relationship is an aesthetic education of astounding possibilities. Carol Mavor gives the idea of close reading a new genealogy. She has written a marvelous book."—ADAM PHILLIPS, psychoanalyst and author of *Side Effects*

"From time to time a book comes along that totally changes the way we look at things in the humanities and does it less by manifestos than by quietly doing its work or singing its song in another voice. Anyone taking the time to look into Carol Mavor's fabulous meditation on Edwardian culture and its discontents will not have to ponder such problems as the relation of history and literature, fact and fiction, the image and the text, reading and looking, past and present, and even nature and culture in abstract, theoretical ways. Carol Mavor has first dreamed what she has then deeply studied and then dreamed it again, for her readers. This book is performed rather than merely written. And it shows how to do a new kind of cultural historiography that renders most of the theoretical questions raised by postmodernism quite moot."—HAYDEN WHITE, University Professor of History of Consciousness, Emeritus, University of California, Santa Cruz, and Professor of Comparative Literature, Stanford University

"*Reading Boyishly* is as complete and mesmerizing a work of reflection on art, time, gender, and family (mothers anyhow) as I have ever seen. It is a remarkable and rare invitation to find ways to extend our nostalgia into a positive mode of being that does not close off the future at all but relocates it within desire."—JAMES R. KINCAID, author of *Erotic Innocence*

Carol Mavor is Professor of Art History and Visual Studies at the University of Manchester.

DUKE UNIVERSITY PRESS

BOX 90660 | DURHAM, NC 27708-0660 | WWW.DUKEUPRESS.EDU

ISBN 978-0-8223-3962-5

9 780822 339625

CAROL MAVOR

READING BOYISHLY

ROLAND BARTHES,
J. M. BARRIE,
JACQUES HENRI LARTIGUE,
MARCEL PROUST,
and
D. W. WINNICOTT

DUKE

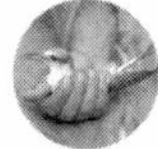

READING BOYISHLY

ROLAND BARTHES, J. M. BARRIE, JACQUES HENRI LARTIGUE, MARCEL PROUST, *and* D. W. WINNICOTT

CAROL MAVOR

Lauren Berlant's *Cruel Optimism* is an example of a simpler book (from a production standpoint) that still illustrates how I like to work.

The text design makes use of two devices: one, the chapter titles start, like the title page itself, at the very top of the page, and, as the book progresses, sink lower and lower with each chapter; two, the descent is marked by a black half-circle that bleeds off the right edge, like the black thumb-cuts of a dictionary or Bible. Berlant's book, a theory-driven examination of how we remain attached to "unachievable fantasies of the good life" in our liberal-capitalist society, brought to mind something like a black balloon falling: a picture of cruel optimism. Michael Hardt's blurb for the back cover calls the book "a how-to guide for living in the impasse." That made me think of reference books; thus the descending black ball became a sort of thumb-cut. It is a very simple design that hopefully makes some connection to the text without getting in the author's (or reader's) way. This is what I hope to do on my best days.

Contents and chapter opening from *Cruel Optimism* by Lauren Berlant (Duke University Press).
Trim: 6.125 × 9.25.
Text: 9.8/14 × 25 Quadraat.

CONTENTS

INTRODUCTION **AFFECT IN THE PRESENT**

A relation of cruel optimism exists when something you desire is actually an obstacle to your flourishing. It might involve food, or a kind of love; it might be a fantasy of the good life, or a political project. It might rest on something simpler, too, like a new habit that promises to induce in you an improved way of being. These kinds of optimistic relation are not inherently cruel. They become cruel only when the object that draws your attachment actively impedes the aim that brought you to it initially.

All attachment is optimistic, if we describe optimism as the force that moves you out of yourself and into the world in order to bring closer the sat-

FOUR **TWO GIRLS, FAT AND THIN**

1. *When You Wish Upon A Star*

History hurts, but not only. It also engenders optimism in response to the oppressive presence of what dominates or is taken for granted. Political emotions are responses to prospects for change: fidelity to those responses is optimistic, even if the affects are dark. It is usual to think of critical theory as dark, not as an optimistic genre, not only because, traditionally, it's suspicious: but also since it creates so much exhausting anxiety about the value of even the "thinkiest" thought.[1] But the compulsion to repeat optimism, which is another definition of desire, is a condition of possibility that also risks having to survive, once again, disappointment and depression, the pro-

The time for theory is always now.
—Teresa de Lauretis

SIX **AFTER THE GOOD LIFE, AN IMPASSE**

Time Out, Human Resources, and the Precarious Present

1. *Always Now:* Situation, Gesture, Impasse

This chapter extends to the bourgeois family our attention to the relation between the reproduction of life and the attenuation of life in lived scenes of contemporary capitalist activity. Laurent Cantet's assessments of French labor in the late 1990s—*Ressources humaines* (1999) and *L'emploi du temps* (2001)—have been extolled as aesthetic reenactments of the impact of neoliberalism on the everyday life of formerly protected classes.[1] Documenting the shifting up of economic precarity into what Giorgio Agamben has called the new "planetary petty bourgeoisie" (PPB) comprised of unionized populations, entrepreneurs, small property owners, and the professional managerial

Chapter opening pages from *Cruel Optimism* by Lauren Berlant (Duke University Press).

Designing Fiction

I have often felt more frustrated designing fiction than working on more complicated manuscripts; there are generally so few design elements to work with. For me, finding that exactly right typeface, one that feels appropriate to the text, is more critical than it might be for a scholarly monograph. No matter what I am designing I always set a few pages of the author's words to see how they look and feel. Using different fonts or different sizes of the same font with the actual text gives an accurate idea of how well the text fits the format, such as how few line breaks there might be, how even the word spacing seems, how few paging problems show up. I take it as an omen that if I encounter awkward problems in the first half-dozen pages I should reconsider the design.

Designers often refer to typefaces as being masculine or feminine, a kind of aesthetic sexism: sans serif or slab serif types being masculine, italic supposedly being feminine. An editor I worked for forbade me ever to use italic display in books by women as she felt it was a cliché to do so.

Much of the fiction I have designed is meant to fit into a template design. Designing model specifications for a book of fiction is somewhat like designing for a journal except there are usually fewer problems to anticipate. The main consideration is to find a neutral typeface such as Minion that offers a complete range of weights, sets reasonably well without much adjustment, and has a display version that feels as if it was meant to be a display face (instead of seeming a blown-up version of the text size).

Volumes of short stories and fiction anthologies offer a bit more of a design challenge than a novel with simple breaks having only numbers or simple titles. Anthologies have titles, authors, perhaps dates of original publication, different structures from one excerpt to another.

The Wesleyan Anthology of Science Fiction was a 780-page compilation that had to be designed to be reasonably attractive to a general reader but had to have 2,900 characters per page. The trim size is 6.125 × 9.25, text face is 9.9/13.5 Miller × 27, headnotes in 9.7/13.5 Scala Sans, with Filosofia Unicase display: not a standard look for a university press.

According to Virginia Tan, recently head of interior design at Knopf:

> The choice of a text font is based both on readability and that "flavor" factor—I like the font to be historically relevant as well as to capture the feeling of the plot, especially in fiction. If the story is masculine or feminine, noir, romantic, adventurous, comic or tragic; the environment, etc.,

A page in a book must not look like a collection of letters. At least it should look like a collection of words, at best a collection of phrases. To achieve this, not only must the right letter-design for the language and text be chosen, but it must also be used in a way that allows the easy flow . . . of phrases. That is the basis of designing a page . . . for the reader to read.
—John Ryder, *The Case for Legibility*

Edited by Arthur B. Evans,
Istvan Csicsery-Ronay Jr., Joan Gordon,
Veronica Hollinger, Rob Latham, and
Carol McGuirk

WESLEYAN UNIVERSITY PRESS
Middletown, Connecticut

NATHANIEL HAWTHORNE

Rappaccini's Daughter

. . . .

{1844}

Nathaniel Hawthorne (1804–64) was born and raised in Salem, Massachusetts, and used his family's history there most famously in his novel *The Scarlet Letter* (1850), which drew on his ancestor's role as a judge in the infamous Salem witch trials. According to his biographer James R. Mellow, Hawthorne borrowed from his own life for "Rappaccini's Daughter." Like Giovanni, Hawthorne was a handsome and intense man prone to romantic entanglements who had an affair with the metaphorically poisonous Mary Silsbee. Beatrice's personality, however, seems closer to the character of the woman he eventually married, the secluded and intelligent Sophia Peabody. Peabody suffered from health problems that may have stemmed from her physician father's overuse of drugs in treating her ailments as a child, so Dr. Peabody may have served as a model for Dr. Rappaccini.

Hawthorne was part of the American Romantic movement of the mid-nineteenth century and was friends with other major figures in American Romanticism such as Emerson, Thoreau, and Melville. In the spirit of the times, he did not draw distinctions between art and science, using both in ways that would now be considered science fictional, not only in the story collected here but also in other stories such as "Dr. Heidegger's Experiment" (1837), "The Birth-mark" (1843), and "The Artist of the Beautiful" (1844). As Hawthorne himself put it in "The Custom-House," his introduction to The Scarlet Letter, his literary concern was with "a neutral territory . . . where the Actual and the Imaginary may meet and each imbue itself with the nature of the other." In this neutral territory, Hawthorne allows science to be imbued with evocative metaphorical significance and offers plausible explanations from the world of the Actual to undermine seemingly impossible events from the world of the Imaginary. Hawthorne was part of the American Romantic movement of the mid-nineteenth century and was friends with other major figures in American Romanticism such as Emerson, Thoreau, and Melville. In the spirit of the times, he did not draw distinctions between art and science, using both in ways that would now be considered science fictional, not only in the story collected here but also in other stories such as Just as in *The*

(15

JULES VERNE

from *Journey to the Center of the Earth*

. . . .

{1864}

Jules Verne (1828–1905) was a prolific French novelist often identified as one of the "Fathers of Science Fiction," the other being the British author H. G. Wells. During the nineteenth century Verne popularized an early brand of "hard" science fiction in a series of novels called the *Voyages extraordinaires* (1863–1919), which depicted adventure-filled quests to the ends of the Earth and beyond, with heroes making use of scientific knowledge and the latest technology to explore "known and unknown worlds" (the subtitle for this series). Expertly marketed by his publisher and mentor Pierre-Jules Hetzel, Verne's novels became best sellers in France and around the world. Today he is ranked as the third most translated author of all time, according to UNESCO's *Index Translationum*.

Verne's career began in the theater: he was a struggling playwright in Paris during the 1850s. He also penned articles on scientific topics and wrote occasional short stories such as "A Voyage in a Balloon" (1851) and "Master Zacharius" (1854) for French magazines. After the publication and success of his first novel, *Five Weeks in a Balloon* (1863), about an aerial trek across the continent of Africa, Verne told his friends at the Paris Stock Market, where he had been working part-time: "My friends, I bid you adieu. . . . I've just written a novel in a new style. . . . If it succeeds, it will be a gold mine." And a gold mine it was, not only for Verne and his publisher but also for world literature as the many Extraordinary Voyages helped to give birth to a new literary genre.

Verne's next book manuscript, a futuristic but dystopian story called Paris in the Twentieth Century, was rejected by Hetzel as being too unrealistic and depressing. Verne promptly locked it in a safe and never looked at it again (it was discovered and published only in 1994). Verne's career began in the theater: he was a struggling playwright in Paris during the 1850s. He also penned articles on scientific topics and wrote occasional short stories such as "A Voyage in a Balloon" (1851) and "Master Zacharius" (1854) for French magazines. For his subsequent novels, Verne agreed to return to the successful narrative template of Five Weeks—that is, educational adventure tales heavily flavored with scientific didacticism, mixed

18)

E. M. FORSTER

The Machine Stops

. . . .

{1909}

E(dward) M(organ) Forster (1879–1970) was one of the most critically acclaimed British novelists in the first quarter of the twentieth century. His novels *A Room with a View* (1908), *Howards End* (1910), and *A Passage to India* (1924), are considered canonical works of modernist realism—*Passage* is one of the first to openly confront the racism of British colonial rule in India.

"The Machine Stops," Forster's only foray into science fiction, has become a classic of dystopian literature. Forster's image of a future society of human beings governed by an autonomous Machine built to satisfy all their needs, and consequently sapping them of all natural drives, was the first in a long line of dystopian visions based on the model of the beehive that would eventually include the Russian Yevgeny Zamyatin's One State in *We* (1921), Aldous Huxley's *Brave New World* (1932), George Orwell's Oceania in *1984* (1949), *Star Trek*'s Borg, and *Wall-E*'s Axiom. Forster claimed that he was inspired to write "The Machine Stops" as "a counterblast to one of the heavens of H. G. Wells"—probably to *A Modern Utopia* (1905)—in which Wells imagined a future utopian society managed by a technocratic elite. Forster had been influenced by Samuel Butler's satirical utopia, *Erewhon* (1872), in which human beings, expecting their machines might someday evolve into intelligent beings destined to dominate humanity, ban them from society. "The Machine Stops" is one of the first examples of a dystopia, a futuristic monitory parable that dramatizes the consequences of a troubling social trend in the present day. Distant echoes of its vision of an empty, closed-off, claustrophobic future can be heard in Harlan Ellison's "'Repent, Harlequin!' Said the Ticktockman" (1965).

Adapting the Frankenstein theme of a science usurping the powers of nature to Plato's myth of the cave, "The Machine Stops" became the model of the "if this goes on . . ." story that became one of the dominant forms of later science fiction. Although Forster was personally not unsympathetic to socialism, the diction of "The Machine Stops" clearly links it to the conservative Victorian tradition that viewed technology as a threat to traditional humanistic values.

(19

by women writers in the early years of the genre, such as an androgynous byline and male point-of-view characters. At the same time, Moore injects her own disturbing elements into what begins as a conventional adventure story. Played out against the background of her raucous frontier Mars is the nearly silent and intensely erotic seduction of Northwest Smith by the Shambleau in her role as exotic femme fatale. The Shambleau remains one of science fiction's most intriguing aliens, forerunner of the erotic mind-parasites of Robert Silverberg's "Passengers" (1968). At the heart of the story is her ambiguous promise to Northwest Smith: "Some day I—speak to you in—my own language."

Man has conquered space before. You may be sure of that. Somewhere beyond the Egyptians, in that dimness out of which come echoes of half-mythical names—Atlantis, Mu—somewhere back of history's first beginnings there must have been an age when mankind, like us today, built cities of steel to house its star-roving ships and knew the names of the planets in their own native tongues—heard Venus' people call their wet world "Shaardol" in that soft, sweet, slurring speech and mimicked Mars' guttural "Lakkdiz" from the harsh tongues of Mars' dryland dwellers. You may be sure of it. Man has conquered Space before, and out of that conquest faint, faint echoes run still through a world that has forgotten the very fact of a civilization which must have been as mighty as our own. There have been too many myths and legends for us to doubt it. The myth of the Medusa, for instance, can never have had its roots in the soil of Earth. That tale of the snake-haired Gorgon whose gaze turned the gazer to stone never originated about any creature that Earth nourished. And those ancient Greeks who told the story must have remembered, dimly and half believing, a tale of antiquity about some strange being from one of the outlying planets their remotest ancestors once trod.

"Shambleau! Ha . . . Shambleau!" The wild hysteria of the mob rocketed from wall to wall of Lakkdarol's narrow streets and the storming of heavy boots over the slag-red pavement made an ominous undernote to that swelling bay, "Shambleau! Shambleau!"

Northwest Smith heard it coming and stepped into the nearest doorway, laying a wary hand on his heat-gun's grip, and his colorless eyes narrowed. Strange sounds were common enough in the streets of Earth's latest colony on Mars—a raw, red little town where anything might happen, and very often did. But Northwest Smith, whose name is known and respected in every dive and wild outpost on a dozen wild planets, was a cautious man, despite his reputation. He set his back against the wall and gripped his pistol, and

26)

The Wesleyan Anthology of Science Fiction edited by Arthur Evans et al. (Wesleyan University Press).

any of those could influence my type choice. Even within the text I might used mixed fonts in extracts; an italic for passages described in the text as being handwritten, a bold, sans serif for signage, Times Roman set small and narrow for a newspaper article. These are visual stimuli to the reader which, I hope, draw the mind's eye into the story. I, personally, am a slow reader because I unconsciously view a story like a movie in my head as I read. I want to give that to the readers of books I work on.

The same applies to the display. Readability is less of a consideration as there is so much less of it and it is larger. I don't always use the same fonts, but I do use a rather limited number of text faces as I feel that there are not that many that I think are both comfortable to read as well as attractive. There are authors who have some knowledge of type and want their books all set in the same font.

Some publishers such as Knopf design each book. However, at other publishing houses such as Faber, where over 200 titles are handled by a very small design staff (at this writing there is no internal design staff for text design), they have standard, relatively straightforward models and mostly use the same typeface for all fiction. In the original model design for Faber by Gerry Cinamon, Palatino was used. As the publishing plan changed and new format sizes were required, Minion, Sabon, and Ehrhardt were used instead. Palatino, possibly because of its ubiquity, seems to be less favored by many designers.

Of course, not all fiction fits so neatly into a format design. As former Faber design manager Ron Costley noted, "Sometimes a unique design would be demanded by the text and/or the author. One example was a narrative by three characters each given a different voice through a change of typeface. I doubted the effectiveness of this approach."

The production department is often preoccupied with length because of the cost of paper and printing. At Faber there is greater concern by marketing and editorial about the size of the type. Virginia Tan at Knopf said the primary concern of the designers was to fit the book into the desired page count. She said, "However, if I find that fit is either too tight (the text having to be too small to be readable by our usual standards) or too loose (when it looks like a book for young readers or approaches a large type format) I will argue strenuously for a change of page count."

Costley at Faber said, "My primary concern has always been an attractive, readable page with an extent that makes a working (i.e., signature), give or take a blank or two. If serious adjustments have to be made, my first move is to look at lines per page, always working to the divisible by 3 rule (e.g., 36 lines or 33 lines)."

The designer Mindy Hill said, "I've had a couple of font-opinionated authors. One poet insisted that I set her book in Helvetica. I've also had a couple that have insisted that they wanted Times Roman, but after a little detective work, they really just wanted a seriffed font. (No problem there.) As far as I know I've never had an author really hate the font that I've used. I think that most don't even have that aspect of the design on their radar."

Then there are those like a Knopf author who insisted the book be set all in Optima caps with the leading so that the space between the lines was the same as the height of the caps.

Anne Winslow, art director at Algonquin, says that her choice of text face is first and foremost legibility and the reader's experience:

> I don't want the font style, size, or setting to distract the reader from the reading.
>
> In the past, there was more of a correlation between the themes and audience for a book and the feel of the design. For instance, we had a book on one list called *The Jew Store*. It was a memoir about a southern Jewish family. I used Berkeley Book, which is a warmer rather more playful font, than, say, Times Roman. Headings, running heads, and so forth complemented the text, and I remember our managing editor commenting that I'd "nailed" the feeling. Conversely, I once set a whole novel, which was historical fiction, in ITC Cheltenham Book. The sample page looked OK, but when the pages came in—I was dismayed. Ironically and unrelated to my misadvised font choice, the book became an Oprah pick and was a best seller.
>
> Today, because 99 percent of our titles will also EPUB, to avoid problems down the line, we try to set text in Adobe pro fonts—and other OpenType fonts. In the EPUB version, the reader can change the font, so what matters most there is the styling of bold, italic, small caps, but not individual fonts.
>
> For print, I keep in mind the audience and feel I'm going for, but my choice of font is based on more general criteria: i.e., serious or more whimsical—masculine or feminine or crossover—literary or not. For chapter openers I may use a display font, instead of a pro font, but gone are the days when I'd have art ghosting under a chapter title—or anything floating on the page. Now, everything is set in line, and every bit of type has a style sheet.
>
> I rely on Adobe Garamond Pro and Minion Pro. I have also used Adobe Jenson, and I like Bembo. For sans serif I like Univers, Trade Gothic, and Gotham. I have used Myriad Pro as well with its many variants, but I prefer Univers. As for special fonts, I have used Fairfield, Electra, and Galliard. I used Fairfield for a couple of celebrity biography/memoirs. It sets nicely and has lots of weights. The celebrities loved it because it looks a bit special.

I begin with the front matter because (for fiction) this is most customized, is more fun to design, and it sets the tone.

I make sure I know the complexity of the manuscript and the general feeling to go for. In all cases legibility is primary. We want a perception of value and ease of reading. I am looking for the best possible way to hit a projected page count. Usually I am trying to flesh out a short manuscript, but sometimes the challenge is to take a 600-page manuscript and make it into something manageable.

MINDY BASINGER HILL

When I tell people that I design books, they are often confused. "Do you draw the pictures that go in books? Are you an illustrator?" they ask. This is not really surprising considering that book design, for the most part, is meant to be a fairly invisible art. Even the most complex text should never overshadow the content it presents. The underlying subliminal utility of the book is part of the wonderful challenge of creating an elegant book design.

Within that architecture, the design of fiction books is refreshingly straightforward. Compared to other genres, fiction text designs tend to be structurally simple. While other types of manuscripts come to me with lists of coded elements that stretch several pages, fiction titles may have only six or eight design elements, and some of those may even overlap. There is no matrix of subheads, multiple tables, or complex mathematical equations. They rarely have notes or footnotes. Illustrations are unlikely, and if there is back matter, it is usually brief. The simplicity allows me to focus on capturing and revealing the personality behind the writing.

Without the constraints of a complex set of elements, I am free to focus on the overall feel of the written text. Because fiction deals more with emotion than fact, it is important to portray some sense of those feelings in the design. However subliminal that visual tie might be, I like to think that even the most subtle connection between the design and the text will help convey the author's intent.

General Design Process

I almost always begin by designing the book's cover. While the text design and the cover design are definitely two distinct processes, in my experience, designing the cover first lays a good foundation for the design of the text. During the process of designing the cover, I not only do a lot of image research but also begin examining the text itself. Even though I get a synopsis of the book from the acquisitions editor, I read parts of the manuscript as well, to ensure that I really get a feel for the book. I try to understand the tone, the characters involved, and the setting. While we do not necessarily involve the author directly in fiction text designs, I interact with the author on some level during the cover design process. By the time I have finalized the cover design, I have a fairly clear picture of his or her likes and dislikes and can apply that to the text design. Another benefit of beginning the design process this way is that the cover and interior design can be integrated and hold together as a package. Again, any visual support that reinforces the stories, however subliminal, is a good thing.

Usually by the time I have designed the cover, I have thought through the fonts that I would like to explore for use on the interior. While my display fonts almost always tie into the cover design directly, the text font choice is a little more fluid. I might lean toward a font with a more historic feel, or I might look for something clean and optimistic. I always try to relate the font to the personality of the text in some way. I find that this is usually a pretty intuitive decision on my part, and I generally draw from the fonts that I have on hand. I am an admitted fontaholic, so matching the tone of the text to that of the text font is an enjoyable task. Rarely in this genre do I find the need to choose fonts that might aid in lengthening or compressing the page count of the book.

I work in Adobe InDesign for page layout and begin the physical design process there. I always start by setting up the grid for the basic text spread. Generally the trim size for the book has been determined before I get the project, and while I might revisit past projects that are likely to have similar grids, I set up a new file for each design. I always begin with a gutter margin and a head margin of 4.5 picas each and adjust accordingly to get the line length and the text depth that I want. The 4.5 picas is really just a starting point; it often changes as I make the necessary adjustments. In general, I want my head margin and my gutter margin to be smaller than the outside margin of the page. I always leave more space at the bottom of the page to add some visual weight. After I have designed a basic text spread, I design the title spread and chapter title pages in tandem, often working back and forth between the two. I may also make slight adjustments to the basic text spread, so that everything works in concert. After I have those solidified, I turn my attention to the secondary elements that need to be designed, sometimes an extract or verse extract or the first level heads.

I should note that there are a couple of structural challenges I generally try to keep in mind during the design process. Fiction text is often punctuated by short, choppy paragraphs and may have dialogue to consider. Chapters or individual short stories, depending on the book, can be short, making the chapter breaks frequent. Careful attention to the line length and hyphenation will usually address most of these slight nuances. To allow myself flexibility to address any paging issues, I almost always allow a short, normal, and long page grid. This means that if my optimum spread has 36 lines, I will occasionally allow a short, or 35 line, spread, or a long spread, 37 lines in length. I try to maintain the normal lengths as much as possible, running no more than three long or short spreads in a row, and never allow short and long spreads to run consecutively. Since fiction text often has few elements to allow for adjustment, the varied grid gives some flexibility.

Since I almost always compose the books that I design myself, I rarely write specs for my designs. Instead I set up complete sets of both character and paragraph styles within the InDesign file during the design process. This has two advantages. First, any changes suggested during the design approval process are quick to make and apply. Second, especially in simple books like these, composing the book itself is a fast process. After the design is approved, working closely with an editor to make sure that the manuscript files are set up accurately, the styles can be applied automatically when styled text is imported into the page layouts. With this production model, setting a book of fiction can be streamlined.

Design for *The Theory of Light and Matter* by Andrew Porter

The Theory of Light and Matter is a collection of short stories by Andrew Porter peopled by characters negotiating the gray areas between right and wrong. The stories are snapshots of middle-class Americans set in the subdivisions and shopping malls of today's suburbia.

At the beginning of the design process, I received the final manuscript and text files, which is usual for our workflow. I had access to an earlier version of the manuscript while I was designing the cover, so I was already fairly familiar with the tone and cadence of the text. The trim for this book is 5.25 × 8 inches, and it was designed for and initially printed on a traditional offset press.

Since these are modern stories, I wanted a font with a clean, contemporary feel. I turned to Electra LT Standard, a personal favorite, and used both the text and display weights in the design. While Electra LT can be wonderful at both large display and text sizes, I should note that this cut was designed for use with the traditional offset processes. It has extremely thin strokes originally meant to benefit from the gain that inevitably happened throughout the letterpress process. My experience is that current processes have reduced this gain and can leave it a little anemic on the page, difficult to read at smaller sizes. Recently I have found Parkinson Electra to be a good substitute for Electra LT Standard for use as a text weight font. It is slightly heavier and is a better cut for today's printing technology.

With this design I began with the usual 4.5 picas sink from the trim to the top of the first text line and the same for the gutter margin. I ended up adjusting the gutter margin to 4p0, allowing enough width for the text box and the folio that I wanted to run up beside the text box. I knew that this book would be fairly short and I would not lose much of the margin in the gutter. The text is 10 pt on a 15.25 pt leading with a line length of 22 picas. I often

Title page spread from *The Theory of Light and Matter* by Andrew Porter (University of Georgia Press).

winner
of the
flannery
o'connor
award
for short
fiction

the theory of light & matter

ANDREW PORTER

the
university
of georgia
press
athens
and
london

Text page spread from *The Theory of Light and Matter* by Andrew Porter (University of Georgia Press).

the shopping malls and bars popping up along the highways near their farms. Leola was expanding quickly then, it was becoming more common, and it worried the elders in the Amish community. And I think it explains why that spring some of the Amish teenagers were given permission to leave their farms for a few hours on Friday nights.

Out on the other side of town there was an intersection on the rural highway where they would go to hang out. It was a remote area. A strip mall with a Kmart sat on one side of the intersection and across the road there was a twenty-four-hour diner. You would sometimes see them on Friday evenings traveling in a long line like a funeral procession, their buggies hugging the shoulder of the road as tractor-trailers rubbered by. They would park out of sight behind the Kmart, tie their horses to lampposts or the sides of dumpsters, and then the younger ones would go into the Kmart to play video games and the older and more adventurous would cross the street to the diner.

The diner was a family-style place, frequented only by local farming families and truckers, and it was usually empty. Inside, the Amish kids would immediately disappear into the bathrooms and change into blue jeans and T-shirts that they had bought at Kmart, clothes which never seemed to fit their bodies right. Then they would come out, their black wool clothes stuffed into paper bags, and order large platters of fried food and play country songs on the jukeboxes, and try to pretend they weren't Amish.

That spring Tanner and I had begun stopping by just to see them. We never bothered them, just watched. And it never occurred to us that there might be something unnatural about what we were doing, or even wrong. We were simply curious. We wanted to know if the rumors we had heard in school were true: that there were

98 departure

99 departure

spectacular deformities to be found among the Amish, that few of the children possessed the correct number of fingers, the results of extensive inbreeding.

We would sit in a booth at the far end of the diner and glance at them from behind our menus. We were amazed to hear them curse and see them smoke cigarettes. Some of them even held hands and kissed. Sometimes other people, people from town like us, would stop by, just to watch—and you could tell that it worried them. People were still scared of the Amish then, they were still a mystery and a threat because of their wealth and the tremendous amount of land they owned—and so naturally they were disliked, treated as outsiders and freaks.

At eleven o'clock, they'd change back into their clothes and very politely pay their checks. Then they'd cross the street in a big group, climb back into their buggies and leave. And Tanner and I would stand out in the diner parking lot and watch them, still not believing what we had seen, but also somehow sad to see them go.

Once the other kids at school found out about the diner, they started coming regularly in their Jeeps and BMWs—not to watch like Tanner and I, but to mock and torment. It was cruel and it saddened us to see, though we never once tried to stop it. Instead we sat back in the corner and watched, angry, but also privately relieved that for once it was not us who were being teased or beat up. In the midst of targets so uncool and vulnerable as Amish teenagers, the popular kids seemed to have practically forgotten us.

There was one Amish kid who looked older than the rest. He could have been in his twenties. Tanner and I had noticed him the very first night because of his size and because of his face which always looked angry. He came every week with the rest of them, connecticut

THE SUMMER HE WAS RELEASED from the hospital my father moved to our family's summer cottage on Maquesett Island, off the coast of Connecticut, and for most of my childhood that is where I remember him living. He managed to reside there year round, even through the desolate winter season, among the small gray shingled houses at the far end of the beach. My sister and I grew up with our mother in eastern Connecticut, in the house she had inherited, and every few weeks we would take the ferry out to the island to visit him. These trips were often brief, never longer than a few hours, and their purpose was usually to bring my father his medications or later to make sure he had not had what my mother referred to as a "setback." My sister and I were told that our father was in a recovery period, that he was taking some time

Chapter opening from *The Theory of Light and Matter* by Andrew Porter (University of Georgia Press).

make the size, leading, and line length adjustments visually to make sure that they work, which means that sometimes the final type sizes are not nice, neat whole numbers. Instead of traditional running feet or running heads, I ran the folios and running head text down the sides of the text block. I base-aligned the verso folio with the last text line of each spread and aligned the one on the recto with the ascenders of the first text line. This allows a modern look and gives the spread a very open feel. Turning them also tends to deemphasize the folios and removes them from the flow of text during the reading process. In this case the number of text lines on a normal grid is 30 lines per page, and I did run spreads one line shorter or longer, as necessary. The verso folio bounced up and down to align with the last line when the page varied from the normal depth.

When I turned to the chapter openers, I decided to sink the first text line substantially and aligned it on the eighteenth line of the normal text grid. I was under no obligation to keep this book within a certain number of pages, so I opted for the extra visual space on the chapter opening spreads. Apart from the story that the book borrowed for the title, all chapter titles were very short. Because these are short stories, the text did not include chapter numbers. This allowed me to track the text of the chapter titles tightly and run them at a large size. While using all lowercase on these also permitted the large text size, it also reinforced the informal nature of the stories. The chapter titles are screened at 25 percent black so that they don't become an overpowering focus on the page. The last line of all chapter titles base aligns with the fourteenth text line of the normal depth page. You will see that I used this sink as a standard part of the architecture in the front matter as well. To further focus the reader on these openers, I dropped the folio altogether, and I highlighted the first text line of the chapter opener by setting the first phrase in small caps. I wanted to direct the reader's eye subtly to the beginning of the text. I kept these pages simple, open, and approachable. I did not differentiate between the chapter openers and the openers in the front matter and back matter and extended this part of the design to include them. I prefer to simplify the organization of the book's information into as few elements as possible. If there is no valid reason for the openers to be differentiated, doing so will just muddy the design.

I wanted to echo the demeanor of the chapter openers on the title spread. Although slightly larger, the title of the book, like the chapter titles, base aligns on the fourteenth text line of the normal depth page. Playing on the title itself, I flooded the page with a 20 percent black screen on the verso and dropped out the first part of the title. I downplayed the imprint line and the award line by turning them and hanging them visually from the x-height of the title. By turning them in different directions, the focus can remain on the title. The turned text also relates to the turned running feet in the body of the book. I wish I could say that it visually relates to the different odd perspectives

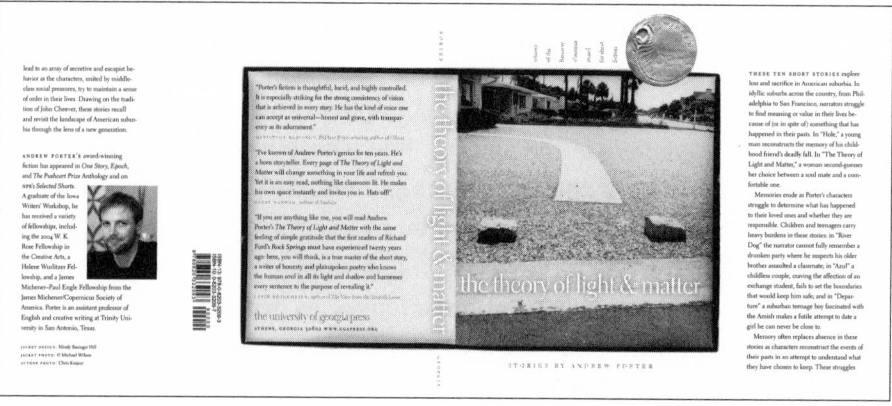

Jacket for *The Theory of Light and Matter* by Andrew Porter (University of Georgia Press).

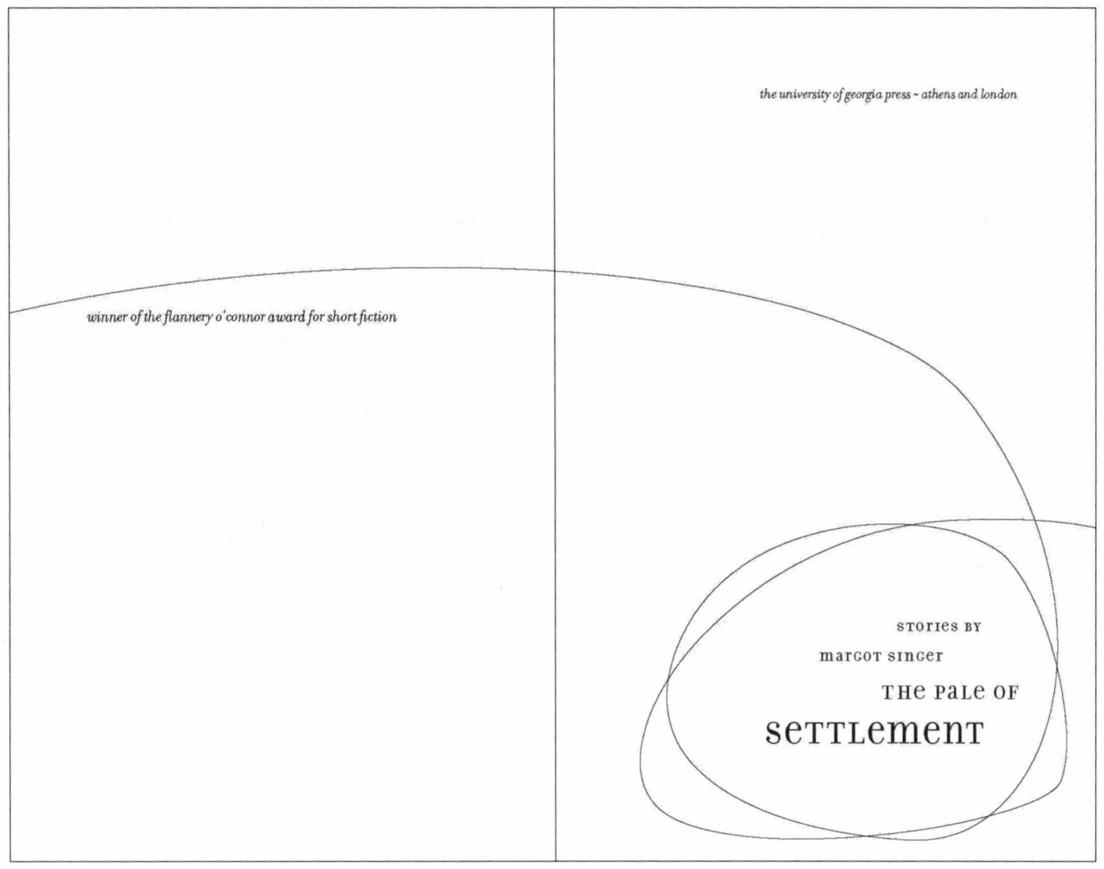

the university of georgia press ~ athens and london
winner of the flannery o'connor award for short fiction
stories by
margot singer
the pale of
settlement

Title page spread from *The Pale of Settlement* by Margot Singer (University of Georgia Press).

presented in the book, but really, as often happens, it was just something that I tried that worked for me. It is a happy accident that can easily relate visually to the stories.

Design for *The Pale of Settlement* by Margot Singer

Part of the same series as *The Theory of Light and Matter*, this book shares the same 5.25 × 8 trim size. *The Pale of Settlement* is a collection of stories by Margot Singer in modern settings ranging from Jerusalem to Manhattan, always against a backdrop of Jewish history and culture. One of the most fascinating aspects of this collection is that each stands alone as a short story, and, while the settings and perspectives change, each story includes the same group of characters.

This text includes a few more elements and has a different personality than the Porter. The design itself might be classified as a bit more embellished.

I chose to use the font Filosofia for this text design. To me, its rounded serifs and oval letterforms seem almost feminine, while its slight compression and high x-height are very readable. Filosofia seemed like a good fit for stories that document the straightforward and reflective experiences of the main character, Susan. I do not often use Filosofia as a text font, mainly be-to the Israeli Arab students he'd had over the years—their politeness, their rather old-fashioned courtly ways, so different from the brash Israeli style. It was impossible, but now that the thought had entered his head, Avraham couldn't get it out again. He could hear the throaty ayins, the rolling rs, as he lifted her off the ground, his eyes locked on hers.

Is it really you?

Of all people. Shit.

By 1959, Leah was in New York. She left the apartment blocks of Sanhedria, the crumbling stone walls and dusty lots littered with curls of rusted wire and weeds, for the steel and glass of Manhattan, the unbounded energy of the States. She stood on the tarmac at Idlewild and felt her lungs expand. She wasn't of the generation who had longed from exile for a mythic land of olive trees and Bedouins roaming with their flocks, for the desert wind, the sound of camel bells. She hadn't realized just how confining Israel was until she got away.

Still, she longed for him. *Last night I dreamed that I was at the beach, singing songs to a guitar. Y. was there and then he began to play and I started to cry. Why am I still thinking so much of him after all this time? I wonder—is he thinking of me, too?* She crosses Washington Square Park in the half-light of a November afternoon, dead leaves swirling before her on the path. She looks up at the brick townhouses with their imposing stoops, the windblown sky. She's fixed up her dorm room with a new bedspread and a potted cyclamen, tacked a travel poster to the wall—*for the first time, I have a room that looks like my own!*—but even so there is something loose inside her, sliding around like broken glass. She clings to the edge of indepen-

136 ~ HAZOR

dence, too frightened to look down. *At moments I almost enjoy New York, being here on my own and free. But then there are so many nights like this, when I just feel lonely and self-pitying and sad.* She tries to fill her emptiness with pain, holding Y inside her like an open wound, hating herself for her weakness, welcoming it as evidence that what she felt was real. But already she is having trouble conjuring up the image of his face. It is cracking like old paint.

Soon there's Herb or Richard, Len or Bill, flirting in the college library, taking her out to parties or Greenwich Village clubs. To them, she's an exotic, with that alluring accent and her long dark hair. *Had a fun time being bubbly, losing my voice over all the music and the noise! But I'm afraid I've been too free. . . . Before I knew it he had his arms around me and all I could think was, oh no no no you can't, even though for the first time in forever, I actually felt alive.* These American Jewish boys are nothing like the men back home—with their ties and blazers, their rosy cheeks and slouchy ways, they seem barely formed. They are like newborn rabbits, blinking in the light. What do they know of the world? She lies awake at four a.m., cold and restless, listening to the clicking of the radiator, a distant siren's scream. She has not been back to Israel in more than two long years. In the grainy dark, she tries to picture home. She tries to remember the smell of the kerosene heater in winter, the feeling of the stone floor underneath her feet, the crackly call of a muezzin from a distant minaret. She thinks of her mother, knitting in the rocking chair in the alcove outside her room. If there is another woman there now with Abba, she doesn't want to know. She pulls out her memories of Y, replays them like a tape. She listens for that soft choked sound deep in his throat as he touches her face and whispers, *Is it really you?*

HAZOR ~ 137

Text spread from *The Pale of Settlement* by Margot Singer (University of Georgia Press).

cause I do not have an OpenType version. I generally lean toward my OpenType fonts for body text because the extended character sets eliminate the need for extensive search and replace regimes. Nevertheless, sometimes I feel strongly enough to endure a little inconvenience. In this case, I used Filosofia Unicase, which is a version of the face that combines elements from the upper- and lowercase letters of the font, on the cover and knew I wanted to use it as the display. Using the text weight, as well, was the most natural decision and very appropriate.

The text spread was based on a very simple grid. I used 10 pt Filosofia on 15 pt leading at a line length of 23 picas. The ascender height of the first text line falls 4.5 picas from the trim, and the gutter margin is again 4p0. There are 30 lines on the normal text grid, and running feet fall below the text block and flush to the outside. I specified that this design grid would have a short and normal depth only, because I felt that allowing a long depth would extend the text too close to the bottom trim and crowd the page.

The openers and front matter were a little more interesting to design. The chapter openers had a few more elements than *The Theory of Light and Matter*

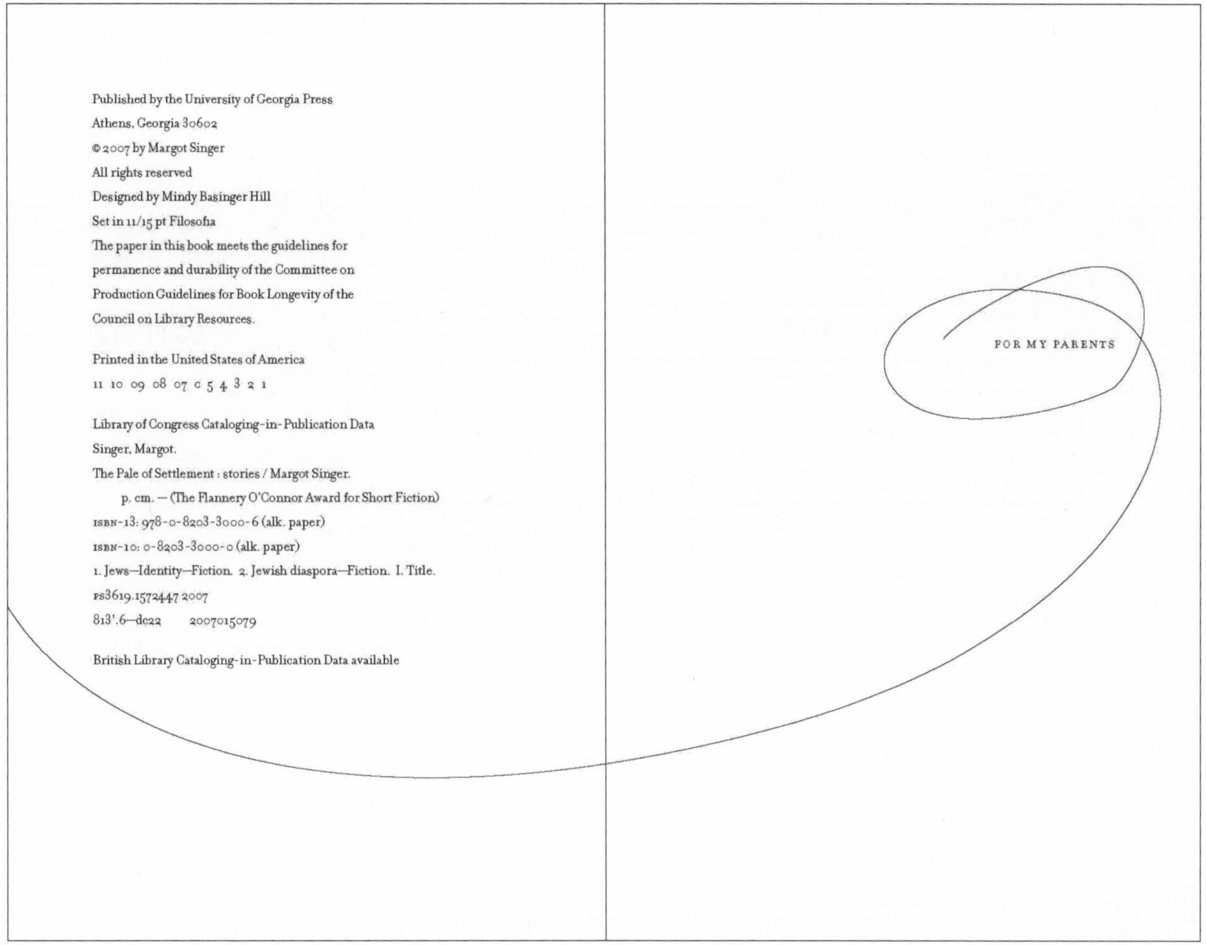

Published by the University of Georgia Press
Athens, Georgia 30602
© 2007 by Margot Singer
All rights reserved
Designed by Mindy Basinger Hill
Set in 11/15 pt Filosofia
The paper in this book meets the guidelines for
permanence and durability of the Committee on
Production Guidelines for Book Longevity of the
Council on Library Resources.

Printed in the United States of America
11 10 09 08 07 c 5 4 3 2 1

Library of Congress Cataloging-in-Publication Data
Singer, Margot.
The Pale of Settlement : stories / Margot Singer.
p. cm. — (The Flannery O'Connor Award for Short Fiction)
ISBN-13: 978-0-8203-3000-6 (alk. paper)
ISBN-10: 0-8203-3000-0 (alk. paper)
1. Jews—Identity—Fiction. 2. Jewish diaspora—Fiction. I. Title.
PS3619.I572447 2007
813'.6—dc22 2007015079

British Library Cataloging-in-Publication Data available

FOR MY PARENTS

Front matter from *The Pale of Settlement* by Margot Singer (University of Georgia Press).

text design. While many of the openers had only a chapter title, a couple opened with a second level head, a couple with an epigraph, and at least one had both. To allow all options I decided to flush the chapter titles right and allow the epigraphs and second-level heads to remain flush left with the text. This separated the elements and allowed legible space for every possible combination of the opener's elements. To emphasize the chapter titles, I circled them using one of the vector drawing tools in InDesign. For simple vector elements I often bypass Illustrator altogether and just create them in InDesign. In this case I wanted them to be very informal, and I wanted each to be a little different. I just scrawled a circle for each opener and adjusted them according to the length of each chapter title. Although I did not do it in this case, I have also hand-lettered chapter titles using the vector tool. A little handwork adds individuality and personality to the design and is especially appropriate with fiction that is much less formal than a regular scholarly title.

In the front matter, I used the linear element similarly but actually connected the lines from spread to spread, using the line like a string to tie each page to the next. Where the line bled off the edge of the page on one spread,

I look everywhere for grandmothers and find none.
ELIZABETH BARRETT BROWNING

LILa'S STORY

Israel 1997

In my memory, my grandmother is framed by flowers. Head-high stalks of gladioli, a backdrop of hibiscus, anemones at her feet. My grandmother is smiling, cheek to bloom. Here are the flowers still: tricolor lantana bordering the sidewalk, vermilion bougainvillea overhanging the second-story stairs. Here are photographs, a pile of black-and-white snapshots taken in the 1940s, not long after my grandparents arrived in Palestine. I flip through them like tarot cards, lay them face up on my hotel room bed. Here is my grandmother in a full skirt and blouse and walking shoes, kneeling in the Carmel woods called Little Switzerland. Here she is, arms linked with her two sons, posing on the beach. She is beautiful, or almost, cat-eyed and slim, with an aquiline nose and prematurely white hair. Here she is leaning against a railing by the sea. Her hair is blowing across her face and she is squinting just a bit. The sea behind her is flecked with white. The camera has caught that fleeting moment that precedes the self-consciousness of a smile, and that,

36

Maternity is proved by the senses whereas paternity is a surmise based on a deduction and a premise.
SIGMUND FREUD, *Moses and Monotheism*

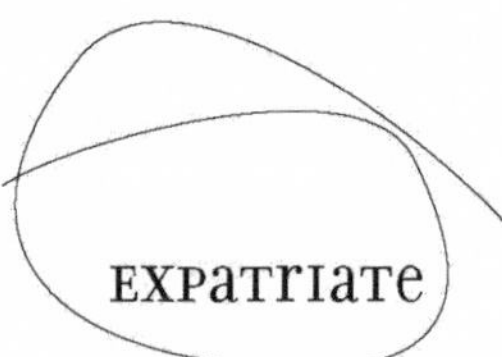

EXPaTrIaTe

What Leah remembered many years later was that it was May and it was snowing and throughout the city the branches on the budding trees were snapping under the weight of leaves and blossoms and the unexpected snow. She didn't really remember the pain of the contractions or the shaking or the numbness of her legs, other than the fact that these sensations had occurred. She remembered the milky light, the clumps of falling snow. You're nearly there, the nurse had said. She held up a mirror and said, Look!

But Leah didn't look. She turned her face toward the wall. It was only afterward, after they'd placed the baby in her arms, washed and checked, that she drew her breath and looked and saw: skin the color of eggshells, eyes a murky, indeterminate blue. The baby gazed up at Leah, the faintest shadow of perplexity traced between her brows, as if she might have been thinking, Who the hell are you?

148

Chapter openings from *The Pale of Settlement* by Margot Singer (University of Georgia Press).

it would begin again on the page that followed. While I was designing this, I kept thinking about how these seemingly unconnected stories were bound together by a specific set of repeated characters. While I never actually expected readers to relate that to the design element, it was my inspiration.

Designing Cookbooks

In the autumn of 2011 I was invited to talk to some university students in a culinary studies course about cookbook design. Having assumed they would have some interest in cookbooks, I was surprised to learn that many of them never used them. When they needed a recipe, they went to the Internet. That same week the *New York Times* ran a story about how publishers were increasingly producing cookbooks as apps for devices like the iPad. I began to wonder what cookbooks were for if they were increasingly not to be thought of as instruction manuals. With hundreds of new cookbooks published every season, what were they intended to be: something to read about food, a souvenir from a favorite restaurant, food porn? Do home cooks really cook from glossy, full color, beautifully produced books? Do gorgeous photographs of carefully styled plated food help or intimidate?

In cooking, each recipe is a unique operation to be followed step by step. It is this feature that makes cookbooks a special problem in design.
— Marshall Lee, *Bookmaking*

As a modestly skilled cook I still find cookbooks useful manuals—even those that violate what I would consider ideal. Ideally I would prefer:

the ingredients set as list with fractions as full-size numbers
(not as case fractions)
the yield (e.g., serves 4) clearly expressed close to the list of ingredients
the instructions as short sentences, perhaps as a numbered or unnumbered list
the entire recipe on one page.

Of course there are cookbooks that are not meant to be so explicitly instruction manuals. Elizabeth David, for example, describes a recipe as a narrative and assumes that cooks will get the general idea how to prepare a dish.

As university presses began to seriously consider the cultural aspect of the culinary arts, the content of cookbooks has often become more than a collection of recipes and can require considerable design involvement. One such project is *The World in a Skillet* by Paul and Angela Knipple, designed by Kim Bryant for the University of North Carolina Press. Another is *Daring Pairings*, designed by Nola Burger for the University of California Press.

Overleaf:
Kim Bryant's design specifications for *The World in a Skillet* by Paul and Angela Knipple (University of North Carolina Press).

Title: *The World in a Skillet* by Paul & Angela Knipple
Description: Profiles first-generation immigrants who are chefs, food entrepreneurs, and restaurateurs in the South. Features 50 recipes.
Trim: 7 x 10-inches
Main text: 9.7/14 Odile x 25p, justified, 42 lines   Recipes: 2 columns x 33p, 1p ditch
Ink: black throughout; screens used to add color

Allowed for a 5p gutter should the book become a strip and rebind.

Main text (set justified) consists of profiles, each beginning with the individuals name screened and hanging in margin. Profiles run a few paragraphs to several pages. Run-in recipes follow each profile.

B. J. Chester-Tamayo, Memphis, Tennessee

B. J. Chester-Tamayo was born in the small town of Meridian, Mississippi. While she's been cooking soul food professionally in her downtown Memphis restaurant, Alcenia's, for over twelve years, she says that she's been "dibbling and dabbling" with cooking for at least twenty-five years.

She was brought up on "good southern cooking" that her mother prepared, feasts that celebrated the seasons and local flavors. Some of the dishes she remembers best include fresh corn, yams, potato salad, roast with gravy, fresh crowder peas, buttermilk, cornbread, and apple cobbler that was so good it "would make you want to slap somebody."

B. J. learned to cook by watching her mother. In her restaurant today, she uses many of the simple dishes she learned to make growing up, serving them as soul food to her customers. She explains soul food as food cooked with intention. "Soul food is about how you really feel about what you want and what you want people to take away from that meal. That's what food here is to me; making it is an action to show how you care about people, how you love them."

Screened ornament signals end of each profile.

Recipes set ragged right in 2 columns to distinguish them from the main text. Cooking times and yield run-in and moved to follow titles for greater visibility. Recipes begin with a headnote (serif), followed by ingredients and instructions (sans serif).

Whenever possible, each recipe is confined to a single page or spread so no turning is required (this can sometimes be accomplished by rearranging recipes)

GREENS

Active cooking time: 30 minutes | Total cooking time: 3 hours | Yield: 4 1-cup servings

Collards. Mustard. Turnip. A mess o' greens.

The first greens cooked by enslaved Africans in the South were likely cast-off turnip greens or the collard greens they brought to the South with them. Other greens were available, though, and did become part of the slave diet in part because they grow well in the South, even well into the winter. In addition to turnip and collard greens, mustard greens are very popular, and all of them are a great part of southern cuisine today.

Collards are the mildest greens with an almost creamy flavor. Turnip greens are more bitter and also tend to be stringy. Mustards are also more bitter, but they tend to have a spicy flavor.

A mess o' greens is defined as a serving of greens large enough to feed your family. This recipe can easily be doubled if you have a big family or a family of big eaters. The recipe works well for any of these greens or a combination of the greens. Even spinach works, but cut the cooking time back to about ten minutes for spinach because it is so much more tender than the other greens.

According to B. J., you really can't overcook greens as long as you don't let the water cook away. When you are seasoning your greens, err on the side of caution. As she says, "You can always add more, but once it's in there . . ." Greens can obviously be prepared as a vegetarian dish, but B. J. always prepares her greens with meat. "Some people say they don't use any meat in their greens. I don't know how they do that."

6 *Introduction*

The page grid is flexible, allowing for single-column main text and double-column recipes. Sidebars are able to take advantage of the single- or double-column format depending on their length and placement.

Ingredients are listed in the left column and set in a heavier weight than instructions for better readability. Stacked fractions are set at a larger size. Heads are in caps and screened.

I find most stacked fractions available in fonts inadequate for cookbooks—they are just too small. (I will forever remember Rich saying they look like mouse droppings!) I now use fonts with customized fraction sets to better control their appearance.

2 pounds collard greens or mixed turnip and mustard greens (about 3 bunches)
1 medium yellow onion, chopped (about ⅔ cup)
1 ham hock or 1 pound smoked turkey pieces
3 teaspoons Greek seasoning blend
½ teaspoon crushed red pepper
4 teaspoons salt
Pinch of sugar

TO SERVE

Chow-chow (tomato relish) or pickled tomatoes

Wash the greens thoroughly and remove the tough stems and ribs.

Slice the greens into 1-inch wide ribbons or keep the leaves whole. Place the greens in a stockpot and add the onion to the greens.

Rinse the ham hock in cold water to remove any excess salt and add it to the pot with the greens and onion. Add the Greek seasoning, crushed red pepper, salt, and a pinch of sugar. Add 1 gallon of water to the pot.

Cook over medium heat until the greens are tender, about 2½ to 3 hours.

Season to taste with salt.

Serve in bowls with plenty of potlikker, the cooking liquid, for sopping with cornbread. Serve chow-chow or pickled tomatoes on the side.

Instructions run in right column with minimal hyphenation. The same capped, screen heads used in ingredients list are also used within the instructions.

Kitchen Passport **So you've tried greens before and didn't like them? You're not alone. They're an acquired taste.**

The younger your greens are, the less bitter they will be. To reduce bitterness, you can pour off some of the cooking liquid and replace it with fresh water halfway through the cooking time. Don't pour off too much liquid, though, because that liquid, the potlikker, is as valuable a taste treat as the greens themselves. All you need are some hoecakes (recipe follows) to soak up the potlikker. This is one of those cases where sopping is not only acceptable but encouraged.

Another way to cut the bitterness is to add more sugar—just a pinch at a time because a little can go a long way and no one wants sweet greens. Make them spicier if you like. Experiment with using different fresh peppers or hot sauces instead of the crushed red pepper flakes.

If you want to prepare your greens without using meat, add a tablespoon of vegetable shortening or butter to give the greens the richer flavor that the fat from the meat provides in this recipe.

If you're still not a fan of greens and potlikker, try this method. Bring a large pot of salted water to a boil. Blanch the greens by cooking them in the boiling water for 2 minutes and then immediately transferring them to a bowl of ice water. This way you'll have tender greens after only a brief time in the skillet. Cook 4 to 6 slices of bacon in a large skillet over medium heat. Transfer the bacon to a paper-towel-lined plate, leaving the grease in the pan. Cook the greens, stirring constantly, in the skillet with the bacon grease for 10 minutes. Crumble the bacon back into them and finish them with a pat of butter for a decadent treat.

Sidebars of varying length follow several recipes throughout and are isolated by a screened background. Text size is smaller than that of recipes but set in bold face. Sidebars set in 1–2 columns or full text width, depending on best fit.

Generous foot margin

Introduction 7

Running feet set flush with outside margin. Running foot screened for added color.

Chose two fonts, a serif for main text and recipe headnotes and a sans serif for recipe ingredients and instructions. Both fonts have good color. Kept leading generous and used different sans serif weights to distinguish recipe elements and sidebars.

NOLA BURGER

Many projects look similar at the beginning. At the University of California Press, a manuscript arrives on my desk as a box of paper with a memo from the editor. Several months before, I will have heard a description of the book and discussed the publishing plan at the launch meeting. And I may have also heard informal comments from the editor—either praise for the project or perhaps tales of woe about editing difficulties. Mostly, I learn about the book when I open the box.

Higher-profile projects such as cookbooks are a more complex story. UC Press publishes a small number of cookbooks, and they tend to come with unique requirements. Often there's an involved author or organization spearheading the project, high expectations internally and from the author, and a multifaceted manuscript. As a scholarly press, their cookbooks require a cultural, regional, or historical component. For example, *Encarnación's Kitchen* was a translation of *El cocinero español*, the first cookbook by a Hispanic in the United States, written in 1898. This book included introductory sections about the author and the era, a translation of her original recipes plus bilingual titles, a photo essay, glossary, and bibliography encompassing cooking and historical sources. Each section had its own requirements that drove the overall design.

The book I've chosen to discuss in detail is *Daring Pairings* by Evan Goldstein. California published an earlier title with Evan, *Perfect Pairings,* which I also designed. Both are wine reference books as well as cookbooks. Over several meetings Evan and I discussed which aspect to emphasize, because Evan's forte is wine but he knows food really well too, and the recipes are top-notch. The decision was a 50/50 hybrid that would hold its own with both cooks and wine readers. Two markets sound bigger than one, but that's deceptive. Making a book that speaks to two distinct types of readers can fail to attract the attention of either.

Having worked together previously, Evan and I had a positive track record. The acquiring editor and I met with him over the course of two years as he completed the text. Our goal was a manuscript that would require less intervention in editing. The early meetings also familiarized me with the components of the manuscript, making it much easier to get started on the design when it reached my desk.

With Evan's books I read small amounts of each kind of section. This was enjoyable because his writing is great, I'm interested in wine, and I like to cook. I'm not always so fortunate! His manuscript had several introductory chapters about pairing wine and food, charts, and an in-depth chapter for each of the thirty-six grape varietals with an accompanying recipe and wine-pairing notes. Back matter included five reference sections and two indexes. There would also be a 36-page color section.

This is exactly the type of project I love digging into. The text was well written and consistent from section to section, so the design wasn't called upon to pull together a problematic manuscript. I knew that incisive design solutions could do a lot for the information, though, and Evan had already shown that he was receptive to design input. So, for example, in *Daring Pairings* I could suggest whether to structure the book in two parts, white and red wines, or run everything A to Z, like a dictionary. And the editor and I could refine material, such as in the charts, to fit elegantly within the format.

As I first skim any manuscript I sketch with pencil on paper, making thumbnail drawings for each type of spread. My sketches are small and loose, a few lines and boxes that allow me to try a number of scenarios. The directness of hand and pencil allows ideas to come together quickly. After going through the manuscript this way, I'll have several pages of thumbnails that map out the whole book in overview. It's my starting point, and although I haven't read the entire manuscript I'm ready to sit at the computer and begin working with type.

I consider all factors at the outset—what the manuscript is, what the book could be, what strengths and drawbacks the project holds. In the later design stages I work at a micro level, adjusting in tiny increments, so in the early stages I try to stay at macro level.

I look for inherent design challenges in the manuscript and art program. Evan's manuscript was packed with concentrated information, in lists, short subsections, and charts. There are thirty-six contributing chefs with their names repeating prominently in several places throughout the book. I wanted an accessible and inviting design, but the publishing plan called for a 350-page book length, so "airing" elements with white space wasn't an option. When I don't have a lot of space to play with, typefaces have got to really function. In this case, Univers gets a workout as the display face. Its clean, distinctive letterforms look great in multiple weights, styles, and situations.

The publishing plan presents its own challenges, and I look for ways to minimize and fold the shortcomings seamlessly into the design. The largest hurdle here was color printing; for cost reasons I had to gather all color photos in one section. We had an excellent team for the photo shoot, and their creatively styled images would have logically appeared within each of the thirty-six sections. By gathering images they're less integrated in the book, so I gave this a lot of thought as the design emerged. I ultimately devised a framing element around recipes and photos, and both share a common type treatment.

I also consider how I can put the book's assets to best use. Our publishing plan allowed for a second ink color to aid subhead hierarchy and add visual appeal. The book was titled *Daring Pairings;* I experimented with assertive oranges and greens, but they looked offbeat rather than bold in the context of a wine book. I kept returning to red, choosing a versatile salmon-red shade, more refreshing than the typical "wine book burgundy." Once I have my color I determine how much to use, and where. The temptation is to maximize it, but I'm always happier when color is used sparingly. On most spreads red type adds an accent, and on chapter and part opening pages it's used assertively.

And, of course, with a cookbook I'm thinking about recipes. Evan's manuscript was approximately 15 percent recipe to 85 percent text, but regardless of quantity the recipes had to be supremely functional. Recipes are read while standing and cooking, and a cook needs to be able to easily return to the right place in between chopping onions and stirring the pot. Type, leading, and text alignment choices are crucial. And since the ratio of recipes to text was low, recipes needed to distinctly stand out from the main text.

Once I start working with text, I look for a typeface that works well with the subject matter. I may want to invoke an era, region, or attitude, or I may follow visual intuition. If I were to set a page of text in ten fonts (even ten of my favorites), for any given manuscript there will be standouts as well as uninspiring or incompatible results. I work with real text from the actual manuscript, and I read several paragraphs to see how text-block color (light, heavy, textured, even) looks in context with the writing.

Italics are an important factor. Even if they occur infrequently in the manuscript, they're expressive and attract attention. In *Daring Pairings* the text font is Chaparral, which has even-textured italics that are nicely integrated with the roman face. Since numerals appear often in cookbooks, they're a consideration as well. Some old-style figures are easily confused with text (in some typefaces, the old-style figure 1 is notorious for resembling a small cap "i"), but Chaparral's old-style figures were clear and well suited for recipes.

Equally important is a typeface that supports the book's target length. If I've been asked to expand a short manuscript into a longer book, I'll choose a font that reads well at a relatively large size. But I'm usually in the opposite situation, where I need to fit a lot of text on the page, in which case I'm looking for good readability at smaller text size. Lastly, to my tastes a text face shouldn't draw attention to itself, nor should it make the book look dated in ten years . . . or fifty years.

I have typefaces I use consistently, perhaps fifteen if I include sans serif. These are faces I find beautiful and workable—by that I mean I can make them look good. There are wonderful faces that just don't work out for me, but other designers use them with beautiful results. My staples include Scala, Fournier, Bembo, Electra, Adobe Garamond, Granjon, Janson, Jenson, and Requiem. In sans serif I gravitate to Interstate, Univers, DIN, Akzidenz Grotesk, and Benton Sans.

My "desert island" fonts are undeniably favorites, but they don't fit the bill every time, and I would never limit myself to just them. Chaparral, used for Evan's book, isn't a face I've used frequently, but it was a great fit for his writing style: inviting and friendly.

At the start of a project I have an open mind. I'll make a list of faces that intrigue me and try them all. Usually I come back to one of my favorites . . . but not always. And sometimes I know from the outset that I need to find something special. In other cases, it's not the typeface but how it's used, such as choosing sans serif for text, or using flush left rather than justified alignment. I can count on two hands the books I've designed with sans serif or ragged text, but it's exciting when the opportunity presents itself.

My choice of text font begins with the overall text block color on the page. Also, how well the text reads—which means truly reading it, not just glancing at it. Italics. Proportion and x-height. Classical and timeless beauty, nothing too old-fashioned, nothing too obviously of-the-moment. And if I'm planning to use the text font for display purposes then I want characters that look pleasing at larger size.

I begin with the text spread and work my way outward. This is how I was initially taught by Steve Renick (at the time, art director at the University of California Press) and Tom Ingalls (adjunct professor at the California College of the Arts), and for me it's the best approach. The brilliance is that the all-text spread, though seemingly simple, is actually a complex construction. So once the text block, margins, folio, and running head/foot are figured out, the grid becomes evident and provides the framework for the rest of the design.

Over the years I've modified Steve and Tom's sequence in small ways. The classic process is to design the text spread and then build outward from small to large: text elements (lists, extracts), then subheads, chapter openings, part openings, front matter, back matter. But by working gradually toward display elements, I would find myself painted into a typographic corner, since decisions made early tend to limit flexibility later. I could get out of a tight spot by reworking the early pages, but that's frustrating when it means losing a lot of time. So after establishing the text spread I now jump to the strongest display pages—chapter and part openings, title page, and artwork with captions. Since these pages are visually prominent, I can determine display typography here and then carry it through to subheads and text elements.

I begin each book design with a unique page layout. A book's trim is my starting point—the page size. The book's ideal length is my goal—meeting the castoff. With those two parameters, I take a rough guess at line length and see how the typefaces I've chosen look. I always work in spreads and consider margins as well as text block. I make printouts and trim them out; I tape pages together into spreads; then I look, take notes, adjust, and repeat. I check castoff figures when I've developed some spreads that I like. I might work this way for half a day or longer to get one or two spreads that I truly like. From there I start working outward. I'm always aiming for balance—readability, pleasing margins, good color on the page, but no excess.

A display font needs to contrast harmoniously with the text font and add personality without calling too much attention to itself. Again, timelessness matters. There are books I designed in the 1980s with display type that looks so dated now. I regret that! I can't be sure that my current designs will hold up in thirty years but I aim for it. The versatility of a typeface also influences my choice; display fonts that work in a wide range of styles or sizes are better for complicated manuscripts.

In *Daring Pairings*, Univers Ultra Condensed is used for display type on chapter and part openers and title page. It's elegant at large sizes, and the tall, narrow letterforms are substantial enough to hold a soft graduated grayscale tone. The smallest it's used in the book is 32-point; much less than that and it becomes difficult to read. All remaining display type is set in uncondensed versions of Univers, which look great at petite sizes.

For non–visually oriented books, there is usually no author input about text design. On occasion, an author may want to discuss the jacket. But with trade, art, and food-related books, author contact seems to come with the territory. Evan and I never specifically discussed text design, although a good deal of information (spoken and nonverbal) is exchanged in any meeting. I got a sense of his personality and how the design might convey the correct tone. I knew the book had to look unintimidating—not for wine experts only. And although he didn't spell out likes and dislikes, he wanted a handsome book.

The marketing department affects what a book will look like, both by what's allotted in the publishing plan (i.e., four-color printing; paper quality) and what they request ("must look trade-y"). Sometimes there's a disconnect between marketing and author vision. As designer I don't manage the book's budget or marketing plan, but I will advocate for whatever seems necessary.

Since cookbooks are visually oriented, their authors see preliminary design layouts and offer feedback and/or approval. I've had authors who were pleased with everything and authors who wanted a redesign to their specific vision. I always try to incorporate requests for text readability, recipe clarity, and design features, although it sometimes boils down to perception: the press likes it, the author doesn't. My recollection with Evan is that he was pleased with everything as designed. He also ran a careful check of final photographs to confirm that the prepared food presented the recipes correctly, and the right wine glasses were in each shot.

It makes a difference who the typesetter will be. UC Press usually works with compositors, rather than having in-house designers format and compose books. I'm fairly exacting as I flesh out the design, getting everything just as I want it. Then I spec concisely so the compositor doesn't have to guess my intent. The goal is for a good result the first time around, in sample pages.

I go through the same careful process when I'm going to set a book myself. Writing specs is where I iron out inconsistencies of spacing and sizing. Years of working with compositors has taught me to fully resolve the design at the design stage, so when I'm composing pages I don't need to reformat a lot of text. I may adjust a few specs based on the way pages are fitting together—perhaps caption size or subhead spacing—but typically nothing major.

Specs by nature are dense reading material. It's kind of like reading a phone book. A compositor who knows my tendencies and UC Press's house style will interpret specs with amazing accuracy.

There are no text-only spreads in this book, but I designed one anyway because it provides the foundation (grid) for all layouts. The manuscript was

whites has encouraged winemakers in other countries to experiment with it. A small but increasing number of winemakers in California are vinifying the grape with ripe quince-like fruit and varying levels of acidity, creating a range of wines from good to flabby and occasionally almost off-dry. In Oregon, despite the grape's potential, only one winery, Ponzi Vineyards, seems to be daring enough to bottle it. In Australia, things are more hopeful: more than thirty wineries are planting Arneis, although it's premature to say that it's found a home in any specific area. There seem to be more plantings in Victoria's Mornington Peninsula and King Valley than in other areas.

Vintner's Choices Aged vs. not aged, early vs. late harvesting, oak vs. no oak, sandy vs. clay soil, vineyards at low altitudes vs. high altitudes

Arneis means "difficult" or "stubborn" in Piedmontese dialect, and any winemaker who has worked with this grape probably thinks the name is apropos. For a white grape, it's a relatively late bloomer (ripening at the end of September), and, to add insult to injury, those who are patient are rewarded with consistently low yields. Picking at just the right time to maximize both ripeness and acidity is key because of the grape's naturally low acidity. It is claimed that vineyard location and soil type are critical to maintaining the acidity (and thus the verve of the wine).The best locations tend to be in clay soils, which seem to preserve the acidity, while sandy soils bring out more of the floral aromatics. In practice, most producers are working myriad soil types. Higher-altitude vineyards are also said to be superior.

Although a handful of producers use oak, most believe (as I do) that avoiding oak better maintains the character of the fruit and doesn't push too hard on the wine's structure. Some of the barrel-aged wines I have tasted were oaky and flaccid. The wine's naturally low acidity means that it's best drunk as young and fresh as possible, and not cellared away for your kid's twenty-first birthday.

PAIRING WITH FOOD

The greatest challenge in pairing Arneis with food is coping with its often-underwhelming acidity. The best wines are refreshing and reasonably zippy, but many are barely balanced or lacking. Low-impact cooking methods are best. A pasta tossed with simply blanched peas and a little olive oil and lemon zest or a fillet of fish poached in a court bouillon would be an excellent accompaniment to Arneis. The relatively low alcohol enables Arneis to pair with piquant and often-problematic dishes like Chinese salt-and-pepper shrimp or spaghetti puttanesca, with its olives, anchovies, hot pepper flakes, and tomato. Most fish are a good match—from the simplest of pan-roasted black cod to a good old plate of lightly battered fish and chips, and treatments involving green herbs (such as salsa verde) or a simple wedge of lemon or lime are especially successful. Basic shellfish is also quite happy with Arneis, as are lighter types of poultry, such as Cornish game hen or quail or a simple breast of chicken.

ARNEIS 40

The cuisines of the eastern Mediterranean seem to pair well with Arneis, including Lebanese, Israeli, Turkish, and Greek. Tabbouleh, dolmas, and falafel are all nice options. This variety seems to match up well with many vegetables, though it is less happy with the always-problematic artichokes, asparagus, and Brussels sprouts. Finally, it's not a stretch to have milder charcuterie with Arneis, especially when served with fruit that's not overly sweet (prosciutto with watermelon or Crenshaw melon, as opposed to the traditional sweet, ripe cantaloupe, would be a tasty example).

PAIRING POINTERS

Arneis goes well with:

- A range of starter dishes. It's a wonderful wine to pair with the assortment of flavors and textures in an *antipasto misto,* tapas, and especially Middle Eastern mezes.
- Composed salads. Keep the dressing low in acid (opt for cream- or citrus-based dressings) and have at it. Scallops and grapefruit on mixed greens, almost anything with avocado, and a refreshing couscous salad with lightly grilled vegetables are nice pairings with this wine.
- Almost anything that swims. From fillet of sole to swordfish, most fish, especially milder types, go well with Arneis. Stick to low- to medium-impact methods of preparation so as not to overwhelm the wine.
- Dishes with mild, fresh herbs. Rosemary and thyme are too assertive, but sweeter herbs like sweet basil, chervil, and Italian parsley show well with Arneis.
- Mustard, believe it or not. A simple roast chicken with a dab of Dijon mustard, a scaloppine of veal with a light mustard sauce, or a mustard-and-breadcrumb crust on a loin of pork are three treatments that will show the wine well.

Arneis isn't good with:

- Tart dressings and green salads. While fresh and generally bright, most Arneis can't handle acidic vinaigrettes and sharp sauces.
- Heavily smoked or grilled foods. A rich tea-smoked duck or intensely flavored smoked salmon or trout will overpower most Arneis. So will items that have been grilled over powerfully flavored mesquite or other charcoal.
- Very rich dishes.
- Strong spices. Arneis gets lost behind chiles, many Asian spices (five spice, star anise, or garam masala), powdered ginger, and clove, to name a few. If you must include these spices, use a very light hand.
- Very briny shellfish. The wine simply doesn't have the oomph to handle salty oysters, strong clams, or intense *goût de mer* mussels, which make the wine taste off.

ARNEIS 41

Text pages from *Daring Pairings* by Evan Goldstein (University of California Press).

long, and we were aiming for 350 pages using a 7.5 × 9.5 inch trim. Here the text is 10.25/14 Chaparral × 33 picas. Chaparral reads well even at this long line length, in part because its letters have a substantial and even stroke weight. And its italics are distinct without being attention hogs—a great feature since the text includes a lot of italicized foreign terms. This spread shows the three levels of subhead. The all-cap 1-heads print red, and cap/lowercase 2-heads and 3-heads print black (a 2-head sits on its own line; a 3-head runs with text at paragraph level). Subheads are streamlined to recede, since they occur so often.

Recipe page from *Daring Pairings* by Evan Goldstein (University of California Press).

Evan enlisted thirty-six chefs, matching each one with a particular grape varietal. In the Tempranillo section the chef is Dan Barber, and this recipe is his suggested pairing. Since recipes would not run together (i.e., new recipe begins on new page) my first step was determining the number of pages they

tempranillo | ROAST RACK OF LAMB WITH CREAMY RICE WITH PARSNIPS

DAN BARBER Blue Hill, New York City, and Blue Hill at Stone Barns, New York

Makes 4 to 6 main-course servings

CREAMY RICE

1 cup basmati rice
2 cups water
1½ teaspoons canola oil
½ pound parsnips (2 small), peeled and cut into ½-inch chunks (about 1 cup)
Salt and freshly ground black pepper
2¾ cups vegetable stock, or as needed
Chopped fresh chives for garnish

LAMB

Canola oil for searing
2 (8-bone) lamb racks
Salt and freshly ground black pepper

Preheat the oven to 425°F for the lamb, then begin cooking the rice. In a saucepan, combine the rice and water and bring to a simmer over medium heat. Reduce the heat to low, cover, and cook until the water has been fully absorbed and the rice is tender, 17 to 20 minutes. Remove from the heat and set aside. You should have about 3 cups cooked rice.

In another saucepan, heat the oil over medium heat. Add the parsnips, season with salt and pepper, and sauté gently until beginning to soften, about 10 minutes. Do not allow the parsnips to color. Add 1½ cups of the stock and bring to a simmer. Cook, uncovered, until the parsnips are tender and the stock has reduced by about half, 5 to 10 minutes.

Transfer the parsnips and their cooking liquid to a blender and process until smooth. If the purée is too thick to flow freely, add a little more stock. You should have about 1 cup purée. Set aside.

Begin roasting the lamb while the rice is cooking. Film the bottom of a large skillet with the canola oil and place over medium-high heat until hot. Season both sides of the lamb racks liberally with salt and pepper. When the oil is hot, place the racks, fat side down, in the pan and sear until golden brown on the first side, 3 to 4 minutes. Turn and sear on the second side until browned, about 4 minutes. Transfer to a rimmed baking sheet, place in the oven, and roast for 20 minutes for medium-rare, or until done to your liking.

TEMPRANILLO **290**

required. I look at extremes first, in this case placing the longest and shortest recipes in the text grid. Each recipe required two or three pages when roughly formatted. This became my parameter as I addressed the specifics of each text element.

The manuscript had fourteen distinct recipe elements, which fell loosely into categories of title, ingredient, instruction, and chart. Several of the title elements meshed nicely into a header that anchors the recipe and deals with four elements in one shot. Below that is the ingredients list. Although it's text-level information, a cook refers to this list repeatedly. It's in Univers bold for emphasis, and to further clarify the list, I manually constructed slash fractions and inserted hard line breaks where needed. After the ingredients come recipe instructions and wine-pairing notes; they use the same Chaparral font as text in the main book. (These pairing notes were formerly headnotes, but they were unwieldy at the start of the recipe; Evan and Dore Brown, the editor, were amenable to moving them to the end.) The wine producers' chart ends the recipe in sans serif, to distinguish it as reference material rather than part of the overall recipe.

Our press commissions new photography rarely, so we wanted to maximize the opportunity. The thirty-six photos are the creation of a talented team: photographer Joyce Oudkerk Pool, chef Pouké, and stylist Carol Hacker. In advance of the shoot I prepared thumbnail layouts showing sequenced spreads as they'd appear in the book, so we could see which grape varietals would face each other. Joyce photographed the recipes in a completely nonlinear sequence over the course of eight days, but she and Carol set up the shots so facing images would be complementary. We poured the correct wine for each shot, and paid close attention to detail so images would be faithful to recipes. The white border in the design provides separation between images and echoes the gray border around recipes.

The thirty-six chapters are the heart of the book and needed to pop. Chapter titles are grape varietal names, very concise. I used them large, reversing type out of the red-saturated grape leaf photo. Red wine openers use one detailed crop and whites use another. I placed a grayscale version of the grape leaves in the letterforms to give descenders (such as the letter "p" in the example on page 152) some tone against white paper.

Below the chapter title is a pronunciation key. This was originally part of the main text, but the editor was willing to pull it out for display use.

I like when the table of contents can fit on one page, but if wine listings, recipes, and chef's name ran together it would clearly take at least three pages. By breaking up the text we devised a main table of contents (one page) followed by a recipe contents list on the following spread. The main contents page shows the organizing principle of whites and reds in one glance. The contents page is one of the last I design, and it can take a surprisingly long time

tannat | ROBERT DEL GRANDE'S RUSTIC BEEF STEW WITH PRUNES AND GUAJILLO CHILE SAUCE PAGE 281

DAN BARBER'S ROAST RACK OF LAMB WITH CREAMY RICE WITH PARSNIPS PAGE 290

Pages from *Daring Pairings* by Evan Goldstein (University of California Press).

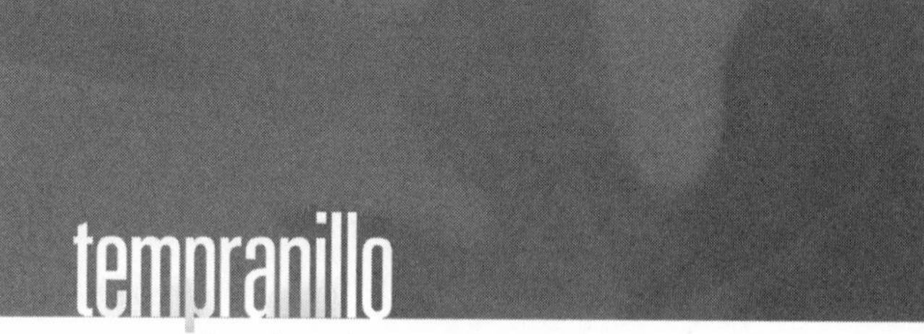

tem-prah-*nee*-yoh

When I'm asked which is my favorite wine, I usually reply in one of two ways: it's like your kids—it depends what day; or, as long as it's balanced, varietally correct, and true to its specificity of place, I'm happy. But at the end of the day, I suppose I'm a Pinot Noir guy and—a Tempranillo guy. I love Pinot Noir because of its seductive charm, intoxicating complexity, and amazing peacock's tail of flavor (when it's at its best). But Tempranillo I rate equally high because of its incredible food-friendliness, range of styles, and unique character.

The most important grape of Rioja, Spain, Tempranillo has rich red to black fruit, signature *balsamico* flavors (see below), and an ability to age gracefully. Like Tuscany's Sangiovese, which it resembles in some ways, Tempranillo is wonderful on its own and in blends. It varies from easy-drinking to age-worthy and serious, and is made according to so many classifications (in Spain) that the wine lover has a wide range of age and flavor profiles to choose from.

Alternative Names Cencibel, Tinto Fino, Tinto del Pais, Tinta del Toro, Ull de Llebre (Spain), Aragonez, Arauxa, Tinta Roriz (Portugal)

Styles Light-medium to full-bodied dry red, medium-bodied dry *rosado*

Sometimes Blended With Mazuelo/Carignan, Garnacha/Grenache, Graciano, Viura, Cabernet Sauvignon, Merlot, Monastrell/Mourvèdre (Spain), Touriga Nacional, Touriga Franca, Trincadeira (Portugal), Bonarda, Malbec (Argentina)

Flavor Lexicon *Fruit/vegetable:* Black olive, dried cherry, fennel, fresh cherry, red plum • *Floral:* Herbs (dill, marjoram, mint, oregano, thyme), laurel, patchouli, tobacco • *Earth:* Dust • *Wood:* Cinnamon, cocoa, masala mix, vanilla

Similar Sips Pinot Noir, Sangiovese, lighter-style Syrah

Where It's Grown Argentina (Mendoza), Australia (South Australia: Adelaide Hills, McLaren Vale), Chile, Mexico, Portugal (Alentejo, Dão, Douro), Spain (Castilla–La Mancha: Valdepeñas; Castilla-León: Ribera del Duero, Toro; Catalonia: Penedès; Navarra; Rioja),

284

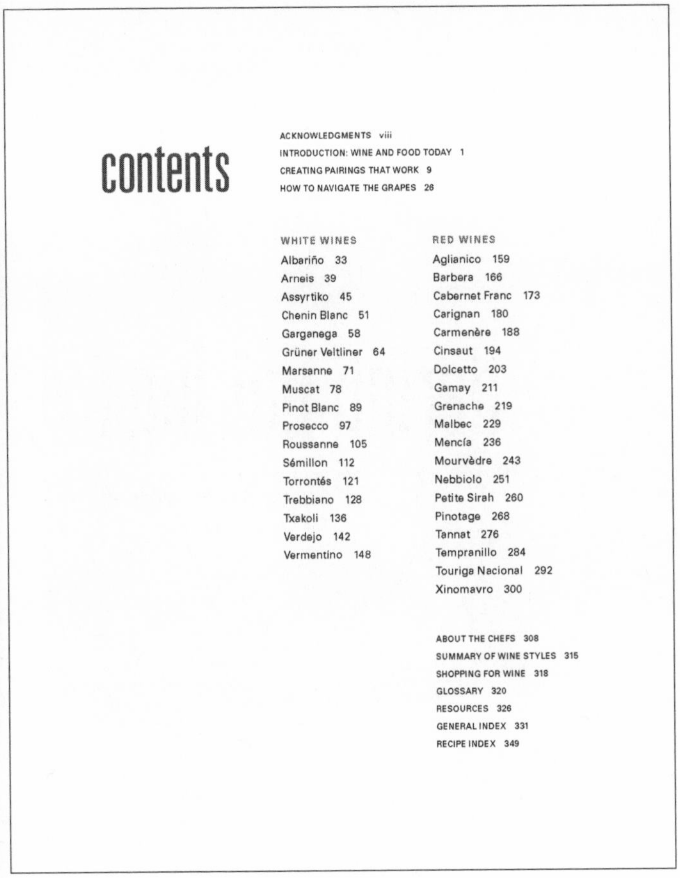

contents

recipes

vi

to get it right. It follows type conventions from the main design but is also a unique layout with its own requirements.

Most back matter uses type conventions established elsewhere in the book, but I do need to decide what to apply where. A two-page chart was originally a series of small graphs that our editor was able to distill into a straightforward list that fit on one spread. In the "Resources" section, text size jumps down a few points, and remains at that smaller size for the remainder of the book.

I worked on the title page at the same time as part openers, adjusting each until they were in correct balance. The title page is a notch more prominent and provides a visual link between the image-heavy jacket and text-heavy interior.

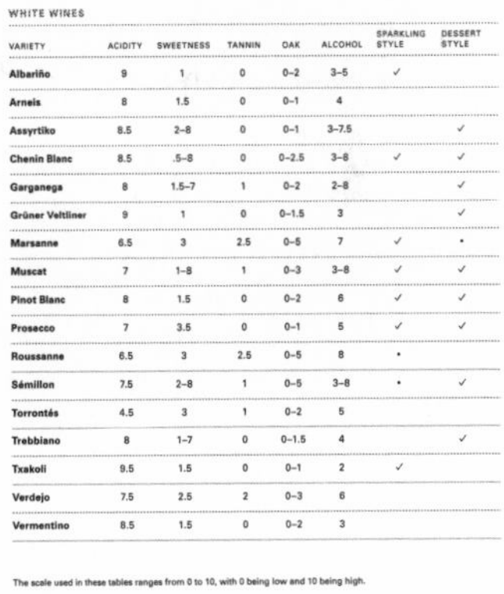

WHITE WINES

VARIETY	ACIDITY	SWEETNESS	TANNIN	OAK	ALCOHOL	SPARKLING STYLE	DESSERT STYLE
Albariño	9	1	0	0–2	3–5	✓	
Arneis	8	1.5	0	0–1	4		
Assyrtiko	8.5	2–8	0	0–1	3–7.5		✓
Chenin Blanc	8.5	.5–8	0	0–2.5	3–8	✓	✓
Garganega	8	1.5–7	1	0–2	2–8		✓
Grüner Veltliner	9	1	0	0–1.5	3		✓
Marsanne	6.5	3	2.5	0–5	7	✓	•
Muscat	7	1–8	1	0–3	3–8	✓	✓
Pinot Blanc	8	1.5	0	0–2	6	✓	✓
Prosecco	7	3.5	0	0–1	5	✓	✓
Roussanne	6.5	3	2.5	0–5	8	•	
Sémillon	7.5	2–8	1	0–5	3–8	•	✓
Torrontés	4.5	3	1	0–2	5		
Trebbiano	8	1–7	0	0–1.5	4		✓
Txakoli	9.5	1.5	0	0–1	2	✓	
Verdejo	7.5	2.5	2	0–3	6		
Vermentino	8.5	1.5	0	0–2	3		

The scale used in these tables ranges from 0 to 10, with 0 being low and 10 being high.

Detail of chart (reduced at 30%) from *Daring Pairings* by Evan Goldstein (University of California Press).

RESOURCES

RECOMMENDED BOOKS

Dorenburg, Andrew, and Karen Page. *What to Drink with What You Eat*. New York: Bulfinch Press, 2006.

Fletcher, Janet. *Cheese and Wine: A Guide to Selecting, Pairing, and Enjoying*. San Francisco: Chronicle Books, 2006.

Herbst, Ron, and Sharon Tyler Herbst. *The New Wine Lover's Companion*. 2nd ed. New York: Barron's Educational Series, Inc., 2003.

Jenkins, Steve. *The Cheese Primer*. New York: Workman Publishing, 1996.

Johnson, Hugh, and Jancis Robinson. *The World Atlas of Wine*. 6th ed. London: Mitchell Beasley, 2007.

Robinson, Jancis. *The Oxford Companion to Wine*. 3rd ed. New York: Oxford University Press, 2006.

Stevenson, Tom. *The Sotheby's Wine Encyclopedia*. New York: DK Publishing, 2007.

———. *Wine Report 2008* and 2009. New York: DK Publishing, 2008 and 2009.

Werlin, Laura. *Laura Werlin's Cheese Essentials: An Insider's Guide to Buying and Serving Cheese*. New York: Stewart, Tabori & Chang, 2007.

ONLINE RESOURCES

WINE-RELATED SITES

There are hundreds of wine websites, but here are a few that consistently deliver useful and accurate information.

***Decanter* online** www.decanter.com The website for one of the most respected wine magazines in the world. Includes articles, news, and tasting notes.

eRobertParker.com The subscription-only site of perhaps the world's best-known wine critic offers tasting notes, articles, vintage charts, reviews, and other useful information.

JancisRobinson.com This website, much of which is accessible only to subscribers, is a wonderful combination of tasting notes, news, food information, and opinion from possibly the most influential wine journalist in the world.

National Grape Registry http://ngr.ucdavis.edu A great resource for amateurs, providing information on grapes of all colors, shapes, and sizes.

***Wine and Spirits* online** www.wineandspirits magazine.com Much of the valuable, well-researched information on this site is available to subscribers only. A useful alternative to the *Wine Spectator* and Robert Parker.

326

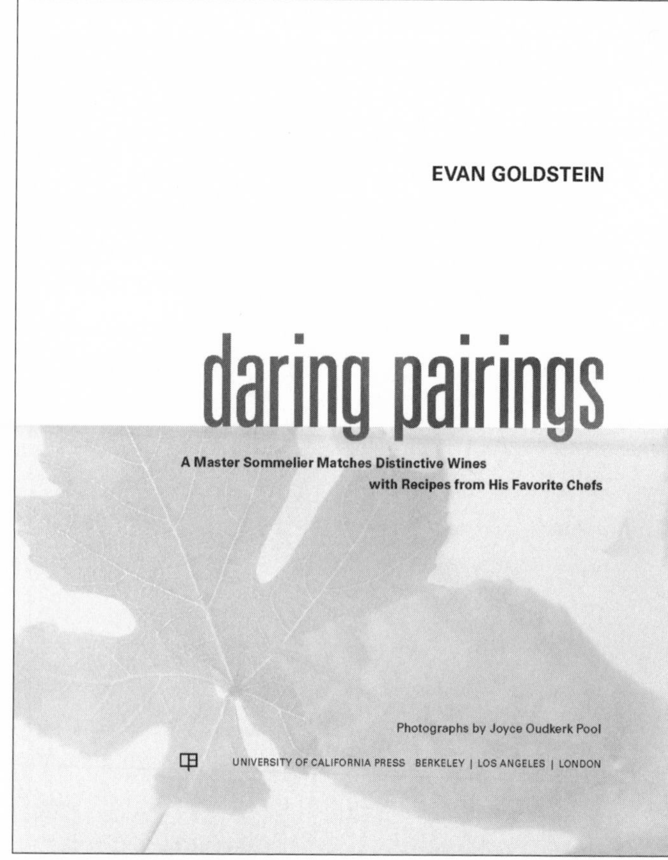

EVAN GOLDSTEIN
daring pairings
A Master Sommelier Matches Distinctive Wines
with Recipes from His Favorite Chefs
Photographs by Joyce Oudkerk Pool
UNIVERSITY OF CALIFORNIA PRESS BERKELEY | LOS ANGELES | LONDON

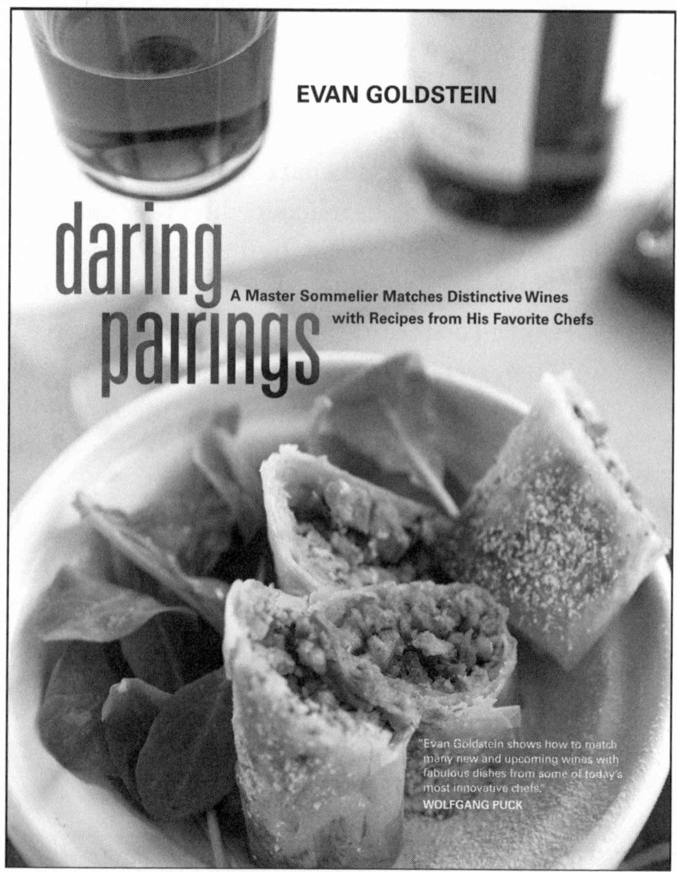

EVAN GOLDSTEIN
daring
pairings
A Master Sommelier Matches Distinctive Wines
with Recipes from His Favorite Chefs
"Evan Goldstein shows how to match many new and upcoming wines with fabulous dishes from some of today's most innovative chefs."
WOLFGANG PUCK

Back matter page, title page, and jacket from *Daring Pairings* by Evan Goldstein (University of California Press).

Designing Plays

Whenever I am going to the theater I like to read a play before I see it, especially plays by Tom Stoppard, where the clever dialogue flies by so quickly that some of the best wordplay can be missed. I wonder how many in the audience at the opening night of *Pirates of Penzance* really understood W. S. Gilbert's brilliant Major General's patter song without having first read the words. Reading and seeing a play are quite different experiences, especially for Harold Pinter, where pauses on the page are very different experiences from what pauses on the stage are like. There are, of course, plays that are meant to be read as well as performed. It is said that George Bernard Shaw was just as happy to have his plays read as seen.

Individual play texts are generally as thin as a book of poetry, and so the text face and text size can often be a bit more generous. With many short lines of dialogue, stage directions, and extra space between dialogue, keeping the integrity of the text page can be difficult to balance.

The most conventional way to indicate speaker names is to set them in small caps; stage directions are usually set in italic. When stage directions are integrated into dialogue, they are often set within square brackets or parentheses. My own preference is for square brackets to avoid any parenthetical observation in the actor's dialogue.

Given these conventions, having a good italic font is a necessity. Small caps in some fonts look a bit too small against the lowercase. Occasionally it is useful to make the small caps a fraction of a size larger. I nearly always letterspace the small caps. Charles Ellertson, in his chapter, writes about setting up character styles for handling this.

In conventional play setting, the speaker names begin flush left, and the dialogue is unhyphenated ragged right with turnover lines indented. Character names within stage directions are also set in small caps, same as the speaker names. Often there is extra space between dialogue and between dialogue and stage directions.

There are always anomalies. If the dialogue is verse, the speaker name may be on a line by itself, and words spoken may begin on the next line. Occasionally long speaker names are abbreviated, but rarely these days.

Acts and scenes are treated as if they were parts and chapters, though scenes are usually run on with extra space or an ornament. Acts usually begin a new page in books of individual play texts, as space is not a problem.

Quite the opposite are books of multiple plays. *The Complete Pelican Shakespeare* designed by Hans Schmoller (Penguin Books, 1969) is a fine example

The question of designing plays, as in poetry and art books, is better resolved in favor of the spirit and essence of the work than the period. . . . The indiscriminate use of contemporary style and dynamics is just as bad as blind application of period trappings according to the date of composition.
— Marshall Lee, *Bookmaking*

III, ii KING

And can make vile things precious. Come, your hovel.
Poor fool and knave, I have one part in my heart
That's sorry yet for thee.

FOOL *[sings]*

He that has and a little tiny wit,
With, heigh-ho, the wind and the rain,
76 Must make content with his fortunes fit
Though the rain it raineth every day.

LEAR True, boy. Come, bring us to this hovel.
Exit [with Kent].

79 FOOL This is a brave night to cool a courtesan. I'll speak a
prophecy ere I go:
81 When priests are more in word than matter;
82 When brewers mar their malt with water;
83 When nobles are their tailors' tutors,
84 No heretics burned, but wenches' suitors;
When every case in law is right,
No squire in debt nor no poor knight;
When slanders do not live in tongues,
Nor cutpurses come not to throngs;
89 When usurers tell their gold i' th' field,
And bawds and whores do churches build –
91 Then shall the realm of Albion
92 Come to great confusion.
Then comes the time, who lives to see't,
94 That going shall be used with feet.
95 This prophecy Merlin shall make, for I live before his
time. *Exit.*

*

III, iii *Enter Gloucester and Edmund.*

GLOUCESTER Alack, alack, Edmund, I like not this unnatural dealing. When I desired their leave that I might
3 pity him, they took from me the use of mine own house,
charged me on pain of perpetual displeasure neither to
5 speak of him, entreat for him, or any way sustain him.

EDMUND Most savage and unnatural.

7 GLOUCESTER Go to; say you nothing. There is division
8 between the Dukes, and a worse matter than that. I have
received a letter this night – 'tis dangerous to be spoken
10 – I have locked the letter in my closet. These injuries the
11 King now bears will be revenged home; there is part of a
12 power already footed; we must incline to the King. I will
13 look him and privily relieve him. Go you and maintain
talk with the Duke, that my charity be not of him perceived. If he ask for me, I am ill and gone to bed. If I die
for it, as no less is threatened me, the King my old mas-
17 ter must be relieved. There is strange things toward,
Edmund; pray you be careful. *Exit.*

EDMUND

19 This courtesy forbid thee shall the Duke
Instantly know, and of that letter too.
21 This seems a fair deserving, and must draw me
That which my father loses – no less than all.
The younger rises when the old doth fall. *Exit.*

*

III, iv *Enter Lear, Kent, and Fool.*

KENT

1 Here is the place, my lord. Good my lord, enter.
The tyranny of the open night's too rough
For nature to endure.
Storm still.

LEAR Let me alone.

108

Detail from *The Complete Pelican Shakespeare* (Penguin Books), designed by Hans Schmoller.

of how to do it.[1] Schmoller's concerns were to avoid turned lines, to preserve the flow of the blank verse, to let the speaker names stand out, and to avoid absurd abbreviations (where Hamlet is a "ham" and Tititania a "tit"). He used Ehrhardt, a typeface that is slightly condensed, and even in 9 pt has enough weight. Speaker names were in letterspaced small caps flush left run in except when followed by verse. Turnovers in prose were indented 1 em. Verse began a new line indented 1 em. Stage directions were set ragged right in italic indented.

RON COSTLEY: FABER PLAYS

You changed Faber play style from Plantin to Sabon.
Was Plantin always used?
Plantin had been used for plays for many years. I changed to Sabon when a new drama editor was keen to refresh the look of the list. Small caps for character names went out, semibold came in.

As Faber published many of the most prominent playwrights,
did any of them have any design requirements or requests, other
than Pinter's, to center the speaker names?
No. Playwrights, other than Pinter, seem to have been happy with the new house-style.

If you were not designing a play in the series,
what would influence your choice of font?
I would have to use a type that I was reasonably familiar with and that had the necessary sorts to meet the demands of the text.

Would you ever choose a font to reflect the content?
For example, would you ever use a sans serif for a play text?
I cannot think of a text where sans serif might be appropriate. For a "one-off" I might think of reflecting the content. For example: setting a Restoration play in Caslon. It's a different matter when designing a template that must be suitable for many different genres. The point of a play is that it really exists when it is acted or spoken, not as printed text in the way a novel is.

[1] A full discussion of Schmoller's working methods designing the *Pelican Shakespeare* is the informative "Hans Schmoller and the Design of the One-Volume Pelican Shakespeare" by S. J. M. Watson, in *Typography Papers* 3 (University of Reading, 1998).

Typesetting Specifications New PLAYSTYLE ff

Designer RC Date Feb 1995

New M/s Offset

M/s complete

Series

Linotype Postscript SABON

Text type 10½/12pt ranged left unjustified x 22 picas

~~Verse~~ thin word #

– use o.s. figs throughout

verse ~~Extracts~~ 10½/12pt r. left ~~full out~~ indent 1em begin on line following speaker.

~~Drama~~ ½ line # between stanzas

198 mm · 126 mm · measure 22 picas · 3 3 picas · full page = 36 lines of 10½/12pt exclusive · 3½ picas head

Notes end page / end ch / end book 8/10pt

indicated in text by

References

indicated in text by

Tables

Special sorts

Part title 12pt CAPS, letter #d centre on 2nd line

Part number

new part – new recto, verso blank

Act heading

Appendices

Bibliography

Epigraphs

Glossary

Illustrations line tone

Integrated Non-integrated

Captions 9/12pt ~~r. left~~ centred

Chapter title

Acts begin new page / ~~run on~~

Chapter number

text lines on ch opening page = 30 lines

Act heading 12pt u & l.c. centred on 2nd line

Sub-headings Spacing –

A head

B head

C head

D head

E head

scene heads: 12pt s.cs letter #d centred, 2 line # above, 1 line # below.

scenes run-on

Running heads – for collected plays only: 10½/12pt s.cs #d, centred ½ # above text

Verso AUTHOR Recto PLAY TITLE

Folios 10½pt o.s. fig, centred, 1 line # below text

~~with running heads~~ / at foot

Spec pages Notes

– see also separate marked up specimen pages

Specifications for the new style for Faber plays.

12pt

Act One

2nd line

< 2 line#

SCENE ONE

5th line

< 1 line#

7th line

A tall, fresh-faced man of about thirty sits by the fire in his room in Christ Church, lost in thought: this is **Lewis Carroll.** *It's some time in the 1860s and he's formally, not to say sombrely dressed. After a time he shifts position in his capacious armchair and looks up.*

< ½ line#

Carroll I've always been fond of children: except boys.

Character's name bold followed by en #

A movement catches his eye and he looks across at the fireplace. Above the fire is a substantial marble amntelpiece bearing a clock and a number of ornaments; and above the mantelpiece is a large gilt-framed mirror. And in the mirror is a small girl, eight or nine years old: **Alice.** *He watches her for a moment and then she disappears. He moves to the table and begins arranging the tea things. Presently, there's a knock at the door. he crosses to open the door: it's Alice.*

< ½ line#

Alice Hello, Uncle.

Carroll My dear.

Alice (*sweetly*) I'm sorry if I'm late.

Carroll (*gruffly*) Stuff and nonsense.

Alice And I've forgotten to bring the sonnet. (*dejectedly*) Well, really, I forgot to copy it out. (*Alice gets up and walks around.*)

Carroll (*wearily*) What a tiresome child you are.

Alice (*angrily*) Don't you call me tiresome, you old pervert! (*She goes to the sideboard, opens a drawer, takes out*

Pages may fall ½ line short. Do not feather such pages.

< 1 line#

1

< 10½pt o.s. fig

– opening scene setting directions italic, fullout, unjustified
– Stage directions within dialogue italic, in rom. parens; usually no opening cap nor closing stop.
– All other stage directions italic, indent 1em, unjustified.
~~Characters' names on their first appearance to be bold u&l.c., italic u&l.c. thereafter.~~

28/iv/95 RC

Faber plays: Opening Act 1/Scene 1.

Faber plays: Scene 2 and verse.

plays2 18/1/95 5:46 pm Page 2

3picas back margin

3½picas head margin

a gun, turn around and shoots Carroll in the stomach, three times.) That'll stop you asking me to take my clothes off.

Carroll Aaaagh.

< 2line #

SCENE TWO

< 12pt scs letter#d

< 1 line#

Alice Hello, Uncle.

Carroll My dear.

Alice (*sweetly*) I'm sorry if I'm late.

Carroll (*gruffly*) Stuff and nonsense.

Alice And I've forgotten to bring the sonnet. (*dejectedly*) Well, really, I forgot to copy it out. (*Alice gets up and walks around.*)

Carroll (*wearily*) What a tiresome child you are.

Alice (*angrily*) Don't you call me tiresome, you old pervert! (*She goes to the sideboard, opens a drawer, takes out a gun, turn around and shoots Carroll in the stomach, three times.*) That'll stop you asking me to take my clothes off.

< ½ line#

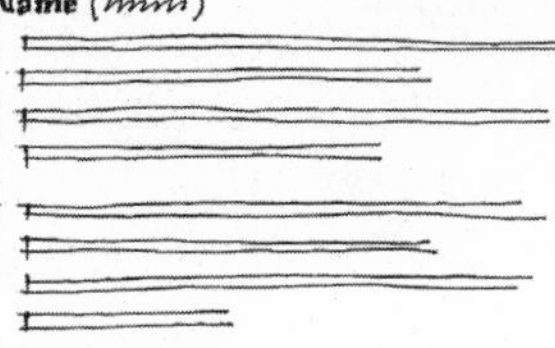

style for verse 10½/12pt indent 1em ½ line# between stanzas

< ½#

Alice mmm/mmm

2

style for verse in plays

Flies of silver.
He can only whinny
To the hard mountains
From the dry river
Dead in his throat.
Aye, the great horse
That will not drink the water.
The sorrow of the snows,
The horse of dawn.

Mother-in-law
Keep away, stay
Close to the window
With a branch of dreams
And a dream of branches.

Wife
Now my baby sleeps.

Mother-in-law
Now my baby rests.

Wife
Horse, my baby
Has a soft pillow.

Mother-in-law
A cot of iron.

Wife
A cover of linen.

Mother-in-law
Hush, baby, hush.

Wife
Aye, the great horse
Will not drink the water.

10

When it came to designing the plays of Harold Pinter, Costley changed to Pinter's preferred style where the speaker names are centered above the dialogue. This resembled the style of screenplays, which followed the layout of typed film scripts, a genre familiar to Pinter. Courtesy of Faber and Faber Ltd.

Typesetting Specifications for Pinter plays – reset ff

Designer Ron Costley Date 26/xi/99

New M/s Offset

M/s complete

Series

Text type Linotype SABON 10½/13pt r. left x 21 picas use o.s figs

Verse

Dialogue: r. left x 21

Extracts

stage directions: italic r. left

Drama

Notes end page / end ch / end book

indicated in text by

References

indicated in text by

Tables

Special sorts

Part title

Part number

new part – new recto, verso blank

Act heading

Sub-headings Spacing –

A head character name: 10½/13pt scs centred, ½ line # above

B head

C head

D head

E head

198 mm; measure 21 picas; ½ picas; full page = 33 lines of 10½/13pt exclusive; 3½ picas head; 126 mm; un-sewn

Appendices

Bibliography

Epigraphs

Glossary

Illustrations line tone

Integrated Non-integrated

Captions

Chapter title

new page / run on

Chapter number

text lines on ch opening page = 27 lines

Act heading 12/13½pt italic centred T.L.2

scene heads: 12/13½pt scs ltd centred, 2 line # above, 1 line # below

Running heads

Verso Recto

Folios 10½/13pt o.s. figs centred

with running heads / at foot 1 line # below text

Spec pages Notes

Basic style for Pinter plays

3½ picas head

immediate experience. I mean, for example, when the hairdresser takes your head in his hands and starts to wash your hair very gently and to massage your scalp, when he does that, when your eyes are closed and he does that, he has your entire trust, doesn't he? It's not just your head which is in his hands, is it, it's your life, it's your spiritual . . . welfare.

Pause.

So you see what I wanted to know was this . . . when your lover had his hand on your throat, did he remind you of your hairdresser?

Pause.

I'm talking about your lover. The man who tried to murder you.

REBECCA

Murder me?

DEVLIN

Do you to death.

REBECCA

No, no. He didn't try to murder me. He didn't want to murder me.

DEVLIN

He suffocated you and strangled you. As near as

43

T.L.2 T.L.5 T.L.7

3½ picas back

< ½ line # only if follow

] centre

33 lines 10½/13pt Sabon r. left x 21 picas

Do not separate name from speech at the foot of a page

centred folio

< 1 line #

Designing Poetry

There are often more design problems lurking in a 64-page book of poetry than in a history book ten times that length. Until I could convince publishers it was easier for me to set the entire book myself, I often had to write unique specifications for more than half the poems in the manuscript. Not all poetry books are so design intensive, but increasingly poets seem partial to eccentric spacing, changes of font midstream, mixing prose and verse, adding subheads and epigraphs within a poem, presenting poems without titles, etc. I'm not sure what this eccentric typography is meant to represent. I wonder what readers are to make of it all. Are poems meant to be read aloud like a verbal score? Or are they meant to be looked at as art?

For the very look of verse on the printed page excites definite expectations in the mind of the reader, just as a glimpse at a bill of fare excites certain digestive juices in one's body.
— Walter de la Mare, *The Printing of Poetry* (quoted by Oliver Simon in *Introduction to Typography*)

What does a reader think when coming across an occasional poem, within a book of poems, that has extra space between lines of text? Are you meant to blink an extra time before reading on? Or on a page of poetry with but a single line or even a single word, is the reader to pause? How long is too long? It's like the finale to Sibelius's *Symphony 5*: how much time do you take between the notes/words?

As a designer my job is to present the author's words in type, but I never quite understand the need for such curious typography. I still subscribe to the old-fashioned notion that *words* were what poets were about. As the poet and illustrator Debora Greger wrote: "Negative space can be so powerful in visual works of art—and yet on the page in a book [it] seems to read as a production error or pretension. In my own work, I've come to discover the power not just of what things you can include in a poem, but of what can be left out. So my 'blank space' happens in the content, not in the form. I hope the presence of what's unsaid is felt."

Sometimes it is very clear why a poet has a page with little type on it. As Greger noted, section V of Baudelaire's *Voyage* has but four words, and even I understand why.

As with any manuscript I try to get a sense of the author's intent in writing the book: Is there a theme? What is it about? If only my education had been better. I often find poetry the most difficult text to get a handle on. It helps when the publisher provides the editor's statement for publishing or the marketing blurb. With that in mind I first consider which of my handful of most useful text fonts would seem visually suitable. For example, I might not use Quadraat if the manuscript called for much italic as Quadraat's italic is a bit too calligraphic for my taste; also, the Quadraat italic figures are so subtly different from the roman that editors occasionally question their style.

Perhaps even more than with fiction, I find it curious that poets don't know more than they seem to know about different fonts. Many poets with whom I work are concerned about the way their poetry is positioned on the page, kinds of eccentric spacing, whether I use caps or caps and lowercase for titles, etc. But as for typefaces, when they do suggest one, it often seems like a font wildly inappropriate (Comic Sans!).

Many publishers I work with are receptive to my using slightly different trim sizes as long as they fall within a range from as small as 5 inches wide × 8 inches deep to as large as 6.125 × 9.25, which are standardized sizes. I look for the poems with the longest lines to avoid as many turnovers as possible and find the poems with the most lines. If the poems have long lines but have few of them, I might make the book 6.125 × 8 (wide and short); correspondingly, for a book of poems that are predominantly narrow but are fairly long I would opt for 5.5 × 9.25. Of course, poets being poets, they are usually not so consistent. As Debora Greger once told me, poets are writing what they consider the ideal poem without concern for the printed book. Yet poets do seem as concerned about the sequence of their poems as photographers do about the sequence of their images. Long poems necessitate running over to a new page, so that it is not always possible to have certain poems face each other. Just as it is not possible to keep from breaking long lines that could never fit a text page no matter how small or compressed the font.

Manuscript page from "Live Oak with Moss" by Walt Whitman, reproduced in *Walt Whitman's Songs of Male Intimacy and Love* edited by Betsy Erkkila (University of Iowa Press). Courtesy of Alderman Library, University of Virginia.

Turnovers are sometimes a problem if the poet has also used many indented lines, and I have never found a solution I am really happy with under those circumstances. I have tried making the turnover lines flush right but that seemed awkward and did not seem to me to be a natural place for a turned line. Most of the time I simply resort to a 1 pica or 1 em indent. I have designed many books of poetry about Walt Whitman where editors include his exceptionally long lines. I had never thought about how Walt must have written these until recently when I saw photographs of his handwritten manuscript showing that he obviously was untroubled by letting lines turn over indented. When I mentioned this to the poet, critic, and teacher William Logan he said, "Though the manuscript you saw was narrow and the lines all runovers, I'm not sure this provides a crucial insight. Whitman knew a lot about typesetting and preferred to have his drafts set in type, so he could see what they would look like in print. He was ahead of his time. Most poets now have the advantage of him—they set their poems on computer and revise. Longhand writing and revising is now a rarity. Every poet is now his own Gutenberg, if not blessed with the taste of the early printers."

Since poetry is one of the most personal kinds of writing, and poets are more particular than most authors about how their text is presented, I asked Logan and Greger their thoughts about being designed.

William Logan wrote:

I try to specify, within reason, some of the elements of design. I ask for a large, open, serif font (Baskerville, Dante—I'm willing to be surprised), preferably in at least 10.5 size. I want no sans serif types. Many young designers prefer a tiny font size, often with a large amount of leading between lines. The older I get, the less I want to squint while reading a poem, particularly one of my own.

I usually ask to see three different settings of a single page, choosing the one I prefer. I rarely ask for changes—sometimes a designer has put in flourishes that seem unnecessary or made the margins smaller than I like. Sometimes the designers squeeze the gutter margin so that the text half disappears into the binding. In general I'd prefer larger gutter margins than I'd get—perhaps I'm whimsical in this matter.

If I'm noticing design while reading the poem, the designer has failed—design should augment, clarify, even provoke, but never distract. Fine press books in particular sometimes suffer from unnecessary elegance, from fussiness of intention, and unfortunately the designer's understanding of design is sometimes far more sophisticated than his taste in poetry.

I've had books set in Baskerville, Goudy Old Style, Fairfield, Fairfield Light, Poliphilus, Palatino, and Bodoni Book. My favorites were Fairfield Light and Palatino. Some of the others were set too small for my taste—I'd have liked them better if set a full point larger. I should not give the impression that I am at all knowledgeable about these things—I wouldn't be able to tell Monotype Baskerville from the Hound of the Baskervilles. That does not mean I think the differences between fonts are unimportant or that a more sensible author wouldn't spend more time familiarizing himself with those differences.

My lines are not usually so long that a runover is necessary. Still, typesetters have been dealing with runovers for centuries. The conventions are plain, and shouldn't bother a reader any more than the lack of a closed quote at the end of a paragraph, when the character's speech continues into the next paragraph. That said, runovers are more the problem of the poet than of the designer. Most poets who write the occasional long line would not expect the poem to be laid out so the line is not curtailed—a runover is an elegant way of bringing order into disorder.

Editors who have asked the designer to miniaturize the font size to avoid runovers are idiots. They have no sense of the history of typesetting or the conventions that have made design an art.

I've heard of a poet who reordered her whole book so that every poem on two pages started on a verso. Adding blank rectos, so that all poems start on a verso, lets text triumph over design, a mistake just as bad as letting design triumph over text.

As for a one-size-fits-all design, I suspect that it matters, but perhaps not as much as a designer would think. If the poems are themselves different, the design will fade into the background. The implicit point, that in an ideal world every design would enhance the text without competing with it, is inarguable. I'd certainly take a decent standardized design, however, over some of the monstrosities I've seen.

Debora Greger wrote:

All I say before Penguin sends me two or three sample faces and pages is that I'd like serifs and I'd like to be able to read the book without a magnifying glass. Some book designers have used such small point sizes that to me it feels as if they regard the print as just a graphic element on the page, not something to be read.

Of my three books from one publisher, each succeeding book was set in smaller type. On seeing proofs of the third one, I burst into tears on the phone with the editor, which did the trick. It was not the last time I would hear an editor say, "We've had this problem with this designer before." So I guess I'm feeling that some designers make too little of the text, not too much.

Beyond liking a font—and here I don't have the terms I need—that's big and open in relation to its height, and has serifs, and looks fairly classic, I don't have favorites.

Well, for whatever reason, I don't seem to write very many long lines that run over. I try to vary my line length, but I do seem, at this point, to have a sort of default length, one that happens not to need to be broken.

The place it bothers me is in the narrow columns of the *New York Review of Books* when a poem is quoted in a review—and every single line has to be broken. By the time they've done that, it reads like a different poem. Which is interesting, but not fair to the original poem.

I'm perfectly happy to let poems fall where they may, trusting the reader to keep the previous page in mind. But I do prefer to have the non-poem pages that begin the sections of the book fall on the recto.

I guess I've never felt that a universal design [such as at Faber] didn't fit a particular poetry book. On the other hand, I do love it when a great designer is given pretty free rein on the design of my book. Is it like having an haute couture gown made to measure? It's you underneath, but you're exquisitely turned out.

At this point in the history of the book, I feel so lucky still to have a publisher, let alone one like Penguin. Will mine be the last generation to go through a whole career being published like this? Even a print run of just 1,500 or 2,000 seems huge in the face of print-on-demand and the e-book. Strange days.

Once I have decided on the text face, size, and leading, I set the most problematic poems as samples to see not only how the words feel but how they fit the space. Unless the poems are short, I try to keep the stanza breaks to an extra half-line space. Where to break stanzas when poems run on to a new page also has to be considered. I would prefer not to break a stanza of approximately six lines and instead let the page run short. Another issue is where on the page the continued part should begin: at the top of the page to align with the poem title or sink to align with the first line of the poem. If the poet, as they sometimes do, includes poems without titles, they need to be distinguished in some way from continued parts of poems. I have used a simple ornament like a closed box or a small rule in place of where the title would normally go to indicate the start of a new poem.

Poem titles are just as problematic as chapter titles in that authors are not concerned with consistency, so that one title may be a single word and another many words. Shorter titles offer more possibilities for design and placement (for example, using small caps flush right at the top of the page), but long titles seem better to me as caps and lower case aligned somewhat left with the poem. Centering titles over poems can be a visual nightmare in that there is no fixed visual width of the text lines. Epigraphs and dedications only compound the problem and need to be distinguished from the poem text. They cannot be too small if they are short (e.g., To Vicky) but not so long that a later epigraph runs to many lines and thus seems to be part of the poem itself. Using italic and indenting dedications and epigraphs can be a useful solution.

If the poem titles are reasonably consistent in length, all the poems can begin on the same place on the page, but if poem titles vary greatly in length or there are many dedications or epigraphs, it is better to let the poems begin at an approximately similar space (i.e., approximately three lines from the last line of the title).

Occasionally I have to deal with authors who refuse to acknowledge that books are upright rectangles. They write long lines and order that none can be broken. On a recto page I will let the text overset into the front margin, but this is a problem on a verso page where the line would get too close to the spine. On rare occasions I have had to set an entire book in a typeface I consider too small or one far more condensed than I like.

Inevitably at least one poem will run one line long for the page. If there are stanza breaks, they can be reduced a bit to fit an extra text line. If there are no stanza breaks, I have been known to remove just a bit of leading between the text lines and let the page run a bit long (something my design colleagues would no doubt view as typographic heresy) .

Some poets have unusual theories regarding space between stanzas, as if a reader might understand a poem differently if some had an extra line space between them. One poet insisted that the stanzas have progressively more space as the poem progressed. As I said, I wondered if readers would pause for the exact amount of time before tackling the next stanza.

Other poets want poems to face each other even at the expense of having a blank recto. To me, a blank recto is a design solecism, and I feel the need to have something on the page. I don't mean the sort of thing one finds in a financial prospectus that has the paradoxical statement: "This page is intentionally blank." I often run a 10 percent black screen especially when an otherwise blank recto is meant to be the start of a new section.

To avoid problems of slightly long pages, it is important to place the folio in a relatively unobtrusive place. Most books of poetry are short so folios need not be as prominent as in other kinds of book design.

Authors differ in their preference for prose poems. Some prefer ragged right without hyphens while others prefer justified, hyphenated text. I always ask the editor or author to confirm what should be done.

Poetry anthologies only increase these problems. Collections of poems obviously have more inconsistencies than single-author collections, with the added complication of where to place author names and deciding on whether the emphasis should be on the authors or the titles. When the poems run on, it is even more important to plan where to break the text. The designer needs to decide whether spacing between entries can be flexible to make the pages align or whether uneven pages are preferable. If there are multiple poems by the same author, should the author name precede each, or can some other device indicate these are a group of poems by the same author?

There is no solution that would apply equally well to all poetry collections, and though I am never convinced that standard designs are the best solution, Faber has used model templates for much of its poetry.

RON COSTLEY: FABER POETS

When Ron Costley was design manager at Faber he preferred to work with a self-imposed restricted list of fonts that he felt met most, if not all, eventualities: Sabon, Minion, Utopia, Baskerville, Imprint, Janson, and Garamond. Costley has said, "I prefer to get to know a typeface to the point where it becomes as familiar as my handwriting." Thirty years of designing books left him with a "deposit of formats" in his head that he would refer to consciously or unconsciously when looking at a new text. He invariably uses the same font for display as for the text, generally two point sizes larger than the text. Costley feels that the title is part of the poem and to separate it too much works against that idea, that using a title that is too bold or too large draws the eye to the title on the page rather than to the whole page. Even when one poet wanted the titles of his poems to be in full caps, Costley chose to use small caps but in a slightly larger size than the text. He sometimes centers the poetry block on the page. To determine this, he centers the poem on the maximum text measure and adjusts it so it visually centers under the title. This, of course, assumes either the designer is setting the type or has a chance to see proof and make adjustments. There is always the question: is the poem title to be centered, flush left on the poem, or in some bizarre position that the designer would think visually "interesting"? One poet Costley worked with likened the centered title to a coat hanger, but his preference for a flush left title looked like a hinge opening the poem.

About specific problems, he said he had no general specification about where to break stanzas at the bottom of the page. In cases where a poem ran to a new page, he would begin on the first line at the top of the page. But if it began a new stanza he would drop it to the second line. For turnover lines he preferred to indent 1 em. For a while he put the turnover flush right, but he felt that just introduced another line of white.

At Faber one problem that he had to deal with was poetry set with line numbers. The numbers had to appear close enough to the text to be useful, but not so close as to be read as part of the poem. His solution was to put the numbers on the left of the text and set them smaller than the text.

Costley's specifications for the poetry series are shown on the following pages.

Following pages:
Layouts for Faber poetry series by Ron Costley. Courtesy of Faber and Faber Ltd.

Typesetting Specifications for Faber Poets [previously Poet to poet]

Designer Ron Costley

Date 12/viii/2003

New M/s Offset

M/s complete

Series

Text type Minion 9½/12pt × 84 mm use o.s. figs throughout

Verse 9½/12pt r. left ½ line# between stanzas *

Extracts 9½/12pt indent 1em (9½pts) ½ line# above & below

Drama

Notes end page / end ch / end book 8/10pt r. left × 84 mm

indicated in text by

References

indicated in text by

Tables

Special sorts

Part title 11/12pt CAPS l.#d r. left on T.L.2

Part number

new part – new recto, verso blank

Act heading

198 mm

measure 84 mm ~~picas~~

15 15 mm ~~picas~~

full page = 36 lines of 9½/12pt exclusive

16.5 mm ~~picas~~ head

119 mm

narrow B format

Appendices

Bibliography

Epigraphs see B head

Glossary

Illustrations line tone

Integrated Non-integrated

Captions

Indexes 8/9pt r. left

Chapter title

new page / run on

Chapter number

text lines on ch opening page = 33 lines

Act heading

Sub-headings Spacing –

A head [poem title] 11/12pt rom u&l.c r. left on T.L.2 — new page

B head [epi/dedi] 9½/12pt italic r. left, indent 1em (9½pts)

C head [section nos] 9½/12pt s.c. rom figs or o.s. arabic, indent 1em, 1# above, ½# below

D head [source/date] 8/12pt rom u&l.c, r. left indent 1em, ½# above

E head

AA

Running heads —

Verso —

Recto

Folios 9½/12pt o.s. figs, r. left & right, indent 9½pts, 1½ line# below text

with running heads / at foot

Spec pages

Notes

* indent turned lines 9½ pts

Signed RC 13/x/2003

8/10pt r. left

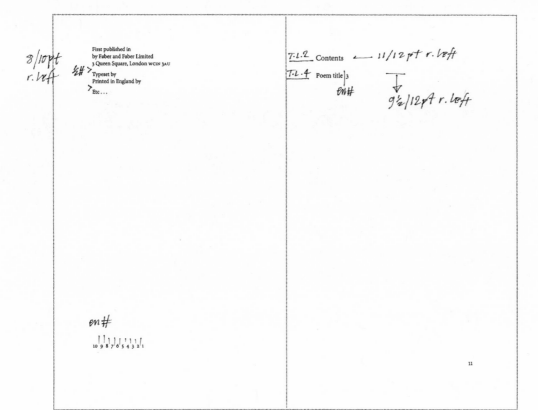

First published in
by Faber and Faber Limited
3 Queen Square, London WC1N 3AU
½# >
Typeset by
Printed in England by
> Etc . . .

en#

10 9 8 7 6 5 4 3 2 1

T.L.2 Contents ← 11/12pt r. left

T.L.4 Poem title 3

en#

9½/12pt r. left

11

T.L.2 (A) Poem Title Range Left

(B) *Epigraph or dedication, etc italic ranged left* – 9½/12pt ital r. left indent 1em

Poem begins

Poems set in 9½/12pt r. left
turnovers indent 1em (9½pts)

4

Poem Title Line — 11/12pt r. left on T.L.2

< 1 line#

Now this particular girl
During a ceremonious April walk
With her latest suitor
Found herself, of a sudden, intolerably struck
By the birds' irregular babel
And the leaves' litter. < ½ line# between stanzas

Now this particular girl
During a ceremonious April walk
With her latest suitor
Found herself, of a sudden, intolerably struck
By the birds' irregular babel
And the leaves' litter.

Now this particular girl
During a ceremonious April walk
With her latest suitor
Found herself, of a sudden, intolerably struck
By the birds' irregular babel
And the leaves' litter.

Now this particular girl
During a ceremonious April walk
With her latest suitor
Found herself, of a sudden, intolerably struck
By the birds' irregular babel
And the leaves' litter.

Now this particular girl
During a ceremonious April walk
With her latest suitor
Found herself, of a sudden, intolerably struck
By the birds' irregular babel
And the leaves' litter.Now this particular girl
During a ceremonious April walk

5

style for anthologies

T.L.1 POET NAME (1890–1960)

< 2 line#

Poem Title

< 1 line#

Now this particular girl
During a ceremonious April walk
With her latest suitor
Found herself, of a sudden, intolerably struck
By the birds' irregular babel
And the leaves' litter.

< ½ line#

Now this particular girl
During a ceremonious April walk
With her latest suitor
Found herself, of a sudden, intolerably struck
By the birds' irregular babel
And the leaves' litter.

Now this particular girl
During a ceremonious April walk
With her latest suitor
Found herself, of a sudden, intolerably struck
By the birds' irregular babel
And the leaves' litter.

Now this particular girl
During a ceremonious April walk
With her latest suitor
Found herself, of a sudden, intolerably struck
By the birds' irregular babel
And the leaves' litter.
Now this particular girl
During a ceremonious April walk

Footnotes 8/10pt
glossary set here ranged left in roman and *italic*
blink o' licht, *beam of light*

f.n. 8/10pt
r. left

14

15

T.L.2 (A) Poem Title Range Left

(B) □ *Epigraph or dedication, etc ranged left 9.5pt*

< 1#

(C) □ [King David]*

< ½#

Now this particular girl
During a ceremonious April walk
With her latest suitor
Found herself, of a sudden, intolerably struck
By the birds' irregular babel
And the leaves' litter.

< ½

Now this particular girl
During a ceremonious April walk
With her latest suitor
Found herself, of a sudden, intolerably struck
By the birds' irregular babel
And the leaves' litter.

< 1#

□ [The Jews]†

< ½#

(C) head

Now this particular girl
During a ceremonious April walk
With her latest suitor
Found herself, of a sudden, intolerably struck
By the birds' irregular babel
And the leaves' litter.

Now this particular girl
During a ceremonious April walk
With her latest suitor
Found herself, of a sudden, intolerably struck
By the birds' irregular babel
And the leaves' litter.

f.n. 8/10pt

*Charles II□†The English

em#

4

1.2

Alexander's Feast; or the Power of Musique

An Ode, in Honour of St Cecilia's Day

(B) head 9½/12pt indent 1em

< 1#

(C) I

< ½#

Now this particular girl
During a ceremonious April walk
With her latest suitor
Found herself, of a sudden, intolerably struck
By the birds' irregular babel
And the leaves' litter.

< 1#

II

< ½#

Now this particular girl
During a ceremonious April walk
With her latest suitor
Found herself, of a sudden, intolerably struck
By the birds' irregular babel
And the leaves' litter.

Now this particular girl
During a ceremonious April walk
With her latest suitor
Found herself, of a sudden, intolerably struck
By the birds' irregular babel
And the leaves' litter.

Now this particular girl
During a ceremonious April walk
With her latest suitor
Found herself, of a sudden, intolerably struck
By the birds' irregular babel
And the leaves' litter.

Now this particular girl
During a ceremonious April walk
With her latest suitor

5

T.L.1 FROM THE GREEK OF HOMER 9½/12pt scs #2

< 2 line#

(A) *from* The Iliad, Book I 11/12pt

< 1 line#

(C) [The Invocation]

< ½#

Now this particular girl
During a ceremonious April walk
With her latest suitor
Found herself, of a sudden, intolerably struck
By the birds' irregular babel
And the leaves' litter.

Now this particular girl
During a ceremonious April walk
With her latest suitor
Found herself, of a sudden, intolerably struck
By the birds' irregular babel
And the leaves' litter.

Now this particular girl
During a ceremonious April walk
With her latest suitor
Found herself, of a sudden, intolerably struck
By the birds' irregular babel
And the leaves' litter.

Now this particular girl
During a ceremonious April walk
With her latest suitor
Found herself, of a sudden, intolerably struck
By the birds' irregular babel
And the leaves' litter.
Now this particular girl
During a ceremonious April walk

f.n. Footnotes 8/10pt
glossary set here ranged left in roman and *italic*

15

Designing Illustrated Books

The first job I had after finishing art school and three years in the army was as designer for the Toledo (the one in Ohio) Museum of Art. Little did I realize that the curators I worked with there were not typical of what I would later encounter. They had some sense of production, kept within budget, made few changes, and knew that schedules actually mattered. In the many years since I worked in Toledo I have not always had such good fortune when working with museum curators.

But on the whole, one should not make books unduly large. One rarely encounters the reverse case: books that are too small.
— Jan Tschichold, *The Form of the Book* (1975), translated by Hajo Hadeler

By their nature, illustrated books are usually far more problematic, requiring uncommon materials, special printers, and larger budgets, and are too often running late. As if those were not already problematic issues, the expected outcome of perfection from artists, editors, and curators is the stuff that makes designers crazy. Even with the tightest of deadlines, editors and authors seem to need alterations up to the last possible minute (and beyond). Aesthetic visions don't always match, catching designers between what they think is right and the taste of the others. The English designer Alan Bartram noted that for him the best artist to work with was a dead one.

When I have asked authors of nonillustrated books about their thoughts on design, most seem concerned only about two things: is the typeface large enough, and what will the jacket look like? However, as many poets care excessively about the way their words are presented, those who create heavily illustrated books are far more invested in the total design.

Designers for nonillustrated books can most often count on having a complete manuscript, even though they might have an unedited version. With illustrated books I have often had the smallest fragment of a project to build a design. Recently a major museum sent me a few manuscript pages with a handful of scans and asked me to design sample pages for a new catalog. They had wanted the book to make 176 pages, but there were 85 images that each took two text pages no matter how small I made the type. I hoped they would see the problem from my samples, but the only reaction I got was the curator didn't think my typeface choices would work well with the ones being used for the exhibit (how would I have known?) and they wanted much larger margins in a design that was already too tight to accommodate additional text.

■ Incomplete information about the contents is just one of the problems on projects like this. Not knowing who the printer might be has its own complications: How should the scans be dealt with? Who would supply the profiles to adjust the scans for proper color in printing, and at what point in the process? What trim sizes might be best for the eventual printer? Is there time to manufacture off shore?

Unlike nonillustrated books, which are most often done to standard book sizes, there is more flexibility in the formats for art books. Jost Hochuli in his splendid *Designing Books* (Hyphen Press, 1996) rightly says that illustrated books need to be large so that images are large enough to see the details clearly. He suggests that the reader should be able to take in the image "with one look." However, he warns that such a book is best not larger than 30 cm (11.8 inches). Mitchell and Wightman in their very useful manual *Book Typography* (Libanus Press, 2005) say: "As with all publishing decisions, it is a matter of finding a balance between aesthetic, practical, technical, and business considerations."

Large format books call for different thinking about how type is arranged, often in multiple columns, sidebars, and extended captions. A grid system as described by Kristina Kachele in this chapter is the best way to organize a lot of information. The choice of a typeface for the text and for the captions should relate visually both to each other and to the artwork by their weight and color and possibly to the period of the art itself. Mitchell and Wightman suggest sans serif because of its "neutral feel."

I agree with Jim Wageman's position noted earlier in this book: a design approach that ignores the demands of the material is a design failing. At the same time Jim could also see the value in placing historical art in a context of our present day, giving it, as he said, "renewed life."

Authors and editors of illustrated books have an ideal vision for the way the art should be sized and sequenced, but sometimes what they think will happen cannot be done. Art that should be on facing pages ends up not being possible for many reasons. I always ask for guidance on sizing for illustrations (which ones should be large or small) and if photos may be cropped, bled, or run across a spread. It is also one of the only times I have the temerity to ask if text can be edited, especially for captions. I truly dislike both abbreviations (for example, in., fig.) and inch marks (″) and loathe making the "x" indicating measurements a sans serif if the caption is otherwise set in a serif type.

While it is always nice to have a beautifully illustrated, lavishly produced art book as a sample of one's work, I'd much rather have an encyclopedia to design. In the following section two designers who are far more patient (and skilled) than I write about how they work.

KRISTINA KACHELE

I came to book design through photography. My early interest and training were in fine-art photography, and when I began learning book design, I could think of no better combination than designing fine-art photography books. As a book designer, I seek to enhance and enliven the content without interfering with or complicating the author's intent. As a means of facilitating communication with clients, authors, photographers, and editors, several years ago I devised a comprehensive checklist (see next page) that details every aspect of a book's design and production, including questions like who will approve the design, what the author's expectations are, what limitations exist on the use of illustrations in the text or on the cover, and whether the illustrations will be provided as digital files or original art.

■ I begin a design by reading the supporting material provided by the publisher, including editorial memos, new-book descriptions, transmittal forms, estimates, author's requests and preferences, and comments from the production manager or art director. I have in the past—though less frequently now—received copies of readers' reports, the outside reviews that most scholarly manuscripts must undergo before publication. These materials together convey the author's content and ideas, the publisher's marketing strategy, and the press's preferences and aspirations for the design. Once I've read through the background material, I thumb through the manuscript to get a good grasp on the content. For collections of short stories, I'll read at least the title story and a few others; for longer fiction, as much of the manuscript as possible; for anthologies of essays, the volume editor's introduction and a sampling of other chapters; for nonfiction, the same. For illustrated books, I read key sections of the manuscript to help me understand the author's interpretation of the pictures or plates.

Most monograph and trade book assignments have the trim size and desired page count already set, but for illustrated books, I may be asked to suggest these specifications after I review the art, text, and background materials. In such cases, early communication (such as my checklist initiates) really helps. For example, I was once asked to design a long text with many lovely illustrations of the work of a well-known stained-glass artist. The publisher did not envision a coffee-table book so planned for a 7 × 10 inch trim. I suggested opening the width to 8½ inches to allow more room for the horizontal art while keeping within a similar price range for printing a 7 × 10 inch book. The publisher was agreeable, in part because the increased trim fit the book into fewer pages and roughly compensated for any increase in the cost of printing a larger size.

When designing photography books, one of my primary concerns is to be sensitive to the artist's preferences concerning stylistic decisions that will in-

Design

INTERIOR

Trim size
Estimated (or target) page count
Cast-off or desired characters/page
Schedule for
- rough sketches to client? *(if applicable or needed)*
- comments back to design?
- final layouts?

- can layouts be delivered as pdfs or are printouts required? if pdfs, by email ok?
- how are layouts presented in-house and to author
  - by art director or production manager? by editor?
  - in group meeting?
  - by circulation?
- who approves layouts?
  - art director / production manager
  - editor / author
  - marketing / sales
  - press director
  - others

Please list all text elements (or attach in-house checklist)

Please list all text elements to be shown in samples (or attach in-house checklist)

How are illustrations to be handled?
- Are there any restrictions on use, especially if this is a fine art book?
  - ok to crop? bleed? can type overprint?
- Are illustrations to be full page, 1/2 page, quarter page?
- Can details of illustrations be used as design elements? any to be avoided?

- Will the author/artist or institution have approval of page proofs? color proofs?
- Other concerns/issues?

(continued)

INTERIOR *(continued)*

ART DIRECTION

Please give as much detailed information as possible about what is desired in this text design. Color palette (if applicable), degree of complexity in design, specific art or imagery to be used or avoided, typographic style (classic, historical, modern, post-modern, scholarly, etc). Sample books/titles that express your desired style, feel, or look are especially helpful. Also useful are titles of competing books.

(please continue on the back or attach additional pages as needed)

Please describe the author's expected involvement in the design process and/or the author's expectations for this design. This is especially relevant for fine art/photography and illustrated books.

FEE

Can this job be billed in stages, such as a % at approval of design layouts, then at first page proofs and the final bill at delivery of final files?

COMPOSITION

Has compositor been selected yet?
- if so, please give contact info
- if not, please provide list of possible suppliers
  - if not, will designer see sample pages? page proofs?
- will designer be compositor?
  - if so, will written specs be required? when will these be needed?
- will detailed layouts with specs be required or will InDesign files provided to compositor, with additional needed instructions, satisfy present and future needs?

Has manuscript been fully copy-edited?
- do you expect corrections at page proofs to be light or heavy?

Please attach any house style sheets for composition
- or include instructions for: acronyms, running heads, rules for hyphenation, house guidelines for widows/orphans, old style vs. lining figures, number of lines on the last page of a chapter, etc.

Method for supplying page proofs:
- Will you need pdf files, printouts or both?
- If printouts, how many sets?
- If larger than 8-1/2 x 11, can printouts be scaled down to 8-1/2 x 11 with one master set at full size?

SCHEDULE
- Final manuscript and specs to comp or design
- Desired date for first proofs (or no. of weeks from delivery of final mss files)*
- First pass back for corrections (or no. of weeks from delivery of first proofs)
- Second pass due to Press (or no. of weeks from receipt of corrections to first pass)
- Final corrections to design/comp (or no. of weeks from last pass)
- Final files due to Press / Final files to printer
- Number of weeks to bluelines/first proofs from printer
- Desired ship date of bound books

If more than two passes of proofs/corrections are anticipated, please note how many passes and how many weeks between each pass.

**If Kachele Design is compositor, please allow at least 4 weeks from final manuscript and/or approved design samples to first page proofs and 2 weeks between each pass. If faster turn-around times are required, please let us know at the start of the project and we will do our best to accomodate your needs.*

FEE

Production

ART

How will the art be supplied? *(please list the number of each)*
- digital? transparencies? slides? prints?

IF DIGITAL:
- Are files consistently sized?
- Is the resolution of the files consistent (at least 300 dpi)?
- Who will be responsible for sizing? prepress?*
  - **prepress would include conversion to cmyk, any needed adjustments for color balance, dot gain, contrast, etc.*
- What is the color space and file format of the files (rgb/cmyk; tif, jpg, eps)?
  - *Please supply an art log if possible. If not, please advise if one will be needed by your press.*
- Will designer or compositor place final lo- or high-res image files?
  - If not, what is the prepress plan?

Has the printer been selected for this project?
- Will this book be printed domestically or overseas?
- Will designer solicit and/or evaluate printers' estimates, assign the job, or otherwise oversee the manufacturing of this book?

Have text stock and binding materials been selected?
- If so, please supply
  - ppi of paper
  - list of binding materials (if designer will be selecting colors, etc)

SCHEDULE FOR PROOFING ART

What kind of proofs, if any, will you receive from the printer or prepress house?

Will designer be asked to review proofs?
- If so, what will the turnaround time be?
- Will designer give final approval of proofs?

How many rounds of proofs do you anticipate?

ARCHIVING

What will you need for your digital archive for this book?
What are your e-book requirements, if any?

FEE

fluence the conceptual tone of the book or impact how the work is presented. Many photographers have begun their collaboration with me somewhat on edge, anxious about what fate their art will suffer during design and production. For some artists, a book is akin to an exhibition between two covers, and they are apprehensive about their work being cropped, bled over, made too small (or large), unnecessarily edited, and/or resequenced. As a former photographer, I understand these concerns, and try to reassure authors, editors, and photographers that I will incorporate their ideas and preferences into the design as much as possible. In general, a collaborative approach fosters a productive and satisfying relationship between me and the author/artist.

Designing *The Plazas of New Mexico*

The Plazas of New Mexico presented the challenges inherent in both a long, scholarly text and an art/photography/illustrated book. This book combines cultural history, historic preservation, architecture, urban planning, and photography, and includes architectural plans, drawings, maps, elevations and diagrams, as well as historic and contemporary photographs. There are eight essays by various authors in each of these disciplines describing the history and culture of plazas in New Mexico, followed by a longer section that presents a portrait of each plaza in detail (twenty-two in all). The tricultural nature of New Mexico and its plazas (Anglo, Hispanic, Pueblo) is one of the key features of the book and something I wanted to capture in the design, requiring solutions similar to those in most art and photography books: how to merge image and text to meet the expectations of a highly visual audience (author, artists, and readers) and how to keep the book within a manageable budget while creating a visually appealing object. At the same time, as a multidisciplinary study of every town and city plaza in the state of New Mexico, the text is not secondary to the art and needed to be legible and inviting, yet weighty in appearance and tone.

The design of *Plazas* began with a conference call between the press director, the main author, the photographer, and me. Using my checklist, we discussed overall design and production parameters, including the general size and shape of the book, approximately how many illustrations would be included, what format I would need for the electronic files, and a general timetable. Two years later, the manuscript was ready for design. With the press's permission, I then met with the authors to discuss in greater detail the approach they wanted in the design. We looked at other titles similar to their book, making note of effective solutions to design issues we expected to face. We chose the trim size based on several factors: the shape of the contemporary photographs (all wide, narrow panoramas); our desire for a pleasing shape—something almost square, rather than the long rectangle of a standard 9 × 12 inch trim; and the need to fit enough text on the page to keep the length of the book manageable *and* be big enough to accommodate detailed architectural plans and elevations. An 11 × 10 inch book satisfied each of these needs: it was close to a square shape; wide enough to fit the panoramas and plans; deep enough to fit (if needed) several illustrations and text on a page; and not so oversized that it was unwieldy to hold or that it would send the budget through the roof.

Next, the lead author, Chris Wilson, requested a roman/classical ("chiseled") approach to the typography. He later followed with this note to me and the other contributors, intended to summarize our conversation and invite input from the others before I began to design in earnest: "A serif type for the text, and either a san [*sic*] serif type or a very clean serif type for the headings. The overall sensibility for the book, typefaces, etc., is something contemporary but grounded in history. Perhaps type subtly evoking roman chiseled lettering, Spanish Colonial documents, 1920/30s city beautiful/architectural monographs but with a contemporary feel."

Finally, during that meeting I realized that while we had planned to print duotone (two colors), we could likely print four-color process for approximately the same price since the difference between prepress, proofing, and printing two or four colors would be minimal. The photographer liked this idea and was excited by the possibilities that four-color printing offered. I reported our discussion to the press director and the editor, who were enthusiastic about printing in color but concerned about cost. They shared their vision for the design of the book with me at that point: "We'd like a contemporary, elegant design with a traditional typeface that has distinction; nothing trendy; contemporary but esteemed/classic."

Meanwhile, research conducted in bookstores, online, in book show and other design catalogs, and elsewhere had provided some inspiration for my work on this book, but a few ideas in particular, gleaned from a session at the annual meeting of university presses that year, largely informed my approach:

- maximum *effectiveness* of the shape of the page
- maximum *use* of the space *on* the page and spread
- the importance of restraint but also of playfulness
- use of small type for captions to simplify the layout, create variety in the color of the type, and establish hierarchies of information
- faith and trust in the reader to understand the page: that is, place all captions in one grouping on the spread, or in a central/consistent location (rather than under each image), in order to minimize "noise" on the spread and simplify the grid
- careful consideration of front matter pages (so they don't look like an afterthought): the contents page, the dedication page, the copyright page, etc.

I began sketching the page layout for *Plazas* while exploring typefaces, since text fit was an essential consideration for this long book. With a 450-page manuscript, one column text would have been inefficient, and three columns, too hard to read, yielding too much type on the page, and a look that was too "textbook." Two fairly wide columns created the right look and feel, and allowed comfortable, efficient pacing of art and text, especially in the long first chapter, which has the greatest number of run-in images, and in the third section on communities, where all the drawings are at the same scale yet vary widely in size.

For the most efficient placement of elements on the page, I set the captions in the foot margin, sometimes in one group for the entire page or spread. This space is often used for running feet, especially in illustrated books in which running *heads* would interfere with the placement of illustrations or create a busy-looking page. I could do this in *Plazas* because most of the captions are only one or two lines and the illustration they describe is generally clear. The decision not to place captions under every illustration created more room on each spread for art to run as large as possible and to extend illustrations into the head and side margins as needed, allowing a lot of flexibility during page makeup. Given these factors (the head and foot of the page reserved for images and captions) and the nature of the material (architectural plans), I set the part and chapter titles together as a side-head on just the recto page, with part titles in a heavier weight. This treatment still gave the reader enough information to navigate this long book and added a pleasing visual accent to each spread (see Figure 1).

As I mentioned earlier, *Plazas* combines the demands of a long, scholarly text with those of an architecture/photography book, and presents a somewhat different set of demands than many fine art/photography/illustrated books. In many illustrated books—especially fine art/photography books—the text is placed apart from the images, in front or in back, with the images in a gallery as the central focus of the book. Such an arrangement reflects a gallery or museum exhibition with wall text to be read before entering the main exhibition space where the art is presented unencumbered by words. This is a very traditional approach to the photographic monograph, and many photographers envision their book in this light. In *Plazas*, the art is engaged in a continual dialogue with the text and may illustrate specific facts and ideas or provide additional visual information that adds to the reader's understanding. In the case of the contemporary photographs, which often do not *directly* illustrate the text, they serve an emotional, social, or conceptual purpose by presenting a moment in contemporary life, helping the reader see the plazas as lived-in spaces. In either case, it was important to place the art on the same page or spread as its accompanying text as much as possible, and my challenge was to create a grid that could support these multilayered conversa-

HISTORY | CENTER PLACE, PLAZA, SQUARE

1960 Chevy low-rider with its top down, dragging a turban-wearing effigy of Osama bin Laden.

The spectators two or three deep along main street at the start, fall in at the tail of the parade as it ambles the eleven blocks to the old plaza. As the parade crosses the Gallinas River—demarcation between east and west—and climbs the final block to the plaza, rock music, and fire engine sirens echo off the brick and stone business fronts. The crowd six to eight deep along Bridge Street joins those already trailing the parade as perhaps 2,500 people spill into the plaza. One-story adobes standing shoulder-to-shoulder with two- and three-story rail-era business blocks enclose the plaza. Overhead, mature elms and a scattering of sycamores form a tall, arching canopy. Each multigenerational family soon sets out blankets and folding chairs to define its own small territory and settles in to await the program of historical reenactments and music on the central gazebo.

Las Vegas's Fourth of July Fiesta—embedded as it is within a historic plaza and Main Street—resembles the annual celebrations of a hundred other New Mexico communities. Many studies of public spaces focus on their physical attributes, and the cultural, economic, and political forces that have shaped those spaces—what theorists term the "production of space." But this study, like other recent scholarship, also examines the more ephemeral web of memory and myth, of celebrations and everyday interactions that combine with the physical setting to create and sustain a community's identity—what is sometimes referred to as the "social construction of place."[1]

People have been creating plazas in New Mexico for over a thousand years, and with its three distinct cultural traditions, the state may well have the most varied set of community spaces in the United States. As early as 700 AD, ancestors of Pueblo Indians were building compact villages, and by 1000 AD, these surrounded clearly defined plazas. To this day, the cycles of ceremonial dances of the eighteen pueblos in New Mexico focus in each village plaza. Spanish colonists brought their own urban tradition, and from the founding of Santa Fe in 1610 to La Union in 1882, and in dozens of settlements between, the Spanish and their descendants initiated new villages by laying out a plaza. Even in Anglo-American towns that clustered along Main Streets after the arrival of the railroad in 1879, civic boosters avidly developed courthouse squares much like those of the South, Midwest, and Great Plains states.

Each of these three town-planning traditions includes both a public space form and the particular building types that conventionally shape the uses of those spaces. Terraced residential blocks and ceremonial *kivas* mark Pueblo plazas as primarily domestic and religious spaces. A prominently located church and surrounding courtyard houses imparted a similar character to the earliest Spanish and Mexican communities, while business blocks surrounding a courthouse and its square reflect the growing importance of commerce and government in Anglo-American towns at the end of the nineteenth century. Each cultural tradition, likewise, reinforced community identity with characteristic celebrations: ritual dances to ensure bountiful crops and hunting at the pueblos; religious processions asserting Catholic beliefs, and folk dramas recalling local conquest history in Spanish plazas; and Fourth of July and Old-Timers Day parades around Anglo courthouse squares celebrating national and local identities. Indeed, as people sought to establish and sustain their communities, these ensembles of open space, special building types, and community celebrations provided a vessel into which they could pour their energies, aspirations, and shared dreams.

PUEBLO CENTER-PLACES

Puebloan Villages

The characteristic components of a Pueblo village—and by implication the Pueblo worldview—began to coalesce about 700 AD. Earlier hunter-gatherers had lived in semi-subterranean pithouses at dispersed seasonal camps. But villages became more fixed and substantial after corn, beans, and squash arrived from central Mexico. At first, people continued to live in pithouses, and built above-ground, rectangular rooms to store agricultural surpluses. But in time, they moved into these above-ground rooms and began to excavate their pithouses deeper until their roofs were flush with the ground. These underground chambers were likely the first kivas.[2]

A typical village of the 700s and 800s had from ten to twenty connected rooms organized in a southeast-facing arc with a few circular chambers—whether pithouses or kivas—to the southeast. From 900 to 1050, the largest villages grew to two stories and one hundred rooms with a few kivas. Builders turned the tall blank walls of their multistory buildings to the northerly winter winds and stepped down to the southeast to absorb the warmth of the rising sun. These southeast-facing, stepping forms protected outdoor living spaces on the roof terraces and in the sheltered plaza. The remains of cooking hearths placed in front of them, and the presence of kivas nearby, suggest that these packed earthen plazas were the sites of everyday domestic life as well as religious ritual.

The number of rooms and formality of village plans increased significantly in the years 1050 to 1300, especially in the so-called Great Houses of up to a thousand rooms. If earlier villages had been constructed incrementally a few rooms at a time, the Great Houses rose in organized building campaigns over a few years. The unifying, highly finished stone veneers and geometrically precise D-shapes and rectangular villages suggest formal planning and an

11

Figure 1

tions, with at least some text on almost every spread, and illustrations on most (see Figures 2 and 3).

I decided on Arnhem (Blond) for the text. Its strong color and tight fit made it a good choice for a two-column format. Additionally, Scala Sans had been used in some of the drawings following a decision made two years prior as the preparation of plans and drawings got under way. At that time, Scala Sans seemed an appropriate choice among typefaces available to the architects preparing the art. It was a face I was accustomed to working with, and I thought Scala would be relatively easy to incorporate into the rest of the book's design later. I decided to use Scala Sans for the captions as well to give the book some continuity between art and text (see Figure 4).

Figure 2

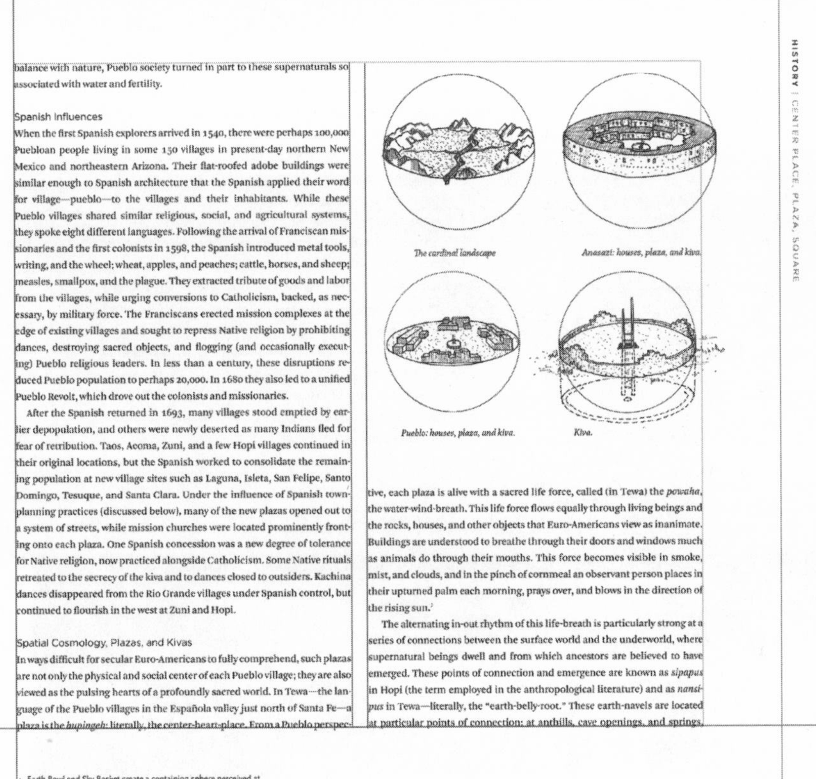

balance with nature, Pueblo society turned in part to these supernaturals so associated with water and fertility.

Spanish Influences

When the first Spanish explorers arrived in 1540, there were perhaps 100,000 Puebloan people living in some 150 villages in present-day northern New Mexico and northeastern Arizona. Their flat-roofed adobe buildings were similar enough to Spanish architecture that the Spanish applied their word for village—pueblo—to the villages and their inhabitants. While these Pueblo villages shared similar religious, social, and agricultural systems, they spoke eight different languages. Following the arrival of Franciscan missionaries and the first colonists in 1598, the Spanish introduced metal tools, writing, and the wheel; wheat, apples, and peaches; cattle, horses, and sheep; measles, smallpox, and the plague. They extracted tribute of goods and labor from the villages, while urging conversions to Catholicism, backed, as necessary, by military force. The Franciscans erected mission complexes at the edge of existing villages and sought to repress Native religion by prohibiting dances, destroying sacred objects, and flogging (and occasionally executing) Pueblo religious leaders. In less than a century, these disruptions reduced Pueblo population to perhaps 20,000. In 1680 they also led to a unified Pueblo Revolt, which drove out the colonists and missionaries.

After the Spanish returned in 1693, many villages stood emptied by earlier depopulation, and others were newly deserted as many Indians fled for fear of retribution. Taos, Acoma, Zuni, and a few Hopi villages continued in their original locations, but the Spanish worked to consolidate the remaining population at new village sites such as Laguna, Isleta, San Felipe, Santo Domingo, Tesuque, and Santa Clara. Under the influence of Spanish town-planning practices (discussed below), many of the new plazas opened out to a system of streets, while mission churches were located prominently fronting onto each plaza. One Spanish concession was a new degree of tolerance for Native religion, now practiced alongside Catholicism. Some Native rituals retreated to the secrecy of the kiva and to dances closed to outsiders. Kachina dances disappeared from the Rio Grande villages under Spanish control, but continued to flourish in the west at Zuni and Hopi.

Spatial Cosmology, Plazas, and Kivas

In ways difficult for secular Euro-Americans to fully comprehend, such plazas are not only the physical and social center of each Pueblo village; they are also viewed as the pulsing hearts of a profoundly sacred world. In Tewa—the language of the Pueblo villages in the Española valley just north of Santa Fe—a plaza is the *bupingeh*: literally, the center-heart-place. From a Pueblo perspective, each plaza is alive with a sacred life force, called (in Tewa) the *powaha*, the water-wind-breath. This life force flows equally through living beings and the rocks, houses, and other objects that Euro-Americans view as inanimate. Buildings are understood to breathe through their doors and windows much as animals do through their mouths. This force becomes visible in smoke, mist, and clouds, and in the pinch of cornmeal an observant person places in their upturned palm each morning, prays over, and blows in the direction of the rising sun.[2]

The alternating in-out rhythm of this life-breath is particularly strong at a series of connections between the surface world and the underworld, where supernatural beings dwell and from which ancestors are believed to have emerged. These points of connection and emergence are known as *sipapus* in Hopi (the term employed in the anthropological literature) and as *nansipus* in Tewa—literally, the "earth-belly-root." These earth-navels are located at particular points of connection: at anthills, cave openings, and springs,

The cardinal landscape

Anasazi: houses, plaza, and kiva.

Pueblo: houses, plaza, and kiva.

Kiva.

Earth Bowl and Sky Basket create a containing sphere perceived at various scales in the Pueblo landscape. Jeremy Iowa and Rina Swentzell.

Figure 3

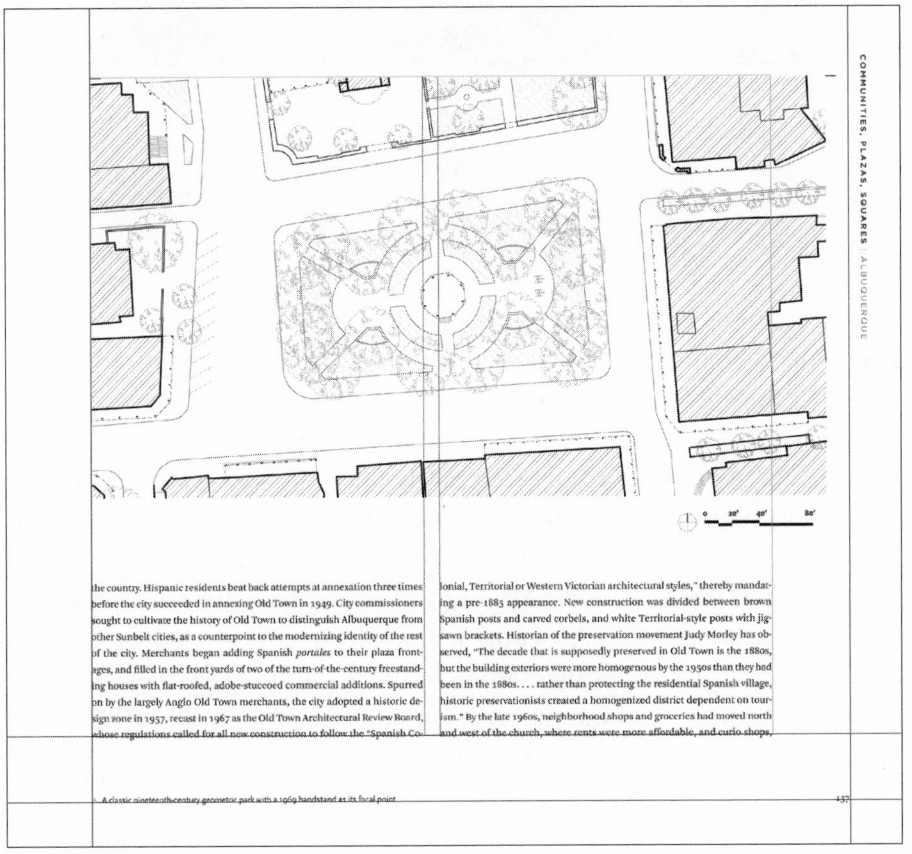

the country. Hispanic residents beat back attempts at annexation three times before the city succeeded in annexing Old Town in 1949. City commissioners sought to cultivate the history of Old Town to distinguish Albuquerque from other Sunbelt cities, as a counterpoint to the modernizing identity of the rest of the city. Merchants began adding Spanish *portales* to their plaza frontages, and filled in the front yards of two of the turn-of-the-century freestanding houses with flat-roofed, adobe-stuccoed commercial additions. Spurred on by the largely Anglo Old Town merchants, the city adopted a historic design zone in 1957, recast in 1967 as the Old Town Architectural Review Board, whose regulations called for all new construction to follow the "Spanish Colonial, Territorial or Western Victorian architectural styles," thereby mandating a pre-1885 appearance. New construction was divided between brown Spanish posts and carved corbels, and white Territorial-style posts with jigsawn brackets. Historian of the preservation movement Judy Morley has observed, "The decade that is supposedly preserved in Old Town is the 1880s, but the building exteriors were more homogenous by the 1950s than they had been in the 1880s. . . . rather than protecting the residential Spanish village, historic preservationists created a homogenized district dependent on tourism." By the late 1960s, neighborhood shops and groceries had moved north and west of the church, where rents were more affordable, and curio shops,

A classic nineteenth-century geometric park with a 1969 bandstand as its focal point

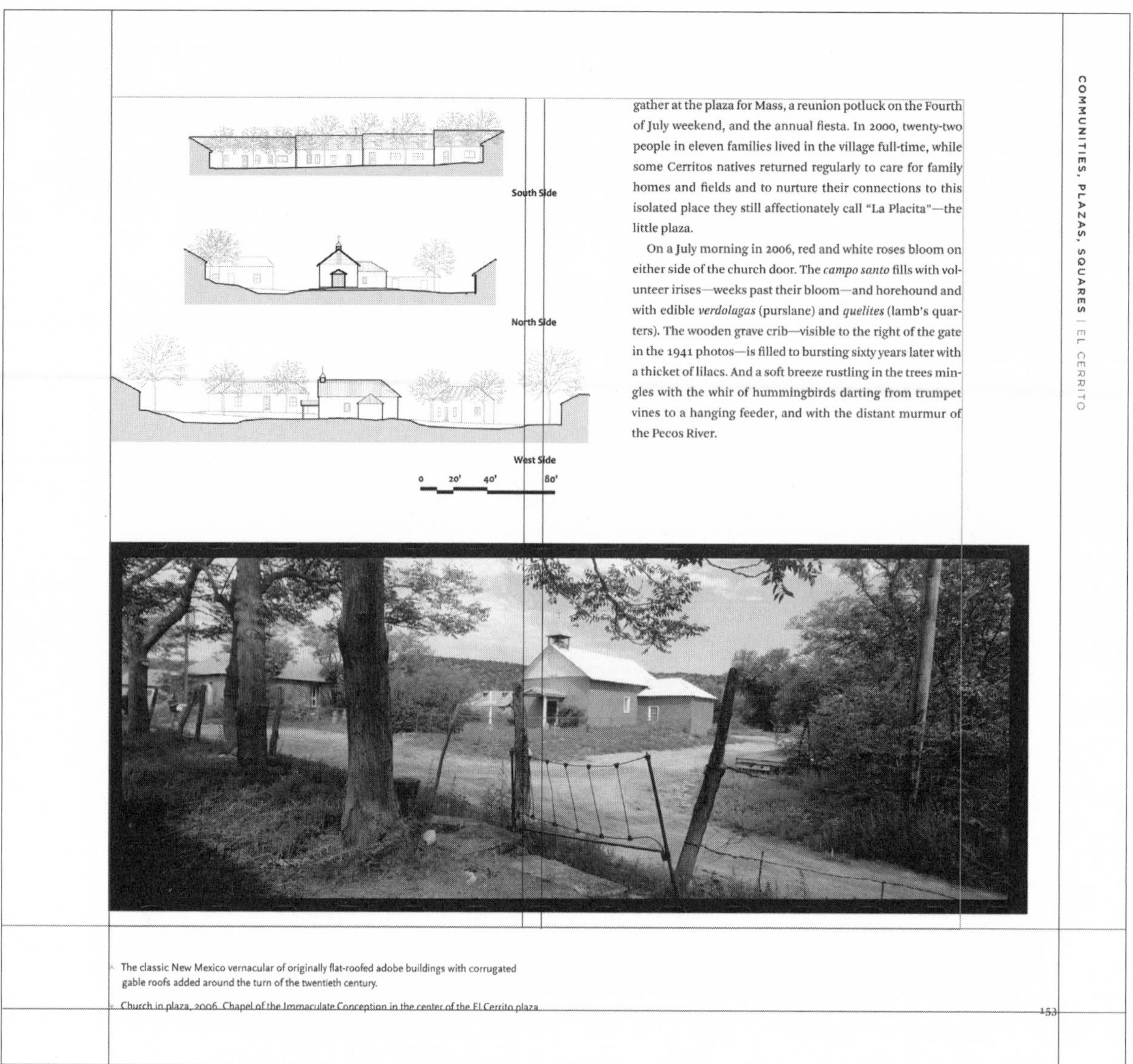

COMMUNITIES, PLAZAS, SQUARES | EL CERRITO

gather at the plaza for Mass, a reunion potluck on the Fourth of July weekend, and the annual fiesta. In 2000, twenty-two people in eleven families lived in the village full-time, while some Cerritos natives returned regularly to care for family homes and fields and to nurture their connections to this isolated place they still affectionately call "La Placita"—the little plaza.

On a July morning in 2006, red and white roses bloom on either side of the church door. The *campo santo* fills with volunteer irises—weeks past their bloom—and horehound and with edible *verdolagas* (purslane) and *quelites* (lamb's quarters). The wooden grave crib—visible to the right of the gate in the 1941 photos—is filled to bursting sixty years later with a thicket of lilacs. And a soft breeze rustling in the trees mingles with the whir of hummingbirds darting from trumpet vines to a hanging feeder, and with the distant murmur of the Pecos River.

^ The classic New Mexico vernacular of originally flat-roofed adobe buildings with corrugated gable roofs added around the turn of the twentieth century.

v Church in plaza, 2006. Chapel of the Immaculate Conception in the center of the El Cerrito plaza.

153

Figure 4

In choosing a display face, after researching roman-inspired type for many days to find something suitable (a contemporary face that referenced the chiseled look the author requested), I concluded that "roman chiseled" typography (like Trajan) was not appropriate for this topic. This book is a monumental study of the history and cultural significance of New Mexico's plazas; but the plazas themselves are not monumental spaces—not, for example, like the National Mall in Washington, D.C., which from a visit the previous summer was fresh in my mind. Plazas and building types here in New Mexico are more human in scale. The grand nature of "roman chiseled" typography did not seem to represent these more intimate public spaces. Since the authors and the press also wanted a design that was clean and contemporary, elegant and learned, once I determined a chiseled face did not work, I felt free

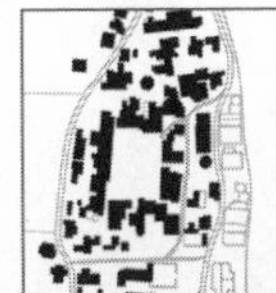  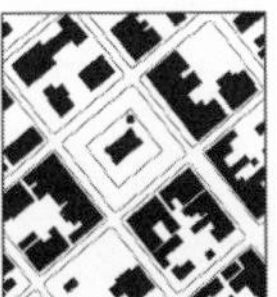

2. CENTER PLACE, PLAZA, SQUARE | Three Traditions of Place Making

CHRIS WILSON

Saturday morning, the sixth of July, 2002—an election year, and the first celebration of the annual Fourth of July Fiestas since 9/11. A parade is making its way down Main Street on its way to the plaza. It is a short journey from east Las Vegas, the 1879 Anglo-American railroad new town, to the heart of west Las Vegas, the 1835 Mexican colonial village less than a mile away. Many of the forty-eight parade entries celebrate a Hispanic identity rooted in northern New Mexico. Others promote businesses or political candidates. Many, of course, express a heartfelt patriotism.

Police cars, an American Legion color guard, and the Grand Marshall riding in a Humvee lead the way. Then comes a four-foot-tall portrait of the Virgin of Guadalupe mounted on a decorated pickup, the Fiesta Queen and her court, and two men dressed as Franciscan friars on foot accompanied by four conquistadors, and an Indian chief (wearing both face paint and aviator sunglasses). One float features a young woman dressed as the Statue of Liberty, another a boy in poncho and sombrero with three girls in buckskin dresses, headbands, and long, tightly braided pigtails.

Convertibles carrying Miss Las Vegas 2002, fiesta queens and their courts from neighboring Mora and Taos, and both toddler and senior-center royalty intermix with cars carrying soon-to-be-governor Bill Richardson, U.S. Representative Tom Udall, and State Attorney General Patricia Madrid. Government and business entries include a Smokey Bear mascot and a huge Las Vegas Towing truck, pulling a medium-sized truck, pulling an average-sized tow truck. One float carries a young man on a cross, wearing a crown of thorns and a blood-soaked sheet, accompanied by a young Hispanic evangelist exhorting the crowd over his PA, "If you let him into your heart, Jesus Christ will save you."

Two northern New Mexican bar bands on flatbed trucks blare out not only "Stairway to Heaven" and "Johnny B. Goode" but also "El Mosquito" and "Rancho Grande." One group of nine horseback riders carries U.S., state, and sheriff posse flags, while a second group of nineteen ride quietly by, two abreast. La Familia Racing stockcars gunning their engines and firetrucks flashing their lights announce the end of the parade, followed by a polished

9

Figure 5

to explore a variety of contemporary faces from my collection. Not long before, I had added Gotham to my type library. I originally avoided it for this book because it seemed too urban (too "New York") for New Mexico. But I tried Gotham and realized it had the look, weight, and feel I wanted. And in the end its own story as an American vernacular face connected to notions of urban renewal seemed to fit with the agenda of *Plazas*, which is not just to preserve plaza spaces as historic moments in New Mexico's past but to present them as vital communal spaces for New Mexico today (see Figure 5).

The design was beginning to take shape yet still I needed a unifying visual strategy to express the grandeur of the project, the open space of New Mexico land and sky, and the multiple layers of information this book brings to light. I attended a talk by the designer D. J. Stout, who shared his view that effective

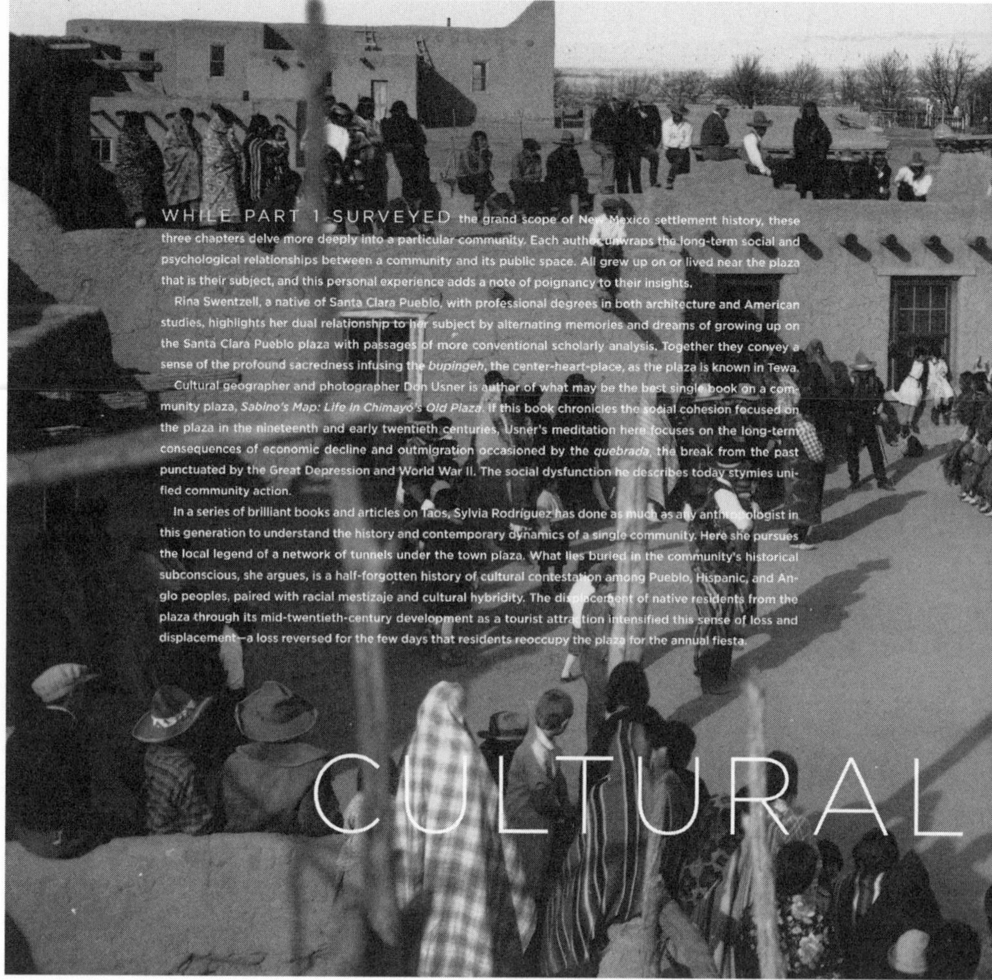

WHILE PART 1 SURVEYED the grand scope of New Mexico settlement history, these three chapters delve more deeply into a particular community. Each author unwraps the long-term social and psychological relationships between a community and its public space. All grew up on or lived near the plaza that is their subject, and this personal experience adds a note of poignancy to their insights.

Rina Swentzell, a native of Santa Clara Pueblo, with professional degrees in both architecture and American studies, highlights her dual relationship to her subject by alternating memories and dreams of growing up on the Santa Clara Pueblo plaza with passages of more conventional scholarly analysis. Together they convey a sense of the profound sacredness infusing the *bupingeh*, the center-heart-place, as the plaza is known in Tewa.

Cultural geographer and photographer Don Usner is author of what may be the best single book on a community plaza, *Sabino's Map: Life in Chimayó's Old Plaza*. If this book chronicles the social cohesion focused on the plaza in the nineteenth and early twentieth centuries, Usner's meditation here focuses on the long-term consequences of economic decline and outmigration occasioned by the *quebrada*, the break from the past punctuated by the Great Depression and World War II. The social dysfunction he describes today stymies unified community action.

In a series of brilliant books and articles on Taos, Sylvia Rodríguez has done as much as any anthropologist in this generation to understand the history and contemporary dynamics of a single community. Here she pursues the local legend of a network of tunnels under the town plaza. What lies buried in the community's historical subconscious, she argues, is a half-forgotten history of cultural contestation among Pueblo, Hispanic, and Anglo peoples, paired with racial mestizaje and cultural hybridity. The displacement of native residents from the plaza through its mid-twentieth-century development as a tourist attraction intensified this sense of loss and displacement—a loss reversed for the few days that residents reoccupy the plaza for the annual fiesta.

CULTURAL

design impacts its audience on an emotional level and changes its perception of the content. His ideas articulated the questions I was trying to answer in designing this project: How to infuse emotional resonance in this design? How, through the design, to affect the reader's perceptions of the topic? I knew that I could secure scans of the contemporary photographs at large sizes if I needed them, and that the photographer would allow me to use his images graphically. Plus the expanse of his panoramas suggests the sense of open space that is part of the experience of living in New Mexico. I arrived at what now seems an obvious solution and enlarged the images to bleed fully across the spread in the front matter and at each part opening. The first several pages of the book show images from two of the three cultural traditions described in the text as a way of suggesting the dialogue between them (in historical order: Pueblo and Hispanic). In between those images, I placed the title spread, using details of a plaza plan from each of the three traditions—again suggesting that dialogue (Pueblo, Hispanic, Anglo). Hoping to persuade

Figure 6

the press to print in color, I used a full bleed image on each part title with a wash of color over it; the color allowed me to print the part title text on the same spread, saving two pages each time (see Figures 6, 7, 8, and 9).

By this time, I had printing estimates showing the difference between four-color process and two-color (duotone) printing. We knew where the prepress would be done, so I also knew that the color proofs, whether two or four color, would be done digitally. The main difference was in the cost of plates and, possibly, a small difference in setup on press. With this in mind, my final sketches showed two versions of the design: one in two colors (black plus gray) and one in four-color process. The four-color version was so much livelier—and would also allow us to print historical images in color when appropriate to the original—that the press agreed to the slight increase in cost, a difference of about 10 percent (even less as print quantity increased). I could now use color to interrupt the (potential) visual monotony of a 336-page book full of black-and-white images and drawings, adding variety and freshness to the layout in

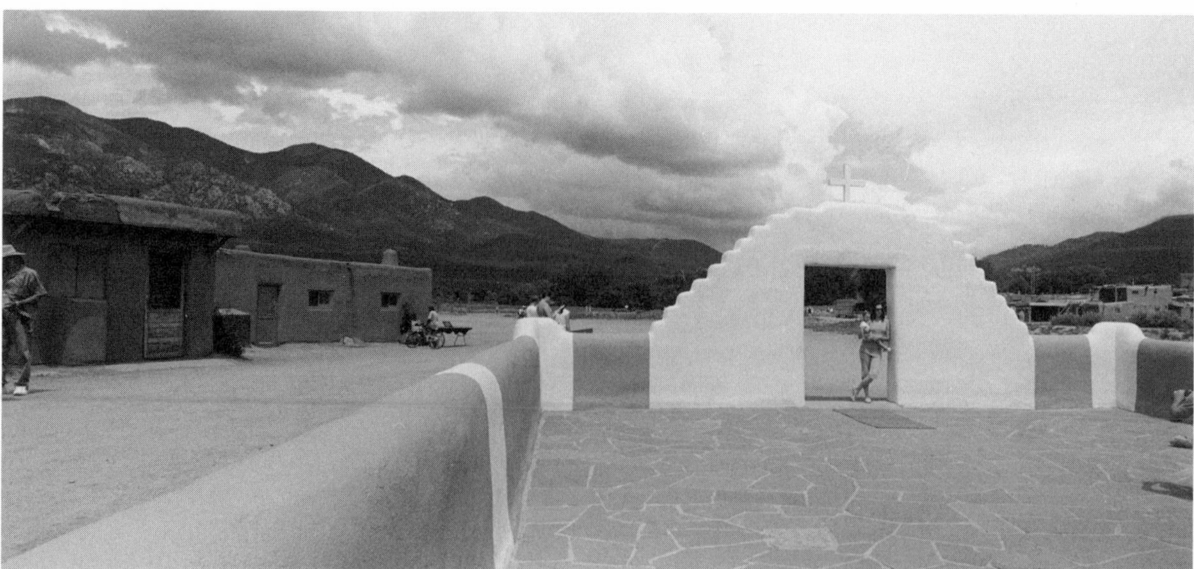

Figure 7

a way that might help the book appeal to the broader audience the authors and the press hoped to reach.

■ Before I delivered the final first pass to the press, with their permission I asked the authors to review the layout and advise me of any adjustments they wanted before we were officially in first proofs. Over several additional rounds of proofs there were additional corrections to the text and adjustments to the layout, but nothing major. With the many parties involved—two main authors, two other main collaborators, a photographer, and a handful of other contributors, in addition to the editorial and sales staff at the press—there were hiccups, false starts, and misunderstandings along the way, but I believe clear communication at the beginning (and throughout) helped avoid many of the pitfalls that can derail a project of this magnitude. Having heard about this book for close to ten years, and then having worked on it for almost three, I was relieved when advance copies arrived and the bound book fulfilled everyone's expectations (even mine).

THE PLAZAS of NEW MEXICO

A PROJECT OF THE HISTORIC PRESERVATION AND REGIONALISM PROGRAM, SCHOOL OF ARCHITECTURE AND PLANNING, UNIVERSITY OF NEW MEXICO
Published in cooperation with the William P. Clements Center for Southwest Studies, Southern Methodist University

Edited by Chris Wilson and Stefanos Polyzoides | Contemporary photography by Miguel Gandert | Documentary drawings edited by José Zelaya

Trinity University Press SAN ANTONIO
PUBLISHED IN ASSOCIATION WITH THE FOUNDATION FOR LANDSCAPE STUDIES

Figure 8

Figure 9

BARBARA WIEDEMANN

Designing the *Seventeenth-Century Dutch and Flemish Paintings* catalog

Designing a systematic catalog of the seventy-seven paintings in the North Carolina Museum of Art's seventeenth-century Dutch and Flemish collection was a rewarding challenge. I began by talking with the author, Curator of Northern European Art Dennis Weller, about his experience as a scholar who holds the National Gallery of Art's systematic catalog series as an ideal. Before I read any of Weller's material, I researched systematic catalogs in our art library and quickly realized the challenges would be threefold. First, to run the color reproductions of each painting with the accompanying essay in a logical way without eating up too many pages, designing a system to begin and end entries efficiently. Second, to keep comparative photos as close as possible to references to the images within the text. Last, to help the reader quickly distinguish one entry from the next and move easily from the main essay or biography into important details like the painting's provenance or the essay's detailed endnotes.

Dennis and I quickly agreed on a roughly 8½ × 11⅛ inch page size that could accommodate horizontal and vertical paintings fairly well—the National Gallery books were our inspiration there, with input from our printer for production considerations. Another quick decision was to go with 100# paper stock. The feeling of gravitas the "baritone" paper weight inspires was appropriate to the in-depth research contained in this book. It makes for a hefty tome, which was brought home to me when stowing the text in my carry-on bag on a trip to Korea, but that's another story!

There are so many layers of extensive research captured in a systematic catalog. My goal was to set a visual hierarchy where the artist's name and his painting came first, followed by the artist's biography and the curator's essay about each painting. I sketched out sample page layouts in pencil. Alongside the biography and essay, I wanted a crisp, narrow column of in-depth data: inscriptions, provenance, exhibitions, references, versions of the painting, and technical notes all ran alongside the main body of text, flowing from one page to the next as needed. Endnotes are an obsession of mine as a reader—if they're juicy, I'll sometimes dip into them before I read an entry—so these would follow the essay in as legible and elegant a manner as I could devise.

I have an aversion to using formulas to set page margins and like to consider every book design as a fresh start to setting up just the right framework/grid. The next step was to take my most successful sketch and think about what page margins, column widths, and horizontal markers would best fit the material and the page size. I did this with hairline rules in InDesign and printed out grids to get a feel for them on the page. I started designing late in the game after undergraduate studies in political science, so my master's degree at North Carolina State University's College of Design coincided perfectly with the school's first Apple lab. I've never traced type. The computer has always been my sketchpad. At the same time, I am wedded to the idea of starting with loose pencil sketches on paper as the most uninhibited way to keep design thoughts flowing.

By this time, I had a number of the author's entries and read through them before making decisions about typeface, point size, and other typographic choices. I don't know that I ascribe to the notion that typeface choices should always reflect a book's contents. Sometimes I want to use the most legible and/or visually relevant or beautiful face for the given task, and the "appropriateness" maxim feels like a crutch. In this case we were working with Michael Beirut and Yve Ludwig of Pentagram on the museum's new logo and graphic identity. I'd fallen for Martin Majoor's Scala typeface back in the 1990s after spotting it in *Eye* magazine, so when Michael and Yve suggested it as a house font alongside Verlag in the graphic identity proposal I almost literally jumped for joy. Scala is such an elegant face with just enough toughness to keep it from getting wispy at smaller sizes. It has a Dutch sturdiness that balances nicely against the crisp artfulness of Hoefler & Frere-Jones's Verlag typeface in all of its incarnations. So yes, Scala is a Dutch typeface in a book about Dutch and Flemish paintings, but the combination of beautifully legible Scala and versatile Verlag has some legs and can hold up to continued use in our ongoing series of systematic catalogs regardless of era or region.

I like the cover and text pages to speak very directly to one another, so I tend to use the same or related faces in display sizes on the cover. Scala is one of those fonts that can be almost invisible as body copy (in a good way) yet is beautiful and strong enough to stand up to display type-size scrutiny. The Odile ornaments that close each biography and essay were an irresistible addition. The older I get, the less I want to gussy up a book design. My biggest regret when looking back on books tends to be overdesigned elements that felt bold and hip at the time and now look brassy, like those orange bell bottoms with brass rivets that were to die for in sixth grade. Of course, that type of minimalist hard line is meant to be crossed, and I admit there is a pair of very flare-legged trousers in my closet, in oatmeal linen instead of orange denim this time around.

Given the density of information in this book, it was important to keep the leading generous and the point size readable, but not so large that it would require an expensive and unwieldy number of pages. Keeping the point size and leading consistent (Scala 10/14) but adjusting column width and settings worked well to unify but distinguish front matter (2-column, flush left/ragged right) from biography (1-column, flush left/ragged right) from essay (1-column, justified).

Changing the running feet to indicate the artist in question's name on each recto page almost came back to haunt me. I ended up with something like sixty different master page options, and the editors and I had to really keep an eye out for relatives like Jan Brueghel I (The Elder) versus Jan Brueghel II (The Younger), for example. It was worth the effort. In a scholarly book like this one I think it is a helpful guide.

Another challenge was finding the right point size for the title of each painting. It was logical to use the size consistently for all seventy-seven entries, but it still frustrates me to see the way graceful *Pastoral Scene* on page 324 holds up against the boxy three stacked lines of *Lady Mary Villiers, Later Duchess of Richmond and Lennox, with Charles Hamilton, Lord Arran* on page 238. I tried to talk Dennis into renaming the painting, but he wouldn't bite.

Fractions were an issue. I longed for OpenType fractions in Verlag and even wrote to the designers to ask about them. Eventually I contacted trusted book designer friends for advice. They suggested setting the fractions in Myriad Condensed Light instead of Verlag Condensed Light. We've since moved to this solution when setting small captions with fractions in Verlag.

I've always loved books best but designed many other types of materials as well. Never having the opportunity to work for a book designer, I've instead learned by studying the work of admired book designers over the years, and continue to learn. I wish I'd felt more comfortable asking these kind of detailed questions years ago. I still cringe to see art catalog work I did in the late 1990s using a lowercase "x" instead of a multiplication symbol between dimensions. I wish I'd asked—of course, an expert eye picks them out immediately, but at the time we didn't know better. Moral of the story: don't hesitate to ask questions of those you admire. This idea of getting advice came up again when I had a bout of anxiety over a tight bottom page margin I was experimenting with early on. Again I called on a designer friend for advice and he gave it. I enjoyed the email wherein he explained that he wasn't "a big bottom man (you should pardon the expression)—but I rarely let the bottom margin get any smaller than the top or front margin."

I ended up typesetting the book myself, followed later that year with the ensuing *North Carolina Museum of Art Handbook of the Collections* and *Rodin: The Cantor Foundation Gift to the North Carolina Museum of Art* catalogs for the museum. This was primarily a budget decision, but I was happy to have the luxury of making decisions per page and per entry that would be difficult to do if I had sent the book out for typesetting. The beauty and curse of fine typography is that there is always more to learn. I have no doubt there are things I would have done differently with this book if I'd designed it yesterday rather than two years ago. That will hopefully always be the case. I never want to be afraid to dive in, but I always want to look back from a place of deeper understanding and insight.

I tend to work on the heart of the matter first (the entries), then work out to the front matter, and then back matter. Generally I save the cover for last.

Good design is a matter of seeking the right balance. There are the expected markers that make reading a book seamless and easy. As Virginia Tan once said, "Good [book] design probably goes unnoticed, as it should." And there are the unexpected aesthetic minor keys, which to me are the asymmetrical amount of white space ending each entry, or the color contrast in subheads consistently using the red, ochre, and warm gray throughout.

Looking back on this book, I'm proud of how it came together as a whole, and of little things like the way the endnote numbers stand out from the notes themselves, but not too much. I like how easily a reader can find a name in the bibliography. The asymmetry of white space on the page depending on the length of each biography and entry pleases me aesthetically. I cringe at the little things, too. Initial caps have always been problematic to me unless they're done with a Fred Woodward *Rolling Stone* magazine–style flair, so why did I use those gratuitous little gray initial caps on each biography? They stand out like special guests who were asked to stand and be recognized at an awards function and never sat down. After consulting with the book's printers, who are wonderful and whom I could bother excessively, I decided to flood the printed pages with an ultraviolet protective dull coating. Less scratching and wear, preserving color without yellowing like varnish, faster drying time and therefore press time. Was it a book design foul not to be able to feel the tooth of the paper underfoot or underhand as it were? These are the levels of detail or eye-rolling minutiae, depending on how you look at it, that designers of all sorts can lose sleep over.

Book designers and typographers can be an intimidating bunch. Rules and traditions can feel meaningful or sometimes, arbitrarily hidebound. It's a cliché but I tell design students that you have to know the rules before you break them, and continually ask yourself "Why?" and "Why not?" I absorb all of the book design knowledge I can, then set it mentally aside and work intuitively on each new book. Maybe that's why the iPad app world that I've recently delved into is so fascinating to me. There are a lot of unwritten rules as we all try to figure out how best to present information in this appealing new way. Books have been my first love, ever since I started checking out a dozen books a week at the Paramus Public Library as a kid. I feel incredibly lucky whenever I can work on a book or other form of publication design, because my passion and my work have come together.

Grid system for *Seventeenth-Century Dutch and Flemish Paintings* by Dennis P. Weller (North Carolina Museum of Art), designed by Barbara Wiedemann.

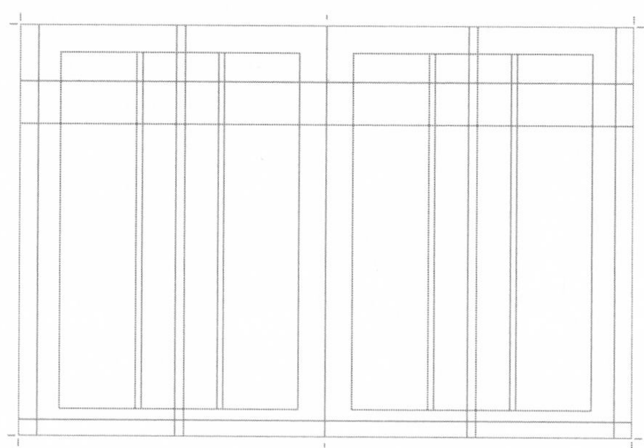

Section title from *Seventeenth-Century Dutch and Flemish Paintings* by Dennis P. Weller (North Carolina Museum of Art), designed by Barbara Wiedemann. 10/14 Scala, 8.5/10 Verlag, and Odile typefaces.

opposite page:
Long and short exhibit titles set in Scala Pro bold italic 18-point type.

WILLEM VAN AELST

1626–1683

Willem van Aelst was a gifted still-life painter active during the third quarter of the seventeenth century. A master in imitating textures, he is particularly well known for his innovations in game pieces, including the trappings of the hunt. Lesser in number, but no less striking in quality, are his fruit and flower still-life pictures. They show Van Aelst to be one of the first artists to introduce asymmetrical arrangements of bouquets. His painting style closely approximates the manner of the *fijnschilders*, as a meticulous finish and refined, handsome light effects are characteristic of his works.

The son of a Delft notary, Van Aelst most likely came from a well-to-do family. It has also been suggested the family was Catholic.[1] The young Willem trained as a painter with his uncle Evert van Aelst (1602–1658), after which he joined Delft's St. Luke's Guild on 9 November 1643. Two years later he undertook a journey to France. He remained there for approximately four years before departing for Florence. Here, he assisted the Dutch still-life painter Otto Marseus van Schrieck (1619/20–1678) in the service of the grand duke of Tuscany, Ferdinand II de' Medici. The pair of Dutch painters returned to their native Holland in 1656.[2] After a brief stay in Delft, Van Aelst moved to Amsterdam. Remaining there the rest of his life, he died in 1683, leaving behind a wife and three children.

His works were greatly prized during his lifetime and highly valued. A laudatory poem by Jan Vos about a flower piece by Van Aelst appeared in print in 1662.[3] Among his students was the flower painter Rachel Ruysch (1664–1750), the artist to whom the Museum's *Vanitas Flower Still Life* was long attributed. He also influenced the art of W. G. Ferguson (1632/33–after 1695), Elias van den Broeck (c.1650–1708), and Simon Verelst (1644–1721).

SELECT BIBLIOGRAPHY

Houbraken 1753, VOL. 1, pp. 228–230, 358.

Swillens 1946.

Bergström 1956, pp. 220–224.

Bol 1969, pp. 324–327.

Sullivan 1984, pp. 51–56, 70–72, 97.

Chiarini 1989, pp. 1–21.

Broos 1996e.

Amsterdam and Cleveland 1999, esp. pp. 242–248, 288.

Paul 2008.

NOTES

1. Published by Swillens 1946, pp. 416–417.
2. Even after his return from Italy, Van Aelst continued to sign works with the Italian form of his name, *Guill.mo van Aelst.*
3. The poem appeared in *Alle de gedichten van den poet Jan Vos*, ed. J. Lescaille (Amsterdam, 1662), p. 566. For the Dutch text and an English translation of the poem, see Goedde in Washington and Boston 1989, p. 44 note 37.

WILLEM VAN AELST 1

CAT. 50 *Lady Mary Villiers, Later Duchess of Richmond and Lennox, with Charles Hamilton, Lord Arran*

INSCRIPTIONS

None.

PROVENANCE

James Hamilton (1606–1649), 1st Duke of Hamilton, Hamilton Palace, Scotland; by descent to William Alexander Louis Stephen Douglas-Hamilton (1845–1895), 12th Duke of Hamilton; (sale, Christie's, London, 17 June 1882, lot 31); to E. B. Denison(?). Baron Alfred de Rothschild (1829–1918), Halston; by descent to Lionel Nathan de Rothschild (1882–1942), Exbury House. (With David M. Koetser, London and New York, by 1952); purchased by Mrs. Theodore Webb, 1952, as intended gift to the Museum.

EXHIBITIONS

Raleigh 1963, cat. 73, illus. (b-w); Baltimore 1968, cat. 6, illus. (b-w); London 1972, cat. 98, illus. (b-w); Montreal 1981, cat. 11, illus. (b-w); Washington 1990, cat. 78, illus. (color); Madrid 1999, cat. 21, illus. (color).

REFERENCES

Bellori 1672, p. 262; J. Smith 1829–1842, vol. 9 (1842), pp. 390–392, cat. 79; Waagen 1854–1857, vol. 3 (1854), p. 297; Guiffrey 1882, p. 275, cat. 794; Cust 1900, pp. 117, 278, cat. 128; Cust 1905, p. 117; Schaeffer 1909, p. 514, under cat. S. 364; Valentiner 1956a, p. 62, cat. 112, illus. (b-w); Millar in Edwards and Ramsey 1957, p. 52, pl. 29 (b-w); Vey 1962, vol. 1, p. 210, under cat. 140; Raleigh 1966, pp. 30–31, cat. 14, illus (b-w); Garas 1967, p. 69, cat. 289; Hardman 1971, p. 555; Raleigh 1972; J. de Bie 1979, p. 183, fig. 35 (b-w); Larsen 1980, pp. 124–125, cat. 946, illus. (b-w); Brown 1982, p. 191; London 1982, pp. 28–29, fig. 32 (b-w); Raleigh 1983, p. 138, illus. (b-w); Waterhouse 1988, p. 274, illus. (b-w); Larsen 1988, vol. 1, pp. 327–328, fig. 340 (b-w), vol. 2, p. 381, cat. 972; Bauman and Liedtke 1992, p. 332, fig. 217 (b-w); Raleigh 1992, p. 77, illus. (b-w); New Haven 1994, p. 13, fig. 11 (b-w), p. 75; Barnes and Wheelock 1994, p. 368; Tel Aviv 1995, pp. 69, 140, fig. 98 (color); The Hague 1997, p. 200, fig. 188 (color), p. 213; Ferrara 1998, pp. 48–49, fig. 21 (b-w); Raleigh 1998b, p. 162, illus. (color); Strong 1999, pp. 264–265, illus. (color); Stewart 2000, pp. 29–31, 33, fig. 11 (b-w); Gordenker 2001, pp. 51–53, 165, pl. 7 (color); Barnes 2004, pp. 588–590, cat. IV.204, illus. (color); Dulos and Griffey 2008, pp. 17, illus. (color).

ELEGANTLY POSED and seemingly mature beyond her fourteen or fifteen years, Lady Mary Villiers (1622–1685) looks out with an expression that carries little emotion.[1] She wears a white satin skirt and bodice with a deep décolletage and French lace cuffs. The bodice is decorated with pearls and jewels extending along a line to her shoulders. Among her accessories are a pearl necklace, double pearl earrings, a "brown fur tippet," and floral decorations attached to her hair with a jeweled pin.[2]

Somewhat more animated is the young boy in the guise of Cupid standing next to her. He is Charles Hamilton, Lord Arran (1634–1640). Shown wearing only a red satin drapery and sandals, his mythological personification is confirmed by his feathery white wings, quiver, and arrows. The outdoor setting, while sparse in its details, is equally elegant. The pair stands on a stone step before a tall fluted column with distant views onto an indistinct landscape. A large architectural element, perhaps a corner of a building, appears to the far right, and the cloudy sky extends between it and the column. While early authors misidentified the boy as the son of Mary Villiers, he was, in fact, her cousin (see below).

Perhaps even more confusing is her identification as Venus to complement his as Cupid. As Arthur Wheelock wrote, "Other than dressing Lord Arran as Cupid, Van Dyck has done little else to convey the allegorical nature of the image."[3] Nevertheless, such associations would not have been lost on contemporary viewers who were conditioned to embrace the interplay between portraiture and allegory. As an example of a *portrait historié*, the canvas represents one of the few surviving examples of this popular type painted by Van Dyck during his years in England.[4]

In *portraits historiés*, sitters are shown in the guise of historical, religious, or mythological figures. This particular instance depicting Mary and Charles appearing as Venus and Cupid earned high praise from the Italian art biographer Giovanni Bellori in 1672. Writing in his *Le vite de pittori*, he likely based his remarks on information supplied on this picture and others from Van Dyck's English period by Sir Kenelm Digby. Bellori explained how the artist "made the portrait of the Duchess of Richmond, daughter of the Duke of Buckingham, and this portrait, because of its unique beauty put in doubt as to whether credit should be accorded to art or to nature. He portrayed her in the manner of Venus. Her portrait is accompanied by that of her son [*sic*], The Duke of Hamilton, completely nude, [portrayed as] cupid armed with his bow and his arrows."[5] Due to its associations with Venus and especially the actions of Cupid, this unique double portrait carried with it a specific message, one closely linked to the eventful life of Mary Villiers. As will be discussed below, the composition's symbolic content may also provide a framework for dating the picture.

The only daughter of George Villiers, 1st Duke of Buckingham (1592–1628), and Katherine Manners (d. 1649), Mary Villiers and her two

Lady Mary Villiers, Later Duchess of Richmond and Lennox, with Charles Hamilton, Lord Arran

ca. 1637
Oil on canvas, 83 1/4 × 52 1/2 in. (211.5 × 133.4 cm)
Gift of Mrs. Theodore Webb, 52.17.1

CAT. 67 *Pastoral Scene*

INSCRIPTIONS

None.

PROVENANCE

Major Sir Hugh Cholmeley, London.[1] (With David M. Koetser, New York, by 1955); Samuel H. Kress Foundation, New York, in 1955; gift to the Museum in 1960.

EXHIBITIONS

Tucson 1957, cat. 22, illus. (b-w); Raleigh 1960, illus. (b-w); Brussels 1965, cat. 258, illus. (b-w); Greenville 1996, illus. (color).

REFERENCES

Raleigh 1960, pp. 142–143, illus. (b-w); Eisler 1977, pp. 124–125, cat. K 2104, fig. 114 (b-w); Toronto 2001, p. 100; Gritsay and Babina 2008, p. 322.

VERSIONS

Versions but not copies of the composition exist, including oil on canvas, 40 3/4 × 30 1/2 in. (103.5 × 77.5 cm), The Hermitage, St. Petersburg, inv. GE 6240; oil on canvas, 49 3/4 × 49 3/4 in. (126.4 × 126.4 cm), The Virginia Museum of Fine Arts, Richmond, inv. 61-50 (fig. 67a).

TECHNICAL NOTES

The painting is executed on linen that has been glue-lined to linen. The structure of the ground could not be determined owing to the thinness of the layer. Some aspects of the composition were blocked in with a gray dead coloring and then built up with a thin but opaque paint. There is little of note in either x-radiography or infrared reflectography. The painting underwent a complete conservation treatment in 2002, including cleaning, revarnishing with low-molecular-weight synthetic resin, and retouching.

NEITHER SIGNED NOR DATED, Jan Siberechts's *Pastoral Scene* is a representative example of the artist's work. Probably painted during the second half of the 1660s, it shows a lush Flemish landscape populated by milkmaids, a few cows, and in the foreground a mother removing lice from the head of her young daughter. As is evident here, Siberechts was especially skilled in capturing the look and feel of the rural Flemish landscape. Today, one still discovers vistas that are remarkably similar to the one described in this painting. On the left light reflects off a slow-moving stream flanked by reeds and grasses. This narrow expanse of water is crossed in the middle ground by a small footbridge, across which a milkmaid and dog walk. Behind the bridge a grassy meadow is interrupted by a row of pollarded willow trees. Other trees fill the distant horizon, their density suggesting their function as windbreaks.

In spite of its topographic charm, *Pastoral Scene* is a genre painting as much as it is a landscape. In this regard Siberechts set himself apart from most of his contemporary Flemish landscape painters.[2] A certain tranquillity and contentment filter through the composition, an effect Siberechts typically provided in equal measure to both landscape and figures. The viewer, little more than arm's length from the mother and child in the right foreground, nevertheless, is asked to remain neutral toward the figures and their actions. One finds "no humor, as in Steen; no begging for sympathy or pity, as in Le Nain."[3]

Despite the picture's quiet appeal, much is happening. A subtle dynamism enters the narrative through its deceptively complex composition and by an assault on the senses. Interlocking triangular planes move the viewer's eye from the right foreground to the left background.[4] In addition, Siberechts has captured the moisture in the air, the breezes moving the branches of the willow trees, the sound of the slowly moving water, and the brightness of the midday sun.

Much of this sensory effect stems from the artist's painting style and his choice of color. Abandoning the Italianate manner that characterized his works from the 1650s, he developed a fresh approach for the representation of his native countryside in the following decade. Evenly dispersed midday sunlight, meticulous paint application, and a palette that showcases a range of harmonious cool green hues are all characteristic of his evolving style. Here, as in many of his works, the greens and related earth tones are contrasted with the bright local colors—reds, blues, and yellow-rusts—found in the figures' clothing.

Once Siberechts had formulated his distinctive style in the early 1660s, he largely continued in this manner until leaving for England in 1672. A few compositional changes did intrude, most notably a growing tendency to open up his compositions by removing some of the trees and bushes that effectively screened vistas into the background.[5] He also demonstrated a predilection for recycling some of his motifs. *Pastoral Scene* serves as a prime example of this practice. For example, nearly identical images of the

Pastoral Scene

ca. 1667–1668
Oil on canvas
23 1/4 × 34 15/16 in. (59.1 × 88.7 cm)
Gift of the Samuel H. Kress Foundation, 60.17.70

mother picking lice from her child can be seen in at least three other examples by Siberechts, including a signed and dated picture now in Richmond, *The Herdswoman and Her Daughter* (FIG. 67A).[6]

In addition to the mother and child, the Richmond work also features a similar stream to the left and the same two cows, which are positioned a short distance behind the mother and child in each painting but differ in the colors and markings of their hides. The date of 1667 on the Richmond painting certainly assists in dating *Pastoral Scene*. Considering the shared motifs and nearly identical painting styles, the Raleigh example must have been executed about the same time as the picture in Richmond. Since *Pastoral Scene* presents a more open vista into the background landscape, it is likely this painting was completed just after the one in Richmond, about 1667 or 1668.

number of his early paintings, Jordaens edited this work.[12] A radiograph of the Raleigh painting (FIG. 55D) shows that a bearded old man, undoubtedly Joseph, occupied the position to the left of the Christ Child. In removing this figure, the artist opened up the composition and reduced the effect of crowding. It also changed the work's identification from a Holy Family to a Virgin and Child with St. John and His Parents.

Such changes reflect a growing maturity on the part of the painter. Considered in light of the stylistic differences between it and the 1616-dated painting (FIG. 55C) discussed above, one can argue for a later date for the Raleigh picture. Consequently, *The Virgin and Child with St. John and His Parents* must have been executed a year or two later, about 1617–1618.

FIG. 55D X-radiograph of cat. 55

Since Jordaens was a prolific draftsman as well as a painter, it would not have been unusual to find preliminary compositional studies for the painting, which in turn could lend additional weight to determining its probable date.[13] Unfortunately, none has been discovered. A single drawing at the British Museum representing the Holy Family with St. Elizabeth and dated by d'Hulst as about 1620–1623 does show a similarly placed wicker chair and lamb, but the figures in the drawing are largely at odds with the ones found in the painting.[14]

NOTES

1. The painting has occasionally been identified as the Holy Family with St. John and His Parents, a description indicating the presence of Joseph. In fact, this seems to have been the artist's original intent. A bearded old man, presumably Joseph, can be seen in the x-radiograph of the picture, but Jordaens painted him out. See discussion and FIG. 55D.
2. A fourth painting, one assigned to Jordaens and his workshop and entitled *Christ and the Pharisees*, oil on canvas, 55 1/4 × 83 5/8 in. (140.3 × 212.4 cm), was previously in the Museum collection. It was deaccessioned and sold at Sotheby's, New York, 5 December 1999, lot 55; see Appendix 2.
3. See Versions. In addition, two other paintings, both designated as coming from the workshop of Jordaens, incorporate some of the elements found in the Raleigh composition. They are both ILLUS. in Antwerp 1993, p. 70, FIGS. A11A, A11B.
4. Brown 1993, p. 584.
5. This wicker chair was clearly a studio prop that Jordaens used on many occasions, including works separated by decades. For example, it appears in the same position in the painting *As the Old Sang, so Pipe the Young* dated 1638, Koninklijk Museum voor Schone Kunsten, Antwerp; ILLUS. Antwerp 1993, p. 179.
6. For a discussion of this source, see Knipping 1974, VOL. 1, p. 115.
7. D'Hulst in Antwerp 1993, p. 70, CAT. A11.
8. A great deal of bibliography is devoted to the impact of Caravaggio's art on northern painting. See Raleigh 1998a.
9. About 1612–1614, for example, Rubens painted *The Entombment*, oil on panel, 34 3/4 × 26 1/4 in. (88.3 × 66.5 cm), National Gallery of Canada, Ottawa, INV. 6431, a work that copies Caravaggio's famous altarpiece at the Vatican.
10. The effects of late mannerist group portraits, including examples by Rubens's teacher Otto van Veen, were among the likely influences to which Jordaens responded early in his career.
11. The detail of the boy blowing on coals has been traced back to the Bassano, a family of northern Italian painters greatly admired by Jordaens. See Bauman and Liedtke 1992, p. 217.
12. Other examples in which the artist removed figures to improve the composition include the painting discussed above (FIG. 55C), where the head of an old woman once occupied the darkened area between Mary and Joseph.
13. For a study of the drawings of Jordaens, see d'Hulst 1974.
14. Ibid., VOL. 1, p. 144, CAT. A50, VOL. 3, FIG. 57.

Just as Esther's name inspired the passions of the Dutch, the growing fame of Holland's painters likewise generated enthusiasm during its Golden Age in the seventeenth century. Today, Rembrandt stands atop this pantheon of artists, so it is not surprising his name was previously linked to *The Feast of Esther*. Rembrandt's elevated position among his contemporaries, however, came later in his career. In the mid-1620s, when *The Feast of Esther* was painted, the artistic prodigy Jan Lievens was held in higher esteem than the young Rembrandt.[6] About the same time, the two painters attracted the attention of Constantijn Huygens (1596–1687), secretary to the Stadholder Frederik Hendrik at The Hague. In his autobiography penned between 1629 and 1631, Huygens fairly accurately described the strengths and weaknesses of this "pair of young and noble painters" [jong en edel schilderduo].[7] Little could he have known that centuries later his words would help scholars to assign *The Feast of Esther* to Lievens rather than to Rembrandt.

> I venture to suggest offhand that Rembrandt is superior to Lievens in his sure touch and liveliness of emotions. Conversely, Lievens is the greater in inventiveness and audacious themes and forms. Everything his young spirit endeavors to capture must be magnificent and lofty. Rather than depicting his subject in its true size, he chooses a larger scale. Rembrandt, by contrast, devotes all his loving concentration to a small painting, achieving on that modest scale a result which one would seek in vain in the largest pieces of others.[8]

The Raleigh picture seems to confirm Lievens's stylistic tendencies as defined by Huygens. "Liveliness of emotions," "audacious themes and forms," and "larger scale" all correspond with what one finds in *The Feast of Esther*. Nevertheless, even a cursory glance at the painting reveals other, less flattering elements. The picture's dissonant colors, nervous execution, and spatial irregularities underscore some of the criticism Huygens also directed toward Lievens. Elsewhere in his autobiography, Huygens wrote, "My only objection is his [Lievens's] stubbornness, which derives from an excess of self-confidence. He either roundly rejects all criticism or, if he acknowledges its validity, takes it in bad spirit. This bad habit, harmful at any age, is absolutely pernicious in youth."[9]

For a young man just eighteen or nineteen years old to take on such a large and complex composition speaks volumes about the artist's ego and enormous ambition. The work's shortcomings, which, to be fair, are exaggerated by the painting's condition (see Technical Notes), suggest that the young painter indeed rejected any criticism he may have received, however well intentioned. Still, the question remains, particularly in light of Huygens's apt description, why so many scholars attributed the painting to Rembrandt.

The Rembrandt attribution must be seen within the context of the accepted connoisseurship practices when the painting was rediscovered in the 1930s. In general, an expansionist view of the artist's oeuvre was in vogue

REFERENCES

W. Martin 1936/1937; Van Gelder 1937; Bauch 1939, pp. 240–241, fig. 160 (b-w); Slive 1953, p. 52 note 2; Van Gelder 1953a, pp. 190, 253, 270, illus. (b-w); Van Gelder 1953b, pp. 281–282, pl. VI, fig. 9 (b-w); Knuttel 1955, pp. 44–46; Bloch 1955, p. 260; Knuttel 1956, pp. 240–242 (as Pieter Lastman); Valentiner 1956a, pp. 51–52, no. 65, illus. (b-w); Gerson 1957, pp. 121–122; Sumowski 1957–1958, p. 225, fig. 15 (b-w); Scharf 1958, p. 304; Judson 1959, p. 82; Bauch 1960, pp. 112–119, fig. 77 (color); Slive 1963, pp. 139–141, fig. 19 (b-w); Judson 1964, p. 151 note 40; Rosenberg 1964, pp. 14, 345 note 7, 364 note 8; Rosenberg, Slive, and Ter Kuile 1966, p. 49, pl. 28, fig. b (b-w); Kahr 1966, p. 229 note 4; Bauch 1966, p. 29, cat. A1, illus. (b-w); Raleigh 1966, cat. 25, illus. (b-w); Bauch 1967, pp. 161ff., fig. 1 (b-w); Arpino 1969, cat. 6; Gerson/Bredius 1969, pp. 398, 616, cat. 631; Held 1969a, pp. 387–388; Rifkin 1969, pp. 31–32, 35, illus. (color); H. Schneider 1973, pp. 344–345, cat. S349; Kirschenbaum 1977, pp. 118, 239, fig. 117 (b-w); Białostocki in Braunschweig 1979, pp. 17–18, fig. 3 (b-w); Brown 1979, p. 742; Nicolson 1979, pp. 81, 244; Corpus 1982–1989, vol. 1 (1982), pp. 446–460, cat. C2, figs. 1–6 (b-w); Sumowski 1983, vol. 3, p. 1776, cat. 1181, p. 1820, illus. (color); Raleigh 1983, p. 97, illus. (b-w); Sutton 1986, p. 249, fig. 370 (b-w); Judson in Utrecht and Braunschweig 1986, p. 57, fig. 51 (b-w); Nicolson 1989, vol. 1, p. 161, vol. 2, fig. 1648 (b-w); Tümpel in Amsterdam and Jerusalem 1991, p. 14, fig. 7 (b-w), p. 16; Leiden 1991, p. 91; Raleigh 1992, p. 87, illus. (color); Stockholm 1992, p. 140, fig. 24a (b-w); Jerusalem 1993, pp. 116–117, illus. (color); Sutton 1995, p. 241; Slive 1995, p. 100, fig. 123 (b-w); Liedtke in New York 1995, vol. 2, p. 8, fig. 5 (b-w), pp. 9–10; Gutbrod 1996, pp. 115–126, 306, 374, 380, fig. 7 (b-w); Dresden and Vienna 1997, p. 186, illus. (b-w); Van de Wetering 1997, pp. 173–174, illus. (color detail); Raleigh 1998a, p. 102, illus. (color); Stechow 1998, pp. 35, 38, 37, fig. 26 (b-w); Judson and Ekkart 1999, p. 226, fig. 76 (b-w); Westermann 2000, pp. 38–39, fig. 23 (color); Liedtke 2000, p. 212, fig. 7 (b-w); Westermann in Boston 2000, p. 36, fig. 28 (b-w); Kassel and Amsterdam 2001, pp. 103ff., 189, 192, 194, fig. 24a (b-w); The Hague 2002, pp. 100, 102; Neumeister 2003, pp. 234–235, fig. 168 (b-w); Van Straten 2005, pp. 27–28, fig. 9 (color); Amsterdam 2006, pp. 189–190, fig. 88 (color); Schnackenburg 2007, pp. 202–205, fig. 22 (b-w); Weller 2008, pp. 257–259, fig. 7 (b-w); Washington 2008, pp. 6, 44, 71, 82, 94, 96, 231, 289; Lopez 2009, p. 83, fig. 2 (color).

Left: An example of endnotes set on a 3-column grid in 8-point Scala Pro regular. Right: Extract and references for *Seventeenth-Century Dutch and Flemish Paintings* by Dennis P. Weller (North Carolina Museum of Art), designed by Barbara Wiedemann.

Designing Journals

There are known knowns;
there are things we
know we know. We also
know there are known
unknowns; that is to say
we know there are some
things we do not know. But
there are also unknown
unknowns—the ones we
don't know we don't know.
– Donald Rumsfeld,
February 12, 2002

The epigraph to this chapter perfectly expresses the dilemma that confronts all designers of journals. The main problem in designing a journal is not being able to know just how many anomalies need to be planned for, so it is best to keep things relatively uncomplicated. With a new journal and a sympathetic editor, the designer can suggest that the editorial program have limits, e.g., no more than three levels of subheads, endnotes or footnotes, style and length of running heads, etc. However, even with the most sympathetic cooperation from an editor, authors always seem to come up with special needs.

I have learned to my dismay that it is best not to make the design for a journal complicated. Keeping it simple means the most important part of the design is the choice of the text typeface. For literary journals I prefer to keep the same typeface (or ones that resemble each other very closely) for text and display. For scholarly journals I prefer to have contrasting fonts for text and display especially when the text requires various levels of subhead.

Before there was OpenType, it was wise to choose a typeface that had a good range of accents, various weights, small caps in both roman and italic, lining and old-style figures. Now, most good text fonts have all of these variants. Editors generally have a target range of how many words per page they would like, and so for me that is where I begin. While literary journals tend to have relatively short article titles and not many subheads, scholarly journals tend to have lengthy titles and subtitles, multiple authors, affiliations, abstracts of the articles, various levels of subheads, and notes.

In designing *The Gettysburg Review*, a literary journal, I had established the original design and then had the chance to completely redesign it after a number of years. In the original design the most egregious mistake I had made was using a display initial to begin each article. Inevitably there were articles that began with a subhead, with a quotation mark, with a figure, or some other kind of text that made the use of an initial less than ideal. Space breaks in the text also needed something more than a line space to indicate the start of a new section because all too often a space break would fall at the bottom of a page and disappear. Where and how to begin a new section after a space break had to be kept simple enough to avoid the same problems as affected the opening text of the article. For me, the most effective solution was to allow for a line space but also set a simple ornament run in at the beginning of the new section. If the line space disappeared between pages, the ornament would signal to the reader that a new section was beginning. Some designers prefer to begin with the first phrase in small caps or caps and small caps. As simple as this seems, I could never decide how many words should be treated in this way. Moreover, for a journal where the designer may never see more than an issue or two, this could be problematic for either the typesetter or the editor.

Journals always have various kinds of extracts. As I have said elsewhere, my own preference is to set extract in the same size and leading as the text, but indented with space above and below. This simplifies things for the typesetter, and I feel no visual adjustment is necessary for the reader. The indent I use matches the paragraph indent of the main text. If extracts are likely to be extensive and run over more than one page, I prefer ragged right. Otherwise indented text on a page by itself simply resembles main text.

Poetry extract is more obvious in its form, but distinguishing prose poetry from prose extract is just one of those problems that defy clarity. I try to keep stanza breaks to no more than a half line and allow the space above and below the extract to be extra as necessary to make up even pages.

If attributions to extract appear as part of the extract, they can be run in within prose extract. With verse extract I usually prefer to place attributions on a new line aligned right with the longest line of poetry. Of course sometimes attributions are so extensive they begin to look like part of the text. Here is where the editor has to take some responsibility in avoiding these kind of situations. I normally set titles of extracts in spaced small caps of the text size.

Literary journals usually have no more than two levels of subhead, but authors for scholarly journals seem to require at least three and often try for more. I usually allow for no more than four levels, which is why I like to have more than one style of typeface (sans serif and serif) rather than try to use various sizes and/or space around versions of the text face. I am not very fond of bold serif fonts and try to avoid anything bolder than semibold if I have no other options.

I used to believe that the only way to unify the design of multiauthored books was to center the chapter titles, subtitle, and authors. In that way long and short titles might not look so different. My current preference is to let titles run ragged right with author names above or below titles, or even sometimes flush right. Occasionally I will use a rule above the title or above the opening of the text to establish the relationship of the title area to the text block. Keeping the title/subtitle relatively small (not larger than 14 pt, for example) but giving the title some space establishes its importance.

Aside from the articles, journals often have review articles, lists of contributors, extensive copyright page information, and a slightly more complex table of contents.

It is impossible to plan for what might be the longest title or largest number of coauthors. It is wise to allow the greatest amount of flexibility in the design

The Gettysburg Review

Volume 1, Number 2 / Spring 1988

Essays and Essay-Reviews

RICHARD HOWARD

Abiding Maturities of Vision

What is often called, in the arts, a movement or a school ("reeling and writhing and fainting in coils"), is as often no more than the energizing activity of one person who has a vision, or a program, of collegial disciplines. That person withdrawn, the light goes out, and the collaboration becomes a languid affair. Since Frank O'Hara's death, there has not been much of an effort on the part of American writers to celebrate, to *assume* the work of American artists. Sontag on photography and dance, Davenport on the aesthetics of still life—slim pickings, set against the vivacity of the School of New York, animated by the zeal of O'Hara and his friends who worked for museums, wrote for art journals, and concurred so boisterously in an enterprise which implied that—as in a perhaps mythical Paris of the cubists and the surrealists, of Apollinaire and of Breton—painting and writing sorted well, or at least willingly, together.

How beguiling, then, that Abrams should publish (in the welter of "art books" by art critics and art historians, while Julian Schnabel writes on himself and Helga takes the cover of *Time* and *Newsweek*) two living painters' works *illustrated* by writers of fiction and poetry, each of considerable glamor and each attending cordially to the pictures, as if such attention were the proper study of imaginative writers, a natural concern. Here, though, the parallel between the projects—Beattie on Katz, Strand on Bailey—must leave off, for nothing in the venture—if it is a venture, if Abrams intends to commission further books in which a poet, a novelist, even a playwright (why not? I presume Albee collects) might offer a view of some compelling presence in an art world so massively unconcerned with literary values—nothing in even the physical layout of the two books suggests that Beattie and Strand have a congruent interest in pictures, or that their (discrepant) editors wanted to beget any sort of community of commentary. Beattie's "reading of Alex Katz" is capricious, a foray into unfamiliar territory; whereas Strand, once a painter and regularly a reviewer of art works, has written a solemn monograph with a bibliography, a biography, and—in two dozen lean pages—offered comparisons with Caravaggio, Zurbaran, Goya, Chardin, Morandi, Gris, Piero della

Alex Katz. By Ann Beattie. Harry N. Abrams, Inc., 91 pp., $27.50.
William Bailey. By Mark Strand. Harry N. Abrams, Inc., 80 pp., $29.95.

265

FREDERICK BUSCH

hero and Mommy and me that he forgets to shift. He told me that. I twitch my nose at him when he says that sort of rubbish. Watch tomorrow when he comes. I'll twitch my nose and he'll stop. It's something about the nose itself, actually. You'll see.

"We're going to Britain's monument, Peter. I want to show you Stonehenge. It's got all sorts of fences and wires round it, but it's quite beautiful, still. You know, when I was a girl, we could run and play on the stones themselves. No one cared. Oh, there'd be the odd initial carved into the rock, that sort of vulgarity, but nothing importantly awful. Then, in the seventies, a group of wild-eyed hippy squatters descended upon it. They said they were claiming it in the name of the people. I never trust anyone who does anything in the name of the people, do you? They camped there. Police vans all round, lights and Alsatians and TV cameras everywhere. When they left, at last, they had sprayed their names and stupid slogans on those great, lovely, timeless rocks. No one knows how they came there still, you know. Taken on boat from Wales, then rolled on logs overland, that's one theory. The stones do seem to be Welsh. Mommy always said it seemed like something perverse only the Welsh would do. Need I tell you that Fox is Welsh? So there it was. They had to sandblast the skin of all that history off the poor stones. That was when they put fences and wires round it all and round each stone.

"When I was a baby I used to wear red rubber boots and I used to dance on the sacrifice stone. That was before they got rational and talked about cosmic observatories and all of that. People believed the Druids sacrificed virgins to celebrate the death of the year, and to pray the sun would come back after winter. People all rigged out in white robes come, still. They dance about and hold knives up in the air, look like a bunch of crazy spinsters, or your Ku Klux Klan. But in *Tess of the D'Urbervilles*—you've read that? Oh, Peter, you *must*! It's my most favorite read of *all* time. Listen. Hardy believed in the Druids. Or in the belief in them, at any rate. And at the end, there's Tess, all pale, a kind of bride, you see, all stretched out on the sacrifice stone, the one they thought the virgins were killed on. Of course, she isn't a virgin anymore. That's part of it. She was betrayed in her *sleep*, Peter. Could we try that some time? I'd love it if you betrayed me in my sleep. Could we *do* it asleep, dear? And Angel loves her truly. They're in flight from the sheriff, I forgot to tell you that. Anyway, she sleeps and he stands guard above her at Stonehenge. Comes the dawn, and the sheriff's men come riding from every direction. And there's Tess, bride of death, lying on the sacrifice stone. It's all but pornographic, it's so marvelous. It's her fate, you see. Come see the stone."

It rose up beside the A303, at first so small as to be disappointing. We parked, and Hilary, like a child at an amusement park, led me through a tunnel that crossed beneath the roadway to a ticket window. She paid for us,

209

The Gettysburg Review 25:4

VOLUME 25,

NUMBER 4

WINTER 2012

PUBLISHED BY

GETTYSBURG

COLLEGE

EDITOR: PETER STITT

Assistant Editor: Mark Drew
Managing Editor: Ellen Hathaway
Marketing & Circulation Manager: Kristin Koontz
Editorial Assistant: Alison Wellford
Intern: Michael Plunkett

ADVISORY & CONTRIBUTING EDITORS
Lee K. Abbott
Rita Dove
Donald Hall
Rebecca McClanahan
Richard Wilbur
Paul Zimmer

ADVISORY BOARD
Fritz Gaenslen
Fred Leebron
Kathryn Rhett
Jack Ryan

www.gettysburgreview.com

The Gettysburg Review 25:4 winter 2012

ESSAYS

FICTION

POETRY

The literary journal *The Gettysburg Review* is published by Gettysburg College, Gettysburg, Pennsylvania. Trim size 6.75 × 10. It was originally designed in the dying years of Linotype to be set in Garamond (top three images). The design is centered. Given the inevitable variety of typographic problems, the chapter opening initials were not a good idea. The redesign (bottom two images) is ranged left in Minion.

THE GETTYSBURG REVIEW

feet down, and more than that with the muck. All twenty or so guards searching the shallows, their legs making uniform sweeps under the dock, churning up sediment, blurring my view. The other three guards and I were taught to dive straight down—one of us on each side of the square, Astroturf-carpeted swim platform—then make neat zippers along the lake bottom, propelling only with our feet, keeping our arms outstretched like a T, high-fiving the diver next to us. We would hold our breath as long as we could stand, and then some, not wasting any time before resurfacing. They made us search until someone found the object planted earlier, when none of us were looking. Usually it would be a croquet ball or a coffee can full of cement or something equally inanimate.

After, I would take long showers, rinsing the algae and muck out of my hair, my suit, every crevice. There is a kind of whole-body exhaustion following adrenaline that has run its course. My arms and legs become loose bags of bones and muscle and nerve, my flesh down to the core, completely wrung out with fear, anticipating the worst.

Canadian musician Gordon Lightfoot memorialized the wreck of the *Edmund Fitzgerald* in his ballad of regret. As I listen to the song now, playing all six minutes over and over on repeat, I am reminded of the family vacation we took the summer I turned ten, when I stood, holding the hand of my father in the Great Lakes Shipwreck Museum on Whitefish Point, looking at the green glowing screen of a ship underwater: rusted deck railing, intact windows looking in on the darkened captain's cabin, the blades of the propeller as large as the fins of an orca, forever frozen in time, motionless.

Twenty years after the wreck, two divers had set out on Lake Superior to be the first to descend the 530 feet down to the resting place of the ship without the assistance of a submersible.

It is said the divers took six minutes to descend, six minutes to survey the wreck, and three hours to resurface. They found, down there, next to the bow of the ship, the remains of a crew member fully clothed and wearing his lifejacket, lying facedown in the mud.

Water-ski ropes are seventy-five feet of braided polypropylene. Waxy, plastic to the touch, but sixteen strands strong. I have watched my father splice old ski ropes with his blow torch, melting one strand into the other, then melting the ends so they wouldn't fray.

570

NORMA MARDER

A Good Laugh

A wise oak stood in the forested cemetery across from our summer house, its arthritic limbs spreading above a burl-circled eye, its ancient bark covered with mosses and fungi. Everyone loved that tree. When we returned this summer, it looked crippled, having lost a massive limb in the winter. Another limb fell during a July storm, smashing headstones. Arborists invaded the cemetery with chainsaws and a chipper. "Stop," I screamed. "You're murdering my tree!" It took them a week. Day after day I photographed the fallen parts—the huge recumbent trunk, the wooden flesh, gnarly burls, the inner eye. Its death felt personal, ominous. I heard a pagan clang, a foretelling. The stump weathered from burnt sienna to gray.

In November a heart attack felled my aunt Regina, two weeks after her hundredth birthday. I thought she was immortal.

Her hall closet looks different. Fewer jackets, fewer shoes, a quart of bleach.

"What's bleach doing there?" I ask.

Regina laughs. "You know me—it's easy to get for the kitchen and the bathroom."

"Two bottles would be even easier," I say.

She clears her throat. "Your mother says what do I need two bottles for."

My mother and aunts function as sea creatures, defending themselves from predators. Mama, the eldest, squirts ink; my neurotic aunt, the beautiful one, makes whirlpools; the youngest, the fat one, hides under a rock. Regina, the peacemaker, floats with the tide.

Family, friends—her voice lights up when she says our names. She's always ready for a visit—cake in the freezer, candy dish full. Lately she's been giving things away—"Here, take it, take it," she laughs, "I don't need it." Saturday afternoons friends come over to play May I, a children's card game, turning on the opera so no one should look down on them for gambling. Sometimes Regina loses as much as ten cents.

605

Text page and essay opening from *The Gettysburg Review*.

by keeping the design for the contents page relatively modest. That, in fact, should best be kept in mind for the rest of the design for a journal.

When the *Journal of Scholarly Publishing* was under the editorship of Ian Montagnes, it was in Alan Fleming's elegant design in Palatino (then not quite as ubiquitous as it later has become). After Ian left the journal, Fleming's design was abandoned and replaced with some pedestrian and graceless typography. Sue Hall writes later in this chapter about her desire when redesigning a journal to retain some connection to the previous style. As I came to redesign the redesign, there was nothing I wanted to retain.

The new iteration of the journal has editorial elements the Fleming design did not have (e.g., abstracts, keywords, etc.), and the article titles and subtitles are now far more complicated.

I had thought about using Palatino to refer back to Fleming's design, but in the end chose Minion only because Palatino, to me, has become a bit of design cliché. Aside from the masthead on the opening page, the largest display size I used was 16 point for the article titles. Even though there were many editorial elements to consider, I saw I could keep everything in Minion roman and italic, no boldface. The italic, small caps, and old-style figures offered enough

One of the problems in designing journals is how to plan for the unknown variety of texts that inevitably present typographic problems. Here are three poems from one issue of *The Gettysburg Review.*

Journal design is essentially a compromise. Not every case can be accounted for, so it is prudent for the designer who cannot fine tune every issue to keep the design straightforward.

DIANE SCHENKER

In Gratitude to Frank O'Hara Who Came Before

Here's to you, Frank O'Hara, all nicotine-
stained fingers and fun.
Go forth! (I have you singing.) Go!
Into the hour of lunch. Launch!
Laugh, contemplate, attract!

Oh you *flâneur* of the streets of New York.
Carved marble doorway and dirty cup
crumpled and the lady in furs, fly by
bike guy. Look out! A baby girl's hand,
headline screaming from a fragrant
stack of freshly printed paper. It is lunch!

Let the waist of the day expand. I'll
have some in my cocktail. Crazy elixir,
pigeons and spit. Dance it! Way down
the street till the hour rolls over, and
Frank—thank you for lunch!

LINDA PASTAN

3:00 AM

Sleep has stepped out
for a smoke
and may not be back.

The sun is waiting
in the celestial
green room,

practicing
its flamboyant
entrance.

In the hour of the wolf,
there is only
the clock

for company,
ticking
through the dark,

remorseless
stations
of the night.

ADRIAN GIBBONS KOESTERS

A Nun Eats Out of Turn on a Fast Day

The hunger not in her stomach   this one that arches her back
Under the stiff linen sheeting   designed to fend off just this hunger
Works its way into her stomach   from her lips, her mouth, how to describe
What it means to need   this much as she faces a metal bowl
Of boiled eggs in the peels   she dips her hand, cupped over one
Less its peel, into the second   bowl of cool water to rinse the shell
Bits from the flesh,   pretends to drop the egg in the third bowl
Brings her hand to mouth and coughs,   flips the egg to her tongue behind
Her teeth and closes them, careful   not to allow a bulge in her cheeks
Nor to let the working of the mouth   over the white and yolk
Show to the sister across the table,   or the guardians watching in spirit
She feels again that hunger that bread,   if it were alive, could not ease
As a voice, detached, says,   "I don't want—I can't—"

Design for the *Journal of Scholarly Publishing* (University of Toronto Press).

Top margin: 48 pts top trim to base of running head
Verso running head (when Journal title):

6 x 9" Text: 10.5/13.5 Minion Pro x 25P6. 38 lines. OK one short.
Oldstyle figures (superscripts lining). Paragraph indent: one pi

24 *Journal of Scholarly Publishing*

Folio: 9 pt oldstyle figures Hang in margin one pi

21 pts b/b from running head to first text line — 4P9 gutter

It becomes print only when it is published, because the economics favor electronic formats elsewhere in the publication process. These same Americans had to be made aware that they wouldn't have many of their necessities, let alone luxury goods, if they didn't learn to take care of them. The slogan in the chapter title — "Use It Up, Wear It Out, Make It Do, or Do Without" — was just one of several designed to make people wake up and smell the (rationed) coffee. (EM dash with thin space left and right)

Level 1 subhead: 11/13.5 even small caps lsp 50 units. Flush left. 27 pts b/b above, no extra space below Begin text flush left clc

THE INHERENT VALUES OF ACADEMIC REWARD STRUCTURES

Most conservation ads, both in 1942 and for the rest of the war, told people how to maintain just one kind of product (car, refrigerator, clothing, etc.). Such ads were usually placed by the manufacturer of one brand of the product in question or by the manufacturer of a product, such as motor oil, useful for the conserving another product, in this case an automobile, truck, or farm machinery. Most conservation ads provided useful tips on how to protect whatever product one owned, regardless of make, brand, or model, but /some advertisers discussed conserving only their own product (such as Mimeograph duplicators). While this may seem self-serving, some justification for this kind of advertising was given by Willard Chevalier, publisher of Business Week, in his weekly column "The Trading Post" on November 21, 1942: "The manufacturer who is now selling his goods to the government instead of to the civilian may still have a very proper need for advertising. He can very usefully, for instance, tell his former customers how to use and conserve and service the goods which he has previously sold them. Those goods in service may very well constitute the country's sole remaining stock of such articles. It is certainly right for the manufacturer to use advertising to help make that stock last.[27] (superscripts lining figures)

Only a few advertisers, both in 1942 and beyond, took up the challenge of presenting the case for conservation generally, but they did so in uncommonly eloquent, tough-talking, and powerful language. The Stewart-Warner Corporation in peacetime manufactured everything from refrigerators and electric ranges to lubricating equipment and speedometers. Straight talk characterized almost all Stewart-Warner war ads, but nowhere more so than in their ad in the Post on May 9, 1942, the first ad to make the case for wartime conservation generally: "Your job — your big job — is the prompt elimination of all forms of waste. That job starts right where you are — in your own home. To ask what to save is to admit a total lack of understanding of the crisis we face. Save everything! Waste noth-

26 *Journal of Scholarly Publishing*

It becomes print only when it is published, because the economics favor electronic formats elsewhere in the publication process. These same Americans had to be made aware that they wouldn't have many of their necessities, let alone luxury goods, if they didn't learn to take care of them. The slogan in the chapter title — "Use It Up, Wear It Out, Make It Do, or Do Without" — was just one of several designed to make people wake up and smell the (rationed) coffee.

Prose Extract: 10.5/13.5 Indent one pi from left 20 pts b/b above 20.5 pts b/b below

> Most conservation ads, both in 1942 and for the rest of the war, told people how to maintain just one kind of product (car, refrigerator, clothing, etc.). Such ads were usually placed by the manufacturer of one brand of the product in question or by the manufacturer of a product, such as motor oil, useful for the conserving another product, in this case an automobile, truck, or farm machinery.

Most conservation ads provided useful tips on how to protect whatever product one owned, regardless of make, brand, or model, but /some advertisers discussed conserving only their own product (such as Mimeograph duplicators). While this may seem self-serving, some justification for this kind of advertising was given by Willard Chevalier, publisher of Business Week, in his weekly column.

27 pts b/b author bio. 9/13 ragged right, names in small caps lsp 50 units, affiliations clc

turnovers indent one pi when there are multiple authors

JOAN F. CHEVERIE is Department Head of Digital Library Services at Georgetown University
JENNIFER BOETTCHER is Business Reference Librarian at Georgetown University
JOHN BUSCHMAN is Asssociate University Librarian for Scholarly Services at Georgetown University Library.

26 pts b/b Notes. Subhead 9 small caps lsp 50 units, flush left Notes: 9/13 hang and indent style. Note numbers FL on2 digits followed by period and word space. Align notes

NOTES

1. The Trading Post" on November 21, 1942
2. The manufacturer who is now selling his goods to the government instead of to the civilian may still have a very proper need for advertising. He can very usefully, for instance, tell his former customers how to use and conserve and service the goods which he has previously sold them.
13. Those goods in service may very well constitute the country's sole remaining stock of such articles. It is certainly right for the manufacturer to use advertising to help make that stock last" (127).
14. Only a few advertisers, both in 1942 and beyond, took up the challenge of presenting the case for conservation generally, but they did so in uncommonly elo-

FOR SINGLE AUTHORED ARTICLES

Halfpt rule x 25P6 on line 1

Title: 16/21 clc, begin on line 3

Should Graduate Students Publish?

Variable space to rule. Approx 27 pts from title
One point rule x 25P6 on next text line

ALLAN H. PASCO — Author: 12/19 small caps lsp 70 units

21.5 pts b/b Abstract: 9.5/13.5 italic, indent one pi from left

Most conservation ads, both in 1942 and for the rest of the war, told people how to maintain just one kind of product (car, refrigerator, clothing, etc.). Such ads were usually placed by the manufacturer of one brand of the product in question or by the manufacturer of a product, such as motor oil, useful for the conserving another product, in this case an automobile, truck, or farm machinery. Most conservation ads provided useful tips on how to protect whatever product one owned, regardless of make, brand, or model, but /some advertisers discussed conserving only their own product (such as Mimeograph duplicators). While this may seem self-serving, some justification for this kind of advertising was given by Willard Chevalier, publisher of Business Week, in his weekly column

19 pts b/b keywords Keywords: 9.5/13.5 italic ragged right Do not hyphen

Keywords: digital schlarship, promotion and tenure, trade publishing

Approx 27 pts b/b text Begin flush left,

It becomes print only when it is published, because the economics favor electronic formats elsewhere in the publication process. These same Americans had to be made aware that they wouldn't have many of their necessities, let alone luxury goods, if they didn't learn to take care of them. The slogan in the chapter title — "Use It Up, Wear It Out, Make It Do, or Do Without" — was just one of several designed to make people wake up and smell the (rationed) coffee.

Most conservation ads, both in 1942 and for the rest of the war, told people how to maintain just one kind of product (car, refrigerator, clothing, etc.). Such ads were usually placed by the manufacturer of one brand of the product in question or by the manufacturer of a product, such as motor oil, useful for the conserving another product, in this case an automobile, truck, or farm machinery. Most conservation ads provided useful tips on how to protect whatever product one owned, regardless of make, brand, or model, but /some advertisers discussed conserving only their own product (such as Mimeograph duplicators). While this may seem self-serving, some justification for this kind of advertising was given by Willard Chevalier, publisher of Business Week, in his weekly column "The

Journal of Scholarly Publishing April 2009 doi: 10.3138/jsp.40.3.219

FOR MULTI AUTHORED ARTICLES

Halfpt rule x 25P6 on line 1

Digital Scholarship in the University Tenure Promotion Process

Title: 16/21 clc, begin on line 3
Ragged right approx 18 pi max

Subtitle: 12/19 small caps letterspaced 70 units, ragged right

A REPORT ON THE SIXTH SCHOLARLY COMMUNICATION SYMPOSIUM AT GEORGETOWN UNIVERSITY LIBRARY

Variable space to rule. Approx 27 pts from subtitle.
One point rule x 25P6. Rule should fall on the next text line

JOAN F. CHEVERIE, JENNIFER BOETTCHER, and JOHN BUSCHMAN

Authors: 12/19 small caps lsp 70 units
'and' is lower case not letterspaced

21 pts b/b Abstract: 9.5/13.5 italic, indent one pi from left

Most conservation ads, both in 1942 and for the rest of the war, told people how to maintain just one kind of product (car, refrigerator, clothing, etc.). Such ads were usually placed by the manufacturer of one brand of the product in question or by the manufacturer of a product, such as motor oil, useful for the conserving another product, in this case an automobile, truck, or farm machinery. Most conservation ads provided useful tips on how to protect whatever product one owned, regardless of make, brand, or model, but /some advertisers discussed conserving only their own product (such as Mimeograph duplicators). While this may seem self-serving, some justification for this kind of advertising was given by Willard Chevalier, publisher of Business Week, in his weekly column

19 pts b/b keywords Keywords: 9.5/13.5 italic ragged right Do not hyphen

Keywords: digital schlarship, promotion and tenure, trade publishing

Approx 27 pts b/b text Begin flush left,

INTRODUCTION

It becomes print only when it is published, because the economics favor electronic formats elsewhere in the publication process. These same Americans had to be made aware that they wouldn't have many of their necessities, let alone luxury goods, if they didn't learn to take care of them. The slogan in the chapter title — "Use It Up, Wear It Out, Make It Do, or Do Without" — was just one of several designed to make people wake up and smell the (rationed) coffee.

Most conservation ads, both in 1942 and for the rest of the war, told people how to maintain just one kind of product (car, refrigerator, cloth-

Journal of Scholarly Publishing April 2009 doi: 10.3138/jsp.40.3.219

8/18 flush outside

variety. And my only "decorations" were the swash caps used in the running heads.

SUE HALL

I think that design is design whether I am creating a logo or bringing order to a complicated page that includes four levels of subheads and three kinds of lists. The principles are the same whether I am designing something for print or for the web. My goal is to simplify and organize the variables so the content is as accessible as possible, in a layout that is balanced but not static. I am part of a team that includes editors, production coordinators, marketing professionals, typesetters, printers, and online publishers, whose goal is to disseminate scholarly information.

A print journal appears several times a volume, year in and year out. An online journal updates more often than that. This periodic and ephemeral existence makes designing journals challenging in a way that designing single books is not.

A major part of its challenge lies in the fact that, in order to project a stable and professional editorial identity, a journal's graphic identity has to be maintained consistently. It's not feasible for me to oversee every typeset page of every journal I have designed, so the success of a journal's design and typographic consistency lies in preparing detailed, logical specs and annotated templates.

Like a typographically complex book, the average journal article can include long article titles and subtitles with multiple authors, abstracts, several levels of subheads, lists, poetry and prose epigraphs and extracts, complicated running head information, a variety of figure types and caption lengths, and footnotes or endnotes. In addition to including examples and specs for these existing elements, I also have to plan for how the design can accommodate new sections or unforeseen layout and typographic situations that might arise in the future.

In order to appeal to contemporary readers, a journal also needs to reflect current trends in typography, design, colors, and coatings. But it can't change too often or it will appear disorganized and fickle.

Another complication is that, if a typographic error is introduced, and if it's not glaringly obvious, it can be overlooked by the production team—myself included. If it's not caught and corrected, it will be replicated in future issues.

The positive, flip side of the evolution inherent in journals design is that there is ample opportunity for a do-over. I feel relieved that I can tweak a spec or design element during the first volume of a redesign, to improve the overall design.

So the graphic nature of journals is paradoxical in its need for stability without looking dated, and its ability to evolve without looking chaotic and unprofessional.

Whether I am designing a new journal or redesigning an existing one, my first step is to meet with the editors so I can learn about the publication's audience, editorial content, mission, and competitors in the field.

Before starting a redesign, I need to know what has precipitated the renovation: Is there a change of editorship or mission statement? Has the editorial office decided to appeal to a different audience, or is there a consensus that the design is outdated? I need to know whether the new look should be an evolution of the current design or a complete makeover.

I see the redesign of an established journal as the next phase in its life. As with biological evolution, I think it makes sense to keep any of the elements that work. The "if it's not broke, don't fix it" attitude helps on practical and philosophical levels. For example, using a rule in a new way or retaining either the body copy or display typeface as a point of departure helps define the parameters of the project. A journal might use a specific graphic element that can be updated. Keeping at least one design element also provides a subliminal level of consistency with the previous version, which in turn signals stability and helps maintain the journal's branding.

Like everything related to design, typefaces come in and out of fashion, and sometimes replacing one face is all that is needed to update the look. (See Figures 1A, 1B, and 1C.) Sometimes we can reuse a graphic image by updating its delivery. (See Figures 2A and 2B.)

As satisfying as it is to specify a favorite typeface for a journal, sometimes the choice is based on a process of elimination. I'm often influenced by what faces a competitor journal or our own journals in a similar field might already use. If the journal features math or other special characters or languages, the choices will be further narrowed to those fonts that either include those characters or can display them without disrupting the surrounding text.

If I decide to keep the existing text face when I redesign the journal, it's been a valuable lesson to work with one I don't personally care for, or one that I have previously taken for granted. Sometimes the existing typefaces being used are appropriate for the subject matter, but their current treatment isn't as readable or elegant as it could be. I've found that making one or two adjustments to size, leading, line length, and/or simplifying alignment improves the readability and freshness of the page. Sometimes introducing a different display face that might relate better to the body copy's x-height and shape is what makes the difference. (See Figures 3A, 3B, and 3C.)

I find it logical and natural to design from the inside out, because it allows me more time with the essential elements of the journal before tackling the cover. For one thing, this allows the basic elements of the cover to grow from the typography and layout of the interior pages. And the reality is that produc-

Figure 1A

Typefaces go in and out of fashion

I was asked to update the design of the interdisciplinary journal, *Social Text* (6-3/4"x9"). I had admired its layout for years because its strong, asymmetrical grid and use of white space seemed appropriate for its content and audience.

However, I found the Eras display text difficult to read and thought its pairing with Plantin made them both seem outdated.

Once I replaced Eras with News Gothic—a more straightforward and readable complement to the organic Plantin—I thought the Plantin worked well as body text. The Plantin italic, used for article opening subtitles, added a lively texture to those pages.

Except for the copyright info, I changed the overall structure of the display from flush right to flush left, in order to simplify the page and increase readability. I introduced a right-bleeding rule to the article openings, to offer a cantilevered balance to the flush left alignment.

Free Labor

PRODUCING CULTURE FOR THE DIGITAL ECONOMY

Tiziana Terranova

The real *not-capital* is *labor.*
—Karl Marx, *Grundrisse*

Working in the digital media industry is not as much fun as it is made out to be. The "NetSlaves" of the eponymous Webzine are becoming increasingly vociferous about the shamelessly exploitative nature of the job, its punishing work rhythms, and its ruthless casualization (www.disobey.com/netslaves). They talk about "24–7 electronic sweatshops" and complain about the ninety-hour weeks and the "moronic management of new media companies." In early 1999, seven of the fifteen thousand "volunteers" of America Online (AOL) rocked the info-loveboat by asking the Department of Labor to investigate whether AOL owes them back wages for the years of playing chathosts for free.[1] They used to work long hours and love it; now they are starting to feel the pain of being burned by digital media.

These events point to a necessary backlash against the glamorization of digital labor, which highlights its continuities with the modern sweatshop and points to the increasing degradation of knowledge work. Yet the question of labor in a "digital economy" is not so easily dismissed as an innovative development of the familiar logic of capitalist exploitation. The NetSlaves are not simply a typical form of labor on the Internet; they also embody a complex relation to labor that is widespread in late capitalist societies.

In this essay I understand this relationship as a provision of "free labor," a trait of the cultural economy at large, and an important, and yet undervalued, force in advanced capitalist societies. By looking at the Internet as a specific instance of the fundamental role played by free labor, this essay also tries to highlight the connections between the "digital economy" and what the Italian autonomists have called the "social factory." The "social factory" describes a process whereby "work processes have shifted from the factory to society, thereby setting in motion a truly complex machine."[2] Simultaneously voluntarily given and unwaged, enjoyed and exploited, free labor on the Net includes the activity of building Web sites, modifying software packages, reading and participating in mailing lists, and building virtual spaces on MUDs and MOOs. Far from being an

Social Text 63, Vol. 18, No. 2, Summer 2000. Copyright © 2000 by Duke University Press.

Can You Feel the Beat?

Freestyle's Systems of Living, Loving, and Recording

Alexandra T. Vazquez

"I had been a little girl with two guys on the side and six producers up her ass. It was time for Lisa Lisa to come out on her own and grow up."
—Lisa Velez, *She Bop: The Definitive History of Women in Pop, Rock, and Soul*

Please Don't Go

Nayobe Gomez is a Brooklyn-born and -reared Cuban musician who came of age in the mid-1980s. While she now performs a remarkable repertoire that includes merengue, cumbia, and salsa, Gomez initially made a name for herself as one of the main players in freestyle. Freestyle is both a musical genre and, as a multitude of fanzines will tell you, a lifestyle. The playwright Jorge Ignacio Cortiñas evoked our teenage surround when he called it a "system of living."[1] Described as "android descarga" by music critic Peter Shapiro and "a soap opera set to music" by the vocalist Judy Torres, there is general agreement that freestyle is constituted by a nebulous Latin feel that is spoken about but not necessarily accounted for (beyond its use of Roland TR-808 Claves).[2] But I enter the scene of freestyle with the assumption that it is both tinge and fringe—and by that I mean both marginal part and decorative border. To do so means to surrender the accolade of theorist for stylist, to harbor the hard work of listening from scholarly convention.

I begin with a set of Gomez's early performances, a recording and a cinematic counterpoint, to illustrate how freestyle has been wedged in the trajectory of popular music. At the same time, though, I argue that it is by way of these performances that Gomez troubles freestyle's position-

Social Text 102 • Vol. 28, No. 1 • Spring 2010
DOI 10.1215/01642472-2009-062 © 2010 Duke University Press

Figure 1B
The journal name, issue, and date were added to the running feet. I was disappointed that the pull quotes were to be removed, because they anchored the page visually. The flip side, however, was that I was able to take some space from the outer margin to increase the inner margin, which I thought was tight. The right-bleeding article opening rule is descended from the pull quotes' rules. I used a bold page number to help anchor the page.

Egalitarianism in One Institute: The Structure of an Alternative Conference

Given the history of unequal relations between the global North and the global South, we have tried to keep before us the consequences of regional power differentials, and to jettison the comforting illusion that academic exchange is immune to inequalities among participants. While recognizing the structural limitations in which we all work, we have deliberately installed mechanisms to combat the most obvious obstacles to democratic participation. These are evaluated and discussed with spirit at the end of each summer's session.

The institute opens each year with a full day of sessions dedicated to influential theoretical readings on the questions haunting both transnationally and nationally framed histories. This seminar format establishes a conference lingua franca before we proceed to smaller workshops on attendees' work in progress. Based on nominations from participants, the common theory readings provoke debate about globalization, resistance, and, following the subaltern studies school, the dubious nature of putatively universalist historical narratives. We opened our first year with Dipesh Chakrabarty's critique of the enterprise of Western history itself, of its provincial categories and stages. Since then, we have read Atilio Borón's work on the premature obituaries of the nation-state as well as Michael Hardt and Antonio Negri's *Empire*, and we have tackled works on subjectivity and resistance. Interdisciplinary arguments by María Josefina Saldaña-Portillo, Saba Mahmood, and Alain Badiou critiqued the illusory sovereign individual of bourgeois liberalism. All three of these readings fueled passionate debate on the dangers of defining resistance as liberation from cultural restraint. A session on the relationships among nationalism, tradition, and modernity also proved fruitful, deploying interventions by Néstor García Canclini and Roger Bartra.[8] But the most passionate discussion has arisen around the very category of transnational study itself.

Transnational History and Its Discontents

By equipping the institute with the deliberately vague moniker *transnational*, we have invited two interpretations of the term to coexist in Tepoztlán. One draws attention to stories that spill over, under, or around national boundaries. The other addresses historical questions in a transnational group, regardless of their geographical unit of analysis. Combining these approaches has made us particularly aware of the political ironies inherent to transnational history itself. Even as neoliberalism's opponents, we risk mystifying globalization with our analyses of population flows, amorphous knowledge networks, deterritorialized power, and solid states melting into air. As students of these phenomena, Borón warns us, we may become unwitting accomplices in the neoliberal demonization of the state.[9]

Voekel/Young

Even as neoliberalism's opponents, we risk mystifying globalization with our analyses of population flows, amorphous knowledge networks, deterritorialized power, and solid states melting into air.

But as Seigel underscores, there is no reason transnational analysis cannot center on the nation-state itself and ground power in specific geographical bases.[10] Collective member Bethany Moreton, for example, demonstrates that while Wal-Mart's thoroughly transnational networks are the products of the retailer's Sunbelt homeland, the multinational corporation also facilitated the Washington Consensus—no amorphous flows or deterritorialized power here. That said, the political effects of framing devices vary depending on whether one analyzes an imperialist nation deluded by notions of autogenesis or a third-world nation looking to defend itself from global forces centered in the North.

Given these critiques, the institute has welcomed historical work framed nationally, regionally, and locally. Agrarian struggle in the Mexican countryside; historical memory; philosophy of history; queer subjects' and indigenous peoples' battles for inclusion in the nation—these and other topics have provoked some of the best discussions at the conference.[11] The importance of the institute's ecumenicalism cannot be overstated: doing history transnationally requires accepting the possible provincialism of questions and categories one previously assumed to be universal. As Margarita Silva, a Central American participant, explained, she initially declined our invitation because the term *transnacional* evokes multinational corporations for Spanish speakers: she feared that we were gathering to celebrate neoliberal globalization.

To guarantee substantive and democratic discussions, we distribute the participants' papers a month in advance via a secure Web site, group them into themed panels with three or four papers each, and assign a team of discussants to each session to incite the crowd. Informal feminist strategies for curbing dominance of the discussion are deliberately formalized: each seminar has a panel dominatrix charged with sending the garrulous to the end of the speaking queue, moving first-time speakers to the front of the line, and encouraging discussion in Spanish. The structure recognizes that knowledge production is collective and that social hierarchies have to be combated—they don't magically disappear simply because we recognize them.

The Tepoztlán Institute is also a devoted promoter of family values. We welcome participants' others, significant and frivolous alike. Our

The Tepoztlán Institute 13

crisis of masculinity, transacting sexual violence personally suggests to him a possible means of escape, but the thrill of revenge evaporates fast.

Female characters are given little textual space in Nasreen's novel. The two most prominent women are Kiranmoyee and Maya. Even so, as characters they are underdeveloped; they serve primarily as sites for the performance of violence, physical as well as psychological. While much of Nasreen's literary and journalistic writings focus on cultural, economic, and sexual oppression of women under patriarchy, *Lajja*, surprisingly, withholds any exploration of Maya's or Shamima's sufferings (these characters disappear after the traumatic events). Instead, Maya's abduction and Shamima's violation serve to dramatize and exemplify Suranjan's psychological destabilization when faced with ubiquitous violence and hostility. Kiranmoyee's passivity is a metaphor for the psychological paralysis of minority women, while her silence suggests the marginalization of minority women as citizens. Abjectly dependent on her husband and helpless in the face of his refusal to relocate to India, Kiranmoyee can only grieve, weep, and pray for her daughter's safe return. When she screams, she does so wordlessly—her pain rejects language. The nation and its brutality remain, for all practical purposes, men's business. *Lajja* is a story of the father and son.

While as an antinational allegory *Lajja*'s propaganda value is considerable, its literary status is less certain. The grimly predictable plot, while it presents the transformation of the characters, does so with almost programmatic rigor. The presentation of the narrative, however, is atypical. Nasreen blurs the borders between fact and fiction through the insertion of numerical data and news reports into the text, which insists upon its own factual accuracy. *Lajja*, in this sense, may be described more fittingly as "faction," or, as the writer herself calls it, "a documentary novel."[4] Nasreen transcribes newspaper clippings on the tense communal situation, placing them side by side with census data to chart the history of Hindu emigration from East Pakistan/Bangladesh into India. In order to communicate the brutalities unleashed on Bangladesh's Hindu minority community, she intersperses her account of the violence with copious statistics of rape, murder, arson, and plunder similarly culled from newspaper reports. These frequently suspend plot development, and not infrequently it seems that situations are created in order to enable characters to cite more data.

The use of journalistic reports with sources mentioned is a way for Nasreen to protect her work against charges of fabrication or exaggeration of the terrorization of minorities. Indeed, the veracity of her work rests on the reliability of professional journalism. Moreover, Nasreen's use of numerical data reinforces the idea that the breadth of the violence is strictly unimaginable such that only raw quantification can adequately represent

34 Mookerjea-Leonard · *Nasreen's* Lajja *and the Minority Man*

it. The matter-of-fact prose of the newspaper overwhelms the novel form, suggesting that in this time of barbarism, all a novel can be is the staging of social science; it is reduced to an edited reader of newspaper reports. While *Lajja* lacks the in-depth exploration of a character's interiority that is central to the novel form, the form is nevertheless critical to Nasreen's presentation of the crisis, because the minorities' pain, like that of Maya and Kiranmoyee, is inarticulable through numbers. At one level, *Lajja* evokes the texture of the minorities' experience of the backlash in ways that journalistic dispassion will not allow. The novel form engenders a compassionate and ethically informed understanding of the minorities' suffering through a focused inquiry into the predicament of one (fictive) family. With its evocation of the sentimental and its purposeful didacticism, *Lajja* prompts a moral recognition of their ordeal. On another level, the novel sets out to represent the unrepresentable and banal character of modern social suffering.

A Minority Citizen

Sudhamoy Dutta, the paterfamilias of Nasreen's fictive family, undergoes literal emasculation as a member of the minority Hindu community in East Pakistan during the region's struggle for independence. His body is subjected to prejudices that have both religious and racial dimensions. In what follows I examine the mutually inclusive and blurred nature of social, political, and cultural identities, and the role of violence in isolating strands of identity, and the individuals who bear them; making them visible through and with suffering.

Embodied Identities

> Masculinity . . . is the "taking up" of an enunciative position, the making up of a psychic complex, the assumption of a social gender, the supplementation of a historic sexuality, the apparatus of a cultural difference.
> —Homi K. Bhabha, "Are You a Man or a Mouse?"

Why is Sudhamoy Dutta, we might ask—a dedicated and fully participatory citizen in the nation, involved in the language movement of 1952 and the liberation struggle of 1971—labeled Hindu-Bengali and subjected to prejudice?

Let us turn to the scene of the assault on Sudhamoy by the Pakistani army in 1971. The attack on Sudhamoy is set in the context of Bangladesh's liberation struggle. On his way to the Liberation Army military outpost, Sudhamoy confronts a band of West Pakistani soldiers and, upon inquiry, gives a Muslim name. The soldiers are skeptical and demand proof of

Social Text 108 · Fall 2011 **35**

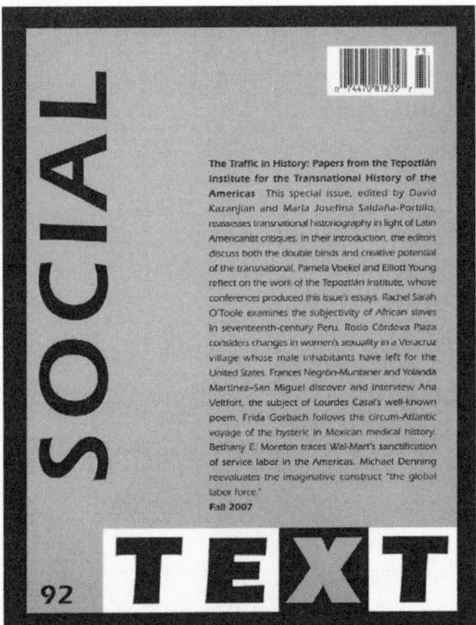

Figure 1C

As graphic and compelling as I found the original *Social Text* cover, the marketing needs of the journal had changed. It was thought that the descriptive copy on the cover should be replaced with art, and that a table of contents should be added to the back.

My first thought was to design a new logo that would retain the angle, and use imagery in the background or in the area defined by the descriptive copy. However, it was realized that the right-angled logo made the journal difficult to display in bookstores, where it would be shown face-out in the periodicals section—only the barcode showed when shorter periodicals were stacked in front of it. This is a case where a redesign instituted a more conventional solution.

Eighteenth Century
Life
PUBLISHED TRI-ANNUALLY FOR
THE COLLEGE OF WILLIAM AND MARY
BY THE JOHNS HOPKINS UNIVERSITY PRESS
Volume 23, n.s., 3
November, 1999

Figure 2A

Maintaining a graphic connection

When I redesigned the well-established interdisciplinary journal *Eighteenth-Century Life* (6"x9"), the editor wanted to continue using the oval vignettes of engravings from *Fables by John Gay* (1793) on the cover. They are rich in detail, so I also enlarged them to create a background and help add depth to the cover. The image changes every volume, and I admit that I enjoy using the ones where humans get their comeuppance.

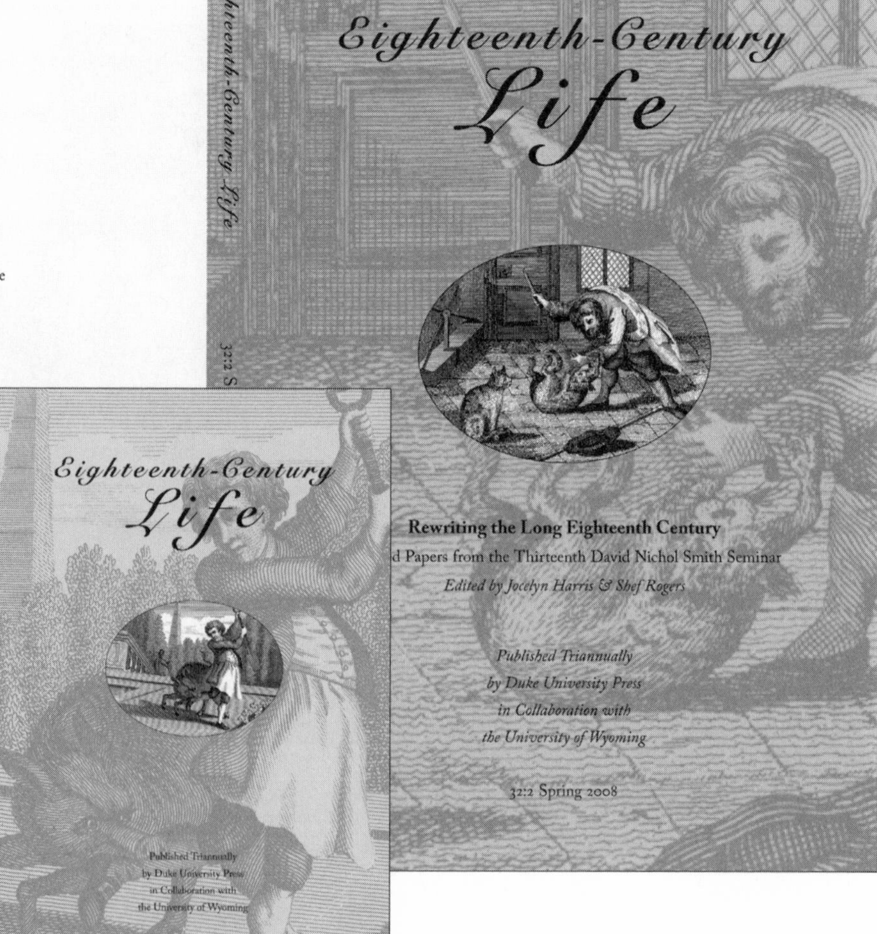

In This Issue
Introduction
Jocelyn Harris & Shef Rogers
Pope's 1723–25 Shakespear, Classical Editing, and
Humanistic Reading Practices
Edmund G. C. King
"A Palpable Imaginable Visitable Past":
Henry James and the Eighteenth Century
Philip Horne
From Pammydiddle to Persuasion:
Jane Austen Rewriting Eighteenth-Century Literature
Olivia Murphy
Rewritten and Reused: Imaging the Nabob through
"Upstart Iconography"
Christina Smylitopoulos
Eighteenth-Century Life
Eighteenth-Century
Life
Rewriting the Long Eighteenth Century
d Papers from the Thirteenth David Nichol Smith Seminar
Edited by Jocelyn Harris & Shef Rogers
Published Triannually
by Duke University Press
in Collaboration with
the University of Wyoming
32:2 Spring 2008
In This Issue
The Scottish Enlightenment and the Politics of Provincial Culture:
The Perth Literary and Antiquarian Society, ca. 1784–1790
David Allan
"Men, Women and Poles":
Samuel Richardson and the Romance of a Stuart Princess
Patricia Brückmann
Private Tutoring in Scotland: The Example of Mure of Caldwell
Henry L. Fulton
The Importance of the Chinese Connection:
The Origin of the English Garden
Yu Liu
Who Can Believe? Sentiment vs. Cynicism in Richardson's Clarissa
Heather Zias
Review Essay
Captivity and Captivation: Gullivers in Brobdingnag
Robert Darby
Books Received
Eighteenth-Century Life
Eighteenth-Century
Life
Published Triannually
by Duke University Press
in Collaboration with
the University of Wyoming
Duke

Ambivalent Judgments in the Proem of Pope's "To Mr. Addison, Occasioned by his Dialogues on Medals"

The opening lines of Pope's "To Mr. Addison, Occasioned by his Dialogues on Medals" compound two types of regret—the nostalgic type associated with elegy and the deploring kind we find in satire. As Howard Erskine-Hill has pointed out, this ambivalence springs from the subject's being simultaneously viewed from Christian and Augustan perspectives: "The emotion of pity, aroused by earlier lines, is modified by Pope's suggestion that Rome suffered chastisement for imperial hubris."[1] One way in which this ambivalence manifests itself can be seen in lines 9–10, the calculated appositive mix-ups of which have (as far as I can tell) not yet been remarked. Here are the lines in context:

> Imperial wonders rais'd on Nations spoil'd,
> Where mix'd with Slaves the groaning Martyr toil'd;
> Huge theatres, that now unpeopled Woods,
> Now drain'd a distant country of her Floods;
> Fanes, which admiring Gods with pride survey,
> Statues of men, scarce less alive than they;
> Some felt the silent stroke of mould'ring age,
> Some hostile fury, some religious rage. (ll. 5–12)[2]

The adjectival clause in line 6 clearly attaches itself to "wonders," and must therefore refer to the forced labor that issued in their erection rather than to the arenas of the circus. A careless reader, tempted to entertain ideas of gladiators and wild beasts before Pope actually alludes to them, would be hard pressed to apply "toil'd" (with its idea of persistent effort through time) to something as brief as a circus spectacle; whereas Rome's criminalization of Christianity *would* account for the martyr's presence among its work-force, the homologous participles—"rais'd," "spoil'd," and "toil'd"—making the dynamics of exploitation abundantly clear.

Even so, the wonders remain wonderful, even on their base of misgovernment, and so too the two nouns that stand in apposition to those "wonders" in the catalogue that follows. Whatever the abuses associated with them, the "Theatres" and "Fanes" clearly compel awe in the Augustan mind, obsessed as it was with environmental control. The word "distant" evokes the stride of aqueducts from a vanishing point on the horizon, an

Eighteenth-Century Life 24 (Winter 2000): 103–107 © 2000 by The College of William & Mary

106

NOTES

1. "The Metal Against Time: A Study of Pope's *Epistle to Mr Addison*," *Journal of the Warburg and Courtauld Institute* 28 (1965): 278.
2. *The Poems of Alexander Pope: A One-Volume Edition of the Twickenham Text with Selected Annotations*, ed. John Butt (London: Methuen, 1963), p. 215.
3. P. J. Chandlery, *Pilgrim-Walks in Rome* (London: Manresa, 1903), p. 205.
4. *Metamorphoses*, trans. Frank Justus Miller, 2 vols. (London: William Heinemann, 1916), 2:82.
5. *The Poems of Gray, Collins and Goldsmith*, ed. Roger Lonsdale (London: Longman, 1969), pp. 125 & 639.
6. *Poetical Works*, ed. Thomas Hutchinson, rev. Ernest de Selincourt (London: Oxford Univ., 1969), p. 509.
7. *English Verse*, ed. W. Peacock, 5 vols. (London: Oxford Univ., 1960), 4:146.
8. *Poetical Works*, ed. H. W. Garrod (London: Oxford Univ., 1970), p. 210.
9. "Euhemerus," *The Oxford Classical Dictionary*, ed. N. G. L. Hammond & H. H. Scullard (Oxford: Clarendon, 1970), p. 415.

— Review Essay —

Social Identity and the Politics of Place in France

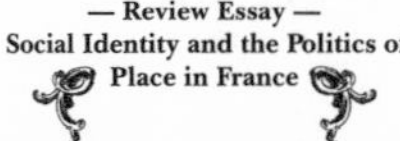

Robert W. Berger. *A Royal Passion: Louis XIV as Patron of Architecture.* Cambridge and New York: Cambridge University Press, 1997. Pp. 224. 160 ills. $23.95 paper. ISBN 0-521-58644-5

Chandra Mukerji. *Territorial Ambitions and the Gardens of Versailles.* Cambridge and New York: Cambridge University Press, 1997. Pp. 420. 150 ills. $80, $34.95 paper. ISBN 0-521-49675-6; 59959-8

Richard Cleary. *The "Place Royale" and Urban Design in the Ancien Régime.* Cambridge and New York: Cambridge University Press, 1999. Pp. 300 194 b&w ills., 12 color. $90. ISBN 0-521-57268-1

Rochelle Ziskin. *The Place Vendôme: Architecture and Social Mobility in Eighteenth-Century Paris.* Cambridge and New York: Cambridge University Press, 1999. Pp. 240. 120 ills. $75. ISBN 0-521-59259-3

The four books under review, all dealing with French architecture and landscape design, were published by Cambridge University Press, which has emerged in the last decade as a powerhouse in the field of scholarly books on art historical subjects. The breadth of Cambridge's book list in this area is astonishing, including highly specialized monographs intended for a limited academic audience, anthologies of essays surveying interpretive methods and debates in specific fields, and survey texts useful for undergraduate teaching. The authors consist both of well-published historians as well as young scholars reworking their dissertations. The Press has managed to keep a grip on the rising cost of producing illustrated art books through its streamlined editorial process and standardized format and layout. Although list prices are high and color plates are few, the books are generously illustrated in black and white and the overall production values are excellent.

Robert Berger's *A Royal Passion: Louis XIV as Patron of Architecture* is a comprehensive chronological survey of the building projects initiated by the Sun King throughout his reign, from 1661 to 1715. All of the major projects are included, from the Louvre and Versailles to Clagny and Marly. Up-to-date information on some of the lesser known commissions, such as Louis XIV's changes to the Château des Tuileries, is available here for the first time in English. The fourteen chap-

Eighteenth-Century Life 24 (Winter 2000): 108–113 © 2000 by The College of William & Mary

Figure 2B
It seemed appropriate to continue using printer's ornaments, but in a way that didn't distract from the titles. They also needed to be practical and sustainable using today's technology. I kept the journal's typography simple and straightforward, while adding back a flourish by using a decorative script for the section titles and page numbers.

The Ghosts of Epigram, False Wit, and the Augustan Mode

Roger D. Lund
Le Moyne College

Despite the efforts of Augustan poets and critics to eradicate false wit, the title pages of eighteenth-century poetic miscellanies offer powerful evidence that the popular taste for anagrams, acrostics, jests, riddles, rebuses, conundrums, epigrams, and cheap witticisms never really disappeared.[1] In a long footnote to the *Dunciad*, Pope complains of Miscellanies

> thrown out weekly and monthly by every miserable scribler; or picked up piece-meal and stolen from any body under the title of Papers, Essays, Queries, Verses, Epigrams, Riddles, &c. Equally the disgrace of human Wit, Morality and Decency.[2]

Following Addison's guidance in the *Spectator*, nos. 58–62 (May 1711), modern readers of eighteenth-century poetry have been trained to recognize puns, anagrams, and acrostics as forms of false wit. Critics have had far less to say about the status of epigram, however, a poetic form advertised in virtually every eighteenth-century miscellany even as critics called its legitimacy into question. Even Pope, who condemns epigram as a "disgrace of human Wit, Morality and Decency," nevertheless produced a significant number of memorable epigrams that were widely reprinted in precisely the sorts of miscellanies he condemns in the *Dunciad.*

Since each epigram might have been reprinted in any number of the

Eighteenth-Century Life
Volume 27, Number 2, Spring 2003 © 2003 by The College of William & Mary
67

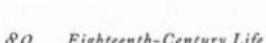

80 *Eighteenth-Century Life*

42. One of the more cutting lines in *Satiromastix* (1601) is when Thomas Dekker has Jonson (as "Horace"), trying to salvage his poetic reputation, desperately enquire "You ha seene my Acrostícks?" (I.ii.90). From *The Dramatic Works of Thomas Dekker*, ed. Fredson Bowers, 4 vols. (Cambridge: Cambridge Univ., 1953–61), 1:318.
43. Robert Lloyd, "A Familiar Letter Of Rhimes to a Lady," from *The Poetical Works*, 2 vols. (London, 1774), 2:82–83, ll. 107–18.
44. James William Dodd, *Ballads of Archery, Sonnets, etc.* (London, 1818), ix–x.
45. Lloyd, "The Puff," *Poetical Works*, 1:175, l.103.
46. Lloyd, "The Puff," *Poetical Works*, 1:175, ll. 99–105.
47. William Cowper, "Table Talk," from *The Poems of William Cowper*, ed. John D. Baird and Charles Ryskamp, 3 vols. (Oxford: Clarendon, 1980), 1:254–55, ll. 506–10.
48. Steele makes his comment in *Guardian* 10; Richard Cumberland is quoted in Field, *King's Nurseries*, 30.

Review Essay

Eighteenth-Century Aesthetics in New Perspective

G. Gabrielle Starr
New York University

Tom Huhn. *Imitation and Society: The Persistence of Mimesis in the Aesthetics of Burke, Hogarth, and Kant* (University Park: Pennsylvania State Univ., 2004). Pp. 216. $55. ISBN 0-271-02468-2

Nigel Leask. *Curiosity and the Aesthetics of Travel Writing, 1770–1840* (New York: Oxford Univ., 2002). Pp. 338. 19 ills. $29.95. ISBN 0199269300

Arnaud Maillet. *The Claude Glass: Use and Meaning of the Black Mirror in Western Art*, translated by Jeff Fort. (New York: Zone, 2004). Pp. 300. 37 ills. $26.95. ISBN 1-890951-47-1

Virginia E. Swain. *Grotesque Figures: Baudelaire, Rousseau, and the Aesthetics of Modernity.* (Baltimore: Johns Hopkins Univ., 2004). Pp. 268. $45. ISBN 0-8018-7945-0

In four new books on aesthetics in the eighteenth century, historicism is blended in striking ways with analytic philosophy, formalism, phenomenology, and the study of empire. Tom Huhn, in *Imitation and Society*, undertakes careful analyses of the development of aesthetic thought in the mid and late century, pursuing the history of ideas as it is rooted in both philosophical discourse and the ongoing play of social forces; Nigel Leask, in *Curiosity and the Aesthetics of Travel Writing*, Arnaud Maillet in *The Claude Glass*, and Virginia

Eighteenth-Century Life
Volume 29, Number 3, Fall 2005 © 2005 by Duke University Press
97

GET THEE TO A BIG CITY

SEXUAL IMAGINARY AND THE GREAT GAY MIGRATION

Kath Weston

On a temporary stage erected in San Francisco's Castro district, Meg Christian leaned toward the microphone. Whether the occasion was a rally or a street fair I can't recall, for I was all of nineteen and had yet to become a sociocultural anthropologist or take my first field note. I had never particularly liked Christian's genre of "women's music." Yet there I was, new in town, and here she was, a recognizable face and a star. I stopped to listen. Following a spirited rendition of "Ode to a Gym Teacher," a comedic ballad about a young girl's crush on her physical education instructor, the singer paused to comment on the difficulties of "growing up gay" in a rural area. Her advice to onlookers who had friends or relatives still struggling to "come out" in the countryside: Tell them to take the next bus or train to a big city. Whistles, cheers, and nodding heads greeted this clarion call.

In the late 1970s, unknown to myself at the time, I was riding a wave of lesbian and gay male migrants to the Bay Area. After finishing college in the Midwest, my girlfriend and I piled all our worldly possessions into a drive-away car to head for the gay metropolis on the coast.[1] The incongruities of age and class in this scenario were apparent to the first patrolman who chanced to observe my raggedy T-shirt-clad self at the wheel of a brand-new Cadillac with twelve miles on it. He pulled us over and demanded to see registration papers within a mile of the agency that had assigned us the car. Time in the streets had left me wary of police, so it took me a while to relax after that initial altercation. But once we hit the highway, I remember taking pleasure in climbing out of that Caddy to walk into cafés in small towns across the United States where a white woman in jeans and boots was not nearly enough to turn a head.

During my years of work and graduate school in California, the occasional cross-country trip with its truck-stop cafés was the closest I got to "rural life." When I chose the San Francisco Bay Area as the site for a research project on lesbians, gay men, coming out, and (as the project evolved) kin-

GLQ, Vol. 2, pp. 253–277
Reprints available directly from the publisher
Photocopying permitted by license only

EXISTENTIALLY SURPLUS

Women of Color Feminism and the New Crises of Capitalism

Grace Kyungwon Hong

What does "crisis" look like under contemporary capitalism? This is a particularly vexing question because contemporary capitalism's signal characteristic is the *incorporation* of the formations that constitute crisis in an earlier moment. In this essay, I examine the shift from an earlier manifestation of capitalism in the United States in the late nineteenth and early twentieth centuries organized around production to one organized around speculation, in order to describe how racialized, gendered, and sexualized difference operate in the contemporary moment.

The previous era of capitalism was organized around the production of difference through surplus labor. In the industrial period of the late nineteenth and early twentieth centuries in the United States, the contradictions of capitalism were sublated through a particular nexus of gendered and sexualized racialization that emerged by exploiting *labor.* As Lisa Lowe observes, the US nation-state required a homogeneous citizenry while US industrial capital required a heterogeneous workforce, differentiated by categories of race that were articulated through gender and sexual nonnormativity.[1] This contradiction was managed by creating a citizenry defined around whiteness and masculinity, subtended by the production of racialized and nonnormatively gendered and sexualized workers who provided the labor force. This differentiated labor force was excluded from citizenship, thereby allowing the nation-state to define itself as homogeneous. Lowe situates the Asian immigrant as the paradigmatic figure for this worker alienated from citizenship.

Extending Lowe's argument, Roderick Ferguson identifies *surplus labor* as producing the very forms of racialized, gendered, and sexualized difference that capital requires but cannot entirely manage. Following Karl Marx, Ferguson observes that these differences are necessary to the production of surplus labor,

GLQ 18:1
DOI 10.1215/10642684-1422152

Figure 3A

Designing with typefaces that are not one's first choice

When I redesigned the interdisciplinary journal *GLQ: A Journal of Lesbian and Gay Studies* (6-3/4"x9-3/4"), the goal was to update its look and increase its readability.

I thought the size, leading, and spacing of the Bodoni body copy made the pages difficult to read, and it would not have been my first choice for an accessible typeface. However, since this face was an integral part of *GLQ*'s well-established look, I thought it was important to make it work. I chose a different cut, reduced the size, increased the leading, and shortened the line length by widening the page margins. I used the script typeface from the cover for the article opening drop cap and page numbers, and chose a less-condensed sans for the rest of the display text.

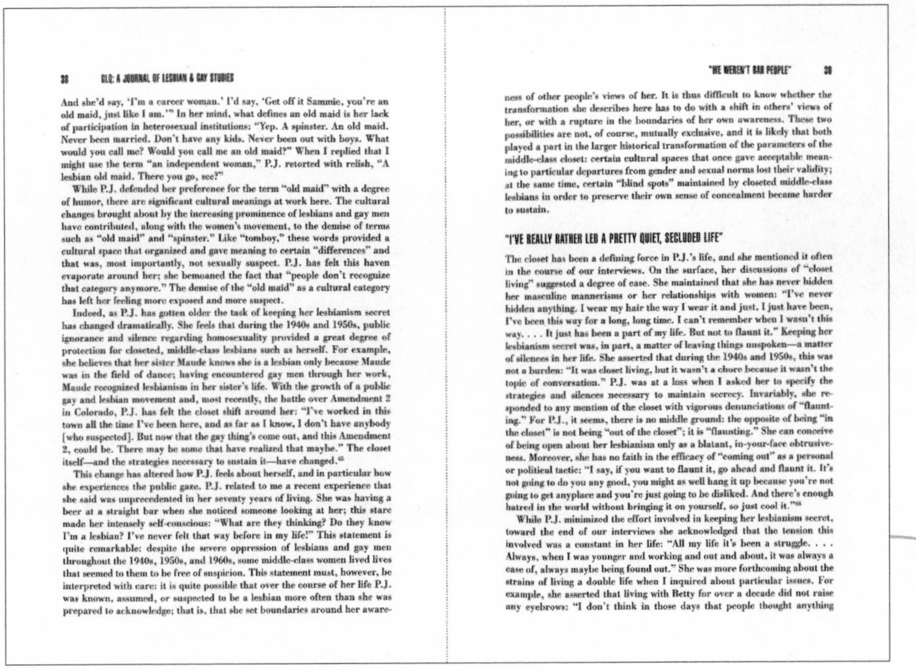

38 GLQ: A JOURNAL OF LESBIAN & GAY STUDIES

And she'd say, 'I'm a career woman.' I'd say, 'Get off it Sammie, you're an old maid, just like I am.'" In her mind, what defines an old maid is her lack of participation in heterosexual institutions: "Yep. A spinster. An old maid. Never been married. Don't have any kids. Never been out with boys. What would you call me? Would you call me an old maid?" When I replied that I might use the term "an independent woman," P.J. retorted with relish, "A lesbian old maid. There you go, see?"

While P.J. defended her preference for the term "old maid" with a degree of humor, there are significant cultural meanings at work here. The cultural changes brought about by the increasing prominence of lesbians and gay men have contributed, along with the women's movement, to the demise of terms such as "old maid" and "spinster." Like "tomboy," these words provided a cultural space that organized and gave meaning to certain "differences" and that was, most importantly, not sexually suspect. P.J. has felt this haven evaporate around her; she bemoaned the fact that "people don't recognize that category anymore." The demise of the "old maid" as a cultural category has left her feeling more exposed and more suspect.

Indeed, as P.J. has gotten older the task of keeping her lesbianism secret has changed dramatically. She feels that during the 1940s and 1950s, public ignorance and silence regarding homosexuality provided a great degree of protection for closeted, middle-class lesbians such as herself. For example, she believes that her sister Maude knows she is a lesbian only because Maude was in the field of dance; having encountered gay men through her work, Maude recognized lesbianism in her sister's life. With the growth of a public gay and lesbian movement and, most recently, the battle over Amendment 2 in Colorado, P.J. has felt the closet shift around her: "I've worked in this town all the time I've been here, and as far as I know, I don't have anybody [who suspected]. But now that the gay thing's come out, and this Amendment 2, could be. There may be some that have realized that maybe." The closet itself—and the strategies necessary to sustain it—have changed.[45]

This change has altered how P.J. feels about herself, and in particular how she experiences the public gaze. P.J. related to me a recent experience that she said was unprecedented in her seventy years of living. She was having a beer at a straight bar when she noticed someone looking at her; this stare made her intensely self-conscious: "What are they thinking? Do they know I'm a lesbian? I've never felt that way before in my life!" This statement is quite remarkable: despite the severe oppression of lesbians and gay men throughout the 1940s, 1950s, and 1960s, some middle-class women lived lives that seemed to them to be free of suspicion. This statement must, however, be interpreted with care: it is quite possible that over the course of her life P.J. was known, assumed, or suspected to be a lesbian more often than she was prepared to acknowledge; that is, that she set boundaries around her aware-

"WE WEREN'T BAR PEOPLE" 39

ness of other people's views of her. It is thus difficult to know whether the transformation she describes here has to do with a shift in others' views of her, or with a rupture in the boundaries of her own awareness. These two possibilities are not, of course, mutually exclusive, and it is likely that both played a part in the larger historical transformation of the parameters of the middle-class closet: certain cultural spaces that once gave acceptable meaning to particular departures from gender and sexual norms lost their validity; at the same time, certain "blind spots" maintained by closeted middle-class lesbians in order to preserve their own sense of concealment became harder to sustain.

"I'VE REALLY RATHER LED A PRETTY QUIET, SECLUDED LIFE"

The closet has been a defining force in P.J.'s life, and she mentioned it often in the course of our interviews. On the surface, her discussions of "closet living" suggested a degree of ease. She maintained that she has never hidden her masculine mannerisms or her relationships with women: "I've never hidden anything. I wear my hair the way I wear it and just, I just have been, I've been this way for a long, long time. I can't remember when I wasn't this way. . . . It just has been a part of my life. But not to flaunt it." Keeping her lesbianism secret was, in part, a matter of leaving things unspoken—a matter of silences in her life. She asserted that during the 1940s and 1950s, this was not a burden: "It was closet living, but it wasn't a chore because it wasn't the topic of conversation." P.J. was at a loss when I asked her to specify the strategies and silences necessary to maintain secrecy. Invariably, she responded to any mention of the closet with vigorous denunciations of "flaunting." For P.J., it seems, there is no middle ground: the opposite of being "in the closet" is not being "out of the closet"; it is "flaunting." She can conceive of being open about her lesbianism only as a blatant, in-your-face obtrusiveness. Moreover, she has no faith in the efficacy of "coming out" as a personal or political tactic: "I say, if you want to flaunt it, go ahead and flaunt it. It's not going to do you any good, you might as well hang it up because you're not going to get anyplace and you're just going to be disliked. And there's enough hatred in the world without bringing it on yourself, so just cool it."[46]

While P.J. minimized the effort involved in keeping her lesbianism secret, toward the end of our interviews she acknowledged that the tension this involved was a constant in her life: "All my life it's been a struggle. . . . Always, when I was younger and working and out and about, it was always a case of, always maybe being found out." She was more forthcoming about the strains of living a double life when I inquired about particular issues. For example, she asserted that living with Betty for over a decade did not raise any eyebrows: "I don't think in those days that people thought anything

Figure 3B
Increasing the leading improved the readability of the page by lightening the "color" of the body copy so it had more contrast with the display text. I further increased readability by making subheads upper and lowercase instead of all caps.

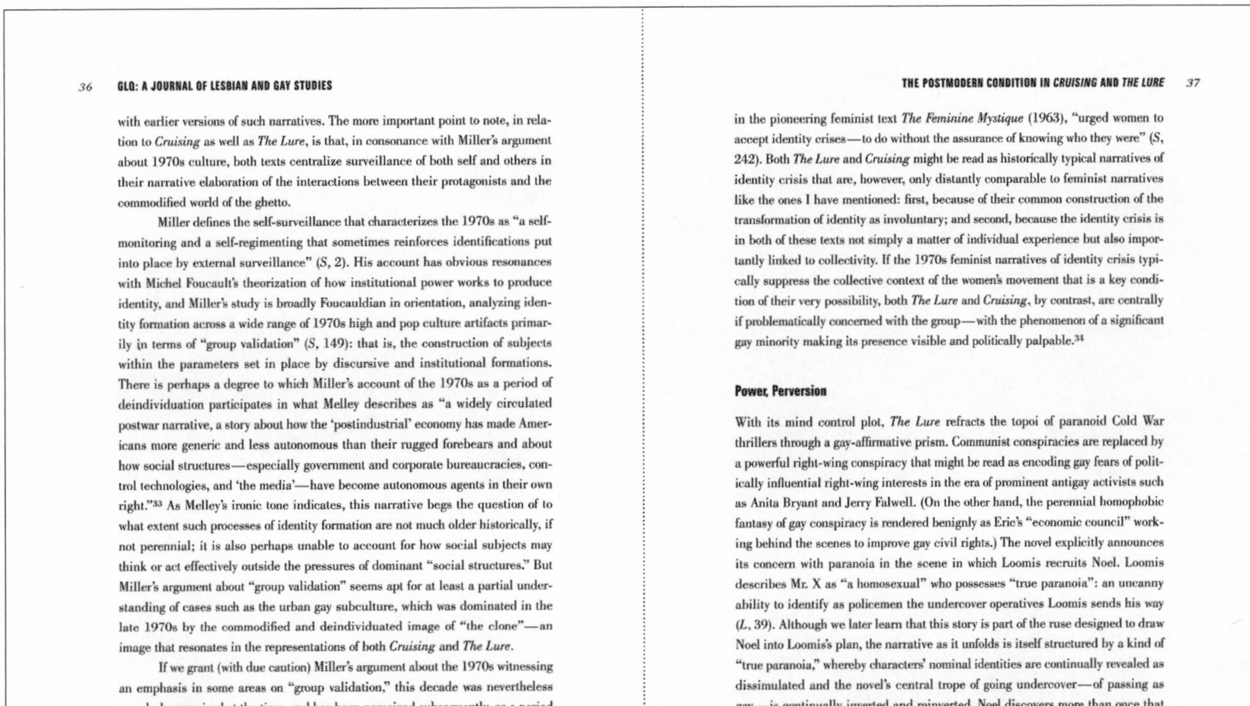

36 **GLQ: A JOURNAL OF LESBIAN AND GAY STUDIES**

with earlier versions of such narratives. The more important point to note, in relation to *Cruising* as well as *The Lure*, is that, in consonance with Miller's argument about 1970s culture, both texts centralize surveillance of both self and others in their narrative elaboration of the interactions between their protagonists and the commodified world of the ghetto.

Miller defines the self-surveillance that characterizes the 1970s as "a self-monitoring and a self-regimenting that sometimes reinforces identifications put into place by external surveillance" (*S*, 2). His account has obvious resonances with Michel Foucault's theorization of how institutional power works to produce identity, and Miller's study is broadly Foucauldian in orientation, analyzing identity formation across a wide range of 1970s high and pop culture artifacts primarily in terms of "group validation" (*S*, 149): that is, the construction of subjects within the parameters set in place by discursive and institutional formations. There is perhaps a degree to which Miller's account of the 1970s as a period of deindividuation participates in what Melley describes as "a widely circulated postwar narrative, a story about how the 'postindustrial' economy has made Americans more generic and less autonomous than their rugged forebears and about how social structures—especially government and corporate bureaucracies, control technologies, and 'the media'—have become autonomous agents in their own right."[33] As Melley's ironic tone indicates, this narrative begs the question of to what extent such processes of identity formation are not much older historically, if not perennial; it is also perhaps unable to account for how social subjects may think or act effectively outside the pressures of dominant "social structures." But Miller's argument about "group validation" seems apt for at least a partial understanding of cases such as the urban gay subculture, which was dominated in the late 1970s by the commodified and deindividuated image of "the clone"—an image that resonates in the representations of both *Cruising* and *The Lure*.

If we grant (with due caution) Miller's argument about the 1970s witnessing an emphasis in some areas on "group validation," this decade was nevertheless popularly perceived at the time, and has been perceived subsequently, as a period of intense individualism—the era of the "Me Generation." The 1970s are often thought of as distinguished by a cultural preoccupation with the volitional invention and reinvention of selves, demonstrated, for instance, by the popularity of narratives of bourgeois feminist self-liberation, such as the Lisa Alther novel *Kinflicks* (1976) and the Paul Mazursky film *An Unmarried Woman* (1978). The usual catalyst for the remaking of the self in these narratives is the identity crisis, which was an invention of the existentialist 1940s and 1950s but the positive ramifications of which were, Miller notes, established during the 1960s; for instance, Betty Friedan,

THE POSTMODERN CONDITION IN *CRUISING* AND *THE LURE* *37*

in the pioneering feminist text *The Feminine Mystique* (1963), "urged women to accept identity crises—to do without the assurance of knowing who they were" (*S*, 242). Both *The Lure* and *Cruising* might be read as historically typical narratives of identity crisis that are, however, only distantly comparable to feminist narratives like the ones I have mentioned: first, because of their common construction of the transformation of identity as involuntary; and second, because the identity crisis is in both of these texts not simply a matter of individual experience but also importantly linked to collectivity. If the 1970s feminist narratives of identity crisis typically suppress the collective context of the women's movement that is a key condition of their very possibility, both *The Lure* and *Cruising*, by contrast, are centrally if problematically concerned with the group—with the phenomenon of a significant gay minority making its presence visible and politically palpable.[34]

Power, Perversion

With its mind control plot, *The Lure* refracts the topoi of paranoid Cold War thrillers through a gay-affirmative prism. Communist conspiracies are replaced by a powerful right-wing conspiracy that might be read as encoding gay fears of politically influential right-wing interests in the era of prominent antigay activists such as Anita Bryant and Jerry Falwell. (On the other hand, the perennial homophobic fantasy of gay conspiracy is rendered benignly as Eric's "economic council" working behind the scenes to improve gay civil rights.) The novel explicitly announces its concern with paranoia in the scene in which Loomis recruits Noel. Loomis describes Mr. X as "a homosexual" who possesses "true paranoia": an uncanny ability to identify as policemen the undercover operatives Loomis sends his way (*L*, 39). Although we later learn that this story is part of the ruse designed to draw Noel into Loomis's plan, the narrative as it unfolds is itself structured by a kind of "true paranoia," whereby characters' nominal identities are continually revealed as dissimulated and the novel's central trope of going undercover—of passing as gay—is continually inverted and reinverted. Noel discovers more than once that the ostensibly straight cops from Loomis's unit who, like him, are passing as gay really are gay, or at least are really having sex with men. Luis, a married man with whom Noel works in the bar, turns out to be "balling" other barmen and bar patrons. Later another man, Larry, who Noel assumes is one of Loomis's operatives, leads him out of a potentially compromising situation by taking him home from a nightclub where his gayness has been challenged. Noel's relief that his cover has been maintained by Larry (the other men at the nightclub "were certain to think that he and Larry were going home to fuck" [*L*, 96]) turns to bewilderment

A JOURNAL OF LESBIAN AND GAY STUDIES

Edited by
CAROLYN DINSHAW & DAVID M. HALPERIN

"We Weren't Bar People"

Funérailles

Troping the Light Fantastic

All About Eve

Where the Girls Are

Intellectual Desire

VOLUME 3 NUMBER 1

Gordon and Breach
PUBLISHERS

Figure 3C
Part of the redesign included moving the article listings to the back cover, introducing cover art, and refining the typography of the circular logo. I created a wordmark to go with it, and reduced it all to make room for the art.

For consistency, I used the script typeface from the cover for the inside pages' initial drop caps and page numbers.

IN THIS ISSUE

Introduction:
Black/Queer/Diaspora at the Current Conjuncture

Editorial Note: A Conversation "Overflowing with Memory": On Omise'eke Natasha Tinsley's "Water, Shoulders, Into the Black Pacific"

Extract from
"Water, Shoulders, Into the Black Pacific"

Chatting Back an Epidemic:
Caribbean Gay Men, HIV/AIDS, and the Uses of Erotic Subjectivity

Queer(y)ing Freedom: Black Queer Visibilities in Postapartheid South Africa

What the Sands Remember

Of Unexplained Presences, Flying Ife Heads, Vampires, Sweat, Zombies, and Legbas:
A Meditation on Black Queer Aesthetics

"My Father Didn't Have a Dick":
Social Death and Jackie Kay's *Trumpet*

Beyond Ceremony
by Wura-Natasha Ogunji.
Courtesy of the artist

ISBN 978-0-8223-6776-5

GLQ A JOURNAL OF LESBIAN AND GAY STUDIES VOLUME 18 NUMBERS 2–3 2012 *Duke*

A JOURNAL OF
LESBIAN AND GAY STUDIES
VOLUME 18 NUMBERS 2–3 2012

Black/Queer/Diaspora

Edited by
JAFARI S. ALLEN

tion timelines mean I need to provide specs and templates for the typesetter long before I will be designing the first cover.

I start with a representative article, a review, and then I design the table of contents. Like books that contain complicated typographic hierarchies, journal design is about planning for the worst-case scenario. So I create a "kitchen sink" article, which includes such elements as a section title, long main title, subtitle, multiple authors, multiple epigraphs (poetry and prose), acknowledgments, two or three levels of subheads, extracts (poetry and prose with multiple paragraphs or stanzas), bulleted and numbered lists, footnotes or endnotes, bibliographic information, a variety of sized and shaped figures and captions, tables, and running heads that include journal title, author, and article title. I find that if I make a complicated article look inviting to read, then the average, more representative real-world article will be even more so. (See Figures 4A, 4B, and 4C.)

During my design process I do numerous roughs, but I limit my presentation to two or maybe three options. These include variations on such broad-stroke elements as text and display typefaces and how they are aligned, typographic or layout variations of footnotes, figures and captions, running heads and page numbers, whether and how I'm suggesting we use a graphic article opening or ending dingbat. I always show spreads, so the editors can envision how the elements relate across the gutter.

I consider this a collaborative process, where everyone brings their own expertise to the table. I find that the back-and-forth communication between the editors and me helps them understand the design process and have a sense of partnership in the collaboration. This is helpful when they have to explain the redesign or design to their editorial boards.

Conversely, I've found that editors often make good suggestions that might not have occurred to me because I am too close to the design. If their suggestions work from a design standpoint I am happy to include them. Likewise, if I think an editor's suggestion doesn't work from a design or readability standpoint, I've found that the process of my pushing back in a pedagogical and professional manner can be trust-building on both sides. (See Figures 5A, 5B, and 5C.)

Once the interior design is approved, I write typesetting specs and make detailed, annotated double-page spread templates out of the InDesign files I've used during the design and presentation process. The typesetter builds the master pages using my grid and style sheets as a foundation, but usually streamlines them so they conform to best typesetting practices. I include a sample of every type of piece that might be included: usually that will be an article, review, contributors' page, table of contents, and masthead and publication information. I make annotated cover templates with in-depth style sheets.

Figure 4A

Templates for the worst-case scenario

Designing for journals means planning ahead of time for typographically complex content. The hope is always that no article will ever include all these elements and variations—at least in such close proximity to each other—so the real-world piece will be orderly and readable.

Redesigning the *Journal of Music Studies* (6-7/8"x9-7/8") meant including specs for displaying multiple levels of subheads, different kinds of lists, extracts, definitions, theorems, mathematical equations, and an unlimited variety of displays of written music.

When presenting such a template to the editorial office, I include a warning that the text should not be "read," because it is just texture and has been cut and pasted without regard for its meaning.

Engebretsen, Nora Ann. 2002. "The Chaos of Possibilities: Combinatorial Group Theory in Nineteenth-Century German Harmony Treatises." Ph.D. diss., State University of New York at Buffalo.

Hook, Julian. 2002. "Uniform Triadic Transformations." Journal of Music Theory 46: 57–126.

Hyer, Brian. 1989. "Tonal Intuitions in Tristan und Isolde." Ph.D. diss., Yale University.

———. 1995. "Reimag(in)ing Riemann." Journal of Music Theory 39: 101–38.

Klumpenhouwer, Henry. 1994. "Some Remarks on the Use of Riemann Transformations." Music Theory Online 0/9.

———. 2000. "Remarks on American Neo-Riemannian Theory." Tijdschrift voor Muziektheorie 5: 155–69.

Kochavi, Jonathan. 1998. "Some Structural Features of Contextually-Defined Inversion Operators." Journal of Music Theory 42: 307–20.

Kopp, David. 2002. Chromatic Transformations in Nineteenth-Century Music. Cambridge Studies in Music Theory and Analysis 17. Cambridge: Cambridge University Press.

Lewin, David. 1982–83. "Transformational Techniques in Atonal and Other Music Theories." Perspectives of New Music 21/1–2: 312–71.

Gollin, Edward Henry. 2000. "Representations of Space and Conceptions of Distance in Transformational Music Theories." Ph.D. diss., Harvard University.

Hauptmann, Moritz. 1893. The Nature of Harmony and Metre. Translated by W. E. Heathcote. 2nd ed. London: Sonnenschein. Reprint ed., New York: Da Capo Press, 1991. Translation of Die Natur der Harmonik und der Metrik. Leipzig: Breitkopf und Härtel, 1853.

Hook, Julian. 2002. "Uniform Triadic Transformations." Journal of Music Theory 46: 57–126.

Hyer, Brian. 1989. "Tonal Intuitions in Tristan und Isolde." Ph.D. diss., Yale University.

———. 1995. "Reimag(in)ing Riemann." Journal of Music Theory 39: 101–38.

Klumpenhouwer, Henry. 1994. "Some Remarks on the Use of Riemann Transformations." Music Theory Online 0/9.

———. 2000. "Remarks on American Neo-Riemannian Theory." Tijdschrift voor Muziektheorie 5: 155–69.

Kochavi, Jonathan. 1998. "Some Structural Features of Contextually-Defined Inversion Operators." Journal of Music Theory 42: 307–20.

Kopp, David. 2002. Chromatic Transformations in Nineteenth-Century Music. Cambridge Studies in Music Theory and Analysis 17. Cambridge: Cambridge University Press.

Lewin, David. 1982–83. "Transformational Techniques in Atonal and Other Music Theories." Perspectives of New Music 21/1–2: 312–71.

Dora Hanninen is Associate Professor of Music Theory and Chair of the Music Theory and composition Division at the Univesity of Maryland School of Music. She is working on a book titled *A General Theory of Segmentation and Associative Organization for Music Analysis* for the University of Rochester Press. ter Press. Univ Light text and the article ending dingbat run-in on the last line).

Parsimony and Extravagance and Another Line for Good Measure

A Colon is Replaced with an Italic Subtitle

Author Name

Another Author Name

Abstract Among the terminological and conceptual contributions made to current music theory by the work gathered under the "neo-Riemannian" heading, perhaps no other has entered the common parlance so thoroughly as "parsimonious voice leading" and its variants. Richard Cohn first used the phrase to describe the ability of the consonant triad to generate more of its own kind through (1) the movement of a single pitch class by step while (2) preserving two common tones. In either one or both aspects, this ability has been a composiaspects are reciprocal descriptions of the same behavior. Indeed, though Cohn presented each aspect as a separate property on the subject, he then gathered them together as the "P relation" (Cohn 1994). They have since remained essentially together under a single rubric in neo-Riemannian literature.

Among the terminological and conceptual contributions made to current music theory by the work gathered under the "neo-Riemannian" heading, perhaps no other has entered the common parlance so thoroughly while (2) preserving two common tones. In either one or both aspects, this ability has been a compositional desideratum for centuries, so much a habit that it is easy—and warranted—to imagine that the two aspects are reciprocal descriptions of the same behavior.

Hin ist alle meine *Kraft*, alt und schwach bin ich.
—Joseph Haydn, visiting card (1806)

Another epigraph here, they have remained the same since the beginning of time,
allowing the lute to replace the plough. We think that is an abomination.
—Peter Rabbit, *Mr. MacGregor's Garden*

IN THIS ARTICLE, I want to take the opposite approach and see what consonant triad relations look like when we understand stepwise voice motion and common-tone retention to be strictly separate properties. I wish to ask what relations between triads are possible when we insist on two common tones,

This article began as an invited paper delivered at the Symposium on Neo-Riemannian Theory, the State University of New York at Buffalo, July 2001. Part IV draws on Cook 2001. An earlier version of the present text was read at the University of Washington School of Music in April 2005. Thanks to John Rahn, Brandon Derfler, Peter Shelley, and Jason Yust for their insight and suggestions for

Journal of Music Theory 50:1, Spring 2008

DOI 10.1215/00222909-2007-000

The notation in Example 4, on the other hand, transmits[2] an impression of pervasive motion constrained by set-class. I do not include all possible sonorities created by semitonal movement of all voices because, unlike in Example 3, here I am not interested expresses the sense of near-identity between parsimoniously related triads, a in judging the interaction of some or between two triads as in Example 3. Instead, it states, "When I move like this, the type of sonority [set-class] is consistent." Examples 3 and 4 may not reflect the most concise representations of voice leading between triads, but they do a good job of capturing salient aspects of the two sequences.[1]

I. One Extravagant Sequence and One Parsimonious Subhead A

Another epigraph here, they have remained the same since the beginning of time, allowing the lute to replace the plough. We think that is an abomination.
—Peter Rabbit, *Mr. MacGregor's Garden*

Two passages from the first movement of the Piano Quintet in F minor by César Franck, both of which move sequentially by minor third but to different the later passage (mm. 90–102), which I treat first because it serves as the lens "extravagant" that I began to hear the earlier passage as a "parsimonious" [2] complement.

> Extract here. This passage is a sequence in which each iteration consists of a root-position major triad elaborated in neighboring fashion by its own ♭VI♭, Cohn's by a dominant seventh in mm. 93 and 97, and a dominant seventh in mm. 99 and 101, where the sequential unit is abbreviated from four bars to two bars in the third line.
>
> Indent subsequent paragraphs. The fashion by its own Cohn's by a dominant seventh in mm. 93 and 97, and a dominant seventh in mm. 99 and 101, where the sequential unit is abbreviated from four bars to two.
>
> Indent subsequent paragraphs. The fashion by its own Cohn's by a dominant seventh in mm. 93 and 97, and a dominant seventh in mm. 99 and 101, where the sequential unit is abbreviated from four bars to two.

Skip half line before and after extracts. The contrast to common-tone retention, stepwise voice leading has been understood to provide coherence that root-interval transposition when act ic labels and instead naming them while the lower two voices descend from the major third D≤–F to the major third consistently according to the ways they transform triads.

continued note from AO page. July 2001. Part IV draws on Thanks to John Rahn, Brandon Derfler, Peter Shelley, and Jason Yust for their insight and suggestions.

1 For a history of neo-Riemannian theory and a sketch of its transformational character, see Cohn 1998.

2 Hook (2002, 60, 89–93) calls attention to this issue in work that both generalizes and particularizes triad relations.

3 Weitzmann's treatise on the augmented triad is an exception, as Cohn 2000 shows. For a comprehensive survey of the issues sketched in this and following paragraphs, see Engebretsen 2002.

property parsimony and the second property each voice move, but only by nant triads by "priority, with the Klänge [consonant triads] receding into secondary status" (Cohn 2000, 92–94).

"Le vent dans la plaine" this is subhead B

Now, any two consonant triads of the same mode with roots a minor third apart share a common tone. One might reasonably expect Franck at least to make use of this link if not emphasize it. Instead, the mediati even into m. 102, register and texture in m. 98 does not disturb my sense of the voice leading.)

(Subhead C) is run-in. Section 3: mm. 160–255 The earlier first passage, Example 2a, contains the only use of hexatonic poles in the piece before the extravagant however; before that, the voice leading of Example 2a is as parsimonious as 2b and the other one.

This passage is shorter than the other, and I find a place for it more easthat draw me to juxtapose the two sequences analytically:

(1) Numbered list. Until I hear the complete, eight-bar second theme later in the piece (mm. 124–31), these sequences are the only two places I hear the characteristic sound of hexatonic poles.
(2) In both cases, the interval of sequential motion from one iteration to the next is by minor third. The parsimonious passage descends by minor third; the extravagant passage ascends.
(10) The sequences have similar formal roles. The parsimonious passage precedes what eventually shows itself to be a long elaboration of VI–V7–I in F minor (mm. 38–51), leading to the first theme of the movement. The extravagant passage precedes an approach to an elaborated dominant pedal in A≤ major (mm. 115–21), the key of the second theme.

Half space before and after lists, whether bulleted or numbered. In sum, many of the same things happen in each sequence, but to different cumulative effects. D≤ major triad with other tones. I am concerned only with the motion between two triads. Example 4 does not implicitly claim some sort of hierarchical, tonal relation between two triads as in Example 3. Instead, it states, "When I remain substantially the same.[14]

- Bulleted list. I hear the complete, eight-bar second theme later in the piece (mm. 124–31), these sequences are the only two places I hear the characteristic sound of hexatonic poles.
- In both cases, the interval of sequential motion from one iteration to minor third; the extravagant passage ascends.
- The structural major triad in the sequential unit of each passage supports its fifth in the top voice. This support is prolonged in each passage by an upper neighbor tone harmonized by the minor triad.

- The sequences have similar formal roles. The parsimonious passage rated dominant pedal in A≤ major (mm. 115–21), the key of the second theme.

Skip half line before and after lists, whether numbered or bulleted. Both groups, the parsimonious UTTs and the extravagant UTTs, are simply ^–, 8, 4ò, or H.15

Long list elements have a 1pl turnover, eight-bar second theme later in the piece (mm. 124–31).
Another list piece
Another list piece
Another list piece
Lasts list element before text

Skip half line before and after lists, whether numbered or bulleted. Both groups, the parsimonious UTTs and the extravagant UTTs, are simply stage of transformatiExample 4 does not implicitly claim some sort of hierarchical, tonal relation between two triads as in Example 3. Instead, it states, "When I remain substantially.

II. Utter Extravagance Ahead before Bhead

1.2 Bhead directly after Ahead

I define parsimonious relations to be those that retain two common tones when moving between triads. The motion of the third voice is unrestricted; triad. As it happens, there are only three such relations possible, and the three are familiar. Example 3 he third voice moves, he third voice moves

B= [x in X: (x+i) in Y] (Equation, not in proof)

D≤–F while allowing the third voice to move through the rest of the chroin the night relations shown he three relations shown in Example 3 are identical to the neo-Riemannian R, L, and P, respectively.

• • •

No indent after section divider. The different notations of the parsimonious and extravagant relations in The common tones are literally held in common by the pianist's right hand. Example 3 implies a claim like, "This new triad is as much the same as the first triad as possible."11 Example 3 illustrates a lack of concern for how exactly the third sustained notes.

4 *Single note sets to inside gutter.* bass. This is a common way to imagine the Relative relation in a major key. The tonal implications are clear: a sub See Klumpenhouwer 1994; Hyer 1995, 110–11; Mooney 1996, 210–68; Gollin 2000, 210–40; and Engebretsen 2002, 209–51.

Table 1. Set m for each augmented triad

Function	*Result*
m([C, E, A≤])	[E+, D≤–, A≤+, F–, C+, A–]
m([D≤, F, A])	[F+, D–, A+, F≥–, D≤+, B≤–]
m([D, G≤, B≤])	[G≤+, E≤–, B≤+, G–, D+, B≤–]
m([E≤, G, B])	[G+, E–, B+, A≤–, E≤+, C–]

Cheads italic and run-in, chromatic tones in the opening sonority. In Example 6, the opening sonority of a piece contained a chromatic tone. There are matic from diatonic tones.

Distinct formal models of parsimonious and extravagant transforma before theorem title. *Indent Theorem and Proof info. Proof is smaller:*

Theorem 4. (compare Lewin 5.1.6) PROGV (X, TY)=rPROGV(X,Y)

The parsimonious and extravagant transformations are of the sort Julian named by an ordered triple ^w, t+, t–ò, where + indicates mode preservation, acting on it.

Theorem 5. PROGV (X, TY)=rPROGV(X,Y)

Proof. Smaller text here. Define three sets A, B, and C:

A= [x in X: (x+i) in Y],
B= [x in X: (x+i) in Y],
C= [x in X: (x+i) in Y].

Observe that #A=PROGVi(X,Y) and #C=PROGV(X,Y); we see an expression for #C in terms of #A. Given any pc x in X, (x+i) either is or is not in Y; thus sets A and B partition X, and , in particular

#A+#B=#X.

Likewise, given any pc y in Y, there is a corresponding x such that y=(x+i), and this x either is or is not in X; thus sets B and C parition Y, and in particular,

#B+#C=#Y=12

Figure 4B

Skip half line after Theorem text. The triad, and t– indicates the root-interval transposition when acting on a minor triad (63–64). W tively salient connota-

5 Nebenverwandten Akkorde, "neighbor-related" or "adjacent" chords, may be understood as a major triad and its minor subdominant or a minor triad and its major dominant—D≤ major and G≤ minor, for example. Cohn says the two interpretations of the pair are of "equal strength" for Weitzmann (2000, 92). (26–28).

6 Obviously, I have difficulty escaping my habit of hearing a whole tone as a "step," but it is only a step in reference to a particular diatonic collection. On the semitonal and whole-tone whole-tone adjacencies in diatonic and chromatic whole-tone adjacencies in diatonic and chromatic d and the status of whole-tone–related notes in chromatic music, see Proctor 1978, 143.

7 One might reasonably read "same" to mean "identical, but for a contrapuntal transformation," such as a root-position triad transformed through 5–6 motion against the bass. This is a common way to imagine the Relative relation in a major key. The tonal implications are clear: a submediant thus expressed is part of a composing-out of the tonic Stufe. The connection of tonal intuitions about Relative and other relations to neo-Riemannian practices is addressed in Part V of this article.

tions of diverse mnemonic labels, it offers an orderly, analytically transparent means of representing transformations and of grasp here Hook's nomenclaand of grasp here Hoo tions of diverse mnemonic labels, it offers an orderly, analytically transparent means of representing transformations and of grasp intuitively salient of k's nomenclature sacrifices the intuitively salient of hierarchical, tonal analytically transparent means of representing transformations and of grasping their properties.

Definition. Given pcsets X and Y, the *progression vector* PROGV(X,Y) is an array with positions indexed from 0 to e. Position i records the number of distinct pairs (x, y) such that x is giving me a headache.

Indent paragraphs in definitions. The progression vector transformations, as UTTs, are ^–, 0, 0ò (or P), ^–, 9, 3ò (or R), and ^–, 4, 8ò (or L). For each transformation, t+ + t– = 0; that is, each of the parsimonious transformations transposes major triads and minor triads by complementary root-intervals mod 12.

Skip half line after Definition. ansformations, as UTTs, are ^–, 8, 4ò, or H; ^+, 1, 1ò, or T1; and ^+, 11, 11ò, or T11. Figure 1b illustrates the commutative behavior ot interested in judging the interaction of some or part of the D≤ major triad with other tones. I am concerned only with the motion tional third stage of transformational engagement, ths meet, and use it to pick apart the common thread of triad relations in neo-Riemannian thinking.

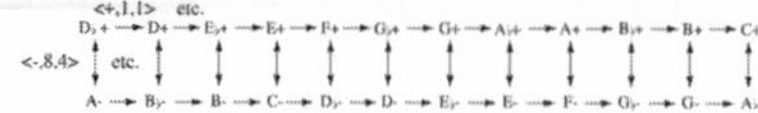

Figure 5. Product networks of the (a) parsimonious and (b) extravagant groups acting on the consonant triads

8 Imagine two parsimonious transformations S = ^–, s, s–1& and T = ^–, t, t–1&. Transforming a triad by ST would be equivalent to transforming the same triad by ^+, s + t–1, s–1 + t& (Hook 2002, 61 and 68–69).

Extract in footnote: overall left indent 1P0. No space above or below. It is clearly the same sort of UTT as the parsimonious transformations because (s + t–1) + (s–1 + t) = 0; that is, the transposition levels of ST for major and minor triads are complementary.

Similar results obtain if the signs of S and T are opposite or if they are both positive. Transforming a triad by ST would be equivalent to transforming.

9 The dualistic character of these transformations has been reflected in neo-Riemannian literature, especially by the ascription of different qualities to progressions by thirds, depending on the mode of initial triad or key. imilar results obtain if the signs of S and T are opposite or if they are both positive. Transforming a triad by ST would be equivalent to transforA recent example: though Kopp (2002, 183–85) takes issue with.

Lewin's (1992, 49–52) networks of progressions by third in Wagner's Ring, both Kopp and Lewin interpret a progression beginning on a minor triad as figuratively opposite in direction to a progression beginning on a major triad.imilar results obtain if the signs of S and T are opposite or if they are both positive. Transforming a triad by ST would be equivalent to transforimilar results obtain if the signs of S and T are opposite or if they are both positive. Transforming a triad by ST would be equivalent to transforimilar results obtain if the signs of S and T are opposite or be equivalent to transform.

that first one note moves down by a semitone and returns to its original position, then the same note moves up by a semitone and returns to its original pits original pits original position. Next, the second note in the triad follows the same routine. Finally, the third note in the triad does the same. We can name a function m to model the motions in this passage. The result of m is a set of six consonant triads. Table 1 shows the four possibilities.[22]

Imagine that there is some passage of music in which the composer has perturbed an augmented triad such that first one note moves down by a semitone and returns to its origiits original position, then the same note moves in the triad follows the sameits origina perturbed an augmented triad such that first one note moves down by a semitone and returns to its origiits original position, then the same note moves in the triad follows the sameits original pits original p routine. Finally, the l pits original p routine. Finally, the third note in the triad does the same. We can name a function m to model the motions in this passage. The result of m is a set of six consonant triads. Table 1 shows the four possibilities.[22]

The definition of m has to do with augmented triads only because we imagined it acting on them. In principle, what m does has to do only with

Example 5. Parsimonious and extravagant UTTs beginning on D≤ major and minor triads

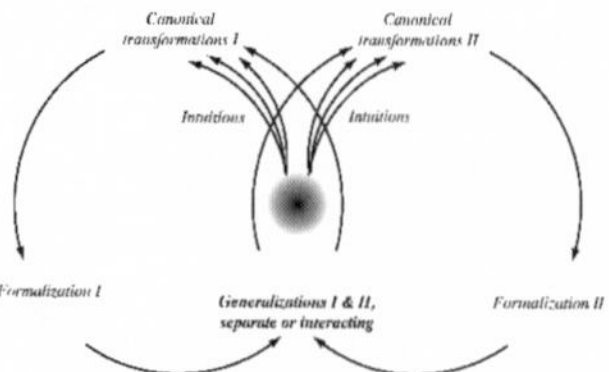

Figure 3. Narrow art: caption matches widest point of art before breaking to the next line.

In that spirit, the approach in this article follows the paths illustrated by Figure 2b, dispersing rather than gathering the intuitional strands into a third stage of transformational engagement, ths meet, and use it to pick apart the common thread of triad relations in neo-Riemannian thinking.

> Extract is the transformational process that relates (E, +) with (A≤, +) and (C, +), then, that prolongs (E, +)'s tonal significance as tonic in these measures. The realization that LP applied three times in succession to an (E, +) tonic produces an equivalent (E, +) tonic thus engages the notion of "closure," both musical and algebraic: $(E, +)(LP)^3 = (E, +)$. (115)

Let us now take a second look at the sequences, but from a transformational perspective. Example 6 reproduces the sketches from Examples 1b and 2b. I have added arrows and labels for the transformations. Example 6a is a sketch of the earlier, parsimonious sequence, and Example 6b is a sketch of the later,

Example 4. Relation between C≥ major and A minor expressed as H between minimal perturbations of augmented triads

extravagant sequence. Each is labeled with transformations from the appropriate group. I mean for these figures to serve as guides to the transformational networks at which we shall look below.

Figures 3a and 3b give network interpreImagine that there is some passage of music in which the composer has perturbed an augmented triad such

entails the tonal relationship between E≤ major and its submediant C minor, which in t laand of grasp here Hoo tions of diverse mnemonic labels, it offers an orderly, analytically transparent means of representing transformations and of grasp urn is parsimoniously inflected by the parallel move to C major.

Example 6. Figures can align with page numbers in face margin relation between C≥ major and A minor expressed as H between minimal perturbations of augmented triads

The "long way" around the right triangle formed by the triad vertices conjures an image of the edge not taken, an image seen *in terms of the two edges* In contrast, Figure 3b transmits the impression that the toggling H pairs of diagonal paths to H; ^+, 1, 1ò, or T1; and ^+, 11, 11ò, or T11. Figure 1b illustrates the commuta illustrate the sort of relationship heard in the parsimonious sequence.

Works Cited

Boretz, Benjamin. 1972. "Meta-Variations, Part IV: Analytical Fallout (I)." Perspectives of New Music 11/1: 172–216.

Callender, Clifton. 1998. "Voice-Leading Parsimony in the Music of Alexander Scriabin." Journal of Music Theory 42: 219–33.

Interior Ahead for Works Cited

Clough, John. 1998. "A Rudimentary Geometric Model for Contextual Transposition and Inversion." Journal of Music Theory 42: 297–306.

Bhead for Works Cited

Cook, Robert C. 1994. "Alternative Transformational Aspects of the 'Grail' in Wagner's Parsiton, IN.Engebretsen, Nora Ann. 2002. "The Chaos of Possibilities: Combinatorial Group Theory in Nineteenth-Century German Harmony Treatises." Ph.D. diss., State University of New York at Buffalo.

Gollin, Edward Henry. 2000. "Representations of Space and Conceptions of Distance in Trans2004.

Dora Hanninen is Associate Professor of Music Theory and Chair of the Music Theory and composition Division at the Univesity of Maryland School of Music. She is working on a book titled *A General Theory of Segmentation and Associative Organization for Music* Analysis for the University of Rochester Press. ter Press. Univ Light text and the article ending dingbat run-in on the last line).

Figure 4C

Dalit Identities and The Dialectics of Oppression and Emancipation in a Changing India: The Tamil Case and Beyond

Jean-Luc Racine

Josiane Racine

Among the many changes that have occured in India during the last two decades, the social dynamics of self-assertion of the so-called lower castes is one of the most significant. The new economic policy that has opened India to global market forces, to a degree unprecedented since 1947, the rise of the Hindu nationalism that has brought the BJP to power, not to mention the open nuclearization of the subcontinent are, of course, major events transforming India in decisive ways. But, there are more profound social changes taking place that affect the very core of Indian society. Its most fundamental and specific character, the caste system, is under tremendous pressure, which can be ascertained in two different ways. Firstly, the caste sytem of regulated hierarchized relationships – the old *jajmani* system – has been virtually destroyed by a series of far-reaching developments: the family/caste relationships which ordered status and professional occupations, the mode of production and the ideological basis on which it has developed for long are now strongly affected by the widespread market relations and by the political maneuvering nurtured by fifty years of universal franchise. Secondly, the decline of caste boundaries – as a system governing and ordering the patterns of relations between the dominant and the dominated, between high status and low status groups, between patrons and clients – has not necessarily weakened the caste *per se*, revealing a specifically Indian social paradox: to a large extent the struggle against the ideological and material

hierarchies of the caste system attacks
caste. To dismantle the prevalent order o
called low castes – the OBCs, Other B
in administrative terminology – have f
based reservations of college seats a
jobs. The OBCs have also used castes
favoring either national parties dedicate
(such as the Janata Dal led by Prime Mi
who launched the Mandal crusade for
vations in 1990), or political formation
OBCs' interests in specific states, such a
Party of Mulayam Singh Yadav in Uttar
Bihar Unit of the Janata Dal (now Rash
run by Laloo Prasad Yadav.

In this context, the changes could n
worst endowed Indians, those traditio
Untouchables, whom Mahatma Gandhi
(the sons – and daughters – of Hari,
names), and whom the Administration
uled Castes. They may also be labele
and generic regional denominations
Dravidians – Adi Dravidar – in Tamilna
Dalits in today parlance. Dalits was fi
militant denomination which appeared
in 1972,[3] and means, in the Marath
trampled down, the oppressed.[4] It is n
edged and politically correct form all
emphasizes the most dominant chara
social and political existence.

State as Socionatural Effect: Variable and Emergent Geographies of the State in Southeastern Turkey

Leila M. Harris

Dams were unique in the scope and manner in which they altered the distribution of resources across space and time, among entire communities and ecosystems. They offered more than just a promise of agricultural development or technical progress. For many postcolonial governments, this ability to rearrange the natural and social environment became a means to demonstrate the strength of the modern state as a techno-economic power.
—Timothy Mitchell, *Rule of Experts: Egypt, Techno-politics, Modernity*

The process of mapping, bounding, containing and controlling nature and citizenry are what make a state a state. States come into being through these claims and the assertion of control over territory, resources, and people.
—Roderick P. Neumann, "Nature-State-Territory: Toward a Critical Theorization of Conservation Enclosures"

Socionatures, Everyday States, and Boundary Work

The relationship between states and environmental change has been a topic of increasing interest over the past several decades. Some have suggested that environmental issues pose a fundamental challenge to the state system and state capacity.[1] Still others have attempted to understand the diverse ways that states mobilize, contest, and negotiate "natures" as a central facet of state power and control, including efforts to make nature legible and controllable.[2] As Mitchell asserts with the above quotation, states demonstrate strength and power through rearrangements of socionatural environments, while Neumann suggests that the very notion of stateness is wrapped up with control of nature and citizenry. Mark Whitehead, Rhys Jones, and Martin Jones open up a broader set of questions to understand the diverse ways that states rely on, manage, and negotiate natures as central to state legitimacy or state building.[3] Building on works of this type, my argument contributes to a

1. See Andrew Hurell, "The State," in *Political Theory and the Ecological Challenge*, ed. Andrew Dobson and Robyn Eckersley (Cambridge: Cambridge University Press, 2006), 165–82; and Hallie Eakin and Maria Carmen Lemos, "Adaptation and the State: Latin America and the Challenge of Capacity-Building under Globalization," *Global Environmental Change* 16 (2006): 7–18.

2. See, e.g., Marius de Geus, "The Ecological Restructuring of the State," in *Democracy and Green Political Thought: Sustainability, Rights, and Citizenship*, ed. Brian Doherty and Marius de Geus (New York: Routledge, 1996), 188–211; James C. Scott, *Seeing like a State: How Certain Schemes to Improve the Human Condition Have Failed* (New Haven, CT: Yale University Press, 1998); and Bruce Willems-Braun, "Buried Epistemologies: The Politics of Nature in (Post)colonial British Columbia," *Annals of the Association of American Geographers* 87 (1997): 3–31.

3. See Mark Whitehead, Rhys Jones, and Martin Jones, *The Nature of the State: Excavating the Political Ecologies of the Modern State* (Oxford: Oxford University Press, 2007).

Comparative Studies of South Asia, Africa and the Middle East

Vol. 32, No. 1, 2012

DOI 10.1215/1089201X-1545345

25

Figure 5A
Collaboration and synergy
Before coming to Duke Press, the interdisciplinary studies journal *Comparative Studies of South Asia, Africa, and the MIddle East* (8-1/2"x11") was self-published, and laid out using a word-processing program. It had a standard two-column design, one serif font family throughout, and very little white space, because they filled each page with as much text as possible.

The editor was enthusiastic about breaking out of the old, constrained layout. He requested that the journal be decorative in a way that reflected the journal's representative regions, and provided photographs of local textiles and architecture for inspiration. He was happy that we could use footnotes instead of endnotes, and asked me to display them in a graphically interesting way. In fact, he asked if we could set them on a 30 degree angle.

310

Comparative Studies of South Asia, Africa and the Middle East

would Muslim women's *anjumans* the following century. A second Armenian women's society, which undertook similar tasks, was established in 1892 in New Julfa by senior students of the Katarinian girls' school and their male teacher. Another society, in the Ghala district of Tabriz, was established in 1895.[91] This was a typical pattern in the early years of new education; many of the early new schools for Muslims, girls and boys, were also founded, funded, and even staffed by private, individual, and small-group initiatives similar in form and modes of action to the Armenian women's. In fact, education initiatives for Muslim girls are commonly viewed as "perhaps the women's parties' [i.e., *anjumans*'] most enduring effort."[92]

Of course, women were not the exclusive supporters of girls' education. There was an intellectual men's discourse on women's education, influenced by various foreign sources. An edited and translated version of Qasim Amin's much-debated (in Egypt) 1899 treatise, *Tahrir al-Mara* (*Liberating the Woman*, translated as *The Liberation of Women*), was published in Iran in 1900 under the title *Education of Women*.[93] French, Japanese, Russian, and other Ottoman influences could also be seen. Some sources on education in Qajar Iran also assert that Iranian men founded at least one public girls' elementary school before the constitutional revolution.[94]

When considering the overall significance of the girls' schools established by Muslim women in the first and second decades of the twentieth century, it should also be recalled that these schools had student populations no larger than those of most of the missionary schools, and classes were often held in private homes.[95] It is also worthwhile to bear in mind that the Iranian discourse surrounding women's education was not driven or, it seems, influenced by an argument deriving from a view that there should be equality—or something akin to it—between the sexes; far from it. Women's education was promoted by men and women alike from the beginning, as well as during and in the years following the constitutional revolution, with a modernizing, nationalist line of reasoning that did not aim to take women out of the home or otherwise alter their traditional cultural roles. Women, it was most often put forth, should be educated because mothers are the first educators of their sons and, thus, could be seen as the backbone—or, perhaps more appropriately, the womb—of the nation. "Backward" mothers could not produce a progressive nation.[96] It was an argument that resounded contemporaneously in other locations in the Middle East, especially in Egypt and Turkey. One indication of the popular existence of this discourse in Iran can be found in Isabella Bird's travelogue of her 1890 six-month journey through central-western Persia. Relating her conversation with

91. Berberian, *Armenians*, 46–47; Ringer, *Education, Religion, and the Discourse*, 128. Also see Berberian, "Armenian Women," 84–85.

92. Bayat-Philipp, "Women and Revolution," 299; also see Afary, *The Iranian Constitutional Revolution*, 207. Amin notes that the issue remained a central focus of women's organizations after the constitutional revolution as well, as "a ticket not only to social advancement, but to their very inclusion in the imagined community of Iranians"; see his article, "Propaganda and Remembrance: Gender, Education, and 'The Women's Awakening' of 1936," *Iranian Studies* 32 (1999): 365.

93. Afsaneh Najmabadi, "Crafting an Educated Housewife in Iran," in *Remaking Women: Feminism and Modernity in the Middle East*, ed. Lila Abu-Lughod (Princeton, NJ: Princeton University Press, 1998), 100–101. Najmabadi notes that the translation, which omitted entire sections, such as chapter 2, on veiling, was well received by "reform-minded intellectuals" but was met with a much quieter reception in Iran than the original was in Egypt (103).

94. Menashri mentions that "the first [public elementary] school for girls" was founded in 1897–98, but he gives no details. Menashri, *Education and the Making*, 60. (The years 1897–98 were significant, since that was when the reform-minded 'Ali Khan Amin al-Daula, a promoter of new education and the founder of the *Anjuman-e Ma'aref*, replaced 'Ali Asghar Khan Amin al-Sultan as chief minister.) Ringer mentions the Sa'adat "free school" (i.e., public school) founded by Motarjem al-Dowleh in Tabriz in 1899–1900 (and later transferred to Yahya Dowlatabadi's management) in the context of other free schools founded by the men's *Anjuman-e Ma'aref*. According to her, it was one of four Tabriz schools whose buildings were destroyed by a mob in 1903. The context of her discussion is boys' schools, however, and she gives no details about the composition of Sa'adat's student body. Ringer, *Education, Religion, and the Discourse*, 170, 174, 177, 199. Paidar, however, states that the first girls' school, named Sa'adat, was founded in 1899, seemingly the school Ringer refers to, although she states the school was in Bushehr. According to Paidar, this school operated until the mid-1960s, but she goes no further in depth. Paidar, *Women and the Political Process* (69). Arasteh, an important early source on the development of education in Iran, makes no mention of such a school. Many women's studies researchers who write on the subject—Bamdad, Bayat-Phillip, Sanasarian, Bahar, Nashat, and Afary, for instance—also do not note the existence of such a school.

95. For an indication of the size of these schools, see the list of girls' schools in Tehran in 1913 in Afary, *The Iranian Constitutional Revolution*, 182–83. The average student population was 39. Three of the sixty-three schools listed were attended by between 110 and 120 students; one had 160 students, and the vast majority had 50 or fewer.

96. See Paidar, *Women and the Political Process*, chap. 2 generally, and 70–73 specifically. For an alternative possible explanation on the reasoning behind the discourse, see Afary, *The Iranian Constitutional Revolution*, 208.

311

Metin Heper

Does Secularism Face a Serious Threat in Turkey?

and the 2007 surveys show that for those who wear the turban, it is first and foremost a symbol of belief in Islam, and for only a few turbaned women is it a symbol of political Islam.

Table 4. Why women in Turkey sport turbans

Reasons	%
Conformity with Islam's tenets	68.0
Displaying one's political preference	14.9
Acting in harmony with others	7.4
Displaying one's identity	4.6
Expression of one's morality	3.1
A means of self-protection	2.1

Source: Tarhan Erdem, "Gündelik yaşamda din, laiklik ve türban" ("Religion, Secularism, and the Turban in Everyday Life"), *Milliyet*, 3–4 December 2007.

Some relatively recent qualitative studies based on in-depth interviews also have arrived at the conclusion that there is no generalized relationship between the turban/*çarşaf* and political Islam. These studies show that in many instances veiling, in fact, enables women to take advantage of the spaces modernity provides and thus to participate in economic, social, and political life, which they otherwise could not be a part of.[30]

Conclusion

In his well-known *Foreign Affairs* article in 1993, Samuel P. Huntington foresaw a clash of civilizations among the constellations of countries divided from one another in terms of religion, history, language, and traditions. In this context, Huntington regarded Turkey as a "torn country" and categorized it as a member of a civilization rival to the Western one.[31]

In religious terms, Turkey is *not* a torn country. For a great majority of its population, Islam plays a role only at the individual level, not at the community and state levels. And the same majority of people support and value the secular republic. Turks as Muslims have a great deal of tolerance toward their co-citizens' ways of practicing or not practicing and living or not living according to their religion. The secularists should not be scared of becoming an increasingly smaller and weaker minority in an increasingly religious society, because those whom the secularists regard as Islamists, in fact, display a great deal of tolerance (with respect) toward those who are different from themselves and, at the same time, show loyalty to the secularist republic.

Since Turkey has gone through a cognitive revolution, Islam for the bulk of the people is not a source of superstitions and dogmas. On the whole, political Islam has no appeal to Turks. They are also not receptive to a community-based political Islam.

If there have been deep divisions in Turkey, those rifts have been around some hard and soft ideologies and only among some members of the intelligentsia. In recent years, the secularists have been rather hostile toward those people and politicians whom they consider retrogressive and who, in their opinion, would take Turkey back to the Dark Ages. In the process, they have held "republican demonstrations" and denounced "the retrogressives." The latter, however, have not reciprocated.

With Turkey having had a democratic revolution, the secularists could not come to power via elections, because for years they have looked down on the majority of people and thus given short shrift to their preferences and demands. Yet in November 2008 Deniz Baykal, the leader of the political party of the secularists (the Republican People's Party, or RPP), admitted women with turbans and even *çarşafs* into his party, and the party was careful to publicize the event.[32] On the face of this "turn of events," this article could have concluded as follows: if this sudden volte-face on the part of Baykal was not

30. Yeşim Arat, *Political Islam in Turkey and Women's Organizations* (Istanbul: Friedrich-Ebert-Stiftung and the Economic and Social Studies Foundation of Turkey, 1999), 61; Ali Bayramoğlu, *Çağdaşlık hurafe kaldırmaz: Demokratikleşme sürecinde dindar ve laikler* (*Modernity Does Not Leave Space for Superstitions: Devout and Secular in the Democratization Process*) (Istanbul: Türkiye Ekonomik, Sosyal ve Siyasal Araştırmalar Vakfı, 2006), 139; Alev Çınar, "Clothing the National Body: Islamic Veil and Secular Unveiling," in *Modernity, Islam, and Secularism in Turkey: Bodies, Places, and Time* (Minneapolis: University of Minnesota Press, 2005), chap. 2; Sema Genel and Kerem Karaosmanoğlu, "A New Islamic Individualism in Turkey: Headscarved Women in the City," *Turkish Studies* 7 (2006): 473–88; Nilüfer Göle, *The Forbidden Modern: Civilization and Veiling* (Ann Arbor: University of Michigan Press, 2001), 137–40; and Elisabeth Özdalga, *The Veiling Issue, Secularism, and Popular Islam in Turkey* (Surrey, UK: Curzon, 1998), 55–85.

31. Samuel P. Huntington, "The Clash of Civilizations?" *Foreign Affairs* 72 (1993): 42.

32. "CHP'den çarşaflı türbanlı şov" ("The RPP Show with Turban and Chador"), *Radikal*, 17 November 2008.

401

Mehrzad Boroujerdi

"The West" in the Eyes of Iranian Intellectuals

historical accuracy to be relaxed."[38] Hence Reza Shah and his intellectual entourage paid great homage to kings such as Shah Isma'il (r. 1501–24), Shah Abbas (r. 1587–1629), Nader Shah (r. 1729–47), and Karim Khan Zand (r. 1747–79) and poets such as Ferdowsi (940–1020) and Sa'di (1213–92).

This article has argued that the inner effects of the impact of Western ideas on Iranian intellectuals were both actual and potential during the interwar years. The intellectual classes became more acclimated with ideas, concepts, and words that had originated in the West.[39] But while their quest to modernize their society was triggered by a growing awareness of Iran's backwardness vis-à-vis the West, the predominant attitude toward the West remained one of ambivalent engagement even though secular nationalist themes dominated the intellectual landscape.[40] If in Turkey the talk was one of Europeanization, in Iran it was all about selective acquisition of modernity's components.[41] In other words, Iran never became a "positivistic mausoleum" like its next-door neighbor.

While this hesitant approach to the West could have been partly influenced by the self-doubts of leading Western thinkers, I have not yet been able to find much evidence to support this assertion. Indeed, there seems to be very little indication that Iranian intellectuals of the interwar years had any awareness of contemporary works such as Edmund Husserl's *Logical Investigations* (1900–1901) or *Cartesian Meditations* (1931); Henri Bergson's *Creative Evolution* (1907) or *Two Sources of Morality and Religion* (1932); Bertrand Russell's *Problems of Philosophy* (1912) or *Religion and Science* (1935); Martin Heidegger's *Being and Time* (1927); or the ideas emanating out of the Vienna Circle (from 1922 to 1938) or the Institute for Social Research in Frankfurt, which was founded in 1923. Nor can one find many references to the works of earlier thinkers such as Søren Kierkegaard (1813–55), Ernest Mach (1838–1916), Friedrich Nietzsche (1844–1900), or Émile Durkheim (1858–1917).[42] Besides unawareness, another factor that can explain the lack of attention paid to these thinkers might have to do with the cultural predispositions of Iranian intellectuals during this era. After all, as the noted historian H. A. R. Gibb has put it, "it seems to be a general rule of history that, when two civilizations come into contact and a transmission of ideas is effected, the recipients are attracted to those elements in the other civilization which are most congenial to their own habits of thought and, on the whole, neglect or reject the other elements which they find more difficult to assimilate."[43]

35. Gavin Hambly, "Attitudes and Aspirations of the Contemporary Iranian Intellectual," *Journal of the Royal Central Asian Society* 51, pt. 2 (1964): 128.

36. To borrow the language of James C. Scott, Reza Shah wished to make Iranian society "legible" through a series of reform initiatives. By simplifying and standardizing people and things he helped to have them amassed, recognized, observed, and recorded. Adopting borders, surnames, census, units of measurement, sanitation standards, and educational levels and eliminating honorific titles were all considered prerequisites for creating an efficient state machinery. See James C. Scott, *Seeing Like a State: How Certain Schemes to Improve the Human Condition Have Failed* (New Haven, CT: Yale University Press, 1998).

37. Thomas Carlyle has argued that hero worship remains "an unfailing act of human experience and the basis of social organization." See Michael K. Goldberg's introduction to Thomas Carlyle, *On Heroes, Hero Worship, and the Heroic in History* (Berkeley: University of California Press, 1993), lxi.

38. Lambton, "The Impact of the West on Persia," 23.

39. For example, Mohammad-Ali Zoka' al-Molk Forughi provides the following partial list of French and English words that had entered the lexicon of the Iranian public by the late 1910s: acid, address, automobile, *billet*, blouse, *bottine* (boot), bottle, *chapeau*, cigar, cinema, class, constitution, cycle, *dictée*, diploma, *esprit*, *faux-col*, gas, glass, *humanités*, kettle, lamp, lemonade, *maison*, *marche*, *merci*, *mode*, *numéro*, park, piano, program, salon, sardine, soup, siphon, telegraph, telephone, theater, and wagon. See Mohammad-Ali Zoka' al-Molk Forughi, *Maqalat-e Forughi*, 2nd ed. (Tehran: Tous, AH 1354/1975), 1:84–85.

40. One reason why in this period there was not much rabid anti-Westernism in Iran has to do with the fact that Iranian secular nationalists had identified the Arabs and Islam as their favorite targets of criticism. The works of Zabih Behruz, Ebrahim Purdavud, Sadeq Hedayat, Ahmad Kasravi, and many others were emblematic of this sentiment.

41. Ali-Akbar Dehkhoda, Mohammad-Ali Jamalzadeh, Seyyed Fakhroddin Shadman, Mohammad-Ali Zoka' al-Molk Forughi, and many others articulated this sentiment. For example, in 1927 Forughi wrote, "Acquisition of knowledge and particularly the sciences of the Western world is both good and necessary yet we should not be so infatuated with European industry that we completely forget our own national arts and crafts." See Forughi, *Maqalat-e Forughi*, 23.

42. The Western thinkers with whom Iranian intellectuals seem to be most familiar are figures such as René Descartes (1596–1650), Auguste Comte (1798–1857), Gustave Le Bon (1841–1931), and Anatole France (1844–1924).

43. H. A. R. Gibb, *Modern Trends in Islam* (Chicago: University of Chicago Press, 1947), 110.

Figure 5B

It wasn't feasible to angle the footnotes, but I set them in columns so they would create different and distinct shapes. They become a visual anchor for the page, like the base of a column or arch.

I angled the display text in the margins, and chose an ornate, calligraphic font for the article opening drop caps and page numbers.

I created a rough-hewn dotted line for the article openings, a decorative section divider, and an organic article-ending dingbat.

Comparative Studies of South Asia, Africa and the Middle East

Vol. XIX No. I 1999

Labor and the Left in South Africa

Lucien van der Walt: The International Socialist League and Revolutionary Syndicalism in South Africa, 1915-1920

Peter Alexander: Coal, Control, and Class Experience in South Africa's Rand Revolt of 1922

Phil Eidelberg: The Shaping of a New African Middle Class and the Transformation of the African National Congress

Andrew Nash: The Moment of Western Marxism in South Africa

Vladimir Shubin: The Mayibuye Centre Archive as a Source on the History of the South African Liberation Movement

Allison Drew: Interview with Leonard Gentle, Manchester, April 1999

Lungisile Ntsebeza: Democratization and Traditional Authorities in the New South Africa

Contradictions of Globalization

Amiya Kumar Bagchi: Dualism and Dialectics in the Historiography of Labor

Amir Arsalan Afkhami: Epidemics and the Emergence of an International Sanitary Policy in Iran

Valentine M. Moghadam: Gender, National Identity and Citizenship: Reflections on the Middle East and Africa

Bonny Ibhawoh: Structural Adjustment, Authoritarianism and Human Rights in Africa

Figure 5C
When I redesigned the cover, I retained the black solid from the original design. I layered as much of the art provided by the editor as possible, to create a collage that represented the regions discussed in the journal. We moved the article listings to the back cover and printed the cover in black and orange.

IN THIS ISSUE

CONTENTIONS

Iran's Hostage Crisis:
International Legitimacy Matters
R. K. Ramazani

RETROSPECTIVES ON THE IRANIAN CONSTITUTIONAL REVOLUTION, 1905–1909
Houri Berberian, Guest Editor

Traversing Boundaries and Selves:
Iranian-Armenian Identities during the Iranian Constitutional Revolution
Houri Berberian

Nineteenth-Century Qajar Women in the Public Sphere: An Alternative Historical and Historiographical Reading of the Roots of Iranian Women's Activism
Susynne M. McElrone

A World Born through the Chamber of a Revolver: Revolutionary Violence, Culture, and Modernity in Iran, 1906–1911
Mansour Bonakdarian

Civil Liberties and the Making of Iran's First Constitution
Janet Afary

Despots of the World Unite!
Satire in the Iranian Constitutional Press: The *Majalleh-ye Estebdad*, 1907–1908
Ali Gheissari

The Bakhtiyari Tribes in the Iranian Constitutional Revolution
Arash Khazeni

The Tale of the Quchan Maidens as an "Originator" Event of the Constitutional Revolution
Mangol Bayat

VARIORUM

Reformation, Islam, and Democracy: Evolutionary and Antievolutionary Reform in Abrahamic Religions
Mohammad Nafissi

Arabic Literary-Scientific Journals: Precedence for Globalization and the Creation of Modernity
Stephen Sheehl

The Issue of Discrimination in Indian Federalism in the Post-1977 Politics of West Bengal
Polly Datta

Satire in Modern Afghanistan
Faridullah Bezhan

Arab Women in Nizar Kabbani's Poetry
Wisam Mansour

Being Palestinian in Israel:
Identity, Protest, and Political Exclusion
Sherry Lowrance

BOOK REVIEWS

FILM REVIEWS

Comparative Studies of SOUTH ASIA, AFRICA *and the* MIDDLE EAST Vol. 25, No. 2, 2005 DUKE

Comparative Studies of
SOUTH ASIA, AFRICA *and the* **MIDDLE EAST**

Volume 25
Number 2
2005

I oversee the first volume's typesetting to make sure the template and specs are interpreted correctly. After that, time constraints and workload make it impossible for me to do more than a spot-check now and then.

As my press acquires more journals—print and online—and I design or redesign them, I naturally have less time to oversee the typesetting of every journal I work on. The good news is that our production coordinators and editorial staff are detail-oriented and quality-conscious, and our typesetters are talented and conscientious.

My experience designing for our journals' online presentation has been a mixed one. On the one hand, it is satisfying to design for the powerful functionality offered through online publishing. However, with today's technology there is only so much a designer can do to affect—much less control—certain aspects of a web site's layout and typography. Providing annotated templates and specs will not necessarily translate into a cohesive page, and that can be difficult to accept. E-publishers are not trying to make life difficult for designers; their software and processes limit their templates to a one-size-fits-all solution. Custom coding that would alleviate some of the awkwardness is expensive.

Whether it is designing an online-only journal like our *Limnology and Oceanography: Fluids & Environments* or art directing how our print journal covers and full-text PDFs are displayed, it can be dismaying to view the final product online. The e-publisher's limitations mean that it does not take many clicks into a site to see clumsy typography and unrelated link colors, or journal covers that have been squashed into a standard, preset format. (See Figures 6A and 6B.)

Custom coding allowed us to maintain a deeper level of typographic and graphic consistency throughout the site of our journal *The Carlyle Letters Online*. There are still instances of awkward typography and graphics, but they are fairly limited. (See Figure 6C.)

I am hopeful that ever-evolving technologies will make this situation obsolete, so that we designers can have more control over how our work is displayed online. Perhaps designers have voiced this same complaint down through the ages—over the built-in limitations of working with chisels on stone, then hot metal type, or the lack of pair-kerning in the early page layout programs. In the meantime, I plan to cross my fingers, keep learning, and hope for the best.

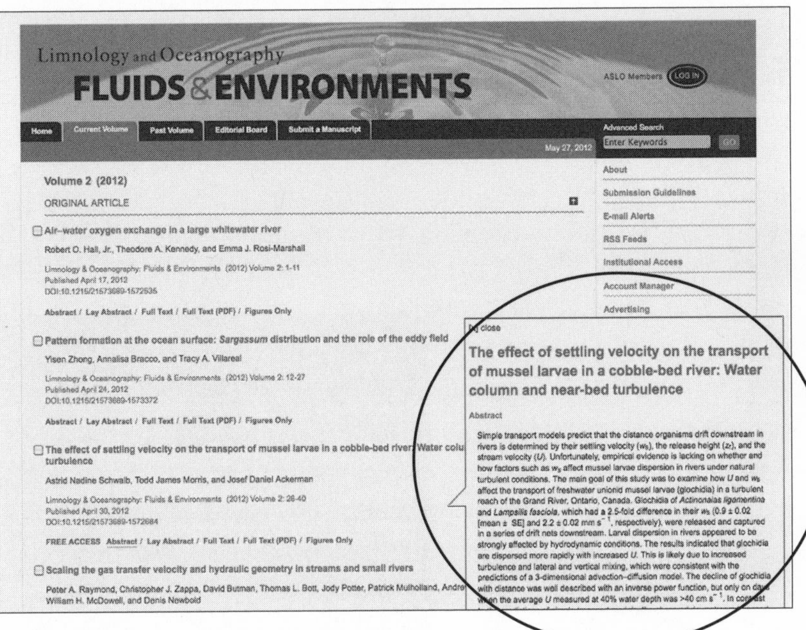

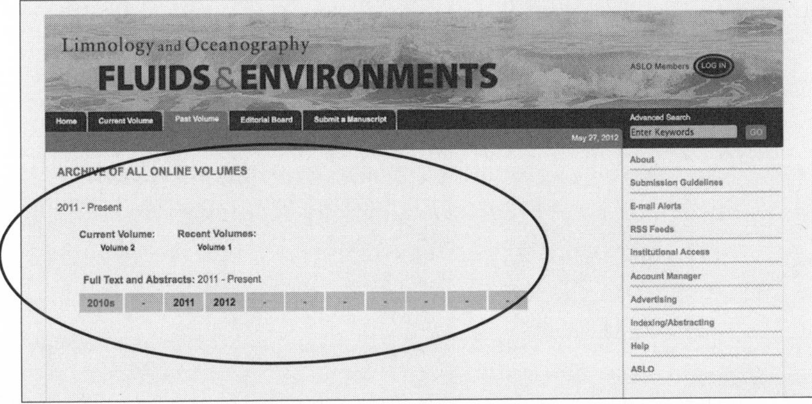

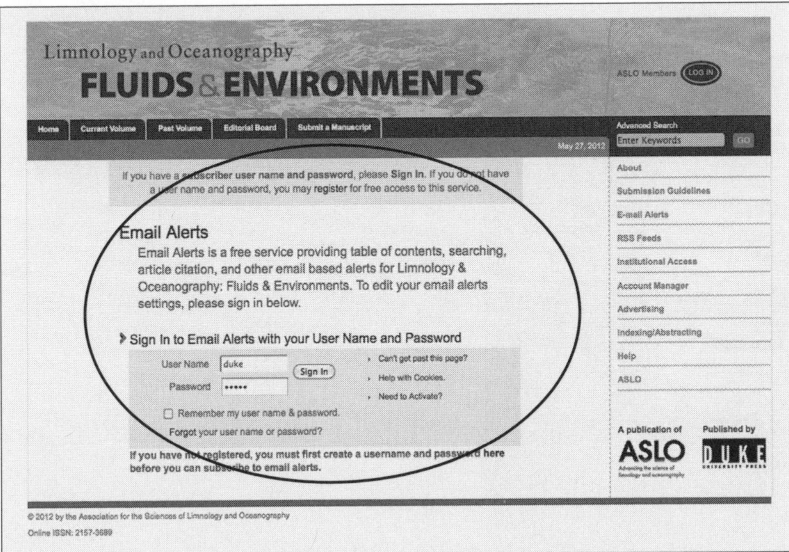

Figure 6A
Trading design standards for online access of content
Designing for online-only journals can be humbling because, beyond a certain point, designers cannot control how the content is displayed.

The online publishers hosting our journals' content are not trying to be difficult; they have to apply a standard template for all material going through their systems. We have found that it is usually not possible to invest in the custom programming that would allow us to override what is provided for basic functionalities like pop-up windows, listings of archived issues, and alerts (all pictured here).

The result is that it doesn't take many clicks into a site to experience canned typography and graphic elements that are unrelated to the basic design of our journal. For more examples, click through the *Free Access* pages at *lofe.dukejournals.org*.

One can only hope that someday soon technology will allow designers to have more control over how their designs are processed and posted. This will only enhance the reader's experience of the online content.

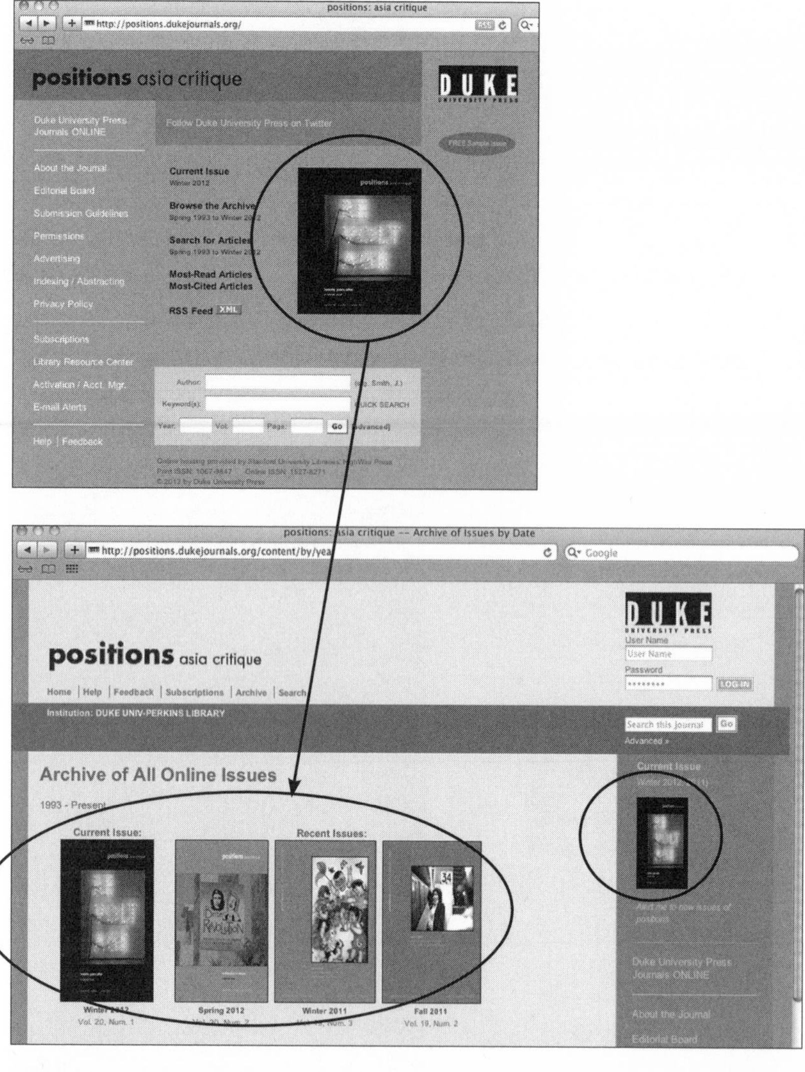

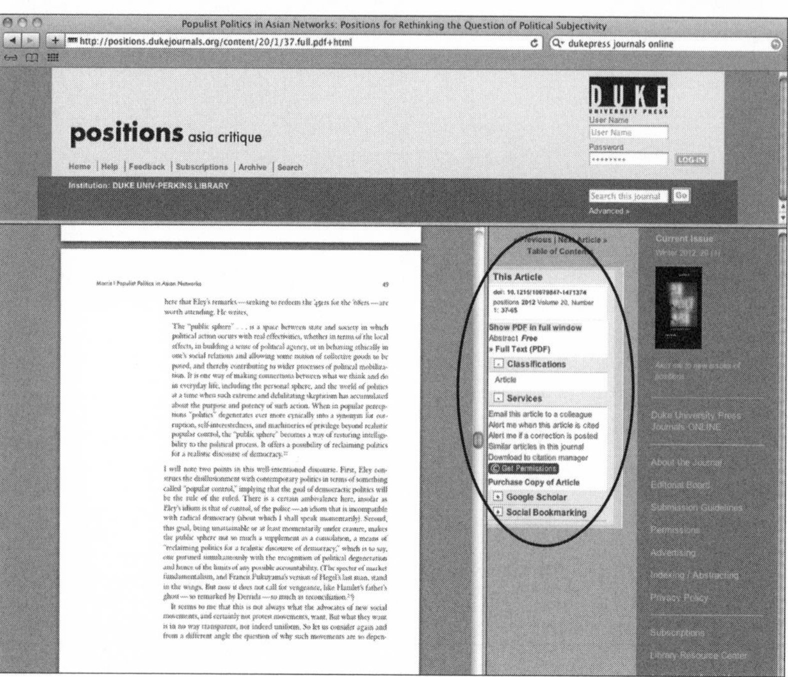

Figure 6B
Trading design standards for online accessibility
Online publishing of print journals is excellent for disseminating scholarly content, but the process can be frustrating from a designer's point of view. Something as simple as displaying a cover's true proportions can be out of reach.

For example, the nearly square proportions of Duke Press's asia critique journal, *positions* (7"x8"), is part of its graphic identity. While it displays properly on its home page (top), one click later and throughout the site it is distorted, because of the limitations of the online publisher's software.

While it offers helpful functionality, the templated "This Article" navigation is graphically unrelated to the rest of the site and the journal itself.

See more examples at *dukejournals.org*.

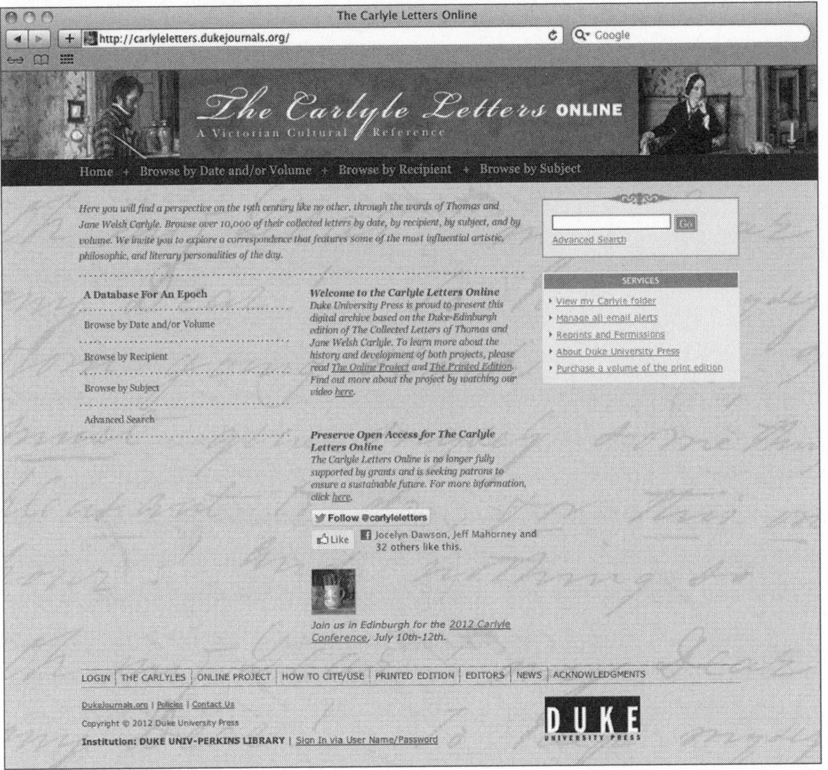

Figure 6C

Custom programming allows more refinement

We were able to provide custom programming and templates for our online journal the *Carlyle Letters Online*. While it is not as refined as it could be as a print publication, the customized templates allowed for more consistent typography, color, and use of graphics throughout the site.

See more examples at *carlyleletters.dukejournals.org*.

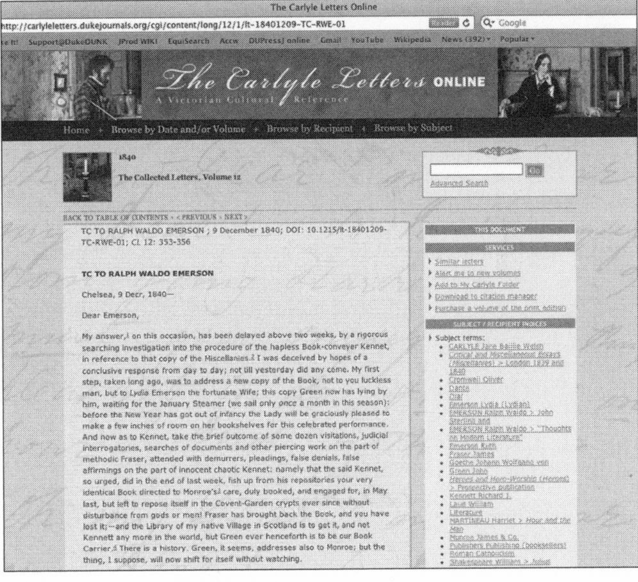

The Conundrum of the E-book

I hardly feel qualified to say anything about e-books, not only because I am an e-book virgin (never having even come close to a relationship) but because at the time of this writing everything is in a state of flux. I first met with Julie Allred, who showed me some of the problems confronting designers of e-books, at BW&A Books. As she is an experienced designer of print books, Julie was able to explain to me the difference between designing for print and designing for e-books. When I naively expressed the complaint that it was not worth the bother to try to design an e-book, Julie told me that it was possible but not always practical to choose a fixed layout.

Julie said:

> Designers are comfortable with fixed layout EPUB because it can be paged to match the print design. It behaves much like a PDF, though it's different under the hood. In reality, text from a print book adapted to fixed layout is often too small for comfortable reading, which means people have to poke to zoom and move around the page, even on children's books. The fact that the text won't reflow or resize has both positive and negative implications. I think there are some cases where it makes sense to use fixed layout, such as books with lots of art and little text. (Though I think a reflowable EPUB3 book with pop-up captions might make even more sense.) But there are also a lot of cases where fixed layout—at least the way we often see it used now—detracts from the reading experience rather than enhancing it. It's just too much work for the reader, and our job as designers is to make reading easy. I am hopeful that we'll have the option of combining sections of fixed layout with reflowable content in a couple of years, but at this point, it's one or the other.
>
> Books should be rethought for the screen size and capabilities, the same way we'd rethink a book for a coffee-table edition versus a pocket guide. I think editorial departments should be involved in format decisions, too. We need to turn off our print production mindset and think about what would make us actually want to read a digital book, all the way to the end. If people get so aggravated that they give up, we're going to lose the audience.
>
> So far there are few profitable instances of heavily illustrated nonfiction e-books. Because attention spans are shorter for digital than print, and the price people will pay is lower, one option may be to release several smaller illustrated e-books. Another option is to create complex

web-based e-books or catalogues. Publishers can charge for access to a website custom designed for the content. Technically savvy designers can take advantage of much more sophisticated control over the organization and display than is possible with current EPUB display.

I strongly believe that some books should be print books, some digital, and some can support both. It will take some time for publishers and readers to sort them out. Even now, early in the transition, many people are placing higher value on beautiful print books.

■ I also consulted with Abbey Gaterud, who answered more of my naive questions.

ABBEY GATERUD

You have said that it was better not *to start with a print design. I assume even with the improvements in software like InDesign CS6 it would still be your advice to begin with a purpose-made e-book design.*

This is a complicated answer, because so much depends on where the technology is at any particular time, and how a particular workflow is set up. One of the nice things about using the most current tools (CS6's relatively easy and clean EPUB export, for instance) is that they (the tools) are constantly getting better and making it easier for one person to produce both the print and e-book. This is good for designers for a lot of reasons, including the very real fact that we should be able to design all formats of a book if we expect to keep our profession and craft afloat.

From a publisher's perspective, I think it makes a lot of sense for the book designers we employ to be designing both print and digitally. There are a lot of quality-control issues that can be avoided if using trusted book designers. Making sure that the files actually work, that they've been proofread, that they follow best-practices for digital design: all of these questions can be addressed if the book designer understands print and digital design.

Best practices in the digital realm are becoming more important than ever. We can get away with lax practices when designing for print, because we understand what we can control in the printing process. You can make a shoddy InDesign file look pretty good on paper. But in the digital world, the display technology is changing and updating faster than we'd ever be able to update all the book files we've made in the past (or even this year). Future-proofing is incredibly important as we think about how to be digital book designers. Making sure that you have clean files, with proper styling and tagging, is going to be so important as new versions of reading technology hit the market. Being a stickler for the hidden code, cleaning it up to make it simple and easily understandable, will be just as important as making it look good on a display.

This is one of the reasons I think book apps (stand-alone pieces of software) are more tenuous, and that we should be thinking with a much longer shelf-life in mind. We make print books to last for hundreds of years. We should be trying to do the same with digital books. While it's a whole lot harder to envision technology in a hundred years—or even five—I believe that being slightly conservative and not so faddish in this area is not a bad thing. Technology is fickle, and for the first time, we're making books that rely on technology not created by the publisher. It's quite possible that apps, like all those Word Perfect documents we have in the archives, or VHS or cassette tapes on our shelves, will not be viable forms of media in five or ten years. But by using international standards (the International Digital Publishing Forum's standards, in this case), there will be a progression in formats and some of that future-proofing will be considered going forward. EPUB3 will lead to EPUB4, and while the latter formats will take advantage of the newer innovations in technology, the standards will be related and transferable.

Thinking about our consumers (readers) from the publisher's perspective, we can't afford to alienate them with bad designs. Publishers, editors, designers, we all have to accept that e-books are still books, they are still the stories and literature and answers that they always were, and we need to invest as much in their design and production as we did in the print edition. We still hear horror stories of two-column e-books being opened on smartphone screens and readers deleting them in disgust. We have to understand what the technology can handle, and what it can't. We can safely assume that technology will get better in the future, so designing (and coding) e-books to work on this relatively primitive technology is akin to a foundational design. Just as print designers should always print their mock-up pages and should be able to translate on-screen design with print production, e-book designers should know how their on-screen designs (just in HTML code now) will translate to the various screens the book is read on.

As far as your question goes, I think that in a workflow, it makes the most sense to tag the text once. Whether using XML, HTML5, or other coding system, going through the process once, with the intention of long-term structure, is our best option. We use this code to tell the translator software that certain tags mean certain things, like "this is a caption," or "this is a title." So really, this part of the design is done for the designer already. It should be an editorial function to properly code a manuscript (and doesn't it already happen that way, just with something called Word instead of XML?).

From there, a designer is simply an interpreter of structure. And that structure is the same, whether in InDesign or in HTML. So yes, you can certainly start with the structure of an InDesign document (since you've already put all the work into making that document's structure correct and apparent), but you just have to realize that the visual displays are not going to be the same.

You have to design each format of the book for its container. It's just like redesigning a hardcover for mass market, or that exercise we all did in school where we were given advertising text and told to design the information for three sizes of production. So I guess the answer to your question is yes, you need to think about the e-book design separately, but you can certainly use the very powerful tools available to you in InDesign's export to take advantage of the structural tagging that you've already done for the print.

Is there really any point in trying to adapt a print design for e-book format? Where/how would you begin?
The first thing I ask about a particular book is the audience. *Where* and on *what devices* are they reading? Ooligan Press recently published a young adult novel that is being used in middle schools in Oregon. While the initial acquisitions process was happening, the buzz in the e-book world was all about "enhanced e-books." We went through an extensive research process to figure out (a) what an "enhanced e-book" is, and (b) whether this format would be relevant for the subject matter and the audience. We discovered that "enhanced e-book," at the time, meant using other forms of media (audio, video) to supplement the story, but that most devices at the time did not support multimedia presentations. But more importantly, we discovered that middle schools were not using e-books in the classroom, and middle schoolers themselves were not reading e-books at home. So if our audience wasn't there, and the technology couldn't do the things we wanted to do, we decided to forgo the "enhanced e-book" (which ended up feeling like a gimmick) and make an e-book that would be available for most everyone that wanted to read digitally.

From there, the question is about the content. If you have what Craig Mod calls formless content,[1] then the best advice is to give up any illusions that you should or would be able to reproduce that print book on a digital device. This is where you should be most aware of what you can control and what you can't in the digital reading environment. Most of the time you won't be able to control the typeface displayed or the size of that typeface. You won't be able to control widows and orphans. You probably won't be able to control whether or not the reader is looking at your book in color or grayscale. Designing simply, for the most basic reading device, is your best bet. You want to be able to reach the most readers possible, right? That's one of the reasons we, as an industry, are so excited about e-books: they bring in new readers (and there's lots of research to support that statement). But if we're designing books that they want to read in forms that are unreadable, we're missing the entire point.

But if you have what Mod terms "definite content," or content that has to follow a certain layout, there are options, but currently these are more limited to certain devices and screen sizes. You can use what's called fixed layout, kind of in the same vein as a PDF, but with more interactivity and scalability. At the

[1] Craig Mod, "Books in the Age of the iPad," http://craigmod.com/journal/ipad_and_books/.

moment, fixed layout designs are only supported on certain tablets. So all of those complicated nonfiction designs with graphs and charts and multiple columns and colors: those may be better served in the future.

We as designers and publishers have to be able to recognize where the limits are, and how to deal with them. But that's been our job all along, hasn't it? We take our limits—whether they be trim size or page length or budget—and make a product that fits within those limits that the audience will enjoy. We'll just be more and more aware of the design choices we're making, and why. The days of a one-size-fits-all book design are gone. Each title should be considered on its own, and publishers need to be able to recognize that not all content is appropriate for all containers.[1] This makes our job harder, but I think we have to stop complaining about it and just suck it up. This is the world we live in, and we can do some pretty amazing things with it.

You mentioned that some fonts (Garamond) were obviously not suitable. What kind of fonts would you recommend?

This goes back to knowing the content and what containers are appropriate for it. If you can embed fonts, then using typefaces designed for the screen is a good idea. Generally, typefaces with less thick/thin contrast are easier to read. Remember that not all digital devices display at the same resolution. A high-definition tablet shows immensely more detail than an e-ink device. Matthew Carter is a digital type genius (as well as a print genius, but he's one of the first in the digital realm). There are other type design initiatives out there that are trying to find the best letterforms for easy screen reading from Microsoft, Adobe, etc.[2]

But if you are dealing with files formats and readers that you can't embed fonts with, then at least find out what the commonly available fonts are on the popular e-readers. Then find the commonalities between them: maybe there are proportions that work well for all the fonts available on the three major devices that are suitable for your content.

The biggest key to remember is that type settings (size, leading, spacing in the print world) are reader-controlled in the digital world. This means that any absolute settings that you choose (pixels or points) can be affected by the default settings of the reading device and by the preferences of the readers themselves. This is why getting the proportions right, rather than the absolute measurements, is the best option for a designer to make the reading experience the best it can be.

Learning about cascading style sheets (CSS) styling is as essential to digital design as learning about picas and points is to print. For instance, in CSS for digital books, type should be set in ems. This em, like our print em, is a proportional measurement. The em's 1.0 (or 100 percent) size is determined by the device screen, whether laptop, phone, or dedicated reading device. So

[1] See Brian O'Leary's *Content First* video and *Breaking the Page* by Peter Meyers (O'Reilly e-book).

[2] http://www.poynter.org/uncategorized/32363/in-search-of-the-best-online-reading-experience/.

when you set your CSS style for type size, you're setting it relative to that 1.0 em measurement. When a reader with bad eyesight increases the text size, they are doing so in relation to that 1.0 em.

Your line-height (aka leading) should also be set to that em measurement. If you set your leading with absolute numbers (as we do in print design), and the reader increases the text size, soon you will have what essentially appears as negative leading, because your type size is getting bigger, but the line-height is staying the same. So if you want to have positive leading no matter the size the reader sets the type at, you want to use a larger em measurement. For example, if you set your type size at 0.8 em, try setting the leading at 1.5 em.

But for this same reason, margins should not be set to proportional measurements. If they are, then as the reader increases the font size, they will also be inadvertently increasing the margin size. Soon this gives the reader huge margins with a very narrow column of words, rendering the book unreadable. Margins should be set in pixels or percentages. But again, learn how CSS thinks of paragraphs and the spacing around them (margin, border, padding) to truly take advantage of these features.

The only other thing that digital designers simply must not do is justify text. It is silly and looks awful on these resizable screens as text gets bigger.

Given that some "books" are read on a smart phone, how does a designer even begin to establish the idea of a page and margins? The New York Times, Guardian, *and* Washington Post *on an iPhone are just in one long stream. On the iPad the* Times *is set up in pages and actually looks nicer than the print version.*
I think in terms of this, we have to give up the notion of the page. We need to be thinking more in terms of content, and how it appears. If you do need a page, then, as I said above, fixed page layout is the way to go.

If designers cannot predict how fonts will be displayed or how the design will look across various platforms, is it best to just keep things as simple as possible—to be more concerned about the technical production rather than the design?
Yes, I think that digital design calls for simplicity more than anything else. There's research out there to suggest that we're just more easily distracted when reading on a screen, even if we're just reading text, and especially if we're reading on multifunction devices like smartphones and tablets. Reading, and true "deep reading" as Maryanne Wolf terms it, needs mental space, mental quietude, and as a designer the best way to give that to the reader is to make it easy for them. We'll eventually evolve to be much better digital readers than we currently are, and hopefully we'll evolve into some of those digital deep

reading skills that we don't seem to have now. But to help us get there, I think we designers need to help the process by keeping that reading process as unhindered as possible.

Do you think this will eventually resolve itself so that there will be an agreed-upon standard (like the Beta/VHS and Blu-ray/DVD conflicts that eventually got settled)? It took about a decade before computer type got sophisticated from the early days of PostScript fonts to OpenType.
I think we're going to have a big fight before it happens. EPUB will be the main standard, but we're also dealing with Amazon and the Kindle as long as they hang on to it. I have a feeling that as EPUBs get more sophisticated and Kindle continues to lag behind, we may end up with a Kindle format that reads EPUB, or some such thing. I think Amazon will hold on to their proprietary format as long as they can, but I have no real support for that, other than my personal opinion. I don't foresee the publishing world and Amazon suddenly coming to some détente long enough to settle the format battle in any spirit of compromise, though. I think we're beyond where the two will see the other as anything but adversarial. But now that Microsoft has gotten behind the NOOK, and Apple is Apple, and now Google has the Nexus tablet, I think that readers will have the choice, and if one works better than the other at about the same price point, then we'll see.

On the Design of Whitman

KENT LEW

The concept behind Whitman might be summed up as a what-if thought experiment: What if Dwiggins had set out to design Joanna?

This idea was the confluence of two streams of inspiration back in 1999. The first was my growing admiration for Caledonia, designed by W. A. Dwiggins for Mergenthaler Linotype Company in 1939. I had not previously held much regard for the whole Scotch category of types (generally regarded as a subspecies of Modern). Many examples of Scotch in metal type tend to be heavy, tight, and closed up. On the other hand, early digital versions of Scotch exacerbated the Modern contrast and were quite spindly. The digital New Caledonia, in particular, seems to me quite brittle and gawky. I didn't think I liked Caledonia.

However, as I became more and more interested in collecting books—both fine and trade editions—from the golden age of American book publishing (ca. 1930s, '40s, and '50s), and as I encountered Caledonia at every turn, I began to find a new appreciation. And in 2000, I acquired an original Linotype specimen booklet for Caledonia. Upon experiencing the type in all its previous glory, I realized that here was a rich, lively, and perfectly comfortable text face. The digital version upon which I'd based my initial opinion was a ghost of the original, a caricature.

This is unfortunately true of many digitizations of metal typefaces and is a criticism leveled at many of the current incarnations of classic book faces. One doesn't really know and can't really appreciate Bembo, Baskerville, Electra, or even Times Roman if one hasn't experienced them in their hot metal incarnations. The current digitizations are mere wraiths of the originals.

So I began toying with creating a digital facsimile of letterpress-printed Caledonia, just as an exercise. This was never intended to have a commercial result. It was merely a way to become more intimate with the original face, perhaps to better understand just what made it tick. It was also an opportunity for me to hone my digitization skills.

The other stream of inspiration came from popular trends of the late 1990s and early 2000s. During that period, *Martha Stewart Living* magazine was emerging as a fashionable design influence, with its generous margins, airy layouts, and stylish typography. Their text face at that time was Eric Gill's Joanna (originally designed in 1930, but not issued to the trade until 1958). Joanna is a light, unadorned face with low contrast and a crisp finish which, when openly leaded, lent the *MSL* pages a refreshing, contemporary feeling.

However, while I greatly admire Dwiggins's work, I have a love/hate thing with Gill's. I sense something provocative and promising in many of Gill's type-

THE EFFORT that matured into
with a strong liking for the S
That sound, workable type ha
craft for a hundred years. But
tures about it that are not q
could one go towards modi
without spoiling the vigor of
the start. . . .
But why modify Scotch? Is
it stands? Well, there was a ki
ness about the modeling of
Wilson letters that didn't seen
And when you got down to o
design had suffered the cha
tings, the woodenness had be
by reason of the 19th century
to strike all his curves with a
everything hard and symme

Caledonia, from the original 1939 Mergenthaler Linotype specimen.

The text for this chapter is set in 11.5/15 Whitman.

etter

FROM MARTHA

THIS IS A VERY BUSY OCTOBER, AND WE HAVE LOTS OF WONDERFUL THINGS to offer you. Ten years have flown by since we started MARTHA STEWART LIVING magazine, and in celebration we have compiled our favorite recipes from those years into our newest cookbook for Clarkson Potter, *The Martha Stewart Living Cookbook.* It can be found in bookstores everywhere, as well as on our website—

Joanna, as employed in *Martha Stewart Living* magazine, ca. October 2000.

faces, but all of them seem to fall well short of the mark for me. Where Dwiggins's typefaces invite me to compose with them and inspire me to emulate his achievements in my own type designs, with Gill's typefaces I have a strong urge to replace each one with something less idiosyncratically *Gill.* (Gill fans will have to forgive my blasphemy.) Joanna is no exception. I admire the light, spare simplicity of means, but I dislike so many of the "Gilliosyncrasies" (in particular, that malformed *d*, for instance).

While working on my Caledonia exercise, I was particularly captivated by Dwiggins's unusual treatment of the counters in the arched letters: *h n m u*. What if I were to combine this kind of structure with a light, contemporary, spartan finish, along the lines of Gill's Joanna?

■ Looking again at Caledonia and Joanna, I think the sources have been pretty well dissolved in Whitman. I really don't think I captured that je ne sais quoi found in the great metal faces. Nor was I necessarily trying to. I wasn't focused

h

Dwiggin's enlarged ink drawing, shown in the Caledonia specimen, was a principal trigger for the development of Whitman.

aphgte

aphgte

aphgte

A direct comparison of Whitman (middle) with Caledonia (top, represented here by my own digital facsimile) and Joanna (bottom) reveals a complete melding of the two influences. The outward impression of Whitman reflects the spare simplicity of Joanna, while the underlying structure is more deeply rooted in Caledonia.

hfgruR7;

kfgrutz&

A digital zeitgeist is revealed in certain details of Whitman—abrupt transitions, such as those inside the arches of *h* and *u* or the neck of *g*; sharp cuts and notches, as under the terminals of *f* and *r*; subtle angles and segments in place of curves, as in the taper of *7* or the cant of some italic stems.

on re-creating the metal warmth of Caledonia. For all my love and admiration of the classic letterpress faces, I'm not generally a nostalgist.

Whitman was more an exploration of what I call a digital vernacular: a language of simplified and often unexpected geometry being applied in otherwise traditional forms. I found a fascination in taking seemingly inexpressive, reductive elements—sharp transitions, line segments, precise arcs—and carefully combining them to create a surprising grace or an organic tension. As such, Whitman is unquestionably a contemporary design for today.

There are several other precedents for this style. In digital type, the trend traces back through faces like Vendetta (1997) and FF Scala (1991) to ITC Charter (1987) and ultimately perhaps to Swift (1985). The earliest digital faces I've cited were, to a large extent, confronting technical constraints, and their simplified geometry comes from efforts to create robustness in the face of coarse resolutions, as well as to conserve processor memory and file size. The character that comes through is influenced strongly by the problems set before the designers. But the technical constraints facing Unger and Carter have now been largely overcome, yet Swift and Charter still seem fresh and vital. The continued exploration of this formal territory in contemporary designs seems primarily for aesthetic effect.

Regulations
Vendetta

Regulations
Scala

Regulations
Charter

Regulations
Swift

Today, another decade on from Whitman, this digital aesthetic is a commonplace in contemporary type design. But only a few of these are suitable for or have found any place in book typography. In his 1930 essay "First Principles of Typography," Stanley Morison observed, "Type design moves at the pace of the most conservative reader. The good type designer therefore realizes that, for a new font to be successful, it has to be so good that only very few recognise its novelty. If readers do not notice the consummate reticence and rare discipline of a new type it is probably a good letter." I'm not sure this holds as much widespread truth today as it did then, but in the realm of book typography I think it still bears some relevance.

Toward this end, many of the radical elements in the early drafts of Whitman had to be sublimated. I wanted the typeface to behave itself well in running text. So, I endeavored to harness the crisp, digital vernacular with some sense of the traditional values I admired in those classic book faces: consistent color, reader-friendly proportions, and ultimately an understated quality.

■ It occurs to me that I frequently focus primarily on the Roman design when speaking about Whitman. But the Italic really is admirable in its own right. Today, this pairing of Whitman styles looks almost inevitable. However, it took a lot of exploration to find the right companion. I think I tried maybe seven variations on an italic before I landed on this direction.

■ Matching an italic to a roman can be a very subjective process. One wants a companion that differs enough to create adequate distinction, for emphasis; at the same time, the complement should ideally possess sufficient stylistic similarity to harmonize in context. With a design that falls within well-established historic categories, traditional pairings may influence one's expectations—e.g.,

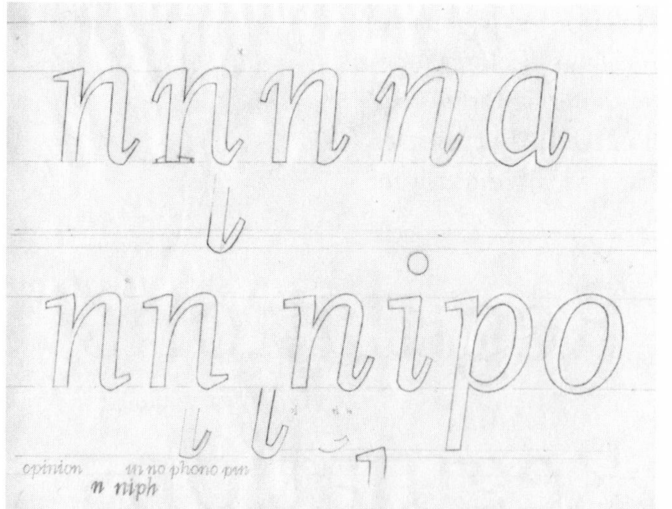

Early exploratory sketches for Whitman italic.

chancery italic with a humanistic old-style roman or copperplate italic with a transitional roman. But often those associations are as much a coincidence of history as they are any sort of structural correspondence. A pure sloped roman (as advocated most famously by Stanley Morison in a 1926 essay entitled "Towards an Ideal Italic") may possess impeccable rationality, but I think history has judged this to be a graceless solution, at least for book work.

As charming as I find Caledonia's italic, I felt that kind of sinuous style too affected and too foreign to the character that Whitman had developed. Whitman Italic has none of the copperplate, split-nib modern stress of the Caledonia italic. Neither is it a radical, attenuated companion like the Joanna italic. Instead, I sought to let the structure of the roman letter shapes themselves inform

Early trial proofs of italic with roman.

Vireo Italic — 10 September 2000 a.m.

Pack my box with five *million* liquor jugs. The quick
brown fox had *no opinion* on the *blind dolphin*. Instead,
he jumped over the incredibly lazy dog. 2
Pack my box with five *million* liquor jugs. The quick
brown fox had *no opinion* on the *blind dolphin*. Instead,
he jumped over the incredibly lazy dog. 3
Pack my box with five *million* liquor jugs. The quick
brown fox had *no opinion* on the *blind dolphin*. Instead,
he jumped over the incredibly lazy dog. 4

Vireo Italic — 10 September 2000 a.m.

no opinion in phono million libido poliphili dolphin bin
no opinion in phono million libido poliphili dolphin bin
no opinion in phono million libido poliphili dolphin bin
no opinion in phono million libido poliphili dolphin bin
no opinion in phono million libido poliphili dolphin bin
no opinion in phono million libido poliphili dolphin bin

Vireo Italic 5 & 6 — 14 September 2000 a.m.

Pack my bag with five dozen liquor jugs. The quick brown
fox jumps over a lazy dog. Back in my quaint garden:
million aluminum phenomenon, pandemonium in braille on
a blind albino dolphin needing repair leopard diverge no
valium opinion revolver.
Pack my bag with five dozen liquor jugs. The quick brown
fox jumps over a lazy dog. Back in my quaint garden:
million aluminum phenomenon, pandemonium in braille on
a blind albino dolphin needing repair leopard diverge no
valium opinion revolver.

Whitman Italic. I chose to keep the italic slope modest, letting small structural details carry the burden of distinction. Although it is slightly narrower than the roman, Whitman Italic maintains an open character that I hoped would help keep it comfortably readable in greater amounts. I hoped it might hold up just on its own—in poetry, for example.

■ To try to make the Whitman fonts as user-friendly and functional as possible, I drew upon my experience as a book designer and an actual *user* of type. I incorporated a handful of options into the fonts in order to enhance their usefulness for text setting that, at the time of their release, were not terribly common.

For example, the minus and multiply characters and the three basic fractions were all already part of the typical character set. But, for whatever reason, these are generally inaccessible from the Macintosh keyboard. I duplicated these glyphs into some of the less-used character slots, so that the average designer could get at them and implement them. In hacking the character slots, I was building on a practice that the Font Bureau (and others, like the Hoefler Type Foundry) had already adopted in order to provide ready access to generally unavailable, but highly useful, characters—the ff-ligatures, for instance. I took many cues from Matthew Carter, who had provided access to minus and multiply in ITC Galliard CC and access to these plus the basic fractions in Miller Text for Font Bureau.

I went a step further by providing a few raised punctuation marks—hyphen, en dash, and parentheses—for use in all-caps settings. I borrowed the idea for the raised hyphen from Matthew Carter (in Big Caslon); but the capital parentheses may have been all my own at the time. Again these had to be placed in hacked character slots.

With the retail release of the Whitman fonts, I pushed for the delivery of two different fonts for every style, each configured with a different figure style—lining figures (LF) and old-style figures (OSF). I think FontFont was producing some fonts similarly configured, but this was relatively uncommon at that time; and I give credit to Font Bureau for offering both versions for a single price (which was even less common) and for not making the customer ask for the alternate arrangement as a special request.

I knew that I wanted the Roman font to have old-style figures by default. They're just generally better for setting extended text. However, this meant that, according to the then-current standards, the lining figures would end up lumped in with the Small Caps font. I don't know who would ever realistically want lining figures with small caps. Moreover, sometimes the lining figures are in fact what you want in your text. The accepted alternative was to leave the lining figures in the Roman font and provide the old-style figures with the Small Caps.

The thing that really annoyed me about that kind of configuration was having to constantly switch back and forth between fonts for a few numbers. I didn't want to have to do that for Whitman. So I developed both configurations in parallel. This turned out to be more complicated than it first seems, since different figure styles also mean different versions of currency and arithmetic symbols, as well as a few others, and it was a challenge to keep track of the variables. However, this way the typesetter could just decide which style of numerals best suited the material at hand and select the appropriate font for use throughout, without needing to keep switching or to set up cumbersome stylesheets specifically for the numbers.

Nowadays, of course, with the expanded OpenType format, all these sorts of options and features are practically de rigueur (and implemented in more robust, standards-compliant ways, without disrupting underlying character encodings), but at the time I was up against the boundaries of the PostScript Type 1 format and had to employ some idiosyncratic solutions.

Unfortunately, some of these idiosyncrasies now make the Whitman fonts less versatile than more recent families that take full advantage of OpenType features. I'm now working on an updated version that will bring these things in line with current standards—e.g., integrated small caps and proper character encodings—and incorporate additional features like arbitrary fractions, true superiors for reference notes, etc.

I think that the opportunities made available by the "intelligent" OpenType format are remarkable advancements, but I worry that type designers are being prompted to overthink situations that are not really their bailiwick. While I like to see niceties like small cap figures or certain alternates, I think it's important to make these available in ways that don't impose too much of a type designer's preconceptions upon the typographer/compositor. I personally don't like layout features that make too many assumptions and that aren't turn-offable.

For instance, while I might personally think it's advisable to use lining figures in a context of all caps, I don't necessarily think that an OpenType font should force lining figures with the all caps (case) feature—at least, not without a reasonably straightforward way for the user to override this and request old-style figures instead, if that's what the design/context calls for. An intelligent font is one thing; an autocratic one is another.

■ There is an oft-repeated bon mot among designers of text typefaces: A good typeface is not a collection of beautiful letters; it is a beautiful collection of letters. That is to say, it's not about how exquisite each individual letterform might or might not be; it has more to do with how they all work together. And it's not just about how various design characteristics—like serif structure, or certain curves, or terminals—are carried throughout the different forms. The success of a typeface has as much to do with how everything fits together to make words—which is, after all, the end objective.

So, I was particularly concerned with the fitting of Whitman. "Fitting" is the process of determining the sidebearings—the amount of space allocated to each side of a glyph. These sidebearings determine how each letter meets up with those alongside. Fitting involves broad decisions, like how overall tight or loose the natural spacing of a face might be. It also involves the minute decisions that balance the spacing of each letter for all possible combinations.

Spacing is not completely independent of shaping. Determining the overall fit of letters is an integral part of the designing, and I tend to establish the general fit of each letter as I'm working out the alphabet. Adjustments to spacing may precipitate changes in letter proportion; changes in a curve may engender adjustments to the basic fitting. Nevertheless, at some point the letterforms are more or less completed, and then the overall design is reviewed and the fitting refined.

I spent probably the better part of a year fitting the original Whitman fonts. That's not necessarily something to brag about. It likely has more to do with my learning curve. Whitman was my first full-fledged typeface design. Since then, I've developed a better sense of spacing from the start. But with Whitman, after the design had been honored by the Type Directors Club and accepted for publication by Font Bureau, I found I still wasn't satisfied with the fitting and I wound up starting almost completely over. I reevaluated every aspect of the fitting, pretty much from scratch, and completely reworked the kerning.

In metal, of course, the allocated space of a glyph was a physical attribute. One sort could not readily invade the space of another, not without incorporating some overhang and overlapping (which, incidentally, was the original meaning of "kern"). This required special handling, as it makes a sort more vulnerable to breakage, and was not feasible in many cases.

In digital, these boundaries become much more malleable and easily manipulated. Nevertheless, the technology still generally follows the same principles. Each glyph has its default fitting, which determines how it sets up next to others, and any overriding departures are handled through kern-pair exceptions. Conventional wisdom advises that a designer get the basic fitting worked out thoroughly before introducing any kerning.

Each type designer has his or her own specific method of fitting. Part of that method will almost undoubtedly involve strings of control characters—abstract strings of letters with the target letter woven into a fabric of known quantities. For example, to evaluate the fitting of the *a*, one might set up a string like "nnonananoaoaonoannaon" or "llolalaloaoaloallaol." Different designers will have different pet strings. In theory, if the spacing of each letter can be made to appear evenly balanced in relation to the regular, more-or-less symmetrical letters, then they will be generally balanced in any combination.

Beyond control strings, though, I think it is equally important to view my letters in real words. The context of a word affects one's perception of the spacing. And the expectations we have of how words should look can influence subtle decisions about fitting. To that end, I have lots of lists of words—for example, a list of words with a preponderance of round letters (words like "coincide compounded decomposed dependence equipped" etc.) and one with a preponderance of straight-sided letters ("aluminum imminent lithium milliliter titillate" etc.). Comparing these can help determine the overall balance and color.

I developed extensive testing documents with long lists of words, real words, presenting each letter in just about every combination and in various controlled combinations—the target pair with a straight-sided letter before and after, with a round letter before and after, with a straight before and round after, with a round before and straight after, etc. So, for example, to evaluate the "ac" combination, I have "niacin placid beacon abacus teacup apache."

It's also important to proof type designs at something close to actual intended size. Perception of space can shift based on relative size; a typeface intended for text requires a different kind of spacing than one intended for display (and not just the rule of thumb that text should be generally looser than display). At text sizes, good fitting is more a matter of balancing volumes of space and pacing the rhythm properly. At display sizes, one becomes much more focused on specific proximities and absolute distances.

One looks for places that go bump in the mind, places that seem not quite even. If there's a recurring pattern to the inconsistency across several similar combinations, then that should probably be solved with an adjustment to the default fitting, the sidebearings. If it's more of a situational, one-off problem, then that's usually a candidate for a kern-pair exception.

Many type designers I know are inveterate collectors of words. We love to discover words that present unusual sequences—especially, it would seem, proper names with uncommon UC-lc combinations, for example: Cnidaria (a phylum of aquatic invertebrates), Txupinazo (fireworks that mark the start of the festival of San Fermin in Pamplona), and Yquem (a variety and producer of sauterne wine). Often these present the potential for rare, but important, kern pairs that become something of a badge of honor among type designers.

Good text performance involves more than just the behavior of the letters. Punctuation deserves and requires just as much attention. Because sorts like periods, commas, quotation marks, and such occupy only a small region of their allotted space, they frequently require kern adjustments in various combinations—and not just in association with letters. Sequences like quotation marks with parentheses (and vice versa), period/comma with quotation marks, asterisk with quotation marks or parentheses or period/comma, and so on all deserve consideration.

That doesn't necessarily mean getting everything as close as one can. Now that space is so malleable in a digital environment, I've seen a tendency on the part of some designers to want to kern everything in sight, to push everything around. I believe that it's entirely possible to overdo things and that in a text face too much can potentially be far worse than too little. After all, the classic metal typefaces managed to perform quite well with very little individual pair kerning. While seeking to remove unsightly holes from the text block, it's important not to sacrifice an appropriate sense of space, of autonomy, for each character. You don't really want every vowel tucked too tightly under a capital T or quotation marks stacked right on top of the period or comma. Every element needs room to be parsed by the reading eye.

As in most endeavors, the goal is Goldilocks's "just right."

■ As a type designer who focuses on text faces, I find it's invaluable to evaluate types not just as isolated words but also in sentences, paragraphs, and whole pages. For any given design I'm working on, I may have several testing pages of real-world text. These are often re-creations of specific book pages, the models for which are usually set in classic faces akin to whatever I'm trying to achieve. This allows me to gauge the performance of my work against references of known quality, comparing overall color, texture, and effect.

I suppose this is similar to my insistence, as a book designer, that page designs not be developed and evaluated purely on the screen or even in single-page printouts. It's important to trim pages and stick them into a dummy, so that one can experience how the inner margins interact with the cascade of the binding and how the outer margins stand against the precipice of the fore-edge.

For Whitman, I made up some replicas of a few Dwiggins book pages originally set in Caledonia, naturally. I would also often take book designs that I might have been working with at the time and change the font to Whitman just to see how it might be working compared to whatever I had actually specified.

I never went so far as to have any of my own designs printed with working versions of Whitman. I somehow felt too self-conscious to make any paying clients into guinea pigs. However, a few publications by a designer in Vermont, working both with her own small poetry imprint and for a trade publisher, used beta versions of Whitman. These examples didn't make it into print in time to be of any practical value to me in terms of evaluating Whitman in actual offset printing. Nevertheless, I think it's valuable, when possible, to partner with adventurous designers who are willing to experiment with new typefaces.

Ultimately, type designers must reconcile themselves with the fact that they are making essentially a tool for others. When a type design is released into the world, it must be let go. Others are bound to do with it what they will. For the most part, I am tickled whenever I discover Whitman in use, even when it may not be handled optimally. I like to see it put into new environments and contexts. These allow me to further discover its strengths and weaknesses, which I like to think help educate me toward making my next efforts that much better.

Overall, I've been happy with Whitman's performance in the real world. It's

bandwidth salamander lithium algorithm
bandwidth salamander lithium algorithm

< > < < >< < > < >< > < > < < >< > > < > >< < < >< > >

bandwidth salamander lithium algorithm
bandwidth salamander lithium algorithm

digitize constitution altruistic fruitfulness
digitize constitution altruistic fruitfulness

digitize constitution altruistic fruitfulness
digitize constitution altruistic fruitfulness

< < >< > > < < > >< > < > < < < > > < > > >< > > << > > < > > >

been extremely gratifying to see it used in books for a range of subjects, from stories and fiction to natural sciences and self-help to crafts and gardening. (I find the latter especially serendipitous given that the initial impetus came partly from the pages of *Martha Stewart Living*.)

I was a bit more surprised to see Whitman taken up by magazines. For whatever reason, it was chosen by a couple of bridal magazines and a prominent women's magazine; I suppose some designers find a feminine quality to it? Perhaps it's just the appeal of the lighter text color. For a while Whitman was used as the text face for a financial magazine.

One thing I will say: it really does bother me when designers enable Adobe InDesign's Optical Metrics. This so-called feature overrides the spacing that is built into a font and applies the application's own algorithm to push and pull letters around, completely obliterating the type designer's careful work and intent. As I have said, I consider the spacing, the fitting, of a font to be an integral part of a typeface design and an important factor in its ultimate success or failure.

I haven't seen this applied so much in books, but apparently some magazine designers have been misled to believe that this feature provides the optimal spacing. It's not true. It's only an algorithm, which cannot replace human judgment. With some typefaces, this algorithm has a minimal, and perhaps largely unnoticeable, effect. With others, however, it can completely disrupt the fitting of the face, to great detriment. Whitman, unfortunately, is one of those that suffers considerably.

I don't claim that my fitting of Whitman is perfect and beyond improvement or adjustment, but I do take exception to a computer algorithm mucking about with it.

"Optical" does not mean "optimal." The first line in each comparison above shows Whitman with its native spacing; the second one demonstrates the sort of back-and-forth manipulation that Adobe's Optical kerning imposes on Whitman at 11 points (the algorithm performs differently at different sizes). It is particularly overbearing with letters like *r*, *t*, roman *a*, and italic *f*. All these inept shenanigans introduce distracting clusters and unsightly gaps into words, disrupting the underlying rhythms and adversely affecting readability.

■ This design wasn't always called Whitman. It existed for more than a year as Vireo. In the beginning, as the typeface was taking shape, it was connected in my mind with the red-eyed vireo. The vireo is a very common woodland bird where I live. One distinctive characteristic is that it sings almost constantly throughout the summer—even at midday, on the hottest days. Its song is so constant that it becomes part of the summer atmosphere and you cease to notice it. Something about that ubiquitous, unnoticed, almost unremarkable quality resonated with my intention for this face. Everyone hears vireos in the summer, but they hardly ever notice and rarely look for them. Like a good text face. There's a contradictory line that a good text typeface walks between being unremarkable and yet distinctive.

It was John Downer who pointed out that Vireo might be problematic as a name in the marketplace, being unfamiliar and easily misread for "video." After some extensive searching, I finally landed on Whitman. It seems to have been a good fit. There's the attendant association with literature; there's Walt Whitman's celebration of the physical, the common, the everyday; there's his plain-spokenness.

I also think of the typeface as having an essentially "American" quality. I hesitate to say it like that because I dislike our society's current nationalistic fervor; that's not the kind of American that I mean. There's a quality of American literature and letters that I think was epitomized in the first half of the twentieth century and exhibited by Updike, Dwiggins, Conkwright, Blumenthal, that whole crowd. I hoped to capture some of that distinctively American voice and spirit in my design and thus make Whitman a worthy successor to that splendid tradition.

Beyond Selecting and Arranging Type

CHARLES ELLERTSON

Beautiful typography. Is there room for this notion outside the rarefied worlds of book shows and fine-print books? I think so. I'm tempted to say that typography is the most important element in presenting the text. The academic in me shudders at such a bald statement. A host of qualifications are surely needed. I'll just have to live with that; here, and other places below, I will make observations fully aware that there are other factors at play, and other points of view.

Unlike design, who contributes to, who *controls* typography, is usually the work of more than one person. Perfunctorily, the type designer and punchcutter, the book designer, the typesetter, and the printer all contribute to the typography of a book.

To some extent, how we judge typography depends on the time period. In the first century of printing, the type founder, the typesetter, and the printer could be the same person. When not, they were often housed in one place. From the early days to the last decade of the nineteenth century, the design of the book was usually the work of the compositor. When speaking of the typography of a book, every aspect of the printed piece was included, and generally summed with the word "printer," as in "printer to the king."

Machine-set type, with all fonts available to whoever owned the machine, began in the late nineteenth century. Perhaps coincidentally, compositors were in a period of typographic excess about this time, where they tended to use an excessive number of fonts and styles within a printed piece. Whether this came from the number of typefaces now available or from boredom with the same old fonts, we'll never know. In concert, and with other factors at play, the new availability of type and the failings of the compositors led to the separate profession of book designer.

Machine-set type and the designer as a separate profession changed our view about the responsibility for good typography. What distinguished one book from another migrated toward the design of the book. The interior designer as analogous to an architect came out of this period. While compositors and pressmen still had some importance, the common view was that their job was to avoid mistakes rather than to make an aesthetic contribution to the book.

This designer-as-architect model, with the typesetter and printer cast in the role of tradesmen and the type designer admired from afar, was apt for the first half of the twentieth century. It fit less well with photocomposition, and with the changes occasioned by digital type has acquired ragged edges.

Now, for good or ill, typography is again understood to be affected by the work of three people—the type designer, the book designer, and the compositor. Oddly enough, once again the interior designer and compositor may be the same person.

Does this mark a return to thinking good typography today is the same as was considered good during the first 400 years of printing? I think not. Too much evolution—from foundry, to hot metal, to photocomposition, to digital type. This affects how designers must think. Even with machine-set metal type the number of typefaces a designer could select was relatively small. In the 1950s, the cost for a full set of Linotype matrices needed for bookwork was almost as much as a new car. A printer would have four or five suitable text fonts, and was not about to buy a new one for a book. With photocomposition, the price for a set of fonts dropped to about the cost of a weekend getaway for two. Not a major purchase, but still one to think about. My point is that how we put the ink on the paper matters. The various machines that replace the scribe's hand matter, just as the change from calligraphy to type mattered.

Photocomposition came with its own set of constraints. Though the costs were lower, the decision to try a new font was limited by the relatively few good typefaces suitable for text. Many text typefaces offered were revivals of older fonts. Sadly, the foundry's execution of those revivals often left much to be desired. In *On Book Design*, Rich Hendel remarked that Janson was once in fashion, then dropped out. One reason was that most photocomposition versions of Janson were terrible. When printed, the fine lines were just too fine—with a 10-point setting, the lowercase "o" looked like two small parentheses. In an extreme case like Janson, there wasn't much a typesetter or printer could do about this.

With photocomposition, however, some fonts could be rescued in ways not previously available. If a font would print well but the character fit was poor, the typesetter could come to its aid. Most photocomposition systems allowed kerning tables to be written. It didn't take compositors long to figure out that kerning could be used to generally refit a poorly spaced font. While the spacing increments one could use were large by today's standards, with work, a poorly spaced font could still be rendered rather nicely. For example, looking at letterforms alone, Linotron 202 Pilgrim was perhaps Gill's best font for setting text. Sadly, the spacing of the characters was terrible. Designers could select it—and should only select it—if they knew the typesetter had written a decent kerning program.

In the 1990s, the introduction of PostScript fonts changed many things. Fonts were now *software*. Suddenly, typefaces were not proprietary to a single brand of typesetting equipment. The fonts were cheap. Soon, the PostScript source code was made public. That allowed other software to be written to allow both creating new fonts and editing old ones. This software could be purchased by anyone. Two things made this revolutionary. On the creation side, almost anyone could try making type. More remarkable to me was the ability for anyone to edit fonts. For the first time, the end-users of type gained control over the type itself. Glyphs could be modified or added. Character fit could be adjusted beyond simple kerns. The extent of the control available was limited only by the skill of the person working on the fonts.

Still, getting the ink on the paper is the final goal. The next change came from the printing side of book manufacturing, direct-to-plate (DTP) printing—also termed computer-to-plate printing. Prior to DTP platemaking, the typesetter ran the type out on rolls of photosensitive paper, called repro paper. While repro paper didn't really allow for gradations in tone, a change in the exposure did result in some variation in the weight of the letters. Since many photocomp revivals of hot-metal typefaces had fine strokes that were too fine, the exposure was usually set to get the most one could out of them. With the increased exposure, the type generally picked up weight. It is not well known, but with type set using a photographic process, the difference in weight that could be achieved by varying exposure and development was about half the difference between a "regular" and "medium" font in today's PostScript world.

The printer affected the weight of the type as well. To make the printing plate before DTP printing, the printer first had to perform another photographic operation, to put all the mechanicals supplied by the typesetter on a copy stand and make negatives. For several reasons, the exposure used for making the negatives was on the underexposed side, which increased the weight of the type a bit more. The final thing to remember in this process is that any negatives for halftone images were separate from the type, so the weight of the type and the dot gain for images were not tied together.

The DTP process eliminated all the photographic steps before making the plate. Since the plate was "exposed" from the computer file, all the weight the type had usually gained with the old system was lost. While the type became clearer, it also became thinner, and many typefaces were already on the thin side. Sadly, most of those who made type did not adjust their fonts for the new printing technology. Just as with the change from metal to photocomposition, some old favorites didn't work as well.

but of affirma	at we could ca
unjustified pr	nony does no
arguments be	difference wl
which traded	litics are refo
falsity. For Ba	of any given s
mortal huma	and can only

The typeface Scala. The sample on the left was printed using repro/negative/plate; the sample on the right was printed direct to plate. Enlarged from a 10/13 setting.

This is where we are today. As a typesetter, I sometimes take the quixotic view that the type designer provides some raw materials, the book designer gives the book form; the details, especially the typographic details, are left to the person who sets the type. While not true, I find it a useful fiction.

■ What is the sum of these changes for typography—where are we now? First, fonts are not as good as they could be. Offsetting this, there are now better tools to let users of type both fix problems and tailor the type to their vision. At the beginning of the PostScript era, most of these tools were available only in font editing programs, but as this is written, some are beginning to appear in layout programs such as Adobe's InDesign. As fonts have become software, the tools too are software; where they are often doesn't matter.

The work of a typesetter is with small detail. Nothing a typesetter can do will save a poor design or make an average design seem inspired. The large spatial relationships established by the margins and display elements are entirely the work of the designer and are the cornerstones of the page. However, while typographic elegance begins with the design of the page, it does not end there. For example, while the typesetter does not specify the leading, he often controls how well the leading works. If this seems odd, consider that all the spacing of the elements on the page interact; it does not take too much contemplation to realize that leading strongly interacts with the fit of the words, which in turn are influenced by the fit of the characters.

We have all run into typefaces that no matter what the setting size, no matter what the measure or margins, we can't seem to get the leading just right. Why is that? Occasionally this is due to the letterforms themselves, but usually, I believe, it is due to the fit of the characters. Hence the importance of kerning. With computer-assisted composition, kerning was first used to replace logotypes (two letters cast together), to adjust the fit of certain very awkward letter pairs where the gap between them competed with a word space, as you typically find with "Vo." However, kerning need not be limited to large gaps; it can also be used to address the small details of fitting type. The farther down this path one goes, the better the leading works. Indeed, as you begin to get the kerning right, you usually find that more than one leading value will work with a particular size of type, so leading choices can be better tailored to the measure and margins.

This may not be clear at first blush. What we read are not letters, or lines, but clumps of words. What lets us read clumps of words are the word spaces. Anything that makes these boundaries less clear, either by obfuscation or distraction, is poor typography. Essentially, I believe that what a good kerning program does is to remove distractions from the word boundaries. With those distractions minimized, the spacing of lines is not as critical.

Technically, kerning is the adjustment of space between two characters. But again, we read clumps of words, not pairs of letters. While writing a kerning program is a technical matter, the ability to see where the work should lead is an aesthetic one. The relationships involved cannot be addressed mathematically. After the type designer has established the general character fit by assigning sidebearings to each glyph, kerning can begin—or more accurately, both kerning and fine adjustments to the sidebearing assignments can be made, as sometimes a small change in sidebearing assignments lessens the need for ever more kerning.

The letters *f* and *e* in Minion, with black lines showing the set width of the characters. The spaces between the character and the black lines are the left and right sidebearings.

With the modern fashion to use as tight word spacing as possible, some rather unfortunate kerning has crept into fonts. Consider the following: generally, you want to kern an apostrophe with a Latin capital A, and you want to kern commas with both single and double quotes. Closing up these spaces helps the word boundaries become clearer.

When looking only at pairs of letters, it is easy to go too far. The first of the following pairs is kerned, the second is not (the font is Adobe's Warnock, using the kerning values from the font as published):

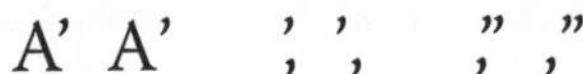

Individually, the kerns look more or less all right. However, if we put all four characters together, A’,” we get

A’,”

which is a mess. I'll allow those four characters do not often occur together, but it does happen.

Another example, this from Adobe Jenson, shows a different problem: what happens when the desire to make word spacing as even as possible tempts one to kern letters or symbols with the word space itself. Whoever kerned the foundry font decided that if the open quotes were tucked back into the word space, word spacing generally would be optically more even. The line below probably shows the intent:

this too “felt good” though in the end, looked bad.

Even if you accept this practice, the kern value used is too large. And it doesn't always work. Below, the first line is again set using the font as it comes from the publisher, the second line after the kerning has been modified:

the beginning of“a good thing.”
the beginning of “a good thing.”

The obvious problem with the foundry kerning is that in effect, the word space dropped out, though technically it is still there. In passing, there are other, rather subtle differences between the two versions—look at the word “the” and how tightly the close quote is kerned to the period.

Unless kerning tables can be programmed more selectively than a single value always used between two letters, the amount of any kern must be limited to accommodate the most awkward situations. To address this issue, Adobe developed contextual kerning for its older GX fonts. Contextual kerning allows for adjusting the space between two letters depending on the other letters that surround the pair. Contextual kerning is supported in the OpenType format, though it is not yet available in one of the most commonly used font development/editing programs.

There are ways to implement contextual kerning outside the font. At our shop, we pre-process text files before composition. That lets us search for a longer sequence of letters than just a pair. For example, to get more optically even word spacing, we search for any of r, v, w, x, and y, followed by a word space and any of a, c, d, e, o, q, and put a small kern. Other triplets are adjusted too, of course. Beyond triplets, this technique also allows us to search across font boundaries—i.e., an italic *d, f, i,* or *l* followed by a roman close parenthesis—and put in a kern: for example, *f*) is automatically kerned to *f*). While we have done this for a long time, more recent releases of InDesign make such a practice available to anyone who can write a script.

■ As mentioned, it is sometimes useful to work on the sidebearing assignments of glyphs. This doesn't necessarily mean there is something wrong with a published font. There can be different, legitimate views on the correct spacing of a particular set of letterforms, especially considering the varying uses of type. Type designers also have to consider that their fonts may be used by people using a text editor, or a simple layout program that does not support kerning. Sidebearing assignments must be made accordingly, again considering the letter fit with worst-case pairings. Those of us setting books with sophisticated layout programs like Quark or InDesign may find that changing the sidebearing assignments reduces the amount of total kerning necessary.

The paragraph below has had work done on both kerning and sidebearing assignments, with an eye toward achieving evenness in both letter and word spacing. In passing, this font is a reworking of Charis SIL, an open source version of Matthew Carter's Charter. The result, I think, demonstrates the effects of good kerning and spacing:

9.5/13.5 × 25.5 Charis. The size and leading shown are appropriate for a 6 × 9 trim. As an open source font family, Charis SIL may be modified, and can be used for print or digital books without concern about additional fees. In addition to the spacing work, we added ligatures, small capitals, and old style figures.

> This designer-as-architect model, with the typesetter and printer cast in the role of tradesmen and the type designer admired from afar, was apt for the first half of the twentieth century. It fit less well with photocomposition, and with the changes occasioned by digital type has acquired ragged edges. Now, for good or ill, typography is again understood to be affected by the work of three people—the type designer, the book designer, and the compositor. Oddly enough, once again the interior designer and compositor may be the same person.

The current standard font format, OpenType, allows a fair number of typesetting instructions to be built into the fonts themselves. In earlier times, these typographic niceties would have to be done in the layout program, often by hand. Moreover, with OpenType, there is usually more than one way to address an issue. For example, you can have more than one glyph for a single character. A *glyph* is a representation of a character. The capital A of Poetica and Baskerville is the same character—a Latin capital A. But the representations of A in the two fonts, the *glyphs*, are quite different. Alternatively, the Latin capital A and the Greek capital Alpha are different characters, but in most fonts have the same representation: two different characters, but the same glyph.

By using multiple glyphs, the problem of "f_space_open quote" can be addressed by using an alternate "f" glyph when that letter is directly followed by a word space.

The story of Jim and Huck, of life, of "a good thing," of ʿAyn.
The story of Jim and Huck, of life, of "a good thing," of ʿAyn.

There is no kerning in the "f_space_(following letter)" in either the first (foundry font) or second lines of the example. But in the second line, an extra "f" has been drawn, with a slightly shorter terminal and more space in the right sidebearing. The OpenType font has been programmed to use it automatically whenever an "f" is directly followed by a word space. I think this a better solution than contextual kerning, since with kerning, the space after the "f" would have to be increased, perforce increasing the apparent amount of white space between words. By shortening the terminal, less space is needed. The trick is to shorten the terminal stroke of the "f" just enough so that it does not call too much attention to being different.

Another case: sometimes kerning simply will not work well. Consider an "ä" following an "f." The fä pair is usually awkward with fonts that have a long terminal on the "f," like Quadraat, or the open-source font Alegreya.

biosfär, biosfääri, gefälscht (Swedish, Finnish, *biosphere*; German, *falsified*)

Since kerning the "f" with the ä requires an unfortunate amount of space,

biosfär, biosfääri, gefälscht;

a better solution would be to draw up a ligature, another kind of alternate glyph:

biosfär, biosfääri, gefälscht.

Again, substituting the ligature can be programmed into the font itself, where it will be used automatically like the more common f-ligatures.

Other situations where alternate glyphs can solve problems are a capital "Q" followed by a comma, a lowercase "f" followed by a word space, and a capital "J"—"of Jewish . . ." etc. For good fonts that have a problem with certain sequences of letters, using a substitute glyph can be the best solution. Examples abound: the worst case of clashing letters I've encountered was in a book about either the Kiowa or Comanches; I've forgotten in just which language it occurred. The book was to be set in Scala. One word contained the sequence i_macronbelow_macron_grave + f + another vowel with an accent. Let's make it a bad case and use an i_acute:

ȉ̱fí.

On reflection, kerning will not work; a special "f" seems required,

ȉ̱fí.

Not ideal, but the best, I think, of the choices available, especially for the 10-point setting used in the text. A different redrawing might be done for display, with the "f" much taller and deeper, its terminals surrounding the other letters, yet standing away from them. Not for text, though.

Is this typography? I think so. When looking at the examples above, remember that they are set ragged-right, where the ideal word space value is used. Consider some of these combinations in a justified setting, especially in a line where the word spacing runs a little tighter.

■ Earlier I mentioned that some layout programs have started to provide for typographic treatments formerly available only through special fonts or by using font-editing programs. In the 1990s, Richard Eckersley began using Minion for a number of his books. Richard was fond of shorter measures, which worked better with slightly condensed fonts. When Minion Multiple Masters was offered, Richard came up with the notion of creating a slightly condensed version. That let him shorten a line without dropping the number of characters on the line quite so much. In the example below, the regular Minion is shown first, followed by Richard's slightly condensed version:

As Richard was fond of narrow measures, a condensed typeface would
As Richard was fond of narrow measures, a condensed typeface would

While the Multiple Masters fonts were withdrawn when OpenType became the standard, the glyph scaling and tracking tools within the layout program InDesign allow small enough increments to duplicate what Richard did with Multiple Masters:

As Richard was fond of narrow measures, a condensed typeface would
As Richard was fond of narrow measures, a condensed typeface would

Here, the first line is from the Multiple Masters, the second shows standard Minion Pro, condensed to 97 percent, then tracked +3 units, all done within InDesign. The same result could be achieved in a third way: use a font-editing program to condense the characters to 97 percent, then add one unit to the sidebearings on the right and two units on the left.

Another nicety that can be done in both a font editor or some layout programs is scaling small capitals. Frequently, the foundry small caps are a bit small. In either program, you can scale them nonproportionally, that is, increase the height a different amount than the width.

J. Edgar Hoover was head of the FBI for almost fifty years.
J. Edgar Hoover was head of the FBI for almost fifty years.

The first line is set in Minion as published; the second has the small caps scaled 102 percent horizontal, 107.5 percent vertical. This was done using InDesign; the font itself is unchanged. Since the instruction to use small capitals can be put in a character style in the layout program, it is easy enough to include glyph scaling as a part of that style—no extra work for the compositor. However, hand kerning may be needed for any transition of scaled letters and unscaled letters, one disadvantage of doing such work using a layout program. There is a second disadvantage: there is a limit to how much scaling you can do with a layout program, because as the glyphs pick up size, they also pick up weight. As the example above shows, any larger and the increased weight of the characters would become objectionable. When using a font editing program, the weight too can be adjusted.

■ Finally, a more complicated modification to fonts, changing the weight. To date, this kind of work is best done in a font-editing program such as FontLab's Studio. You can make a faux bold suitable for a few words using the stroke routine in programs such as InDesign, but smaller values—less than .25 points—may occasion some problems. In any case, the work is best done with relative units rather than the fixed values of points.

Sometimes changing a font's weight is a simple matter of embolding the glyphs using a programmatic value of one or two units. Usually this technique applies to fonts that have a limited amount of contrast and were developed for PostScript before DTP printing. Examples would be fonts such as Quadraat and Scala. The designers of these types got things just right but didn't anticipate the loss of weight that came with DTP printing (see page 245).

On the other hand, photocomp fonts and their PostScript counterparts that are revivals from the metal era often print too thin, especially the fine strokes. Occasionally hot-metal fonts were themselves revivals from foundry type, adding yet another layer of transition. One example is the Monotype version of Dante, which shows that matrices cut with a rotating burr are not quite the same as matrices made with a punch. From the printing side of things—even within letterpress printing—Dwiggins noted significant variations that result from changes in paper, ink, and the dwell of the impression. When working with revivals, one needs to know where to start, what to look at.

Offset printing introduced yet more changes. With letterpress printing, the ink is pushed outward, and the printed letter appears to have a ring of black around its edge. With photocomp/offset printing, the black is more uniform; if it is greater anywhere, it is at the center of the mass of ink, with the edge of the letter a little grayer.

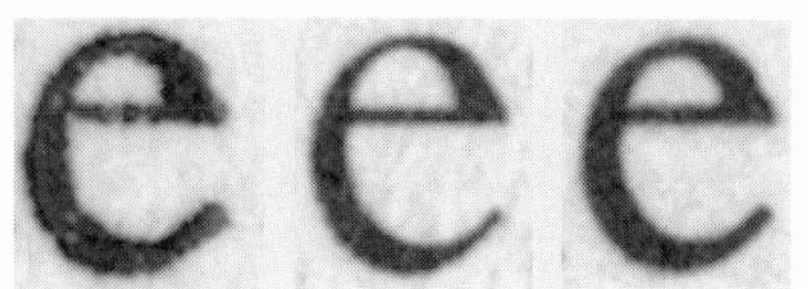

Bembo *e*'s.
The *e* on the left was scanned from a book printed letterpress by the Stinehour Press; the middle *e* was scanned from a book set in PostScript Bembo and printed DTP; the *e* on the right from a PostScript font modified to have more of the weight and thick/thin ratio of the metal Bembo, again printed DTP. Enlarged 1,000 percent, and in this case only, the contrast was increased to show a bit of the outer black ring created by letterpress printing.

To recap: the photocomp revivals were not only too thin generally, but when printed offset, the contrast of the letters—the ratio of the thin to thick strokes of the letters—changed significantly. PostScript fonts usually didn't vary much from their earlier photocomp versions, so the problems with the revivals remained. In fairness, it should be noted that about six or seven years after I made this modified Bembo, Monotype released a new set of fonts called Bembo Book, which addressed most of the defects of the originally published PostScript fonts.

Reweighting glyphs has other uses. Some fonts lack small capitals and superscript numbers. Serviceable glyphs can be created by scaling full capitals and lining figures to the appropriate height, just like with a layout program. Unlike a layout program though, the weight can be increased. With that work, and a little tugging on a few of the control points, very serviceable glyphs can be added to the font, complete with separate and more appropriate kerning values.

This work is not so much difficult as it is time-consuming. Since I have no drawing skill, I was cheered immensely when Matthew Carter once remarked that he had little drawing skill (obviously, he wasn't talking about drawing letters). What such reweighting does require is an understanding of what happens when the ink hits the paper and the willingness to fail at first. The first attempt will be better than the original, but decisions made will usually be improved once one has seen a few books printed with the type. A good eye and a bit of stubbornness are the main requirements for such work.

Opposite:
Three incarnations of Monotype Bembo. With the page turned for proper reading: *Left*, set hot metal, printed letterpress. *Top right*, Foundry PostScript printed DTP offset. *Bottom right*, reweighted Postscript, again printed DTP.

■ Setting justified type is a matter of continually making compromises. Essentially, there are two tools available to justify lines: (1) vary the word spacing, and (2) hyphenate words. With the advent of InDesign and other layout programs where very small values of tracking and glyph scaling are possible, these too can be used. We routinely allow plus/minus 0.1 percent letterspacing and plus/minus 0.5 percent glyph scaling as program values; you simply cannot see the difference. Still, the main choices remain hyphenation and varying the space between words on different lines of type. Of these, hyphenation inherently has the most constraints. There is the constraint of the language itself.

reserved with several black bands concentric around a black disk in the center (chipped off).

Eros and Aphrodite between two women, with a servant girl on the left. In the center a small Eros (two bracelets and three anklets on left, fillet across chest) kneels on the lap of Aphrodite and embraces her. She wears a sleeveless girt chiton, himation, bracelet, polos adorned with circles and dashes, and shoes. A deerskin is draped over the seat of her chair (klismos). In front of her on the right is a woman (himation fallen below the waist, shoes, kekryphalos) holding a phiale of fruits (?) and a thin fillet in her left hand. She sits on two pillows with knobbed ends and decoration of chevrons and hooks. They rest on the ground (covered with tufts of grass below them) which rises in front of Aphrodite to the level of a small bush beside the woman's right hand. Beside Aphrodite on the left is a standing woman (ungirt peplos with long apoptygma, kekryphalos, bracelets, necklace, earrings, shoes) with a small branch in her right hand. A yellow spot under her left arm and numerous short vertical white lines above her waist are apparently the remains of a phiale and its contents once held in her left

cerned, he did not want his daughters to be housewives, th
the point: he was concerned about pregnancy. In fact, he ha
that if this occurred, "Many things you would like to ha
your life will no longer be possible." (Although abortio
Brazil, this was a striking way of stating the outcome of pre
episode concluded after Renato gave his daughter the twen
then reported to me that he had told her she had been inco
that she was lucky he had gone to the bank. (I privately del
this was said for effect, since it seemed Brazilians had to g
almost daily, or whether it simply referred to the rule of

mouthed and unfriendly" [161]); drawn back in fascinati
Roddy from a poker game threatening to turn nasty, T
him from behind to his room where he strips him of the
ing out of his pockets and lying around his hips (162),
ing to the money being safely deposited in a bank. Thi
is reciprocated, as is evident in the reversal that follow
now tends the ailing Tom who had watched over him. I
his job for Tom, does his work for him, finally selling t
(the artifacts excavated on the mesa) and setting up an
Tom's name so that he will be able to afford to go to

Added to this are editorial constraints; don't hyphenate here, don't hyphenate there. The specifics of "here" and "there" vary across publishers, but the more constraints a house style involves, the more justification has to come from varying word spacing

In the first part of the twentieth century, British typography began a movement to constrain word spacing as well. Wide word spacing, it was decreed, was a heresy. This view was best exemplified in Geoffrey Dowding's 1954 book, *Finer Points in the Spacing and Arrangement of Type*. It is remarkable that this view has become so common, particularly among designers who have never examined the extent to which Dowding would compromise everything else to avoid a loose line. It is also remarkable how few have ever looked at the nineteenth-century word spacing that occasioned the rebellion.

Comme deux bourgeons qui restent sur deux arbres de la même espèce, dont la tempête a brisé toutes les branches, viennent à produire des fruits plus doux, si chacun d'eux, détaché du tronc maternel', est greffé sur le tronc voisin; ainsi, ces deux petits enfants, privés de tous leurs parents, se remplissaient de sentiments plus tendres que ceux de fils et de fille, de frère et de sœur, quand ils venaient à être changés de mamelles par les deux amies qui leur

From *Paul et Virginie* by J. H. Bernardin de Saint-Piere (Lon Curmer).

Paul et Virginie (Paris, 1838) was included in Blumenthal's 1973 *Art of the Printed Book*. The sample shown here is reproduced about full size; when seen on the original page (6⅜ × 10 trim) with its generous margins, the typography seems more reasonable, though certainly not in keeping with today's fashion. In any case, it was word spacing of this magnitude that the early twentieth-century British objected to so much.

Finer Points was meant to be an example as well as a treatise. Dowding supervised the composition; the setting met with his approval. Contrast the word spacing of the snippet above with one of the tighter paragraphs in *Finer Points*. What Dowding has done is to make every other compromise possible to avoid the one of larger word spaces. The result is some very tight spacing indeed. While we may share the general belief that tight word spacing is preferable to the nineteenth-century style, what Dowding shows is a far different set trated books. In these settings the spacing between the words is excessively wide in many, if not most, lines, while in others it is non-existent. Frequently the line filling capacity of the words has been eked out with letter-spacing[1]

Three successive tight lines from the Wace edition of *Finer Points*.

Narrow measures, that is, lines of four or five average words or less have always militated against good setting. Very occasionally the disposition and simplicity of the words, combined with the skill of the compositor, make for an excellent setting in a really narrow measure. But such settings are exceptional. Conversely, examples of those cramped, difficult-to-read and patchily-coloured settings confront us daily, not only in newspapers & other ephemeral printed matter of all kinds, but also in publishers' illustrated books. In these settings the spacing between the words is excessively wide in many, if not most, lines, while in others it is non-existent. Frequently the line filling capacity of the words has been eked out with letter-spacing[1] in order to make lines square with their neighbours. In narrow measures word breaks are liable to occur frequently & these cause a ragged hyphen-rash and ugly linear irregularity on the right-hand side of the column.

The entire paragraph, notice the two ampersands used in place of "and" to get things to fit.

Narrow measures, that is, lines of four or five average words or less have always militated against good setting. Very occasionally the disposition and simplicity of the words, combined with the skill of the compositor, make for an excellent setting in a really narrow measure. But such settings are exceptional. Conversely, examples of those cramped, difficult-to-read and patchily-coloured settings confront us daily, not only in newspapers and other ephemeral printed matter of all kinds, but also in publishers' illustrated books. In these settings the spacing between the words is excessively wide in many, if not most, lines, while in others it is non-existent. Frequently the line filling capacity of the words has been eked out with letter-spacing[1] in order to make lines square with their neighbours. In narrow measures word breaks are liable to occur frequently and these cause a ragged hyphen-rash and ugly linear irregularity on the right-hand side of the column.

The paragraph reset, with the only textual change being restoring the "and."

of compromises than I think correct. The three lines in the top of the example are, to my eye, overly tight. Dowding has also replaced two *ands* with ampersands to get his setting to work. This, plus the too-tight lines and hyphenating a word with just two letters taken down, would not usually pass editorial review. Yet all these compromises were needed to avoid a somewhat loose line. Below the full paragraph from the Wace edition, I have set an alternative treatment. What I have used is a PostScript Ehrhardt, not exactly the same as the hot-metal fonts Dowding worked with. But I believe what I've set could be set with the Monotype caster, just as surely as I believe it is a better setting.

What I view as overly tight setting is sometimes encountered today. At play is a different vision about typography. What's my side? As I said earlier, what we read are clumps of words. Reading is not looking at black ribbons on a white background. That one can read *Finer Points* is not the issue. The point, I think, is that a theoretical ideal is being served instead of a reader, and that is regrettable.

■ Much of what I have written involves modifying fonts. I would be remiss if I didn't address the legality of such work. Unlike the days of metal or photocomposition, we no longer own fonts. Fonts are now software; when we purchase them, what we are actually purchasing is the right to use certain software. The End User License Agreement (EULA) is the contract we accept when purchasing the font license, and at first glance, most EULAS seem to prohibit modifying the font software. However, things are not that bleak. At one time—and maybe still today—Adobe's EULA prohibited modifying fonts. However, their published FAQ (www.adobe.com/aboutadobe/antipiracy/ff_faq.html), vetted by the same group of attorneys who wrote the licensing agreement, specifically allows end users to modify any Adobe font software for their own use, though of course not for distribution.[1]

[1]A change in the Adobe license was announced not long ago. See http://www.adobe.com/type/browser/legal/additional_licenses.html

Quoted from the website: "For many years, Adobe's font End User License Agreement (EULA) permitted customers to modify any font licensed from the Adobe Type Library (ATL). However, many fonts in the ATL are sublicensed to us by other companies and we have recently had to stop offering modification rights for some fonts. If you purchased fonts from Adobe prior to August 08, 2011, then you still have the modification rights granted by the EULA that came with your font. However, there is a new EULA for fonts purchased after that date. Please refer to the table below to determine the modification rights permitted for any ATL font."

Font publishers may well give permission when asked. I have been given permission to modify their fonts from a number of the smaller publishers, as well as some of the larger ones. With the larger publishers, permission can be a matter of timing. I received permission to modify some fonts purchased in the mid-1990s; were I to ask today, permission would likely be denied, as font publishers have begun to see making changes or additions to their fonts as a revenue source.

Viewed one way, the "no modifications" clause of the EULA does not make sense. Superficially, what one cannot modify is a piece of software, a font. But font software, without other software, is of no use. While font-editing software is usually the best tool, you can use a layout program to modify the kerning, modify characters through a layout program's glyph scaling and tracking routines, and make many accented characters using kerning and glyph positioning. In short, while it is almost always quicker to do the work in a font-editing program, the result is often the same. It is a bit odd that such modifications can be made through one program, but not another. I believe, and it is a belief only, that the "no modifications" clause for the font software originated to try to forestall font piracy. There should never be a question that as with other software, font publishers are entitled to be compensated for each copy of their product. That the lawyer's choice of words prohibits end users from making changes for their own use, with the most appropriate software, is unfortunate.

Aside from money, there is the matter of reputation. Some font publishers will give permission to modify or add characters only if they can see the work. Their position is they want to retain artistic control. On the face of it, that's a valid argument. But again this doesn't really make sense: I can quickly and thoroughly ruin a typeface with a layout program such as InDesign. Glyph scaling. Tracking. Et cetera.

Unless or until this matter is resolved, before becoming heavily invested in a type family, I believe one should pick fonts from publishers that allow modification. Fonts from publishers that withhold permission should be considered carefully. If you decide to purchase extra characters, it may take weeks to get them, aside from the cost.

There is one intriguing alternative to all these concerns about commercial font licenses, open source fonts. Part of the carrot is that they may usually be modified as needed, can be redistributed to other end users, and are usually free. Open source fonts still have a license, and the terms of that license may vary across fonts in this genre. That said, most allow any desired modifications and unlimited use, including embedding the fonts in electronically distributed material.

When addressing the rest of the carrot, I don't want to debate the use of the term "design." I'll acknowledge that doing the most one can within imposed constraints is a key element of all good design. Perhaps a new term will be needed, "digital book design." I'm all for it. The constraints are so different. That said, and ignoring books presented in PDF format, most books available for the various reading devices are not what most of us would consider typeset. The notion of typography for these books borders on being an oxymoron. To the extent design is possible in the EPUB format, the licensing costs for commercial fonts can be quite high when those fonts are embedded in a digital book. Embedding is necessary if the details of the type and spacing are to be preserved, even temporarily. (The person reading the book can change the fonts and sizes as they choose.) Prices from major font publishers currently range from "no extra charge" to at least a 10-times multiplication factor for each book title or journal issue. In other words, if the basic license for a web font is $40, each book title or journal issue would incur an additional $400 charge for each font used. I have little doubt that both the pricing and the technology will change; the point is that aside from their other virtues, open source fonts are and will continue to be immune to such charges.

■ In some ideal world of book manufacturing, the author, editor, designer, compositor, and maybe the printer sit down and discuss the best way to present the book to the reader. In the real world this rarely happens. As a compositor, my interaction with editors is almost always one of complaint, usually about the structure of the text. One recent example: In a multiauthored book, a chapter has only one occurrence of a B-head, which immediately follows an A-head. In this case, shouldn't the B-head be combined with the A, say after a colon? If the book is released for composition this way, the most a compositor can do is to query it, remembering all the while that should the change be made later, pagination will likely be affected. This in turn could affect the index—and the index will be prepared from the very proof that has the query. Query it, or just let it go?

Another all too common situation occurs when the last paragraph or two in a section calls three, four, or five tables or figures. The general rule for composing pages is that tables and figures are placed on the page where they are called or as soon after as possible, but always before the next subhead. If several tables or figures are called in the last paragraph of a section, one often winds up with quite a puzzle when making up pages. I always wonder what the editor was thinking about—certainly not manufacturing issues. And if an author is referring to a number of figures and/or tables at the end of a section, it usually means they are not an integral part of the argument, but rather data that generally support the argument. Would not the book be best served if such were gathered in an appendix? However, with a change of this magnitude and proof due in two weeks, it is not the kind of issue one brings up, even though the mechanical fitting of the pieces may result in some awkward pages.

Compositor/designer interactions are more common. Probably the most frequent are missing specifications. Yet specifications themselves can be a delicate issue; "delicate" in the sense of "whose job are they?" I have set books designed by older designers like George Mackie, who give you the basic text specification and maybe a few more and assume it is the compositor's job to handle further details. In contrast, there are designers who want to specify everything. Much depends on how often one has worked with a designer and what relationship has been established. For example, if there are a couple of extracts in the notes that were not specified, the treatment of the extracts in the text will usually make quite clear how the note extracts should be set—there is a logic to most designs. If there are to be sample pages, we will set the unspecified element as the design implies and query if the treatment is OK. What if sample pages are not wanted? Stop and wait for answers from the designer? Make what seems the obvious choice and get on with things?

A second complaint arises when the designer has not looked at all the characters needed in a text. If a book has transliterated Arabic, Indic Scripts, Native American languages, etc., there will be characters needed that are not included in most fonts. In such cases the designer could select one of the few fonts that has them; usually they don't check. If they have chosen a typeface that lacks them, I have no choice but to make up the needed characters. Two things give pause. The first is the EULA: if a foundry forbids modifying the font, there are more choices to make. Sometimes the book must be set using the resources of the layout program, though occasionally either an accent or even a character from a different font will have to be used. The second option is to contact the publisher of the font and try to obtain permission to add the characters. This usually pushes back the schedule.

Another matter is in how many fonts do these characters occur? It is one thing to make them up for the text font and companion italic. It is another if there are four weights of a display font used, and the characters are needed there, too. That's enough work to cause one to utter profanities, obscenities, and vulgarities.

Then there are the wonderful times when both the designer and the compositor put on their typographic hats and work together. Recently I was at a book show where a designer picked up a cookbook and remarked that fractions in a cookbook were often a difficult matter. Cookbooks may be read with the book on a countertop waist-high and at arms' length. The fractions in many fonts are a bit small for reading at cooking distance. But using full-size numbers and a solidus doesn't look right either. We thought about this and came up with the notion of drawing up a separate set of cooking fractions, which would be a bit larger, thus easier to read with the book lying on the countertop. Below is an example using Adobe Chaparral. The fractions on the left are from the font as published; on the right, slightly larger variants are used:

use ⅔ cup water	use ⅔ cup water
use 1½ pounds butter	use 1½ pounds butter

■ Working on the subtleties of a font can be seen as an investment. At our shop, we do not charge for extra work that goes into fonts. This is not purely out of a love for good typography. The time taken in composition drops when problems occasioned by the fonts themselves are resolved within the font. Every time the font is used, we get that time savings. Does the work pay for itself? I can make an argument either way. To some extent, our decision to extensively work over a set of fonts does involve a cost/benefit analysis. To fix something that will occur only once or twice, we usually employ handwork in the layout program. The exception is when we believe designers will use this font fairly often for future books; then the work will be done in the font. And beyond any cost/benefit analysis, we do appreciate fine typography.

How long does such work take? From fifteen to thirty hours for the work on a roman font to be used for text, and from six to twenty hours for the italic. This is the initial work; more will likely be needed once we've seen several editions printed on an offset press. You can rarely make final judgments on type based on either the computer monitor or a laser printout.

What do I do as a minimum? There needs to be a serviceable set of superior lining figures for note calls; many fonts lack these. There needs to be a serviceable set of roman and italic small capitals. There needs to be a full set of f-ligatures for most serif fonts. Usually, I'll make up a serviceable set of angle brackets to be used with URLS, to replace the often seen greater and less symbols.

Kerning of punctuation needs to be checked. The fit of capital letters to lowercase letters needs to be acceptable, both roman and italic—remember the notes and bibliography, and King Arthur's mom, Ygraine. Probably I'll take a look at the fit of all lowercase letters, with special attention to vowels and common double consonants—bb, cc, dd, gg, ll, mm, nn, pp, rr, ss, tt—for some reason, the fit of these is often overlooked by the type designer. Sometimes gg requires a ligature, especially in italic.

Does it make sense for book designers who set their own type to add font work to their repertoire? It depends. If they enjoy such work, and if they tend to use a small number of typefaces, I would say yes, both economic and aesthetic sense. If they paint with a broader brush or derive satisfaction with working with a host of new fonts, then probably not. If the answer is no, perhaps the designer should use the services of a compositor. In the end, we all serve two masters: the author and especially the reader. If we can give them something both easier to use and rather more beautiful without significantly raising the cost, why would we choose otherwise?

Uneasy Allies The Designer and the Editor

SEAN MAGEE

Show-and-tell time at a cover meeting at the (then) fine old campaigning publisher Victor Gollancz in London in the mid-1990s. The highly regarded out-of-house designer is displaying his first attempt at a dust jacket for a forthcoming book. The commissioning editor expresses enthusiasm for the overall idea of the design, then suggests that, given the eminence of the author, his name on the cover might—just might—be larger. Scarcely able to disguise his scorn at this effrontery, the designer puts the aesthetically illiterate editor in his place with the gnomic pronouncement: "A designer's job is not to fill all the available space." The editor (who of course has made no such suggestion) slinks back into the gloom from which he had emerged, muttering something that sounded very much like "Give me strength." Or at least I think that's what I was saying . . .

If, according to the final chapter of *Ecclesiastes*, "Of making many books there is no end," nor does there appear to be any end in prospect to the mutual incomprehension that too often exists between book designers and editors. (And by "editors" I mean that army of supposed pedants who might sign themselves commissioning editor or acquisitions editor or desk editor or sponsoring editor or project editor or managing editor or executive editor or copy-editor or field editor or research editor. This is a finely nuanced trade, but we are all editors, more or less.) The two sides should be equally concerned with efficiently connecting the author of a book with the reader, yet there tends to be between them a prickliness that in some extreme cases borders on downright hostility.

■ Some years ago the senior designer Gene Light, vice president and art director at Warner Books, used a *Publishers Weekly* column to pose the question: "Why is it that an editor (with as much art background as the art director has editorial background) feels free to art-direct covers while the art director wouldn't dream of making editorial changes?"

While the inquiry was doubtless intended as a rhetorical question, it is one worth answering, and the obvious response is that the editor considers himself or herself responsible for representing the author at all stages of the production process, and is duty-bound to point out instances where some element of the design is disrupting transmission of the message from author to reader.

It is a commonplace of commentary on book production that design should not be noticed—designer Derek Birdsall produced a nice variation when observing that "in book work, the best layouts appear to have designed themselves"—and while good design can be so pleasing as to persuade buyers to make a purchase they otherwise might have swerved, by the same token poor design can abort a potential sale. A few years ago I located exactly the book I wanted about the history of Hong Kong, but when buying it I had to force myself to overcome my dislike of the text design. The book had been set in some primitive fashion that gave the effect of the whole text being letterspaced—not only setting up the reader for a long-lasting headache but recalling the wise observation of Frederic Goudy that "a man who would letter-space lowercase would steal sheep."

The greatest attribute of a good book designer is not the overarching imagination to wow his or her fellow designers by some typographic *tour de force*, but rather the display of what has been referred to as "design intelligence"—which, like contraception, is often noticeable only when it has failed.

Here is an example. In a volume published in the early 1980s, a distinguished anthropologist has dreamed up a clever structure. The even-numbered chapters of his book, he declares, are an attempt to address some general questions about the hunting societies of the world. The odd-numbered chapters are an account of the eighteen months he has spent on fieldwork in one such society in North America. Neat idea. Trouble is, in the finished book the individual chapters are not numbered at all (either on the contents page or on each chapter opening), which rather spoils the effect. An alert editor would have specifically mentioned to the designer the necessity for numbering, failing which a conscientious designer who had read the preface of the book would have picked up the point.

In a similar vein is the case of the gardening book structured around the months of the year, published by one of London's leading houses a few years ago. When the designer received the copy from the in-house editor he immediately noted that the introduction was given the chapter number 1, January the number 2, February the number 3, etc. It took his design intelligence to suggest that the book would look better were the Introduction to be unnumbered, January to be reunited with 1, the number with which it is inextricably linked, and so on.

And don't get me started on the maddening lack of assistance given to the reader in the monumental *Complete Poems of Philip Larkin*, published by Faber in 2012, in which finding your way from the text of a poem to the notes and commentary about it requires a satellite navigation system. The typography is very fetching, but insufficient thought has been given to how the book will be *used*.

■ The uneasy relationship between what might be called the authorial side of the equation (author, commissioning editor, copyeditor, etc.) and the production side (designer, typesetter, production manager) goes back a very long way, well before the typographic designer was recognized as a creature distinct from the typesetter or compositor. In his monumental *Mechanick Exercises on the Whole Art of Printing*, published in the late seventeenth century, Joseph Moxon declared:

> A good *Compositer* is ambitious as well to make the meaning of his *Author* intelligent to the *Reade*r, as to make his work shew graceful to the Eye, and pleasant in Reading: Therefore if his *Copy* be written in a Language he understands, he reads his *Copy* with consideration; that so he may get himself into the meaning of the *Author*, and consequently considers how to order his Work the better both in the *Title Page* and in the matter of the *Book*: As how to make his *Indenting, Pointing, Breaking, Italicking, &c.* the better sympathize with the Authors Genius, and also with the capacity of the Reader.

Substitute the word "designer" for "compositer," update the language three centuries or so, knock down those initial caps and romanize those italics—wasn't typesetting so much more fun back then?—and Moxon's words ring true today.

Less than a century after Moxon, John Smith's *Printer's Grammar* (1755) exhibits the irritation with authors that will be familiar to many designers and copyeditors today. For example: "It would be kind in Gentlemen to put some mark to the emphatical words in their copy, and either underscore the first letter of such a word, or make some other token, which may inform the compositor of an author's intention. . . . The loss of time, and consequently of gain, which the compositor sustains by not having the emphasis of words pointed out to him till in the Proof-sheet, is very considerable."

Some authors, Smith continues, are so fond of small capitals that "they choose to have whole verses and sentences set in them; but which, as well as matter in large capitals, is perplexing to the reader, especially in books designed for the comprehension of the meanest capacities."

Two centuries later, in 1953, Brooke Crutchley, fabled printer at Cambridge University Press, wisely observed of the designer's brief that

> no typographical astuteness can make clear what is fundamentally confused. [The designer] must make sure first of all that the author's organisation of his material is satisfactory, and this often leads to suggestions of a major or even a minor kind. It might be a proposal about the proper codification of references, the transfer of some semi-relevant passage to an appendix, or the arrangement of certain information in tabular rather than narrative form. To be able to make such recommendations requires an understanding of the author's line of argument and method of exposition—clearly, a lot to ask of the versatility of any typographer.

It is also a lot to ask for publishers to resist the occasionally idiosyncratic design requirements of their most eminent authors, which brings us to The Curious Case of Iris Murdoch and the Line Spacing. When delivering the typescript of her novel *The Sea, The Sea* to her publishers Chatto & Windus, Murdoch insisted that spaces between different portions of text had to allow for a pause of a specifically stated number of lines. Thus a single line of space was to indicate a brief suspension, two lines a longer one, and so on. A space of seven lines would indicate seven times the pause of a single-line space, and no one quite dared to point out that no reader would make any such allowance—nor could the problem of a long pause starting at the foot of one page and continuing to another be easily solved.

Far more logical was Graham Greene's insistence that his books be designed by the late and very great John Ryder, typographer of legend at Greene's publisher The Bodley Head, even after Ryder had retired. Unsurprisingly, Greene's later books retain the compelling simplicity of design you would expect from a designer who declared, in his seminal little 1979 book, *The Case for Legibility*: "Whatever is done must be done for the reader's benefit and for maximum legibility. . . . You must present an author's work to the reader without fuss and with design techniques as invisible as possible."

Appropriately enough in a paragraph following Graham Greene, this observation comes to the heart of the matter, for Ryder's concern that the case for legibility needed making at all—after all, what is book design about, if not about legibility?—was triggered by technological changes surrounding the introduction of computerized typesetting, changes which themselves seem antiquated when compared with modern digital setting methods. It may be too crude to suggest that graphic design, which to a large extent is about creating eye-catching shapes, is usurping typographic design, which is about deploying type in as invisible a manner as possible. But what should govern good book design is the use to which that book will be put and the expectations of a reader that the standard elements of the book will be in the usual places. Ron Costley, late of Chatto & Windus and Faber, famously remarked on "the American designer's relentless quest for a new place to put the folio," while that small but essential component of the page best belongs where the reader's eye will most readily pick it up—and a courageous editor can save the book from the aesthetic excesses of even the most thin-skinned designer.

Most authors do not enjoy the luxury of spelling out the niceties of their requirements to the designer, but that does not stop them having opinions—and in authors a little typographic learning can be a very dangerous thing.

Indeed, letting an author get too close to the design process is a recipe for tears before bedtime. Many authors allow themselves some vision of how their book will look, and to the understandable annoyance of designers, some favor particular typefaces for no logical reason. "Some authors say that they like the use of sans-serif typefaces," reports John Schwartz, founder of London-based design studio SoapBox Communications, "but they can't tell one sans-serif face from another."

One very well-meaning author of mine somehow acquired a pica rule and worked out the type size of the text in his proofs, so that he could correct said proofs with a greater degree of accuracy and diligence. He thought he was being helpful, but unfortunately he was not aware that the size of the type is not the size of the x-height, so all his suggestions for specific sizes were meaningless.

The size of the author's name on a cover can be a contentious issue, the designer often opting for subtlety and the author wanting his name writ large. In my days as commissioning editor at Basil Blackwell in Oxford I had one author who bemoaned the size of his name on the cover proof, and before I could appreciate the idiocy of what I was saying I heard myself telling him that the name would look appreciably larger when the jacket was laminated. The book was published, and I was bracing myself against the inevitable irate call about his name being no bigger (it wasn't), when instead I had a note from him saying that I had been completely right.

(Mind you, this was the same author—let us call him Smith—who on one occasion called me in high dudgeon to report that his book was not placed on a high enough shelf in Foyle's Bookshop in London. When I investigated, it was instantly apparent that the books were displayed in alphabetical order, and in order to be stored on a more elevated level he would have had to change his name to something higher up the alphabet.)

For better or for worse, many authors want to offer their input, from lobbying for the use of their favorite typeface to (a much more common practice) persuading the designer to create just the jacket that the author has had in his or her mind's eye since embarking on the book.

Cue the dreaded word "montage"—or, as one observer memorably put it, the "Italian wedding" approach to cover design. Some authors are wedded to the idea that the cover should somehow reflect the rich nuances of the book by containing a variety of images, whereas the buyers in book stores, and most readers, would go for making an impact with one strong visual element. In that situation, the editor needs to juggle the requirements of the sales and marketing department, the aesthetic sensibility of the designer, and the "let's illustrate the richness of the book" attitude of the author.

Naturally enough, the more eminent the author, the more malleable the publisher. A. Scott Berg's biography of the great editor Maxwell Perkins describes the perfectionist habits of Scott Fitzgerald over the publication of *Tender Is the Night*, relating how Fitzgerald "even complained that the dust jacket, with its reds and yellows, evoked the Italian Riviera more than the Côte d'Azur's white and blue sparkle." Berg quotes Fitzgerald's letter to Perkins:

"Oh God, it's hell to bother you with all this, but of course the book is my whole life now and I cannot help this perfectionist attitude."

There's the rub. Be they ever so famous or ever so obscure, the author has a much greater personal stake in the project than any of the publishing staff working on a book, and it is the role of the editor to filter those authorial anxieties—not only, it must be said, through the design, but equally carefully through the editorial process, where the ability to walk on eggshells is a basic requirement of the job.

But the carping cannot be in one direction, and editors benefit immeasurably from the input of a thinking designer—such as Ron Costley, one of the most thoughtful of British book designers, who was quoted thus in Rich Hendel's *On Book Design*: "If I have a philosophy concerning the design of books, it is that they should be designed for readers. My main concern always is to present the text in the clearest possible way so that the reader can have direct access to the author's text without being inhibited or interrupted by my intervention."

■ Ah yes, the reader. Discussion of design issues and relationships is so much shop talk, so much navel-gazing, that the most important individual in the book production process—much more important than the editor or the designer, and arguably more important than the author, since the author would have no point without the reader—tends to be overlooked.

In 1970 an issue of the *Monotype Recorder* was devoted to the writings of the great typographer and typographical scholar Beatrice Warde, who had died the previous year, under the title "I Am a Communicator." In one piece she wrote: "Reading is a recognition process. Its 'machinery' in the brain is not fully understood, but at least it is possible to distinguish that part of the mind which is busily taking in the sense of the passage and that deeper stratum from which may come, at the same moment, various signals of distress, which translate themselves into impatience with the author's conclusions, or a nagging headache, or simply a conviction that one has read quite enough. It is part of the typographic designer's business to find out as much as he can about the graphic causes of such distress signals."

It is blindingly obvious that in the best interests of a successful and effective final product, designers and editors should enjoy a harmonious collaboration—so obvious that it scarcely needs spelling out. Yet it must be spelled out, and often—not least to prevent a repeat of the frayed emotions at that Gollancz cover meeting.

Bibliography and Further Reading

Bartram, Alan. *Making Books: Design in British Publishing since 1945*. London: British Library, 1999.

———. *Typeforms: A History*. London: British Library, 2007.

Blumenthal, Joseph. *Art of the Printed Book, 1455–1955: Masterpieces of Typography through Five Centuries from the Collections of the Pierpont Morgan Library*. New York: Pierpont Morgan Library, 1973.

Bringhurst, Robert. *The Elements of Typographic Style*. Vancouver: Hartley and Marks, 2013.

Burke, Christopher. *Active Typography: Jan Tschichold and the New Typography*. London: Hyphen Press, 2007.

Dowding, Geoffrey. *Finer Points in the Spacing and Arrangement of Type*. London: Wace, 1954.

Eckersley, Richard, et al. *Glossary of Typesetting Terms*. Chicago: University of Chicago Press, 1994.

Hendel, Richard. *On Book Design*. New Haven, Conn.: Yale University Press, 1998.

Highsmith, Cyrus. *Inside Paragraphs: Typographic Fundamentals*. Boston: Font Bureau, 2012.

Hochuli, Jost. *Designing Books: Practice and Theory*. London: Hyphen Press, 2004.

———. *Detail in Typography*. London: Hyphen Press, 2009.

Jury, David. *Graphic Design Before Graphic Designers*. New York: Thames & Hudson, 2012.

Kinross, Robin. *Modern Typography: An Essay in Critical History*. London: Hyphen Press, 2004.

———. *Unjustified Texts: Perspectives on Typography*. London: Hyphen Press, 2002.

Lee, Marshall. *Bookmaking: The Illustrated Guide to Design/Production/Editing*. New York: Bowker, 1979.

Miller, Cheryl, ed. *Type Works: The Printing, Design, and Writing of Will Powers*. Birchwood, Minn.: Interval Press, 2011.

Mitchell, Michael, and Susan Wightman. *Book Typography: A Designer's Manual*. Marlborough: Libanus Press, 2005.

Morison, Stanley. "First Principles of Typography." In *Books and Printing: A Treasury for Typophiles*, ed. Paul A. Bennett. Cleveland: World Publishing, 1951.

———. "Towards an Ideal Italic." *Fleuron* 5 (1926): 93–129.

Ryder, John. *The Case for Legibility*. London: Bodley Head, 1979.

Simon, Oliver. *Introduction to Typography*. Harmondsworth: Penguin Books, 1954.

Sutton, James, and Alan Bartram. *Typefaces for Books*. New York: New Amsterdam, 1990.

Tschichold, Jan. *The Form of the Book: Essays on the Morality of Good Design*. Ed. Robert Bringhurst, trans. Hajo Hadeler. Vancouver: Hartley and Marks, 1991.

———. *The New Typography*. Trans. Ruari McLean. Berkeley: University of California Press, 2006.

Warde, Beatrice. *The Crystal Goblet: Sixteen Essays on Typography*. Cleveland: World Publishing, 1956.

———. "I Am a Communicator." *Monotype Recorder* 44 (Autumn 1970).

Williamson, Hugh. *Methods of Book Design: The Practice of an Industrial Craft*. New Haven, Conn.: Yale University Press, 1983.

Wilson, Adrian. *The Design of Books*. San Francisco: Chronicle Books, 1993.

Contributors

Julie Allred is a partner in BW&A Books, a full-service book design and production studio. A graduate of the University of North Carolina and the Carolina Publishing Institute, she has almost two decades of experience in all aspects of book production. In addition to design, composition, and project management, she is helping BW&A's clients add electronic books to their publishing programs.

Andrew Barker is an award-winning book designer. In twenty-five years of practice he has designed more books than you can shake a stick at, for companies such as Penguin Books, Faber and Faber Ltd., Pan Macmillan, and the Folio Society. Over recent years his practice has broadened to include other aspects of information design and research, and the questions this work has raised have led him to undertake a rather large research project that investigates how people find their way around print documents such as books and whether the behaviors are at all comparable with how they find their way around built three-dimensional environments and digital environments. Meanwhile he continues to keep busy designing books.

Kim Bryant is the design director and assistant production manager at the University of North Carolina Press. Kim received an M.A. in publishing and creative writing at Emerson College. Her work has been recognized by the Association of American University Presses Book, Jacket, and Journal Show and the Southeastern Library Association.

Amy Ruth Buchanan has been at Duke University Press since 1995. Her text and cover designs have won numerous awards from the Association of American University Presses Book, Jacket, and Journal Show, and a recent title for Johns Hopkins University Press took first place, scholarly books division, at the 2012 New York Book Show. She also runs a one-woman design studio, 3rd Sister Design, doing typesetting and design for university presses, museums, and other cultural institutions.

Nola Burger is a graphic designer specializing in books. As principal designer at the University of California Press, Berkeley, Nola's focus was visually oriented titles including photography, art, poetry, science, and food, as well as scholarly texts. She holds degrees in printmaking and graphic design from California College of the Arts (CCA). She has taught typography and book design at CCA, juried book design competitions, and received awards from organizations including the American Institute of Graphic Arts and the Association of American University Presses. She operates out of her independent design studio in Berkeley.

Ron Costley studied painting, drawing, and lithography before joining the Shenval Press, where he was responsible for the design typography and production of a wide range of printed matter including exhibition catalogs and publicity material for the Arts Council, the Tate Gallery, and commercial galleries. While at the press he designed an anthology of concrete poetry, edited by Stephen Bann, which led to a series of collaborations with the poet Ian Hamilton Finlay that lasted over thirty years. In 1977 he moved from printing to publishing and worked as book designer successively at the Scolar Press, Chatto & Windus, and Faber and Faber Ltd.

Charles Ellertson is co-owner and compositor/designer at Tseng Information Systems in Durham, North Carolina.

Abbey Gaterud is an assistant professor at Portland State University (PSU) and publisher of Ooligan Press, the graduate student–run trade publisher at PSU. She teaches book design, digital design, book business, and various other topics, including her favorite: "thinking about the future." Abbey has an M.S. in book publishing from PSU and a B.A. in English from Lewis & Clark College. She also runs a small publishing company, Blueroad Press. The most recent book from Blueroad Press is *A Song at Twilight: Of Love and Alzheimer's*, which won the 2012 Minnesota Book Award for Creative Nonfiction & Memoir. She thinks that's pretty cool.

Sue Hall has been the journals designer and art director at Duke University Press since 1995. Prior to that she ran her own successful design studio, Number Nine, for thirteen years. It was small—it had one full-time employee—and busy. Clients included entrepreneurs, start-up companies, nonprofit organizations, universities, large corporations, and university presses. Projects ranged from graphic identity and logo work, marketing, and collateral materials, to annual reports and journal design. An economic downturn in 1995 made it unfeasible to continue as a sole proprietor, and when one of her favorite clients offered her the job of journals designer, Sue was happy to join the press.

Mindy Basinger Hill spent her college years as a book paste-up artist and student intern at the University of Georgia Press, and graduated from the University of Georgia with a B.F.A. in graphic design. After ten years of doing more general design, she was given the opportunity to return to the press as a designer. She is currently a senior designer at the University Press of New England. Her work has often been featured in the Association of American University Presses Book, Jacket, and Journal Show.

Kristina Kachele has been designing books for over twenty-five years. She began her career at Farrar, Straus and Giroux when books were still set in hot metal. While pursuing her master's degree in photography, she worked at the University of New Mexico Press, where she stayed for eleven years. She has been freelancing ever since. Over the years, her work has been included in Association of American University Presses, Publishers Association of the West, Chicago Book Clinic, Bookbuilders West, and the Association of American Museums book shows.

Kent Lew has been a designer for more than twenty-five years. He has also worked as an artist and an illustrator. Coming from a family of writers and editors, it seems inevitable that he would gravitate toward the design of words and text. Formerly the creative director at Storey Publishing (a member of the Workman Publishing group), he now works as a freelance book designer, type designer, and typographic consultant. His Whitman typeface family is published by the Font Bureau and has been widely embraced by book, newspaper, and magazine designers.

Sean Magee has worked as commissioning editor at several major British publishers, including Basil Blackwell, Cassell, Victor Gollancz, and, more recently, the independent political publishers Politicos and Biteback. He is also a prolific author, his output including many books born from his passion for horseracing (including the official history of Ascot racecourse) and—most recently—the history of the iconic BBC radio program *Desert Island Discs*. He has long had an interest in book design, an interest nurtured in particular by his old friends Ron Costley and the editor of this volume, and he cannot understand why everyone else on the editorial side does not realize what they are missing by not sharing that fascination.

Cherie Westmoreland was design manager at Duke University Press. Her introduction to book design began in 1982 as a production assistant in a design studio. In 1989 she was hired as a book designer at Duke University Press, working under Mary Mendell, the design and production manager at that time. She was promoted to senior designer and then to assistant design and production manager. Many of her book designs have been selected for awards.

Barbara Wiedemann is the associate director of publications/head of graphic design at the North Carolina Museum of Art in Raleigh, a position she has held since 2008. Prior to rejoining the museum, Barbara was the director of design services for the University of North Carolina (UNC) at Chapel Hill. She received her master's degree in design from the North Carolina State University College of Design. Barbara has also run her own design firm, and taught at North Carolina State's College of Design, Meredith College, and the UNC–Chapel Hill School of Journalism and Mass Marketing. Her work has been recognized by the American Association of Museums (AAM), AIGA, and the Council for Advancement and Support of Education (CASE).

Anne Winslow can find the exact middle of a page and bisect it with a straight line without using a ruler. This now redundant skill, along with writing type specs, has been useful in a career spanning thirty-some-odd years, mostly spent in publishing. She is currently creative director at Algonquin Books of Chapel Hill.

Index